MW01484734

ESAU-EDOM ROME: The Hidden Identity of the Man of Sin

For information contact :

P.O. Box F-60419

Freeport, Grand Bahama

The Bahamas

Website: http://beneyahyasharel.home.blog

Email: bonnievfranks@gmail.com

ISBN: 9781082500596

Third Edition: April 2020

TO
THE MOST HIGH YHWH AND
HIS HUMBLE SERVANT YHWHSHI

And now I know this mystery, that sinners will alter and pervert the words of righteousness in many ways, and will speak wicked words, and lie, and practice great deceits, and write books concerning their words.

But when they write down truthfully all my words in their languages and do not change or minish ought from my words but write them all down truthfully all that I first testified concerning them.

Then, I know another mystery, that books will be given to the righteous and the wise to become a cause of joy and uprightness and much wisdom.

And to them shall the books be given, and they shall believe in them, and then shall all the righteous who have learned thereof all the paths of uprightness be recompensed.

Enoch 104:10-13

"Buy the truth, and sell it not; also wisdom, and instruction, and understanding."

Proverbs 23:23

CONTENTS

PREFACE

I write this book to show the identity of the descendants of Esau, who is Edom. Esau, who is Edom, while an unusual name, shows how Scripture describes him, "Thus dwelt Esau in mount Seir: Esau is Edom" (Genesis 36:8). Esau, who is Edom are, the people who came from the east and rule the earth today. I expect this research to reveal accurate accounts of history. A history that Esau who is Edom has hidden and distorted as it relates to the twin brothers Jacob and Esau, and the purpose for which the Highest YAHUAH created them, and the role they would fulfill on the earth today and in the Kingdom to come.

Esau-Edom has concealed the evidence about their identity by replacing the people of the nations they conquered with the likeness of themselves and then adopting the history as their own. Much of the information available was a challenge to find because Esau-Edom has omitted or inserted historical events to match their narrative. For example, as it relates to the Biblical account of Amalek, and his interaction with Israel, the historians, claim because the Egyptian and Assyrian monuments survived with records which list various tribes and peoples of the area. Still, they did not refer to Amalek or the Amalekites. Therefore they conclude they did not exist. Based on the findings of the archeologist and historian Hugo Winckler, who suggested in 1895 that there were never any such people and therefore the Biblical stories about them are mythological with no historical bases. Because of reports like this, it was necessary to read the entire Books of Scripture available in the context of Hebraic history to determine the truth. Patience and my commitment caused me to persist in finding proof of the identity of the descendants of Esau-Edom, and the places where they migrated and settled on the earth. Through this process, I could put the puzzle pieces in their correct position, which made it possible to see the completed picture, using evidence from Hebrew Scriptures, including the Rabbinic writings along with secular history.

Esau-Edom mixed with every nation and today has rulership over the earth as the revised Roman Empire. They whited out many people of color in the nations they conquered, and because Rome rules the people, appear to be akin to the dominant race. The Edomites are the minority people on the earth, but because they are at the forefront in every nation, it appears they are the majority. Once they enter a nation, Esau-Edom would destroy and change the artifacts and paintings to resemble them. The statues we see today, with noses destroyed, were all vandalized because the people depicted in them all had Negro features. The reader will learn the truth about Esau-Edom. They will also gain knowledge of the thorough job Esau-Edom has done hiding the facts about themselves while impersonating the descendants of Jacob-Israel. Esau-Edom deceived the entire world by making the inhabitants of the earth believe they are the original people who evolved from nothing. They call this theory of evolution, the "Big Bang." Yet, they believe they are the "holy" people, the chosen vessels of YAHUAH, the Highest ELOHIYM of the Universe. Esau-Edom carried out this deception in part, to hide and then replace the chosen people of YAHUAH and to eliminate the Creator of the Universe.

The book will substantiate what is the truth from a Biblical and historical perspective. It will also show and prove the identity of the descendants of Jacob, also called Israel. Hebrew Scriptures identify these twin brothers Jacob and Esau and the prophecies feature them as important characters on the world stage, as we come to the close of this age. Without Esau, there is no Jacob. Both are vital to the prophesied events that have taken place, and prophecies that will come to past. Esau-Edom has tried to hide the identity of Jacob-Israel's descendants. They know who the descendants of Israel are even though the Israelites do not recognize that they are the sons and daughters of the Highest YAHUAH in the true sense. YAHUAH has removed Israel from their heritage and placed them in the hand of Esau-Edom to fulfill his purpose in them. I hope that YAHUAH reveals the truth about both brothers in this writing so we can identify with proof that Esau-Edom is the man of sin, and Jacob-Israel is the truly righteous people of YAHUAH.

My research will also show that all things are according to the will of the Highest YAHUAH, and without him, nothing is complete. YAHUAH gave Esau-Edom the dominion over the earth for a time and allowed them to subjugate the children of Jacob-Israel for the period of their rule. As the rulership of Esau-Edom over Jacob-Israel comes to its conclusion, YAHUAH will reveal the identities of both. This book results from what YAHUAH is illuminating today as Jacob-Israel awakens to the truth about their identity, "For Esau is the end of the world, and Jacob is the beginning of it that followeth" (2 Esdras 6:9). YAHUAH chose Esau-Edom to operate in wickedness. The

Prophet Daniel explains why and how we know this to be true. The dream of King Nebuchadnezzar reveals how the Highest chooses leaders, whether they are good or evil, to fulfill his purpose. "This matter is by decree of the watchers, and the demand by the word of the holy ones: to the intent that the living may know the Highest ruleth in the kingdom of men, and giveth it to whoever he will, and setteth up over it basest of men" (Daniel 3:17).

I have followed the chronological order of the history of Esau-Edom, as found in Scripture. They made this difficult because the events were not sequential, as it included many myths. I concluded that the history of Esau is a mystery wrapped in an enigma having no clear blueprint, and therefore, I had to research and gather the evidence from all of its fragmented pieces. By the grace of the Highest YAHUAH, I have tried to put the parts in its correct order so that a true picture emerges. In this writing, I have also used the set-apart names of YAHUAH and YAHUASHA to identify the Highest ELOHIYM and his Son. Some subjects, to a certain extent, will appear as repeats because I would have dealt with the topics in other areas. The names used to identify Esau, who is Edom differ according to the time discussed. In writing, I identify Esau as Esau-Edom, Edom-Rome, Idumea, the Edomites, and Europeans. I show the identity of the descendants of Jacob as Jacob-Israel, the Hebrews, Judeans, Jews, the Israelites, and the Hebrew Israelites. The support of this research came from many different sources. However, the foundation for this study is the TORAH and TANAKH, the Apocrypha, New Testament Writings, Epistles, and extra-Biblical writings, including those identified as Rabbinic literature. YAHUAH created Esau, who is Edom, for his purpose, and this writing will expose who they are and the lies they told to hide their identity.

I referenced many authors and some authors' accounts I read but did not use as references. However, their ideas informed my understanding and expanded my insight on the topic, which allowed me to write from various viewpoints. I also used the scholarly work of respected authors, but I was not afraid to disagree with them when I believed they knew the truth but pushed a false narrative. I used the information written by those of the modern Jewish thinkers because I realize many of them would have copied the original writings of the ancient writers, then added their perspective or just plagiarized the information and took credit for the work. Because the true writers are all dead, and the children of Israel would not know the truth as they are unaware of who and whose they are. Therefore, the information gathered from these sources helps me in the accuracy based on a Hebrewiac mindset and history.

YAHUAH led me to new information when it was necessary, and I give all praise and honor to him. I have to thank my brothers and sisters for the material I received from their YouTube videos based on research they shared with all of us seeking the truth. The data they publicized was invaluable and confirmed by additional research on my part. I would also like to thank my daughter, who helped me edit the narrative and my readers, who did a phenomenal job helping me organize the story to ensure that my writing was clear and made sense.

I hope that this study activates in the descendants of Israel a desire to know the truth about Esau-Edom because it is imperative for them to identify the true enemy of Israel. The offspring of Israel must then do whatever is necessary to determine if what they read is the truth by proving all things. They must be willing to, "Study to show yourselves approved unto YAHUAH, a workman that needeth not be ashamed, rightly dividing the word of truth" (2 Timothy 2:15). I understand that the lack of knowledge of Israel's identity has contributed to the destruction of Israel at the hand of Esau-Edom.

Israel is the Chosen Nation of YAHUAH, scattered in the diaspora in Africa and to the four corners of the earth. YAHUAH, our ELOHIYM, has not forgotten Israel. He challenges anyone to measure heaven and search for the foundations of the earth, and if they could find the answers to these, then he would cast Israel away. "Thus, saith YAHUAH; 'if they can measure heaven above, and the foundations of the earth searched out beneath, I will also cast off all the seed of Israel for all they have done,' saith YAHUAH" (Jeremiah 31:37).

YAHUAH plans to save Israel because it is His will to save them. He created Israel to fulfill his noble purpose on the earth, just as he made Esau-Edom a vessel for dishonor and to be the wicked upon the earth. The Edomite Christians do not teach the truth about Jacob and Esau; because it does not fit the narrative of them being the superior people on the earth, they teach lies. However, YAHUAH made them a people fit for a fraudulent purpose, which is the reason for this great deception.

As I release this book to my Hebrew Israelite brothers and

sisters scattered to the four corners of the earth and to the strangers who will serve Israel, as it is YAHUAH'S will, I hope that as they read, it will inspire them to take part in further research. Scripture establishes the truth by the mouth of two or three witnesses. I investigated and wrote to confirm in my mind and heart, that Esau who is Edom, is the "white" Europeans ruling on the earth today, identifying as the diverse countries they occupy. They are the enemy of Jacob-Israel and have tried to confuse Israel by changing the history and recasting the people. YAHUAH is awakening Israel from 400 years of lies and deceit. Esau-Edom has used many institutions to keep Israel in this deception, including the Christian church, Islam, Egyptology, the institutions of learning, and by separating us by land borders, so we think we are different nations.

We must not allow them to win. We must overcome by the blood of the lamb and the word of our testimony as we seek the truth in YAHUSHA, our elder brother, and soon coming King. I hope that this writing acts as a catalyst to enlighten the Hebrew Israelites and spur them on to seek the truth and prove all things confirming every word of this study. Truth is singular and eternal and only found in the Highest YAHUAH, and it is not relative to anything else. I pray that the Highest is with you as you read and discern what he is saying to his Chosen people. And I hope that the reader would use this information to increase their knowledge further as it relates to the identity of Esau, who is Edom and Rome, and the purpose of their existence in these "end" times. I say to the Most High YAHUAH be the glory for what he has done, for His mercy endures forever. Shalom!

INTRODUCTION

When I understood that the descendants of slaves were the scattered tribes of the children of Israel, brought to the Americas via the Transatlantic Slave Trade, I thought about writing this book. Not only did I want to know the identity of Jacob-Israel, but I wanted to know for sure with evidence the identity of Esau-Edom and the role they played in the demise of Jacob-Israel. I believed then, I know that the descendants of Jacob are the Negroes, brought to the Americas on Slave ships and scattered throughout the continent of Africa in the diaspora and the four corners of the earth. The people who bought and sold the children of Israel to the Americas from Africa, I now know, are the descendants of Esau. They are the rulers of the earth today. The Bible says Esau is the elder brother of Jacob, twin boys born to their parents Isaac and Rebekah. Isaac, their father, gave blessings to both boys and said the older would serve the younger. In scripture, there are many prophecies relative to Esau and the role he plays in the "Last Days," so it is crucial to identify who the descendants of Esau are. Questions need answering; who is Esau-Edom the Edomites, where did they originate in history, and what effect did they have on the chosen people of YAHUAH, the Hebrew Israelites? Research sets out to answer these questions, because if the word of the Highest YAHUAH is true, and there are many prophecies against Esau, then we need to know the identity of the people of Esau-Edom. I will try to answer these questions using the evidence found in the timeline of Scripture, coupled with historical data, and current events.

The Highest YAHUAH has declared that we consult his word because it stands above his name. In his word, we find the truth about how important his word is. In Psalms 138:2, there is a prayer by King David reminding us of this truth, "I will worship toward thy holy temple, and praise thy name for thy loving-kindness and thy truth: for thou hast magnified thy word above all thy name." Thus, YAHUAH'S word reveals the truth, and should inspire us who want to know the truth to search for the evidence that will identify Esau-Edom, the people who interacted and attempted to destroy Jacob's descendants. To confirm the truth, I will search Esau's genealogy and explore how and when they migrated from place to place and the impact their movement had on the indigenous peoples. I will also use secular history and extra-Biblical text to support the Canonized Scripture to verify the facts.

The first statement made concerning Esau in the book of Genesis 25:25 identifies his complexion. It also establishes that his parents named him for his color. "And the first came out red, all over like a hairy garment; and they called his name Esau." His name tells who Esau is, which shows that Esau looked different from his brother Jacob in his appearance, as Scripture did not describe the color of Jacob. It is also noteworthy that Jacob's name means "plain" and perfect in all his ways. This difference in complexion plays an important role in identifying Esau and the actions he would take against his brother Jacob based on Jacob's black skin color. Esau-Edom has described their skin color as white, a color they believe makes them superior and Jacob's skin color as black, which makes them inferior. Continuing to deny that the white man living and ruling on the earth today is Esau-Edom after learning the facts would be disingenuous. It is Esau-Edom who decided in the 18th century to create a science to support the theory that their white skin color made them superior to all people on the earth, and therefore, we cannot deny they are the people described in Scripture.

When Rebekah was pregnant with the twin boys Esau and Jacob, she inquired of YAHUAH why she was experiencing such difficulty with the pregnancy. He explained in these words; "And YAHUAH said unto her, Two nations are in thy womb, and two manners of people shall be separated from thy bowels, and the one people shall be stronger than the other people, and the elder shall serve the younger" (Genesis 25:23). The prophecy is clear that there would be two Nations, two different people, not ordinary twins that may have been identical or fraternal, as we understand the terms. The Scriptures explain the intentions of YAHUAH. He separated the people of Jacob-Israel, the younger brother to himself for holy use. "Who are Israelites to whom pertaineth the adoption, and the glory, and the covenants, and the giving of the law, and the service of YAHUAH, and the promises; whose are the fathers, and of whom as concerning the flesh YAHUSHA came, who is over all, YAH blessed forever. Amen" (Romans 9:4-5). YAHUAH created Esau for a different role than that of Jacob. He used Esau-Edom as a refiners fire to perfect the righteousness in the children of Jacob-Israel. However, Esau-Edom was brutal in implementing this punishment and went beyond what YAHUAH wanted or thought necessary. Therefore, YAHUAH promises he will have no mercy on Esau-Edom. And, the Prophet

Malachi states what the outcome would be as it relates to Esau-Edom, "The burden of the word of YAHUAH to Israel by Malachi. I have loved you, saith YAHUAH. Yet ye say wherein hast thou loved us? Was not Esau Jacob's brother? Saith YAHUAH: yet I loved Jacob, and I hated Esau and laid his mountains and his heritage waste for the dragons of the wilderness" (Malachi 1:1-3). Esau-Edom will receive their just punishment in return for what they have done to Jacob-Israel because what they sowed they shall reap.

The study will show the color of both Esau and Jacob along with other indicators recorded in scripture and in history that are paramount in determining the identity of Esau in these "last days." Scriptures also identify Esau-Edom with Babylon, and the research will show that they indeed represent Babylon and its mystery religions. "Remember, O LORD, the children of Edom in the day of Jerusalem; who said, Rase it, rase it, even to the foundation thereof. O daughter of Babylon, who art to be destroyed; happy shall he be that rewardeth thee as thou hast served us" (Psalms 137:7-8). The scriptures also show how Esau migrated, moving from Canaan to Mount Seir. And, it shows his grandson Zepho moving into Kittiym, which is Rome. Later in history, Esau-Edom's descendants moved into the lands of Israel in the Negev, south of Judaea. Through marriage, Esau-Edom mixed Arabs, Canaanites, the Assyrians, the Egyptians, and the people of the land of Japheth, including Javan, known as the Greeks. Esau-Edom became the Europeans who conquered and colonized most lands of the earth. It is the will of YAHUAH that gives them dominion over the earth as part of the blessing Isaac gave to Esau, his firstborn son. Isaac told Esau he would live in the earth's fatness with all of its riches and will dominate by the edge of the sword.

My investigation of Biblical and historical records has found that we can observe these blessings and the fact they are warmongers as evidence of the identity of Esau-Edom. Despite many of the descendants of Esau-Edom not believing in the Highest ELOHIYM with many being outright antagonistic toward him, they appear to be more blessed by him than any of the other nations on earth. They are the leaders who have enslaved and destroyed YAHUAH'S people, yet they appear to have it all. They have led Israel into several captivities, with the final enslavement, which has lasted for almost four hundred years. The Targums of Onkelos, an Aramaic translation of the Torah, offers commentary on Genesis 15:12-14 and confirms the prophecy concerning this fact. "And he said to Abram, Knowing, thou must know that thy sons shall dwell in a land not their own because thou has not believed, and they will subjugate and afflict them four hundred years, and also that the people whom they shall serve I will judge with two hundred and fifty plagues, and afterward they shall go forth into liberty with great riches." YAHUSHA, too, reminded the Judeans of the things that would happen to them as they lived the last of their days in Judaea before the Roman wars against them began. Edom-Rome destroyed millions of the Israelites and sent millions more into slavery and exile. As my research will show, the people called Africans living on the continent of Africa are the Hebrew Israelites, exiled into these lands by Edom-Rome from throughout Europe and the Middle

East. Scriptures reveal the children of Israelite descendants would be in exile and go into captivity at the hand of Edom-Rome. Later in history many of the children of these exiled Israelites would be taken on slave ships to the Americas, "And they shall fall by the edge of the sword, and shall be led away captive into all nations: and Jerusalem shall be trodden down of the Gentiles until the times of the Gentiles be fulfilled" (Luke 21:24). The time of Edom-Rome's rule is nearing the end, and the Gentiles spoken of are the people of Esau-Edom and their coconspirators who occupy the land of Palestine. Palestine, named by Rome for the Philistines, is the homeland of the true descendants of Israel whom Edom-Rome expelled almost two thousand years ago.

The historical evidence shows and concludes that Edom-Rome has been the instigator of all the wicked acts perpetrated against the inhabitants of Israel. At the same time, they pretend to be a "holy" nation. However, this is the will of the Highest and Edom-Rome can do nothing except the will of Father YAHUAH, as no one can resist His will. Edom-Rome has tried to change history by revising the history and changing the evidence to make it appear that either these events have already taken place, or they are being fulfilled by the imposter Jewish people living in the land of Palestine, today. But tricks and schemes will not cause YAHUAH to grant Edom-Rome salvation because the word and the will of YAHUAH cannot change as he is not a liar. Therefore, he asks, "Why do the heathen rage and the people imagine a vain thing? The kings of the earth set themselves, and the rulers take counsel together, against YAHUAH, and his anointed, saying, Let us break their bands asunder, and cast away their cords from us. He that sitteth in the heavens shall laugh: YAHUAH shall have them in derision" (Psalms 2:1-4).

The word of YAHUAH will accomplish what it says. Esau is Edom, and Rome and the fake Jewish people, and all those associated with the Babylonian system shown in scripture and history. It is essential to understand the events that will take place in these "last days" as it reveals the identity of Esau, who is Edom and Rome. The Scriptures show the identity of Esau-Edom and make it possible to recognize them since they have no melanin in their skin. "But I have made Esau bare, I have uncovered his secret places, and he shall not be able to hide himself: his seed is spoiled, and his brethren, and his neighbors, and he is not" (Jeremiah 49:10). The evidence will show that Esau has tried to hide among the other nations as they have become a diverse people, even claiming to be the descendants of Jacob-Israel, while also destroying the people who descend from Jacob-Israel. The Prophet Daniel and the book of Revelation tell of the fourth kingdom to rule over the people of Israel. It identifies them as the fourth beast spoken of in the books of Daniel and Revelations. The research will prove that Esau-Edom is that fourth beast system ruling today just before YAHUSHA returns "Thus he said, The fourth beast shall be the fourth kingdom upon the earth, which shall be diverse from all kingdoms, and shall devour the whole earth, and shall tread it down, and break it in pieces" (Daniel 7:23).

This book's outline follows the sequential biblical history of Esau, along with the authentic secular history that helps in substantiating the truth. I have informed the reader using evidence I corroborated with two or more witnesses. However, some information available conflicted with the Scriptural accounts. Thus it became necessary to delve deeper into history. The painstaking process resulted in the completed picture. Making it possible for the reader to identify who the true descendant of Esau is in the earth today as these people continue to destroy and rebuild. The reader will also identify who the true Hebrew Israelites are. "Whereas Edom saith, We are impoverished, but we will return and build the desolate places; thus saith YAHUAH of hosts, They shall build, but I will throw down; and they shall call them, The border of wickedness, and, The people against whom YAHUAH hath indignation forever" (Malachi 1:4).

I established this study on the biblical texts, the Torah and the Prophets, the Apocrypha, the New Testament, and extra-Biblical texts Canonized and Deuterocanonical, including the Books of Jubilees, Jasher, and Enoch. I also used historical data found in; Josephus Antiquities of the Jews, Rabbinic literature, History of the Roman Republic, Chronicles of Jerahmeel, Greek and Roman Mythology, Targums of Onkelos, The Image of the Black in Jewish Culture, Germans and Edom, The Jews in Christian Europe, Jewish Identity in Early Rabbinic Writings, The Two Babylons: Or The Papal Worship Proved To Be The Worship of Nimrod, The Thirteenth Tribe, The Black Jews of Africa, The Letter of Jacob, Hebrewisms of West Africa, Until Darwin Science, Human Variety and the Origins of Race, Bells New Pantheon, Black and White People, History of Arabs in the Sudan, Yawan-the Works of Sir Thomas Browne, Mecca-The

Works of Sir Walter Raleigh, Servius, Commentary on Vergil, The Story of Christianity, The Rise of Christianity, Ancient and Modern Britons, Nature Knows No Color Line, The Black Image in the White Mind, Feats and Wisdom of the Ancients, The Icon, World Religions: A Historical Approach, New Unger's Bible Dictionary, A Comprehensive Etymological Dictionary of the Hebrew Language, From Babylon to Timbuktu, Lost Tribes and Promised Land, The History of the First Council of Nice, Germany's Black Holocaust, Whence the Black Irish of Jamaica, World Religions: A Historical approach, The Flat Earth Conspiracy, Layman's Bible Encyclopedia, The Great Philosophers, Saint Ignatius of Antioch: the Epistles, and many historical articles, found on the Worldwide Web and evidence from Archeological finds and ancient and modern maps and paintings.

The investigation traces the history of Esau and his descendants, the Edomites. It also follows the relationship to Jacob-Israel to Esau-Edom, who, for the past two thousand years of Esau's dominion on the earth, has experienced the brunt of Edom-Rome's cruelty and destruction. It will show how Edom-Rome and Christianity impacted Israel's dispersion and the effect Israel's religion had on Edom-Rome's Christianity. It will clarify in the minds of those who are doubtful of the identity of Esau, who is Edom, while it will also identify the true Hebrew Israelites of Scripture. Esau-Edom, the elder brother of Jacob-Israel, will serve Israel in the kingdom to come. They were each created to have dominion, Esau to live in the fatness of the earth, and Jacob to possess the earth for eternity. YAHUAH created each for his purpose. Everyone born on this earth is subject to YAHUAH because he has a purpose for the creation he made, and no created individual can choose his position. He made Jacob and gave him the position of honor in the earth as he made Esau for dishonor and describes Jacob as the apple of his eye, "When the Highest divided to the nations their inheritance when he separated the sons of Adam, and he set the bounds of the people according to the number of the children of Israel. For the YAHUAH'S portion is his people; Jacob is the lot of his inheritance. He found him in a desert land, and in the waste howling wilderness; he led him about, he instructed him, he kept him as the apple of His eye" (Deuteronomy 32: 8-10).

CHAPTER 1

Identifying Esau

ESAU WAS THE ELDEST OF TWIN BOYS, born to Isaac and Rebekah. Isaac, Esau's father, was the son of Abraham, to whom the Highest, YAHUAH, blessed with the Promise. "And when Abram was ninety years old and nine, YAHUAH appeared to Abram and said unto him, I am Almighty God EL SHADDAI; walk before me and be thou perfect" (Genesis 17:1). YAHUAH made a covenant with Abram to be the father of many nations and then changed his name from Abram to Abraham to reflect his promise. Through this covenant with Abraham, YAHUAH promised to multiply Abraham's seed. "As for me, behold, my covenant is with you, and you shall be a

father of many nations. Neither shall thy name any more be called Abram, but thy name shall be Abraham; for a father of many nations have I made thee" (Genesis 17:4-5). Esau, therefore, was born into an upright family–one chosen to bring forth righteousness throughout the earth.

Despite the promise that he would be the father of many nations, the promised blessing of possession of the earth would pass through only one of Abraham's offspring. "And God said, Sarah, thy wife shall bear thee a son indeed, and thou shalt call his name Isaac: and I will establish my covenant with him for an everlasting covenant and with his seed after him" (Genesis 17:19). Isaac had twin boys, and although Esau was Isaac's eldest son, YAHUAH gave the promise of righteousness and inheritance to Jacob, Isaac's younger son.

"And YAHUAH said unto her, (Rebekah) two nations are in thy womb, and I shall separate two manners of people from thy bowels; the one people shall be stronger than the other people; and the elder shall serve the younger," (Genesis 25:23). According to Rabbinic writings, the two nations would each become its own universe.[1] Jacob would represent the Torah, and Esau would embody sin.

Throughout Rebekah's pregnancy, the two babies struggled within her until the day they were born. "And the first came out red, all over like a hairy garment; and they called his name Esau" (Genesis 25: 25). The Hebrew word used to describe Esau's color, ādōm, and means 'red'. This word, ādōm, refers to blood, such as

2

a garment sprinkled with blood. It also uses this Hebrew word to describe the red heifer or cow, a stew made of lentils, and the complexion of Esau. The color of Esau is significant as he was 'red' and 'covered with hair.' His tone was important in assigning a label to him as a hunter. As a hunter, Esau liked to draw blood. Esau revealed his taste in food when he coveted and sold his birthright for a bowl of red pottage that Jacob had prepared. "Then Jacob gave Esau bread and pottage of lentils; and he ate and drank, and rose, and went his way: thus Esau despised his birthright" (Genesis 25:34). It was during this interaction with Jacob that Esau's name changed to Edom, "And Esau said to Jacob, Feed me, I pray thee, with that same red pottage; for I am faint: therefore was his name called Edom" (Genesis 25:30). 'Edom' means "the Red" (ādōm) because he (Esau) had red hair, red skin, and was bloodthirsty.

In Rabbinic writings, they often note the name equivalence of 'Esau' and 'Edom' throughout the Torah. "Now these are the generations of Esau, who is Edom" (Genesis 36:1). "Duke Magdiel, duke Iram: these be the dukes of Edom, according to their habitations in the land of their possession: he is Esau, the father of the Edomites" (Genesis 36:43). Likewise, it is also essential to understand the distinction between the Hebrew names of 'Esau' and 'Adam.' In Hebrew, 'Adam,' the first man created by YAHUAH means "(hu) man)." It is a proper noun that does not appear elsewhere outside of Genesis chapters 1-5. YAHUAH formed Adam (Heb. 'adam) from the "earth" (Heb. 'adamah), set

him over the Garden, and allowed him to name the animals (Harper's Bible Dictionary). Therefore, the names Adam and Esau derive from different Hebrew words with different meanings.

During Rebekah's labor and the birth of the twins, Jacob was born after Esau. As he was being born, Jacob took hold of Esau's heel. The allusion to the 'heel,' according to Rabbinic writings, is not accidental and relates to Jacob supplanting Esau. By emphasizing the 'heel,' we can explain the name of Esau's younger brother, Jacob - ('âqer), which means 'heel' and 'Yaakov,' which means "it talonnera" complete and in tack. Yaakov then became the first name of Israel because its function was to carry the message of YAHUAH and to attack the snake. By looking at the original meanings of both Esau and Jacob's names, we can understand the unique roles of both of Isaac's sons. "And I will put enmity between thee and the woman, and between thy seed and her seed; it shall bruise thy head, and thou shalt bruise his heel" (Genesis 3:15).

The Zohar also compares Esau with the Serpent in Genesis.[2] This writing explains that, from birth, the hand of Jacob held Esau's heel. It further proves the direction that Jacob would continue with his brother, their rivalry throughout the ages, and that Jacob would crush Esau. Because of this understanding, Rabbi Shimon bar Yochai concludes that Esau's character is one which is such that it is useless to want to behave with those who misbehave; therefore, Jacob will destroy Esau.[3]   As 2 Samuel 22:27 states, "With the pure, you show yourself pure, and with

the crooked you show yourself perverse." He furthers that this adversarial relationship between Esau and Jacob compares as a parallel to the brothers Cain and Abel, who, when YAHUAH accepted Abel's offering yet rejected Cain's offering, Cain became angry and rose against Abel, his brother, and slew him (Genesis 4:8). YAHUAH rejected both Cain and Esau; hence they both took their anger out on the brother that YAHUAH accepted.

According to Alain de Benoist, the relationship between Esau and Jacob refers to the dialectic of the brothers in the Biblical tradition.[4] Following the Hebrew tradition, Benoist explains that the oldest would be first biologically; however, the second would be first spiritually. Benoist's underlying theory is that real hierarchies are unlike hierarchies in the natural sense. Esau dominates the worldly realm and the side of the world reliant on the power of men, whereas Jacob represents the spiritual realm, which includes the power of YAHUAH. Benoist concludes that because the hierarchies are not alike, YAHUAH must break the natural order to give way to its opposite, which is spiritual. Therefore, the natural hierarchy will be reversed because it is the will of the Highest YAHUAH, "And he answered me, saying, the Highest YAHUAH hath made this world for many, but the world to come for a few" (2 Esdras 8:1). YAHUAH made the world of Esau for many people; he will create the world, however, to come, which is of Jacob, for only a few people - those of the righteous of Israel and those chosen by YAHUAH to join Israel as handmaids and servants.

YAHUAH presents Esau in a negative light while He elects Jacob. The natural superiority attached to receiving the birthright he reversed. YAHUAH will bless Jacob in all things, people will serve him, and those who exalt him YAHUAH will bless, while those who curse him will have a curse conferred on them. The blessing that Esau received was that his house would be the fertility of the earth and the dew of heaven above, and by his sword, he would live, and after he has dominated, he will serve Jacob. Benoist explains, "Esau may well conquer the world, but in doing so, he will unwittingly work for Jacob." The elder will serve the younger.

By Hebraic tradition, the history of Jacob and Esau has always revealed the past and predicted the future.[5]   The lesson in this historical tradition is that time, itself, can never destroy the Esau-Jacob relationship and that Jacob will triumph overall. "I have loved you, saith YAHUAH. Ye say wherein hast thou loved us? Was not Esau Jacob's brother? Saith YAHUAH: yet I loved Jacob, and hated Esau, and laid his mountains and his heritage waste for the dragons of the wilderness" (Malachi 1:2-3). The hatred that the Highest has for Esau, according to Mireille Hadas-Lebel, is not only a hatred of his vice to virtue but also his hatred of idolatry for monotheism.[6]   He hates everything about Esau, even when he appears to be virtuous.

YAHUAH established the plan and purpose of the brothers, Esau and Jacob before they were born. After the flood, YAHUAH chose Abraham and declared that he would make him a great nation, and through him, all the nations would receive blessings. However, the ultimate benefit would only come through one seed. "For Ishmael and his sons and his brothers and Esau, YAHUAH did not cause to approach him, and he chose them not because they are the children of Abraham, because he knew them, but he chose Israel to be his people. And he sanctified it and gathered it from amongst all children of men; for there are many nations and many peoples, and all are his, and over all has he placed ruachoth in authority to lead them astray from him," (Jubilees 15:30-31). YAHUAH chose the bloodline of Jacob-Israel to carry his seed. Therefore, the twelve sons of Jacob became the children of the Promise.

In the book "Legends of the Jews," the author provides an account of a dialog between Rebekah and Shem. Shem was Noah's eldest son and the progenitor of the Semitic people. In this conversation, while Rebekah was pregnant, she tells him about what she was experiencing during her pregnancy before Esau and Jacob were born.[7] In this confidential conversation, Shem reveals to Rebekah the destiny of the twins she was carrying.

And Shem replied:

> My daughter, I confide a secret to thee. See that no one finds it out. 'Two nations are in thy womb and how should thy body contain them, seeing that the entire world will not be large enough for them to exist in it together peaceably? Two nations they are, each owning a world of its own, the one the Torah, the other sin. From the one

will spring Solomon, the builder of the Temple, from the other Vespasian, the destroyer thereof. YAHUAH needs these two to raise the number of nations to seventy. They will never be in the same estate. Esau will vaunt lords, while Jacob will bring forth prophets, and if Esau has princes, Jacob will have kings. Israel and Rome are the two nations destined to be hated by the entire world. One will exceed the other in strength. First, Esau will subjugate the world as a whole, but, in the end, Jacob will rule overall. The older of the two will serve the younger, provided this one is pure of heart; otherwise, the older will enslave the younger.

IDENTIFYING ESAU BY HIS DESCRIPTION

As mentioned earlier, Esau was 'red' and 'covered with hair.' But, why was Esau's color described and not Jacob's? History shows that all people had a significant amount of melanin in their skin in the beginning, which means they had dark skin. Adam, formed from the dust of the ground, resembled the dirt that YAHUAH used to make him. Therefore, Adam was the progenitor of all people of color, including Noah and his sons. Esau differed in two marks that identified him. Scripture described him at birth as 'red' and 'hairy.'

Esau was born in Canaan, a boiling tropical climate with an average temperature of 26.4°C. He had no melanin, a built-in, natural form of sun protectant. Instead, hair covered his body, which served as his protection from the sun. Today, to be born without melanin is albinism or, when one loses the melanin, vitiligo. However, in Biblical texts, being melanin deficient was a curse called leprosy, as Moses experienced when YAHUAH told him to place his hand in his bosom, and it turned white. Miriam, his sister, experienced leprosy when she spoke out against Moses. "And the cloud left from off the tabernacle; and, behold, Miriam became leprous, white as snow: and Aaron looked upon Miriam, and, behold, she was leprous" (Numbers 12:10).

Scripture pronounces Jacob as a 'plain man,' "And after that came to his brother out, and his hand took hold on Esau's heel, and they called his name Jacob" (Genesis 25:26). The Hebrew word for plain, (itam: complete Original Word: תָּם) means 'complete, perfect; in beauty; of physical strength.' Jacob lacked nothing; he was perfect in all areas, including his skin color.

The descriptions of Rebekah's newborn twins show the different identities of two nations destined to rule from birth. King Solomon, who descended from Jacob, validates Jacob's appearance when he describes himself in Scripture.[8] He says, "I am black, but comely, O ye daughters of Jerusalem as the tents of Kedar, as the curtains of Solomon" (Song of Solomon 1:5).

The Polemic Writings also confirm a dispute that was contrasting the physical characteristics of the Jews (Israelites) when comparing them to the Edomites who are descendants of Esau.[9] What is instructive is that the Jew (Israelite) does not deny the claim that they are black. The Jew (Israelite) accepts his skin

9

color as an indisputable fact (Melamed, 2003). Sefer of Yosef ha-Mekaneh, written by Joseph bar Nathan, contains the dispute between the apostate Jew and the author's father, R. Nathan.[10][11] It states,

> I made you contemptible, and base before all the people (Mal. 2:9) said a certain apostate to Rabbi Nathan: You are uglier than any people on earth, and our people are very handsome. He (Rabbi) replied: those big plums that grow along the Seine, what blossom do they have? He said to him, white. And what color is the apple blossom? He said: Red. He answered: that is what we are from a pure white seed, and our faces are dark, while you are Edomites, a red race, conceived from menstruation women so that you are yellow and red. Why so? Because we are in exile, as described in Song of Songs 1:6 'Look not upon me because I am black because the sun hath looked upon me: my mother's children were angry with me they made me the keeper of the vineyards, but my own vineyard I have not kept.' But when I kept my own vineyard, I was most beautiful, as it is written: "And thy renown went forth among the heathen for thy beauty: for it was perfect through my comeliness, which I had put upon thee, saith YAHUAH ELOHIYM" (Ezekiel 16:14).

The description of Esau and Jacob's color at birth and the dispute by Nathan the Jew help to confirm the identity of the descendants of both Jacob and Esau today.[12] The explanation also proves that there was a difference in the color of the skin of the Israelites and Edomites. R. Nathan concurs that the Jews may be outwardly dark, but their internal state is pure, unlike the Christian Edomite, who may appear white on the outside, but inside they are dark. Israel prophesied to be among all nations, but would still be identifiable. YAHUAH will gather them from among the Gentiles when he returns, "At that time will I bring you again, even in the time that I gather you: for I will make you a name and a praise among all people of the earth when I turn back your captivity before your eyes, saith YAHUAH," (Zephaniah 3:20). The imposter Jews who say they are Jews and are not have already taken the land away from the Palestinians claiming that the white Edomite Jews are the rightful heirs. But the Scripture states that YAHUAH will gather his people when he returns and take them into the Land of Promise, where they will no longer have to fight any wars.

But, there is a prophecy that shows the descendants of Esau-Edom would fight many wars as they will be a people that the nations will hate. The indigenous people of many nations hated the descendants of Esau, because of how they would come into their homelands with deceit and conquer the lands, destroy many of the people and force those remaining to accept the Edomites' religions. History records that Esau-Edom is the ultimate bully on earth, a characteristic of the blessing Isaac gave to Esau's sons before he died, "And Yitschaq also blessed the sons of Esau, saying, May ELOHIYM cause you to be a dread and terror to all that will behold you, and to all your enemies" (Jasher 47:6). The descendants of Esau-Edom have perfected and fulfilled this role as recent history reveals. The Edomite Jewish converts have taken their bullying to another level as they also have policed even the speech of citizens of all nations as it relates to speaking against them as the true people of YAHUAH. They have formed organizations to condemn what people may say about the Jewish people in Palestine or anywhere else. They decide whatever is said regarding them and may label it hate speech or anti-Semitic. The Jewish Edomites have taken the word Semite and owned as if it belongs to only them alone, but being Semitic only means that the people descend from Shem, the eldest son of Noah. And, many progenies can claim Semitic ancestry. The true Hebrew Israelites never identified as Semitic but as the children of Jacob–Israel or Israelites, Judeans or Hebrews.

Esau-Edom joined with many nations through marriage and conquest and has whited-out many of the indigenous people. They used a theory called whitening, where the white man would have children with the original people. After the third generation, the children will show no sign of blackness, whereby they would breed out the black skin color. Many of these whited-out indigenous people became the replacement leaders of the nations that Esau-Edom conquered. They determined that their white skin color would be the mark of superiority, improving the indigenous people of these nations. These leaders and people would then place a higher value on people with white skin and lesser worth on those of a darker hue.

In, Hebrew culture having white skin was a curse or a disease called leprosy. Howbeit, in this modern-day, Edom-Rome has changed leprosy to mean a chronic infectious disease, which leads to less sensation in limbs with eventual paralysis. They believe and are unyielding in the idea their white color makes them superior. The Israelites' black skin color makes them inferior, even creating a theory in science to confirm their narrative. To reinforce this negative stereotype of black skin in the descendants of Jacob, Edom-Rome labels them Negroes a negative by-word meaning black in Spanish. During the slave trade, they turned Negro into the by-word "niggar" used by Edom-Rome to describe the chosen people of YAHUAH. This distinctive word would serve as a marker that would identify Jacob and define the difference between the brothers Esau and Jacob. What Edom-Rome did illustrates the power of YAHUAH to cause all things to work together for the good of Israel, and that no one can resist his will, not even Esau. YAHUAH made certain not to leave the identity of his people to chance, although they would become dispersed among all nations.

This research reveals it was possible to identify the descendants of Jacob by the color of their skin in the 12th, 13th, 14th to the 19th century based on historical accounts written by Edomites. Jacob and Esau have been on the earth for the same number of generations, and Esau-Edom's skin color can't identify them and not Jacob-Israel by the same identifying mark. The descendants of Esau and Jacob are still people, two different nations, and two manners of people. And, it is not a valid argument to make that because YAHUAH removed Israel from their heritage, and they have forgotten who they are they no longer exist. Today, Esau is still "white," and his descendants identify as Europeans scattered throughout the earth. Jacob-Israel is still the "black" Negro people scattered throughout the earth via various dispersions. However, Esau has mixed with every nation, and the evidence shows in the skin color of the people living throughout the earth. They also tried to white-out Israel, but it is not the will of the Most High YAHUAH that Esau-Edom would white out Jacob-Israel. Therefore, YAHUAH had Edom-Rome scatter the Israelites onto Sub-Saharan Africa, where most of them continue to live today. Edom-Rome has replaced the descendants of Japheth and mixed with the sons of Ham and the Arabs. And, they have whited out the black skin color of many of the people of these nations, so it appears the original people no longer exist. But, they do and are just not prominently displayed in places of authority or sparsely shown as a token, because this is Edom-Rome's white world.

YAHUAH made a choice and determined the physical characteristics of his people. Israel would be a people of dark skin color, and he compared them to the children described as 'the blacks.' "Are ye not as children of the Ethiopians unto me, O children of Israel? Saith the Highest YAHUAH. Have not I brought up Israel out of the land of Egypt? And the Philistines from Caphtor, and the Syrians from Kir?... For, lo, I will command, and I will sift the house of Israel among all nations, like corn is sifted in a sieve, yet shall not the least grain fall upon the earth" (Amos 9:7, 9). Scripture states that although Israel will be among all people, YAHUAH could still identify them by the color of their skin. We should also note that the children of Ethiopia were, and still are, black people. Unger's Bible dictionary defines Ethiopia, as lying south of Egypt, corresponding to Sudan, which is the country of the blacks. The Hebrews call it by the name 'Kush,' and the Online Bible Dictionary further defines 'Ethiopia' as 'having burned faces,' 'the country of Soudan land of the blacks,' 'its inhabitants were the descendants of Ham.' It represents them on Egyptian monuments, and they are all the true Negro.'

In an account of the Edomites' description by Jules Michelet, he confirms the truth about Esau's skin color given by the Athenians when they first met the Romans who were Edomites.[13] They recalled that these Edomites had a fierce face, with red hair, their eyes were green with a red complexion spotted with white, and they found the Romans looks to be amusing, as their physical characteristics were strange because their red appearance was uncommon to them.

IDENTIFYING ESAU IN CHILDHOOD

As a young boy, Esau preferred being outdoors and enjoyed wandering through the fields. He was a skilled bow hunter; he mastered the art of war, and his actions were fierce. Jacob established himself as a scholar who preferred to stay close to home while reading books and learning to write. "And the boys grew up to their fifteenth year, and they came amongst the society of men. Esau described as a designing, and deceitful man and an expert hunter in the field and Jacob was a man perfect and wise, dwelling in tents, feeding flocks, and learning the instructions of YAHUAH and the commands of his father and mother" (Jasher 26:17).

Today, the descendants of Esau display a similar characteristic of individualism, like their ancestor, Esau. Esau was one who disdained tradition and authority. He gloried in his ability to become a confident man while expecting others to do the same. Esau believed in building his future by his toil and effort while subjugating others through calculating schemes and deceiving promises. The Rabbinic writings affirm these characteristics in Esau, "He Esau was a hypocrite" (Shocher Tov 14, 3). They compare the hypocrisy of Esau-Edom to the pig or boar being acceptable in appearance as it has the hoof cloven and split, but impure because it does not chew the cud. It is this hypocrisy that the teachings of the Torah attribute to Edom-Rome, and in fact, the Rabbinic writings confirm that it is Esau who would hunt Jacob down and deceive him with tricky words (Genesis Rabbah 63, 10).

Because Abraham was very much aware of Esau's personality, he insisted on Rebekah ensuring that her first-born son Esau did not receive the blessing that YAHUAH promised. "And Abraham saw the deeds of Esau and knew in Jacob should his name and seed be called; he called Rebekah and gave commandment regarding Jacob, for he knew she too loved Jacob much more than Esau. And he said unto her: my daughter, watch over my son Jacob, for he shall be in my stead on the earth, and for a blessing amid the children of men, and for the glory of the whole seed of Shem. For I know that YAHUAH will choose him to be a people for a possession unto himself, above all peoples that are upon the face of the earth" (Jubilees 19: 16-18).

Abraham loved Jacob very much. He expressed to Rebekah that his love for Jacob was even greater than his love for his sons. He encouraged Rebekah to give favor to Jacob as he was the son that would receive blessings for generations to come. "He shall be blessed forever, and his seed shall fill the whole earth" (Jubilees 19:21). Abraham was persistent in his support for Jacob because he already knew Isaac loved Esau more. Abraham feared that Isaac would bless Esau instead of Jacob. Therefore, Abraham gave Rebekah this significant charge to ensure that Esau would not receive the blessing as his heir. However, those who interpret the story outside of the Hebrew context assert that Jacob received the blessing instead of Esau because he deceived his father. But Biblical evidence is clear that YAHUAH chose Jacob to be his heir before the beginning, and he chose Jacob to receive the promises. "For thou art, a holy people unto YAHUAH thy ELOHIYM: YAHUAH thy ELOHIYM hath chosen thee to be a special people unto himself, above all people that are upon the face of the earth" (Deuteronomy 7:6).

Scripture further exposed Esau's motive and personality when he sold his birthright to Jacob for a bowl of red pottage. Because Esau wanted instant gratification, he never thought about his actions, its consequences, and he did not think about the effect of his actions on the future. The Rabbinic writings explain, "Esau showed to others that (in his opinion) established Birthright order is not morally correct. They should honor rather those who are more talented above others." The writer noted that many of the great leaders of the nations of the world followed Esau's opinion and disparaged the status of birth, rather they believed everything should depend on the natural abilities of each individual (Netziv, Haamek Davar to Gen 23, 34). As a result, Esau has exported his ideas to nations today, where they elect leaders based on their ability to charm voters and make promises they do not keep. In the Western world, and all those influenced by Esau's democratic system, they believe that anyone can become a leader of a nation through this process regardless of pedigree.

ESAU REPLACES NIMROD

The significance of Esau replacing Nimrod is outlined in Scripture and tells the story of how Esau, while out in the field one day on a hunting expedition, came upon Nimrod, the king of

Babylon and his men. Before this encounter, the people knew of Nimrod's jealousy of Esau because he believed that Esau, the grandson of Abraham, would one day replace him as the ruler of the earth since Esau, too, was a very skillful hunter. The Scriptures described Nimrod, "He was a mighty hunter before YAHUAH: wherefore it is said, even as Nimrod the mighty hunter before YAHUAH" (Genesis 10:9). YAHUAH had shown the sign that Abraham's descendant would replace Nimrod in the earth. Thus, upon Esau meeting Nimrod in the field alone where his men had left him resting, Esau saw an opportunity to eliminate his rival and did not hesitate to attack. Esau ambushed Nimrod and killed him. Nimrod cried out for help to his men, but they were too far away, and by the time they arrived, Esau had already murdered Nimrod and stolen the special garments he wore (Jasher 27:1-12).

According to the book of Jasher, we can trace these stolen garments back to Adam and Eve, who had passed them to Enoch, who had given them to Noah. Ham had then stolen them from his father, Noah, and given them to his first-born son, Cush. Later, Cush gave these special garments to his son, Nimrod. "And Nimrod became strong when he put on the garments, and ELOHIYM gave him might and strength, and he was a mighty hunter in the earth, yea, he was a mighty hunter in the field, and hunted the animals, and built altars, and he offered upon them animals before YAHUAH" (Jasher 7:30).

The Scriptures prophesied that Abraham and his seed would replace Nimrod as the power on the earth. They also record that Nimrod died by the sword of Esau in a manner filled with shame and contempt. The seed of Abraham caused Nimrod's death just as Nimrod had seen in his dream, and which confirmed the omen that his wise men saw on the night of Abraham's birth "And they said to each other, this only betokens the child that has been born to Terah tonight, who will grow up and be fruitful, and multiply, and possess all the earth, he and his children forever, and he and his seed will slay great kings, and inherit their lands" (Jasher 8:4).

It was upon returning home from the altercation with Nimrod, Esau, exhausted and hungry, sold his birthright for a bowl of red soup. He first secured the garments he had stolen from Nimrod and then looked to eat something out of fear of dying. He approached his brother, Jacob, who had just finished cooking a pot of lentil pottage. "And he said unto his brother Jacob, Behold I shall die this day, and wherefore then do I want the birthright? And Jacob acted wisely with Esau in this matter, and Esau sold his birthright to Jacob, for it was so brought about by YAHUAH" (Jasher 27:12). Thus, they say Esau abhorred his birthright.

IDENTIFYING ESAU WITH BLESSINGS, HE RECEIVED

After trading his birthright to his younger brother Jacob, Esau expected that he would still receive the blessing designated to him as Isaac's firstborn son, even though he hated his birthright and claimed the pottage was more important because he was near death. So, when Isaac's eyes became dim, and he thought he would die soon, he called Esau. He asked Esau to prepare a savory stew from the meat he hunted, and then he would bless him as the first-born son. Rebekah overheard the conversation between Isaac and Esau. Because she knew the promise of the blessing and heritage was not for Esau, she set a plan in motion to ensure Jacob would receive the blessing instead.

Once Esau left to capture the deer from the field, Rebekah started her strategy that would stop Isaac from doing what he intended to do. She told Jacob to catch and kill two kid goats so she could prepare a savory stew for Isaac, "Go now to the flock and fetch me from thence two good kids of the goats; and I will make savory meat for thy father, such as he loveth: and thou shall bring it to thy father, that he may eat, and that he may bless thee before his death" (Genesis 27: 9-10). Jacob, afraid to follow Rebekah's instructions, hesitated because he thought Isaac would recognize him. It worried him that his father would curse him for deceiving him. He also knew Esau was hairy and that his skin was smooth. Yet, Rebekah assured Jacob that whatever happened, she would take responsibility for it all.

Jacob's protest did not deter Rebekah, and she continued with her plan. She prepared goat's hair skins to cover Jacob's hands and neck and sent him to put on some of Esau's clothing so he could smell like Esau. Then, Rebekah insisted that Jacob take the stew she had prepared for Isaac. Jacob obeyed, and the blessing intended for the first-born, Isaac gave to Jacob instead of Esau.

"And Isaac, his father, said unto him: 'Come near and kiss me, my son. And he came near and kissed him. And he smelled the smell of his raiment, and he blessed him and said: 'Behold the smell of my son is as the smell of a full field which YAHUAH give you of the dew of heaven and the dew of earth, and plenty of corn and oil: Let nations serve you, and peoples bow down to you. Be lord over your brethren and let your mother's sons bow down to you; And may all the blessings wherewith YAHUAH has blessed me and blessed Abraham, my father; be imparted to you and your seed forever: Cursed be he that curses you and blessed be he that blesses you'" (Jubilees 26: 21-24).

As soon as Jacob left his father's presence, Esau entered with the savory meat he had prepared, but Isaac had already blessed Jacob, the younger brother. When Esau realized that Jacob had received the blessing he expected to receive, he cried out, weeping and begging his father to give him a blessing. "Hast thou but one blessing, my father? Bless me, even me also, O my father and Esau lifted his voice and wept" (Genesis 27: 38). Isaac tried to console Esau, but he could not comfort him. He then gave Esau another blessing and told him how he would live from that day forward. "Behold, far from the dew of the earth shall be your dwelling and far from the dew of heaven from above. And by your sword, you will live, and you will serve your brother. And it shall happen when you become great, and shake his yoke from off your neck, you shall sin a complete sin unto death, and YAHUAH shall root your seed out from under heaven" (Jubilees 26:33). The book of

Esdras later confirms how YAHUAH would destroy Esau and his descendants from the earth. Esdras speaks to a woman whose only son had died as he found her weeping inconsolably. She had been weeping for her only son. Still, she represented how the earth would weep for an entire nation of people brought forth by the earth and prophesied for destruction forever "For out of her came all at first, and out of her shall all others come, and, behold, they walk almost all into destruction, and a multitude of them is utterly rooted out" (2 Esdras 10:10).

Because he did not receive the blessing, Esau held a deep-rooted, perpetual hatred for his brother, Jacob, and since then, he has tried to destroy, Jacob and his descendants throughout history. The hatred that Esau has for Jacob led the Prophet Ezekiel to prophesy a stern warning against Esau and his descendants. He explains how and why Esau would meet his end. "Because thou hast had a perpetual hatred, and hast shed the blood of the children of Israel by the force of the sword in the time of their calamity, in the time that their iniquity had an end: Therefore, as I live, saith YAHUAH ELOHIYM, I will prepare thee unto blood, and blood shall pursue thee: since thou hast not hated blood, even blood shall pursue thee" (Ezekiel 35: 5-6).

IDENTIFYING ESAU AND JACOB THROUGH THE PROMISES

Jacob and Esau were both given promises by their father, Isaac. Jacob would rule in the beginning, and Isaac promised Esau that once Jacob's foot came off his neck, he would begin his rule on the earth. History shows that Israel lost its power because of disobedience to the laws, statutes, and commandments. They broke the Covenant that YAHUAH established with them on Mount Sinai. And, because of their disobedience, the Highest YAHUAH used Esau to cast the children of Israel out of the land and scattered them to the four corners of the earth. The complete removal of the great nation of Israel from the Judean territory in 135AD open the way for Edom-Rome, the Edomites, to continue their domination of the earth as the Roman Empire, which arose in 168BC.

IDENTIFYING ESAU BY DIFFERENT NAMES

YAHUAH gave Esau, who is Edom, a mark described in Scripture as the "red" people who later labeled themselves "white." Therefore, the Scripture describes him, "But I have made Esau bare, I have uncovered his secret places, and he shall not be able to hide himself: his seed is spoiled, and his brethren, and his neighbors, and he is not" (Jeremiah 49:10). The mark that YAHUAH gave to Esau prevents him from hiding his shame, anger, his lies, or the people of whom he mingled. However, Esau, who is Edom, has taken the mark that represents a curse and makes it a sign of their superiority. Esau has used this curse to erase the identity and likeness of all historical characters and replace them with the likeness of themselves. Before the capabilities of DNA science, created by Esau, who is Edom, they also claimed humanity to begin with them. They implied that all people emanated from the descendants of Esau-Edom and are carriers of their genes. However, scientifically this is not possible as black cannot come from white.

Besides, Esau-Edom has used various schemes to avoid the truth of their identity from being revealed. They have accomplished this by relabeling and revising the history and changing the land borders on maps, then replacing the people of many territories with the likeness of themselves. They have appropriated all significant accomplishments in history and attribute them to be done by the "white" man. For example, in the history of Nimrod, who was the grandson of Ham, the progenitor of the dark races, they depict Nimrod as a white man or, at least, the modern-day Middle Eastern white man. Through Esau's deceptive morals, he has convinced the world that anyone of Nimrod's stature and prominence could not be black because, according to their narrative, black skin was the curse of Ham. However, the "white" skin of leprosy was the true curse. Esau, who is Edom, has turned everything around and upside down, in his attempt to reclaim Jacob's birthright and declare the superiority of white people. Scripture shows, however, those who are ruling the earth today, to be wicked and are in fact, foolish; "The earth is given into the hand of the wicked: he covereth the faces of the judges thereof; if not, where, and who is he" (Job 9:24)?

For hundreds of years, Esau, who is Edom, has been effective in deceiving the entire world using the lie they are the ones that have brought civilization to all nations on the earth. According to history written from Esau's perspective, they are the people who espouse truth, seek to bring peace on the earth, and are the protectors of all the earth's resources. But, the facts show that Esau-Edom has brought tyranny and death to people in every nation they have conquered. Esau, who is Edom, has been consistent and thorough in their use of the sword, the gun, exploitation, and the religions they have created to destroy the earth's inhabitants, in particular, the descendants of Jacob. Christianity, the religion of Esau-Edom, preaches a message of 'love' in the name of their god, the beast that most of the world follows. The truth is that Esau and his descendants have lied about everything and have recast and renamed people and events to reflect Esau-Edom's identity. They have renamed themselves many times to avoid detection. After the descendants of Esau moved out of Mount Seir to the Negev Valley south of Judaea, they changed their name from Edomites to the translated Greek form Idumeans, which later morphed into Herodians during the time of the Herods who ruled over the Judeans. They also identified as Nabateans, Arabians, Greeks, and Romans. From 600 to 700AD, history identifies a group of them as the Germanic peoples known as the Franks, Lombardi, Vandals, and later the

Khazars. As they spread throughout the earth, they identified by the name of the land, they settled and recognized their heritage as European.

Esau-Edom adopted the name European for the landmass to the north where the sons of Japheth, the original inhabitants, lived. They named the area after the Roman Goddess Europa now called Europe. The sons of Japheth, the original inhabitants of the land that fell to them by lot after the flood, have been whited out and replaced by the Edomites, the descendants of Esau. Thus, history shows that whenever Esau conquered other lands, they took the name of the land they conquered and renamed the areas while continuing to identify as having European lineage. In their recent history, they claim the label Jews, appropriating the name of Judah, the fourth son of Jacob-Israel, to a segment of their descendants said to be converts of the religion of Judaism. And, they identify as the Khazar from the Caucus Mountains of Eastern Europe.

The Edomites changed the original names of the lands to hide the evidence that other people inhabited the territories before they settled in these areas. They now identify by their changed names based on the places they are born. These names include German, Russian, Greek, Brazilian, Italian, Swiss, French, Canadian, Turks, British, Australian, South African, Columbian, Argentinian, and American. They are also the white Arabs, the white Assyrians, the white Jordanians, and the leaders of many other nations. Esau, who is Edom, is a diverse people because they have mixed with every nation and has control over the earth. They have used these name changes to obscure the identity of their blood ties to Esau, who is Edom-Rome. This mingling with the other people has led those deceived to believe that the white leaders among them are now the third race. However, they are all the descendants of Esau because they carry Esau-Edom's mark of having white skin, which they use as a sign of their white power. The nations have made the Negro people living in these lands to feel inferior and encouraged many of them that to improve their race, by mixing with white people. And, although Esau-Edom has mingled his seed with every nation, the Edomites still insists they are an elite people of a pure Aryan race—a race with no mixture.

This clouding of Esau-Edom's identity has also made it possible for Esau, who is Edom, to deflect and blame the other nations for the wicked actions against the Chosen people of YAHUAH. For example, they use the evidence of Arabs persecuting Christians as proof that it is the Arabs that are the descendants of Esau. Many Arabs seen today are not true Arabs because they mixed with Esau and became the white Edomite Arab. However, all Arabs did not mix with Esau but may have mixed with Arabs who mingled with Esau. Therefore, Arabs are white, and some are different shades of brown. Still, some are very black. In Scripture, it was the Canaanites and the Ishmaelites who first mixed with the descendants of Esau. Biblical and secular history shows that the Arabs are the descendants of Ishmael and the six sons of Abraham he fathered with his wife Keturah after the death of Sarah. "And Ishmael and his sons, and the sons of Keturah and their sons, went together and dwelt from Paran to the entering of Babel in all the land toward the east-facing the desert. And these mingled with each other, and they called their name Araviym (Arabs) and Yishmaeliym (Ishmael)" (Jubilees 20:12-13).

The oral and written history of the Arab people tells of these seven tribes that descended from Abraham and make-up the Arab people. In a commentary on Isaiah in the Rabbinic writings, the writer stresses that Edom comes from Rome, which extends pagan Rome. It continues that, Edom appears to have merged with Amalek, who claims to be hereditary Israel as Judeo-Christianity. The commentator further notes that they should not forget that the enemy of the true Israelites is the grandson of Esau (Zepho), not Ishmael, which is the Arab world. It is Esau, who is Edom and Rome, who has tried to change history and the outcome of Prophecy by blaming the Arabs for the destabilization of the nations in the Middle East. Edom-Rome has done this to bring about events of their so-called "end" times. And, it is Edom-Rome who is guilty and has conspired with Edomite Arabs to engage in the tactics of undermining the nations that surround Palestine to support the false narrative that these Arab Muslims are the descendants of Esau who will cause Armageddon and bring about the destruction of the world. However, prophecy shows that it is Esau-Edom-Rome, the brother of Jacob, who has had the dominion over the earth and Israel for at least two thousand years based on the Gregorian calendar, of Rome.

IDENTIFYING ESAU IN PROPHECY

Esau is Edom-Rome, who, in these 'last' days, has revived and revised the Roman Empire. This merged power has established a system of governing that extends the ancient Roman Empire. In this modern-day version of the 'holy' Roman Empire, now identified as the New World Order, exist three different nations that act as the head and form the leadership of this order. They are described as the 'Trinity of Globalist Control' and comprise three city-states - the Vatican, London, and Washington, D.C. These city-states do not belong to any other nation, are self-ruled, and pay no taxes. They have their separate laws, own police, mayors, post offices, separate flags, and their own identities (A Plaintruth Video). A prophecy in 4 Ezra confirms the existences of these nations that YAHUAH would raise up in the last days. "And whereas you saw three heads resting, this is the interpretation: In the last days shall EL ELYON raise up three kingdoms, and renew many things therein, and they shall have the dominion of the earth. And of those that dwell therein, with much oppression, above all those that were before them: therefore are they called the heads of the eagle. For these are they that shall accomplish his wicknedness, and that shall finish his last end" (4 Ezra 12:22-25).

These three nations led by the Vatican holds full authority over the religions of the world and assumes the role as the head of the Babylonian Mystery Religions. Its overall power is controlled by the Pope, who sits in Caesar's seat as King over both state and church. In 1306 Pope Boniface VII and the Vatican congress confirmed this status when he declared the Pope to be the trustee of all of Jesus Christ's holdings on Earth, including the reaping of all lands and souls. These trusts are still in place in our Western legal systems today. The city of London heads the world's finances, and Washington D.C. controls the military arm of this revived Roman Empire. All three entities are separate states within their respective countries and are independent. Therefore, they act without the consent of the people. They all operate under Roman law, known as "Lex Fori." And, the goal of these three system administrators is to operate as a one-world government under Papal Rome, with the United Nations, which is symbolic of the ten toes of the dream of Nebuchadnezzar. They have established a one-world government for centuries ruling the earth under the order of Edom-Rome and have hidden the truth from the unsuspecting citizens of the world. Papal Rome's narrative that they are now planning for a one-world government with a leader, who rules as king, is, in fact, not true as they have always been over the nations. The United Nations is just another organization in this beast system. Rome has never given up its power and authority as king and Pontifex Maximus, although they have made the world believe they only retook control in the 17th century.

The prophet Ezra saw this outcome in a dream he recorded in 2 Esdras 11: 1-2, "Then saw I a dream, and, behold, there came up from the sea an eagle which had twelve feathered wings and three heads. And I saw, and, behold, she spread her wings over all the earth, and all the winds of the air blew on her and were gathered together." Together, these three states make up the Revised Papal Roman Empire known as the fourth Beast of Daniel, and the Revelations prophesied to be ruling at the end of this age. Daniel's vision confirms the events that would take place during Edom-Rome's rule, "and of the ten horns that were in his head, and of the other which came up, and before whom three fell; even of that horn that had eyes, and a mouth that spake very great things, whose look was more stout than his fellows I beheld, and the same horn made war with the saints, (Israel) and prevailed against them; until the ancient of days came, and judgment was given to the saints of the Highest, and the time came that the saints possessed the kingdom. Thus, he said, the fourth beast shall be the fourth kingdom upon the earth, which shall be diverse from all kingdoms, and shall devour the whole earth, and shall tread it down, and break it in pieces" (Daniel 7:20-23). After this time, Jacob-Israel will begin their rulership. "For Esau is the end of the world, and Jacob is the beginning of it that followeth" (2 Esdras 6:9).

Edom-Rome has ruled the earth with deception and an iron fist to ensure their continued dominance over the nations. They have instilled much fear in the nations through intimidation and with deceitful treaties of peace. They have ruled by the sword and false religions. This system has influence over the earth with a strict authority that governs all the important resources needed to survive in their kingdom. The exercise control over the water to drink as well as the places where one may migrate. They have gained the wealth of the entire earth by the sword and will use the sword to protect what they have acquired. The modern-day Edomites Roman Empire is still willing to kill, steal, and destroy using deception while boasting about its success and powerful weaponry. The defense arm of this kingdom, in a report delivered at the Pentagon by General Franklin Blaisdell, a former director of Space Operations and Integration speaking about the Asian region regarding China's rise and an attempt to intimidate them proclaimed;

> I pity a country that will come up against us. The synergy with air land and sea forces and our ability to control the battlespace and seize the high ground is devastating. All countries respect the power of the United States and respect how dominant we are in this region, and we get better and better and better!"[14]

The threat is not at China alone, but to any nation that Edom-Rome considers a danger to them by stepping out of the line of the agreed power system. Edom-Rome has used its dominance to keep the more significant and not so substantial nations in fear because of their willingness to engage in war. Margret Thatcher, the former Prime Minister of Great Britain, describes the story of how the Europeans explored and colonized, without apology and civilized much of the world, as an extraordinary tale of talent, skill, and courage. This statement confirms that Edom-Rome knows they are the fourth beast power of Daniel's vision, and they are aware that all the nations in power today have allied with them if outside foreign forces come against them. They are all part of the system that is against the kingdom of true Israel rising and ruling. Therefore, they pretend to accumulate weapons of mass destruction against each other when, in fact, the war they are preparing to defend against is YAHUSHA, the Lion of the Tribe of Judah. There is no other nation that will fight against Edom-Rome because they are all a part of the one Beast system ruling the entire earth. As President Ronald Reagan stated in a speech to the United Nations General Assembly, "Perhaps we need some outside universal threat to make us recognized this common bond." He continued that the differences would vanish if faced with an alien threat from outside this world. They are indeed waiting for a threat from space that will unite them in their common goal, and they know that the only risk from outside our closed system is YAHUAH. Even though China has risen to become the second-largest economic power next to America, they are still no threat because China needs Esau-Edom as they need China.

The nations of the earth have all joined in the conspiracy against the only government that can intimidate them. That nation is Israel, the true descendants of Jacob. They hope to prevent Israel from rising and ever ruling again. Psalms 83:2 reveals what they have done, "They have taken crafty counsel against thy people, and consulted against thy hidden ones." The scripture also names the nations who have joined Edom in this conspiracy, "For they have consulted together with one consent: they are confederate against thee: The tabernacles of Edom, and the Ishmaelites; of Moab, and the Hagarenes: Gebal, and Ammon, and Amalek; the Philistines with the inhabitants of Tyre; Assyria also is joined with them: they have helped the children of Lot" (Psalm 83:5-8). These nations are still identifiable today, although they have tried to hide behind new names and new land borders to obscure their identities. For example, they made the boundaries of the Hittite Empire and now call it Turkey, and the Phoenician Empire of Carthage shown as a smaller nation called Libya. The rulers of this system have denied their actions. They have instituted a culture of ridicule and mockery of anyone who may suggest there is a conspiracy and identify the co-conspirators. However, their

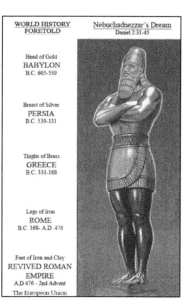

35

denials will not deter the inevitable from happening, when the Highest YAHUAH returns and gathers his chosen ones.

So, in Esau-Edom's quest to keep the identity of Israel hidden, they have covered their own identity and have gone to great lengths to discredit the Hebrew Scriptures as it relates to the covenant YAHUAH made with Israel. They would prefer to believe the etchings they find on rocks before they admit that the Hebrew Scriptures show the real history of the Earth.

PROPHECY PREDICTIONS FOR EDOM-ROME

Many prophecies reference what will happen to Esau, who is Edom because of their wickedness. In the books of Daniel and Revelation, there appear two prophecies that predict and confirm the role the Edomites and the Roman Empire will play as the fourth beast power. YAHUAH ELOHIYM has allowed Edom-Rome rulership over the earth for a certain period and based on prophecy their reign will end at the return of the HAMASHIACH and the coming Kingdom of YAHUAH.

The book of Daniel records an account of Nebuchadnezzar, the King of Babylon's dream. During the time the Judeans were in Babylonian captivity, the king had a dream he could not recall and invited his magicians and soothsayers to not only interpret the dream but also reveal what the dream was because he knew the dream was consequential, but he could not remember it. However, none of these men could figure out the dream, so he ordered Arioch to put them all to death. Arioch, the captain of the king's guard, told Daniel about the king's order and Daniel asked to see the king. He told King Nebuchadnezzar that he would seek the Highest, YAHUAH, to interpret his dream and reminded him that the wise men, astrologers, and magicians could not tell him the dream or know what it meant as only the Highest, YAHUAH, in heaven, could reveal and tell the secrets as he saw in his dream. Daniel sought the answer in prayer and received the interpretation and described to the king what he saw in his dream and what it meant, "Thou, O king, sawest, and behold a great image. This great image, whose brightness was excellent, stood before thee; and the form thereof was terrible. This image's head was of gold, his breast and his arms of silver, his belly and his thigh of brass, his legs of iron, his feet part of iron and part of clay. Thou sawest till that a stone was cut out without hands, which smote the image upon his feet that were of iron and clay and braked them to pieces" (Daniel 2:31-34).

Daniel then explained to the King what his dream meant. "But there is a God in heaven that revealeth secrets, and maketh known to the king Nebuchadnezzar what shall be in the latter days. Thy dream and the visions of thy head upon thy bed are these" (Daniel 2:28). In his explanation, Daniel described that the statue represented four kingdoms that would rule the Earth. Nebuchadnezzar's kingdom was the first, represented by the head of gold, which showed their superiority. The Persian rule would follow, Greece would come next, and the final empire would be Rome, who would have rulership at the time when the

HAMASHIACH returns to set up the Kingdom of YAHUAH. And, according to Legends of the Jews (Vol. 3, pg. 167), "God will call out to the Messiah: Roar at this monster that devours the fat of the nations, that justifies being a descendant of Abraham by his grandson Esau, the nation that kept Israel back from the study of the Torah, and tempted them to deeds that are in accord with the wishes of Satan."

The feet of this statute symbolized this final ruling kingdom represented by the iron and clay. The iron implied the kingdom of Edom-Rome, and the clay signified Israel, the saints of the Most High. Edom-Rome has tried to mix with Israel and, in fact, replace Israel as history has shown down through the ages. However, these two groups of people could never mix. The ten toes represented ten kingdoms that would also try to unite. Still, because of the iron and clay, they will not cleave to one another as iron does not mix with clay, "And whereas thou sawest iron mixed with miry clay, they shall mingle themselves with the seed of men: but they shall not cleave one to another, even as iron is not mixed with clay." (Daniel 2:43). Prophecy shows the descendants of Esau-Edom represented by these ten kingdoms will continue to assert control over Israel until the HAMASHIACH returns; they are all part of the Roman Empire as the former Prime Minister of Great Britain Margret Thatcher admits a partial truth in a speech, "I want to start by disposing of some myths about my country Britain. We British are as much heirs to the legacy of European culture as any other nation. Our links to the rest of Europe, the continent of Europe, have been the dominant factor in our history. For three hundred years, we were part of the Roman Empire, and our maps still trace the straight lines of the roads the Romans built." It is only part of the truth because the people who call themselves British are all Edom-Rome and descendants of Esau who conquered the British Isles, which was first inhabited by the descendants of Jacob. The HAMASHIACH will return during the times of Edom-Rome's rule"And in the days of these kings shall the God of heaven set up a kingdom which shall never be destroyed: and the kingdom shall not be left to other people, but it shall break in pieces and consume all these kingdoms, and it shall stand forever." (Daniel 2:44).

The stone that appeared, while being cut without hands, would come and smite the feet, breaking it into fragments. The stone characterizes the Kingdom of the Most High the final kingdom to come on the earth where Israel with the HAMASHIACH will rule. Both Biblical and secular histories confirm that these four Empires existed and ruled during the time recorded on the statute. However, Edom-Rome, the fourth power still ruling today, has tried to distort the truth by claiming that the Roman Empire ended in 476AD, and the Revived Roman Empire did not resume until 800AD by some historians' accounts and others claim the time to be later. The subsequent period they called the dark ages when they claim people had regressed in their way of living. But evidence shows this did not happen, and Edom-

Rome added this version to obscure the identity of Esau, who is Edom-Rome. All the same, YAHUAH is revealing with historical evidence which they are as we draw nearer to the end of this age. The most ancient Midrashic proof found in the Meghila of Rabbi Ishmael attached to the verse from Genesis that introduced the time YAHUAH appears to Abram (Abraham) shows ("as the sun was going down, a torpor fell upon Abram and behold, a great terror seized him," C. 15:12): "Frightening" describes the Babylonian empire, "chaos," describes the Median empire, which will bring Israel to "desolation," great is the Greek empire which will lead Israel into 'darkness,' "fell" this is the fourth empire, Rome describes 'the abyss' in which it will fall and is found guilty of destroying Israel.[15] Edom-Rome is the fourth and final beast supremacy on the earth, and their rule began in 168AD. There are no gaps in history, although they have tried to insert evidence into the narrative that will support that claim.

The revelation that John wrote and YAHAUH gave to YAHUSHA to show to his servants what would happen during the "end-times" also reveals this fourth beast power when the seals opened. "And when he had opened the fourth seal, I heard the voice of the fourth beast say, Come and see. And I looked and beheld a pale horse: and the name that sat on him was Death, and Hell followed with him. And YAHUAH gave power unto them over the fourth part of the earth, to kill with the sword, and with hunger, and with death, and with the beasts of the earth." (Revelation 6:7-8). The descendants of Edom-Rome, the fourth beast power, have been faithful in committing severe atrocities against the Hebrew Israelites, as stated in this prophecy. Despite their claim of having the power and authority to destroy the entire earth, YAHUAH has only given them control over one-fourth of the land. According to Edom-Rome's historical timeline, they have been ruling and carrying out this destruction for over two thousand years, "And the fourth came, and overcame all the beasts that were past, and had power over the world with great fearfulness, and over the whole compass of the earth with much oppression; and so long time dwelt he upon the earth with deceit." (2 Esdras 11:40).

When the fifth seal was opened, it showed those of Israel killed by the sword, famine, and the beast. These that were martyred called for the Highest YAHUAH to come and avenge their blood, "And when he had opened the fifth seal, I saw under the altar the souls of them that were slain for the word of YAHUAH, and for the testimony which they held: and they cried with a loud voice, saying, How long, O YAHUAH, holy and true, dost thou not judge and avenge our blood on them that dwell on the earth" (Revelation 6:9-10)? History shows that the Edomite-Roman Empire has ruled the earth since 168BC to this present day. They ruled as the Pagan Roman Empire then transitioned into the revived and revised Papal Roman Empire in 325AD after the Council of Nicaea. Edom-Rome, as Papal Rome, continues as the Roman Empire and the Popes occupy Caesar's seat. The Pope keeps the title "King" and Pontifex Maximus, which means

Caesar's successor, with the title Vicar of Christ, which means he sits as the substitute of Christ. It was Pope Pius V, who confirmed this belief in a statement; he asserted the Pope and God are the same. The Papal Roman Empire also teaches and believes it replaces the Highest, YAHUAH'S presence on the earth. But the prophecy declares that Israel will remove them and take their rightful place, "These great beasts, which are four, are four kings, who shall arise out of the earth. But the saints of the Most High shall take the kingdom, and possess the kingdom forever, even forever and ever" (Daniel 7:17-18).

---

[1] Rabbinic literature writings described here in its broadest sense refer to the entire spectrum of Rabbinic writings throughout Israel's history.

[2] The Zohar (Hebrew זֹהַר "Splendor" or "Radiance") is the foundational work in the literature of Jewish thought. It is a group of books including commentary on the mystical aspects of the Torah (The five books of Moses).

[3] Rabbi Shimon bar Yochai also known by his acronym Rashbi was a 2nd century tannaitc sage in ancient Judea, said to be active after the destruction of the second Temple in 70 AD.

[4] Alain de Benoist (2012) is a French academic philosopher, a founder of the Nouvelle Drolte (New Right), and head of the French think tank (GRECE). Benoist is opposed to Christianity, the United States, free market, neoliberalism, democracy and egalitarianism.

[5] Hebraic tradition refers to the traditions and customs of the Israelites and Judeans of Judea.

[6] Mireille Hadas-Lebel is a French academic and historian of Antiquity, specialist in the history of Judaism.

[7] Legends of the Jews are a chronological compilation of aggadah from hundreds of biblical legends in Mishnah. The compilation consists of seven volumes, synthesized by Louis Ginzberg.

[8] King Solomon's relationship to Jacob, who was the father of Judah and his brothers, and Judah, was the kingly line that David the father of Solomon came through.

Solomon's disobedience caused the kingdom to be divided into two – the 10 northern tribes of Israel and Judah, the two southern tribes.

[9] Polemic Writings refer to ideas that stir up controversy by having a negative opinion usually aimed at a group of people.

[10] Sefer of Yosef Hamekaneh the book of Joseph the Official is a 13th century Jewish apologetic text. The book is also translated Book of Joseph the Zealot.

[11] Apostate Jews refer to the rejection of Judaism by the Jews and possible defection to another religion.

[12] Joseph bar Nathan, a Jew, was an official in northern France during the mid-thirteenth century.

[13] Jules Michelet was a French historian. He was born in Paris to a family with Huguenot traditions. He was the first historian to devote himself to anything like picturesque history. His lively imagination and his strong religious and political prejudices made him regard all things from a singularly personal point of view.

[14] General Franklin Blaisdell is a retired Major General in the United States Air force. In 1984, Blaisdell was named Director, Military Strategic and Tactical Relay System Platform, Integration Military Special Programs Office at Headquarters Electronic Systems Center.

[15] Mekhila of Rabbi Ishmael is a halakhic Midrash to the Book of Exodus. The name "Mekhilta" corresponds to the Hebrew "middah" ("measure," rule) and is used to denote a compilation of scriptural exegesis.

CHAPTER 2

Early History of Jacob and Esau

WHEN JACOB LEFT TO GO TO HIS UNCLE Laban in Haran, Esau told Eliphaz, his young son, to follow him and to murder Jacob when the opportunity arose. Esau still held a deep-seated hatred of Jacob, and he intended to execute his plan even if it meant having his young son accomplish the task for him. Eliphaz and some of Esau's brothers-in-law followed Jacob while on his way to Haran, intending to do what Esau had requested once Jacob had arrived at a desolate place. However, when they approached Jacob, he did not resist as he did not know of their intentions. Instead, Jacob greeted them as friends and unnerved them by his kindness. Eliphaz then told Jacob of Esau's directive to kill him, "Thus did my father command me, and now, therefore, I will not deviate from the orders which my father gave me," (Jasher 29:36). However, because Jacob was righteous and gentle in manner, he pleaded with Eliphaz and his companions not to kill him. YAHUAH intervened on Jacob's behalf and allowed him to find favor with Eliphaz and his uncles. Eliphaz then instructed the men not to harm his uncle, Jacob. In return, Jacob offered all of his belongings to Eliphaz, which they accepted along with the silver and gold that Isaac and Rebekah had gifted to Jacob before his journey. When Eliphaz returned home, his report did not please Esau; in fact, it angered him that Eliphaz had spared Jacob's life. Eliphaz then tried to appease his father with the silver and gold, but he could not appease him, because, the only thing that would satisfy Esau was Jacob's death.

When Jacob arrived at his uncle Laban's home, he came with no gold, silver, nothing. As a result, Jacob had to work for Laban for twice as long to pay for his wives' hands in marriage. The expanded version of these events, written in the book of Jasher, helps to fill in the missing pieces of the puzzle, so it forms a complete picture. Many occurrences, such as this incident recorded in the book of Jasher, helps to broaden the story of Esau and Jacob left out of the Canonized version of Scriptures. This omission appears to have been a deliberate attempt on behalf of those seeking to hide the identity of Esau, who is Edom, and the adversarial relationship he had with his brother Jacob from the start. Esau has been the adversary of Jacob ever since, and without this knowledge, the descendants of Jacob cannot understand how it has impacted them. The descendants of Jacob, being awakened today, need to know and understand not only who they are but who Esau is and the effect he has had on their lives.

The Canonized text does not include the story of Esau sending his son Eliphaz to kill Jacob. The Canonized book emphasizes the lie that Jacob stole Esau's blessing when the evidence shows Esau sold his birthright for a bowl of red pottage. Instead, Edom-Rome, the producers of the Canonized version of the Biblical text, does not include the book of Jasher because they claim the writers of the book of Jasher produced too many inaccurate accounts of stories. However, I have found evidence to the contrary. My understanding of how the scribes who wrote Hebrew text conducted their writings show that the writers were meticulous in recording accurate accounts of Hebrew history and would rewrite the entire script if there was one little mistake. Although, I would not put it past Esau-Edom to have added or taken away information to support their narrative. This research shows that the book of Jasher is necessary Scripture in putting the pieces of the puzzle together, so we get the whole story of Jacob-Israel and Esau who is Edom the main characters called by YAHUAH to fulfill his purpose on the earth in these last days before YAHUSHA returns to set up the Kingdom of YAHUAH ELOHIYM.

JACOB TOLD TO RETURN HOME

As Jacob came to the end of his service to his uncle Laban twenty-one years after his arrival, YAHUAH told him to return home, "And YAHUAH appeared to Jacob at the end of the last six years, and said unto him, "Arise, go forth out of this land, and return to the land of your birthplace and I will be with you" (Jasher 31:37). Jacob had received the message earlier from Deborah, her nurse whom she had sent to assist Jacob with returning home with his family. While Deborah brought the message to Jacob, she could not convince him to leave, and so she stayed with Jacob while the other servants returned to Rebekah and Isaac. It was after some time that Jacob gathered enough courage to tell Laban, his father-in-law, of his plan to leave and return to his parents. However, Laban was against the idea and did not give Jacob his blessing to leave and take his daughters and grandchildren away. Although Jacob did not receive Laban's blessing, he was not deterred from preparing to return to his parents. So, one day, when Jacob knew Laban would be away for three days, he made his move and left Haran with his family and servants.

Upon Laban's return, he learned that Jacob had packed up his family and left Haran to return to his home. Laban tracked them down, and as he caught up to them, he inquired, "What is this you have done to flee and deceive me and lead my daughters and their children as captives taken by the sword? And you did not suffer me to kiss them and send them away with joy, and you stole my gods and went away" (Jasher 31:48). Jacob denied stealing the gods and told Laban that if he discovered the gods among his things, he could kill the person who had stolen them and packed them away. What Jacob did not realize, however, was that Rachel had stolen the gods because she knew Laban could use them to track them down. While Laban's men searched Jacob and his family and their belongings, Rachel sat on her father's gods on top of a camel. When they asked her to come down so they could examine the camel she rode, she refused to do so, claiming to have her monthly cycle. Laban and his men searched all of Jacob's belongings but never found the idols he had accused Jacob of stealing.

Once Laban and his servants could not find the gods among Jacob's belongings, Laban suggested to Jacob that they make a covenant together to ensure his daughters' safety, "And it shall be a testimony between you and me; if you shall afflict my daughters, or shall take other women besides my daughters, even ELOHIYM shall be a witness between you and me in this matter" (Jasher 31:51) and me. Following the covenant, Jacob and Laban offered a sacrifice on a heap they had made. They named this place Gilead. That night they shared a meal at this place and rested together. I believe Rachel's subsequent death, during the birth of Benjamin, resulted from her stealing her father's gods, and Jacob telling Laban that he could kill the person he found to have stolen the gods, which implied the threat of Rachel's death or anyone who had the idols.

The following morning, Laban and his servants arose early and wept with his daughters. He kissed them and returned to his home in Haran. However, Laban had not been honest with Jacob, and he soon sought to undermine the covenant he had made with Jacob the night before. Before Laban returned home, he sent his son Be'or and ten other servants who had accompanied him to go ahead of Jacob and advise Esau, who was in Mount Seir, that Jacob was on his way back to Canaan. Laban instructed Be'or to tell Esau that Jacob had stolen his daughters and grandchildren without his blessing after he had done so much for him. By doing this, Laban's goal was to entice Esau into harming Jacob and his family because he knew the hatred that Esau still had for Jacob, "If it be your wish to go to him, find him, and you can do unto him as your soul desires, and Laban's messengers came and told Esau all these things" (Jasher 31:63).

ESAU GOES TO MEET JACOB

Esau and the Horites still lived together in Mount Seir when Jacob returned to Canaan. Once Esau learned what had happened between Laban and Jacob, his hatred for Jacob reignited, and, again, Esau longed more than ever to kill his brother. Esau left his home to find Jacob. He took his sons, his servants, and the children of Seir, the Horites of Canaanite lineage Esau had mixed. Altogether, there were about four hundred men with swords ready for battle against Jacob and his family. Esau intended to go to war and destroy Jacob. However, once Be'or left Esau, he went to

Canaan to tell Rebekah what Esau was planning. Rebekah was excited to hear Jacob was on his way home. She sent seventy men from the servants of Isaac to meet Jacob on his way and to tell him about Esau's plan and to act as his protection.

When Isaac's servants located Jacob, they told him that Esau was on his way to meet him and that he had planned to kill him. Jacob was terrified and he sent a message of peace to his brother, Esau. However, Esau rejected Jacob's olive branch of peace and continued marching toward him and his family. The Highest YAHUAH was with Jacob during this time and sent a host of angels to have several supernatural encounters with Esau and his men during the night. These encounters with the angels frightened Esau and his men so much that by the time they met Jacob, they were humbled and bowed at Jacob's feet, calling him lord and were willing to make peace.

Jacob, too, was humbled and still desired to give his brother, Esau, the many gifts he had set aside from his material possessions. These gifts included cattle, along with gold, silver, and some precious stones. Esau took the goods and shared them with the men he engaged in carrying out the destruction of Jacob. Because the encounter with the angels frightened Esau so much, he invited Jacob to live in Mount Seir and offered to accompany him and his family for the rest of the journey. But, Jacob still did not trust Esau and discouraged him from escorting him the rest of the journey. Jacob refused his offer and insisted that he did not need to do anything else for him and his family. He made the excuse that his children were young and could not travel as Esau would need them to and that they would need to take frequent rests. Jacob assured Esau that everything would be okay once they remained at peace with each other. Esau then took the gifts, left with his men, and returned to Mount Seir.

PROMISES MADE BY ESAU TO HIS PARENTS

Once Jacob had settled in Hebron with his family, he did his best to support his parents. However, Rebekah worried that Esau would return to harm Jacob. She, therefore, petitioned Isaac, on behalf of Jacob, to summon Esau and force him to promise not to harm Jacob after their deaths. "One petition I make unto you: make Esau swear that he will not injure Jacob, nor pursue him with hostility; for you know Esau's thoughts are perverse from his youth and there is no goodness in him; for he desires after your death to kill him. And you know all he has done since the day Jacob his brother went to Haran until this day: how he has forsaken us with his whole heart and has done evil to us; your flocks he has taken to himself and carried off all your possessions from before your face. And when we implored and besought him for what was our own, he did as a man who was taking pity on us. And he is bitter against you because you blessed Jacob your perfect and upright son; for there is no evil but only goodness in him, and since he came from Haran unto this day he has not robbed us of anything, for he brings us everything in its season always, and rejoice with all his heart when we take at his hands and blesses us and has not parted from us since he came from Haran until this day. He remains with us at home honoring us" (Jubilees 35: 9-12). Because Jacob was such a perfect son in the eyes of his parents, they both wanted to ensure that no misfortune would come to him at the hand of Esau.

Isaac agreed with Rebekah, and she summoned Esau to counsel with her. Rebekah said to Esau, "I have a petition, my son, to make unto you, and do you promise to do it, my son." He said: "I will do everything you say unto me, and I will not refuse your petition." She said unto him: "I ask you that the day I die, you will take me in and bury me near Sarah, your father's mother, and that you and Jacob will love each other and that neither will desire evil against the other, but mutual love only, and so ye will prosper, my sons, and be honored in the land's midst, and no enemy will rejoice over you, and ye will be a blessing and mercy in the eyes of all those that love you." Esau replied, "I will do all you have told me, and I shall bury you on the day you die near Sarah, my father's mother, as you have desired that her bones may be near your bones. And Jacob my brother, also, shall I love above all flesh; for I have not a brother in all the earth but him only: and this is no great merit for me if I love him; for he is my brother, and we were sown together in your body, and together came we forth from your womb, and if I do not love my brother, whom shall I love?" Then he continued by asking his mother to make sure that Jacob would not do any harm to him or his sons. "For I know that he will be king over me and concerning my sons, for on the day my father blessed him, he made him the higher and me the lower. And I swear unto you I shall love him, and not desire evil against him all the days of my life but good only." Rebekah then called Jacob and told him while Esau was present, the commandment according to the words which she had spoken to Esau. And Jacob responded, "I shall do your pleasure; believe me that no evil will proceed from my sons or from me against Esau, and I shall be first in naught save in love only" (Jubilees 35:18-27). That night, Rebekah and her sons, Esau and Jacob, ate and drank together, and later into the evening, at one hundred and fifty-six years old, Rebekah died. Together, Esau and Jacob buried their mother in the double cave near Sarah, who was Isaac's mother.

JACOB AND ESAU SHARE THE INHERITANCE

Isaac lived for several years after Rebekah's passing until he died at the age of one hundred and eighty. Once Esau learned that his father's time was drawing near, he went with his sons and household from Edom to the land of Canaan. Jacob and his sons also went from their home in Hebron to be with Isaac. Esau and Jacob and their sons met at Isaac's bedside, and they sat before him. However, Jacob was still mourning the loss of his son Joseph, whom his brothers had sold into slavery, and who Jacob had presumed was dead. The blessing was first given to the sons of Jacob when Isaac placed his hand upon them and said, "May the ELOHIYM of your fathers bless you and increase your seed like the stars of heaven for the number" (Jasher 47:5). He then blessed the sons of Esau and said, "May ELOHIYM cause you to be a dread and a terror to all that will behold you, and to all your enemies" (Jasher 47:6). Isaac then added more blessings to Jacob and his sons, "YAHUAH ELOHIYM of the whole earth said unto me, Unto your seed will I give this land for an inheritance if your children guard my statutes and my ways, and I will perform unto them the oath which I swear unto your father Abraham" (Jasher 47:7). Once Isaac had finished commanding Jacob and his children, he gave up his spirit, died, and was gathered to his people. The blessings to Esau's sons to be a dread and terror to all nations help in confirming the identity of Esau, who is Edom, as they have lived up to that description throughout the ages.

Once Isaac had died, his sons, grandsons and their families mourned for their father and grandfather. Both Esau and Jacob fell on their faces with much weeping, and the kings and people from all the neighboring lands came to accompany Esau and Jacob to bury their father. The whole area of Canaan mourned Isaac's death as they buried him with great honor, like the funeral of kings. At the end of the mourning period, Jacob took all that his father had left in the land and divided them into two parts before Esau. He told Esau to choose for himself the half he wanted. Jacob explained to Esau that YAHUAH ELOHIYM had promised the land of Canaan as an inheritance to Abraham, Isaac, and their seed, forever, and that he could choose between the area and the riches of their father. Jacob said whichever one Esau took, it would satisfy him to take the other.

This proposition concerned Esau because the choices did not appear balance; therefore, he sought the counsel of Nebayoth, the son of Ishmael. Nebayoth asked Esau, "What is this that Jacob has spoken unto you? Behold all the children of Canaan are dwelling in their land, and Jacob says he will inherit it with his seed all the days. Go now, therefore and take all your father's riches and leave Jacob, your brother in the land, as he has spoken" (Jasher 47:22-23). Although Nebayoth questioned Esau, he did not intend to get a reply because Esau already appeared to know the answer. So, Esau took all the riches that Isaac had left, including the souls, the beasts, the cattle, and the property, and all the wealth. He gave nothing to his brother. Jacob was left with all the land of Canaan, from the brook of Egypt to the river Euphrates. He took it for an everlasting possession, for his children, and his seed after him forever. Jacob also reclaimed the cave of Machpelah, from Esau, which was in Hebron, a part of the land of Canaan. Abraham made the original purchase of this cave from Ephron as a burial place for him and his seed forever. Then, Jacob wrote all these things in a Deed of Purchase, and with four faithful witnesses, who would testify on his behalf, he signed it. Jacob bought all these things from Esau for value, for a possession, and an inheritance for his seed after him forever. Esau then took all of Isaac's material goods away from Jacob, and he and his children went home to the land of Seir, where they lived away from his brother and his brother's children (Jasher 47:1-33).

CHAPTER 3

Historical Proof That Esau-Edom Still Exists

THE EDOMITES ARE THE DESCENDANTS of Esau, who was born in 2006BC. Esau grew up in Hebron in the land of Canaan. Before he left Canaan to move into Mount Seir, he married his third wife, Mahalath, one of Ishmael's daughters, also known as Bashemath. Esau married Bashemath to please his parents since his parents had also sent Jacob away from Canaan to ensure that he did not marry a Canaanite woman. Esau realized that it would delight his parents if he married Bashemath, who, like him, was Semitic. "And the women of Esau vexed and provoked Yitzchak and Rivaq with their works for they walked not in the ways of YAHUAH but served their father's Elohim of wood and stone as their father had taught them and they were more wicked than their father." (Jasher 29:14). Before his marriage to Bashemath, Esau had married three daughters of Canaan. His first wife, Yahudith, was the daughter of Berriy. Then, he married a daughter of Elon, the Hittite, and later married his third wife, Oholiyvamah, the daughter of Zibeon, the Hivite, after Yahudith died. "And Oholiyvamah conceived and bared unto Esau three sons, Yeush, Yaalan, and Qorach." (Jasher 30:25).

At the time of Esau's marriage to Bashemath, he was still angry that his brother, Jacob, had received the blessing he thought should go to him being the eldest. Esau was also mad that he again could not kill Jacob because Jacob had gone away, and even before he went to Haran, his parents had concealed him in Eber's house for fourteen years. During Jacob's stay with Eber, one of his grandfathers, Jacob studied and learned the ways of YAHUAH, "And at the end of fourteen years of Ya'aqov's living in the house of Eber, Ya'aqov desired to see his father and mother, and Ya'aqov came to the house of his father and mother to Chevron, and Esau had in those days forgotten what Ya'aqov had done to him, and became incensed against him and sought to slay him" (Jasher 29:20).[1]

After Jacob left for Haran, the place of his mother's birth Esau left his father and mother also, "For in the days when Jacob went to Mesopotamia, Esau took to himself a woman Mahalath, daughter of Ishmael, and he gathered together all the flocks of his father and his women, and dwelt on Mount Seir, and left Isaac, his father at the Well of the Oath alone." (Jubilees 29:18). Although Jubilees records that Esau moved away, the book of Jasher reports he may have moved away after quarrels between the herdsmen of Esau and the herdsmen of the inhabitants of the land of Canaan, as his cattle and goods had become too abundant for him to remain in the area, with his father's household and flocks. Therefore, Esau moved into Mount Seir with his in-laws and lived among the Horites, who were Troglodytes or 'cave dwellers.' "And when Esau saw that his quarreling increased with the inhabitants

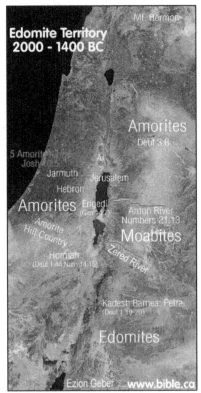

of the land of Canaan, he rose and took his women and his sons and his daughters, and all belonging to him, and the cattle which he owned, and all his property he had gained in the land of Canaan, and he went away from the inhabitants of the land to the land of Seir, and Esau and all belonging to him dwelt in the land of Seir." (Jasher 30:27).

Archeological sources confirm that Esau and his descendants inhabited Mount Seir amid the Horites between the years 1950 to 1926BC. The Horites were Canaanites who descended from Ham's sons and lived in Mount Seir before Esau moved into the area. Esau intermarried within the Horites and gave his daughters to the sons of Seir, "And he gave his elder daughter Marzith to Anah, the son of Zibeon, his wife's brother, and Puith he gave to Azar, the son of Bilhan the Horite; and Esau dwelt in the mountain, he and his children, and they were fruitful and multiplied" (Jasher 30:29).

Mount Seir was a Transjordan territory between Petra and the Red Sea. It was the first place that Esau inhabited after he moved from Hebron, where his father Isaac lived. Petra represented an east-west boundary between Edom and Moab. "Thus dwelt Esau in mount Seir: Esau is Edom" (Genesis 36:1). We can still travel the ruins of the rose-tinted city of Petra today on foot or horseback. According to "Feats and Wisdom of the Ancients," the path through Petra is only three feet in places. Although there are remains of outstanding architectural structures carved in the sides of the mountains today, the Edomites refuse to take ownership for creating the construction. Because, to admit ownership of these massive buildings, its dwellers, the Edomites would then have to own their real history. Therefore, many Edomites claim a mysterious group of people, known as the Nabateans, created the structures throughout Petra.[2]

Edom has tried to remove its people, the Edomites, from history, and one way they have done this is to eliminate the places where they lived from the maps. They have engaged cartographers to change and remove landmarks on ancient maps. In fact, in

1884AD, Henry Trumbull popularized that Kadesh was not at Petra, which they believed for 2000 years before his conclusions, but at Qedis.[3] For Trumbull, it was necessary to redefine the land of Edom. He suggested that Edom was not just limited to the Transjordan region, but next to Kadesh in the land of Judah.[4] However, historian Steve Rudd challenged this idea by pointing out that if Kadesh were at Ein Qudeirat, it would signify errors in the Biblical records of the location.[5] Since the Bible states that Kadesh and Mount Hor were on the border of Edom, Trumbull must have moved Edom west into the Negev without a legitimate Biblical, historical, or archeological basis. Rudd notes that changing where Kadesh was is one of the worst cases of circular reasoning in history. By rewriting maps to bring Edom into the Negev region, where the Edomites had never lived before 800BCE, gives false support to Kadesh Barnea being at Ein Qudeirat. They arranged this misidentification to hide the truth about Esau, who is Edom, and where they lived.

Rudd shows that amateur mappers not only moved Edom from the Transjordan region but also shifted the Negev's position so far north that none of the original Negev regions could be seen on maps of the Negev today. Rudd clarifies that the Negev location ranged from the Ramon Canyon south to Elat, and its edges touched the Arabah valley. Evidence suggests that amateur mappers chose three locations for Mount Hor, none of which are correct. He also postulates they found Mount Seir to be at Jebel esh-Shera about 16 km west of Elat.

Other researchers have found, however, that none of these mapped locations have any historical or archeological validity. It is, therefore, concluded that the underlying reason for causing a change in the location of these places on the map was to conceal the identity of Esau, who is Edom. The Edomites believed by removing the landmark evidence of where they lived, and by replacing it with a made-up history using another group of people, described as the Nabateans, they could conceal the truth about their identity.

HOW BUILDING STRUCTURES IDENTIFY ESAU-EDOM

The attempt by Esau, who is Edom, to distort the true history of humanity has led them to determine that their current achievements are the vanguard of real progress. When looking at structures that the Edomites may have left as evidence of them inhabiting the area of Mount Seir, it is unfortunate for them and the rest of the world that they refuse to take credit for these architectural feats. Although, recent geological discoveries theorize that the structures, called grottoes, found in mountainsides around the world may not have been buildings constructed by people of any nation post the Flood. Instead, these

Structures in the Historical TransJordan Territory

structures they believed may be the remnants of buildings covered by lava left after the Flood catastrophe. Therefore, the Edomites and the Horites may have just expanded and improved the edifices that were already in Mount Seir. Many similar buildings reflect the style of the ruins in Mount Seir, where Esau-Edom first lived and in the architectural style of buildings throughout the ancient Roman Empire. And, these same architectural designs have had a

Buildings with Roman Architecture

profound effect on buildings constructed throughout the Earth today. To hide the evidence that Esau, who is Edom, once inhabited Mount Seir, Edomite historians have made up an elaborate story that the remains of the buildings at Mount Seir are structures built by a nation of Bedouins called Nabateans who conquered Edom and drove them out of their homeland 2000 years ago. David Graf, in his book "Rome and the Arabian Frontier: from the Nabateans to the Saracens," believed the Nabateans were from Mesopotamia (ancient Iraq). He confirms this with the evidence shown in the Assyrian records, which tell how King Ashurbanipal (668-663BC) fought with the Nabateans of Arabia. They report that a few historians believed the Nabateans descended from Nebayoth, the brother of Bashemath, the daughter of Ishmael Esau's wife. The historians report they were nomadic Bedouins who occupied the Mount Seir area for two hundred years, and during this time, built the magnificent structures onto the facade of the mountains. They further report that all the Nabateans could read and write. Still, the written records left by the Nabatean kingdom were sparse, with there being only a few surviving documents with some scattered inscriptions and graffiti. The historians claim that although the Nabateans showed a high degree of technological advancement in building these structures yet, they marvel they left so few written records. However, I believe because there is little known about the Nabateans, Esau-Edom has been able to use their name to obscure the truth about the real occupiers of Mount Seir. By claiming that the Nabateans left little proof of their existence, but there are extensive accounts of their history written by other nations, helps them in substantiating that these people existed, and are different from the Edomites.

Howbeit, the Arab literature from a much later Islamic period report there were at least two distinct groups of Nabateans in the Middle East. The Zenon papyri from 259BC mention that the Nabatu were trading Gerrhean and Minaean frankincense and transporting them to Gaza and Syria. They said the name of a famous city, Rekem, was built by the Nabateans and would become so famous that Chang Ch'ien, the envoy to the Chinese Emperor Wu-ti (138 to122BC), would record it in the chronicles of China. Other civilizations that kept a record of these mysterious people were Greece, Egypt, Rome, Byzantium, and the city known by its Roman name, Petra. However, Petra is the location of

Edom and Mount Seir, which is the actual lands possessed by Esau, who is Edom.

The written historical accounts by the different nations appear suspect. And the question could be asked as to why would these nations have so much information about a mysterious Nabatean people, who left minimal written accounts of their history? Yet, at the same time, there is little to no secular history of the Edomites ever occupying the area. However, the Edomites lived in Mount Seir for thousands of years, and there is much Scriptural evidence that proves they occupied the land of Edom. The land of Edom was given to Esau and his descendants by YAHUAH as an inheritance. And, though Esau, who is Edom, has traversed the earth and has conquered most lands and has taken possession of them, the Mountains of Seir is one piece of real estate they refuse to own as theirs. Therefore, it is safe to conclude that Edom-Rome replaced the Edomites of Mount Seir with the mysterious Nabateans who they said conquered them and remained in the land for about 200 years. I believe the histories held by the other nations are, in fact, the true history of Esau, who is Edom, the Edomites ruling the earth today as the white Europeans claiming Japhetic ancestry.

The Biblical accounts show Edom engaging in wars with Israel but never the Nabateans, other than a report in the Antiquities of the Jews when Josephus registers an incident during the Maccabean period where the Nabateans assisted the Judeans in a battle with the Edomites in Edom after the Judeans had placed the Edomites under subjection. There are also other Biblical accounts of wars between Edom and the Israelites throughout the Israelites' history but not one with the Nabateans. The writers of this made-up history assumed that people would accept what they say without first checking and cross-referencing the information. According to Esau-Edom's version of history, the Nabateans lived in Edom and, after constructing the cities in Petra, occupied them for about two hundred years and abandoned them just before the birth of the HAMASHIACH to resume their Nomadic lifestyle.

There is an ancient Roman theatre located in one of the cities of Petra in Mount Seir reported by the editors of Time-Life Books. This complex is said to have an eerie feeling as it has the remains of thirty-three tiers of seats hewed from a wall of rock pocked with hundreds of Nabatean tombs. They report that these tombs were there at the time the Romans incorporated Petra into their empire in 106AD. The historicity of Edom as a nation and Mount Seir as its territory dates to between 2006 to 1950BC and beyond and is based on the calculations of Jacob's return home from Haran.

Esau, who is Edom, lived in Petra among the Horites centuries before the time of YAHUSHA and was an established nation many hundreds of years before Israel became a nation and before Rome was established as a nation. It was Zepho, the grandson of Esau, who helped to build Kittiym-Rome, as the children of Kittym, the son of Japheth, possessed the land first. Many Edomites remained in the nation of Edom even after they expelled the Judeans from the land of Israel in 135AD. It is my opinion, and some evidence shows that the Jordanians, Saudi Arabians, and all White Arabs and Middle Easterners who occupy the area today are of the mingled descendants of Esau, who is Edom.

HOW ESAU-EDOM TOOK OVER MOUNT SEIR

It was after the death of Jacob in Egypt, while at the funeral and burial in Hebron at the cave of Machpelah that a dispute broke out between the sons of Esau and Jacob. The argument arose when the sons of Esau challenged the sons of Jacob about Jacob being buried in the cave that Abraham had bought as a place for him and his posterity's burial forever. Abraham had deeded the cave to Jacob as part of his inheritance of the land of Canaan. The altercation at the funeral resulted in the capture of Zepho, Esau's grandson, who they took to Egypt and imprisoned along with some of Esau's other family members.

After this incident, the sons of Esau waged further war with Egypt and the sons of Jacob to avenge the capture of their brethren. Esau's sons asked the sons of Seir and others to assist them in their fight against Joseph, his brothers, and the Egyptians. This war resulted in a defeat for the sons of Esau, and because the results were so devastating for the sons of Seir, they demanded that the sons of Esau leave their land. Seir's sons believed because they had engaged in warfare with the Egyptians alongside the sons of Esau, the Egyptians and the sons of Jacob had killed all of their strongest warriors. It concerned them they no longer had enough men adept to go to war for them after the encounter with Joseph and the Egyptians.

Territory Ruled by King Angeas of Carthage - North Africa, Spain, & Islands of the Agean Sea

However, Esau's sons refused to move out of Mount Seir and considered going to war with the children of Seir to chase them out of their land for good. Esau's sons sent a secret mission to Angeas, the king of Africa, for which they name the Aegean Sea. He was king of the Phoenicians. During this period, he ruled the Carthaginian Empire, which extended over much of the coast of North Africa. Angeas also ruled substantial parts of coastal Iberia and the islands of the western Mediterranean Sea. They were the original Phoenicians and the descendants of Phut, one of the four sons of Ham, who established their homeland in North Africa among the lands allotted to Ham and his sons. However, the revised history shows that we now call some of these people Libyans and the land areas they now occupy is contracted. Later in history, the land became divided into different nations, including Libya, Algeria, Morocco, Spain, and Portugal. They divided the Carthaginian Empire to hide the evidence that black people ruled in North Africa and

Spain and Portugal and the islands of the Mediterranean hundreds of years before the descendants of Esau-Edom gained the power of Kittiym-Rome. The descendants of Phut were not Canaanites but, in fact, the cousins of the Canaanites because he was one of the sons of Ham, "And the sons of Ham; Cush, and Mizraim, and Phut, and Canaan" (Genesis 10: 6).

The reason why the sons of Edom reached out to King Angeas was that the Phoenicians were, in fact, cousins of the Canaanites, the family in which Esau had married. The sons of Esau needed help in their war against the descendants of Seir, who were also the offspring of Canaan, so they asked for their help. Although, based on Esau's account of history, Joshua drove the Phoenicians out of the land of Canaan when the children of Israel entered. But the records found in the book of Jasher shows that the Phoenicians had an established Empire on the Northern coast of the lands given to Ham and his descendants. This area they call Africa today was for centuries the Carthaginian Empire before Israel ever became a nation. Therefore, the Edomites could write to Angeas for help, "Send unto us some of your men and let them come unto us, and we will fight together with the children of Seir the Horite, for they have resolved to fight with us to drive us away from the land" (Jasher 57:18).

Since King Angeas and the sons of Esau were allies, he agreed to assist by sending five hundred of his valiant infantrymen and eight hundred cavalries to join them in the battle against the children of Seir. In return, the children of Seir sent for the children of the east in Midian to support their side. The children of Seir came with a great force because they believed Seir, their father, had a right to the land as he was the first to inhabit the area. The book of Jubilees reveals, however, that the land that the Canaanites lived on was the land that fell to Shem and, the Canaanites, including Seir and his descendants, were trespassing on land that did not belong to them. "And there came forth on the writing as Shem's lot the middle of the earth which he should take as his inheritance for himself and his sons for the generations of eternity, from the middle of the mountain range of Rafa, from the mouth of the water from the River Tina, and his portion goes towards the west through the midst of this river, and it extends till it reaches the water of the abysses, out of which this river goes forth and pours its waters into the sea Me'at. This river flows into the Great Sea. And all is towards the north is Japheth's, and all is towards the Negev belongs to Shem. And it extends till it reaches Karaso: this is in the tongue's bosom which looks toward the Negev" (Jubilees 8:12-13). Canaan had moved into this land allotted to the descendants of Shem despite the objections made by his father, Ham, and his brothers telling him not to do so. As a result, when the Children of Israel moved into the land of Promise, they had to fight many wars to remove the descendants of Canaan out of the land. Therefore, YAHUAH allowed Esau, who is Edom, to eject the Horites out of Mount Seir years before Israel entered the land of Canaan because all this territory fell by lot to the descendants of Shem.

Because the descendants of Canaan had lived in the land for hundreds of years before Jacob and Esau, the children of Isaac and Rebekah were born, they believed this land belonged to them as they had occupied it first. In the Babylonian Talmud, written in 332BC, there is a complaint made by the Canaanites to Alexander the Great after he conquered the areas and became the ruler of the Grecian Empire. After Alexander the Great conquered Israel, the Canaanites, who still lived among the Israelites, complained to Alexander that the land of Canaan belonged to them because they inhabited it first. They wanted him to remove the Israelites out of the land. "For when the Africans came to plead against the Jews before Alexander of Macedon, they said Canaan belongs to us, as their father writes it that, the land of Canaan with the coast thereof; and Canaan was the ancestor of these people." However, history shows the land was promised to the Israelites, the chosen people of YAHUAH.

EDOM SECURES KING ANGEAS HELP

After securing help from the King of Carthage, Africa, the sons of Esau went to war in the wilderness of Paran with the help of the men of Angeas to reclaim the land from the descendants of Seir. They were victorious against the sons of Seir after losing initial battles. During this war, they killed the remaining mighty men of the children of Seir, leaving behind only young children in their cities. Because of this, the children of the east and the

Midian people escaped and abandoned the children of Seir, leaving them to fight on their own (Jasher 57: 32-33).

When the war ended, the children of Esau discovered that some of their brethren had become allies with the children of Seir and had assisted them during some battles they had lost. As a result, the sons of Esau were angry because their kindred had betrayed them. The sons of Esau then destroyed all the remaining people who had not escaped the land of Mount Seir. The only people left, according to the book of Jasher, were fifty young girls and boys whom they used as slaves and wives Jasher (Jasher 57: 35).

Therefore, the children of Esau dwelt in Mount Seir, in the place of the children of Seir the Horite. This land became known as Edom. Esau's descendants inherited the land, took control, and seized all that had once belonged to the children of Seir, including their flocks, their bullocks, their goods, and all of their possessions. The children of Esau took the land as a possession that the Highest, YAHUAH, had given them (Jasher 57: 36-37).

They separated the land into divisions for the five sons of Esau, according to their families. Besides, they crowned a king to rule over the entire land they possessed. However, they determined that none of their brethren should ever rule over them. They decided this because of what happened during the war against the children of Seir and the fact that some of their brethren had become traitors and sided with the children of Seir to fight against them (Jasher 57: 39-40).

This rift in the family of the sons of Esau caused them to choose a king from the outside. Their first king came from the troops of Africa. Bela, King Angeas' captain, became the first king of Edom. He was the son of Beor, Laban's son, and Rebekah's brother. Bela was Beor's son with his wife, Adinah. He had fought with Angeas' men when they assisted the children of Esau in the war with the children of Seir. Scripture described him as a courageous man, beautiful and comely and wise in all wisdom, and a man of good counsel. The children of Esau received him, anointed and crowned him as their king, bowed to him, and said, "May the king live, May the king live" (Jasher 57:41-42). The children of Esau built a palace for their King Bela and placed a regal crown upon his head. He ruled as king over all the children of Esau for thirty years, and, during this time, they were secure in their land that once belonged to the children of Seir. Esau's sons and their children remained in Seir until they moved to the south of Judaea into the Negev Valley (Jasher 57:43-45).

IDENTIFYING THE SONS OF ESAU-EDOM

The five sons of Esau and their descendants lived in Mount Seir before they moved into Japheth's territory known today as Europe. Zepho, Esau's grandson, was the first of the descendants of Esau to move into the land of Japheth, "And Zepho reigned over all the children of Kittiym securely, but knew not YAHUAH who had delivered him and all his people from the hand of the king of Africa; and the troops of Africa came no more to Kittiym to plunder as usual, for they knew the power of Zepho who had smitten them all at the edge of the sword, so Angeas was afraid of Zepho the son of Eliyphaz, and of the children of Kittiym all the days" (Jasher 64:6). Later, other descendants of Esau spread into these lands of Japheth. Some identified as the descendants of Heth the Hittite. The Hittites are named for the daughter of Heth the Canaanite that Esau married, and the children identified with their mothers' family lineage and came to be identified as the Hittites. It is said the people occupying the land of Turkey can still trace their lineage back to their Hittite ancestors.

The descendants of Esau today can be identified through tracing the path they took when they left Mount Seir. Although they have hidden their identity among the mythology and traditions of the Greeks and Romans, it is still clear they are the descendants of Esau, who mixed with the descendants of Japheth, Noah's second son. They have also added the narrative, which implies that Esau-Edom has become an extinct race of people. Nonetheless, if you follow the Hebrew contextual timeline of history and trace the movements of Esau-Edom, it will show how they moved and where they still exist today. Esau-Edom has mixed with the people of every nation, replaced some of them, and claims the ancestry as theirs. Esau liked his way and went against his parents' wishes and married Canaanite women. After mixing with his neighbors in Mount Seir, they moved into the land of Japheth, where they also conquered and mixed with the descendants of Japheth, whitening them out and later becoming known as the Europeans. They bred them out the same practice they used in Australia when they conquered the land of the Aborigines. They described how after the third generation of the indigenous people mixing with Esau-Edom, they no longer show any of their aboriginal ancestries and would appear to be of the Edomite lineage.

YAHUAH created Esau-Edom to fulfill a specific purpose of bringing the true descendants of Jacob-Israel back to him as his bride; he used Esau-Edom as the chastening rod in Israel's return to him. YAHUAH described Esau-Edom as a vessel made for common use in contrast to Jacob-Israel being a vessel made for Holy use. Esau-Edom mixed his seed with the other gentile nations, which spread his white color throughout the earth. Scripture describes his seed as spoiled which made it impossible for Esau-Edom's descendants to hide their identity as being from the lineage of Esau, "But I have made Esau bare, I have uncovered his secret places, and he shall not be able to hide himself: his seed is spoiled, and his brethren, and his neighbors, and he is not" (Jeremiah 49:10).

Despite Esau-Edom knowing the truth about their identity did not prevent them from trying to hide this truth even if it meant claiming that their color made them superior to the other people on the earth. They made all nations look to them as a god, even using a white imposter Messiah as the Savior of the world, which they claim as the only way to be saved. Although Esau-Edom is the minority population on the earth, they have made their presence felt as if they are the majority. In their quest to be the greatest, they have created a pervasive media empire where they are the leaders who project themselves as the majority of people with the greatest intelligence and strength. But, according to Wikipedia, the free online encyclopedia, the 2010 World Census reports the "white" people are 850,000,000 plus or 11.5% of the earth's population. These statistics show that Esau-Edom is a small people among the heathen as they report the earth to have a population of about 7 to 8 billion people. As Scripture confirms, Edom would be a small people, "For, lo, I will make thee small among the heathen, and despised among men. For thy terribleness hath deceived thee, and the pride of thine heart, O thou that dwellest in the clefts of the rock, that holdest the height of the hill: though thou shouldest make thy nest as high as the eagle, I will bring thee down from thence, saith YAHUAH" (Jeremiah 49:15-16). They have used their technologies to deceive the nations and claim that they are the majority of people on the earth. They have created an illusion because they have dominated the earth for a long time, and as leaders in the forefront, they control every aspect of everything reported. Besides, they have had great influence over the nations, which includes the Greco-Roman culture that has seeped into every other culture. Through conquest and colonization, Esau-Edom's descendants now occupy and rule over the nations as Edom-Rome. They identify as the people of these lands, and their roots are said to be in Europe, but their true ancestry is in Edom located in Mount Seir. They are the Edomites from Edom, and today they identify as the people of the lands they occupy with the qualifying descriptor "white" in front of the names for which the lands are named. For example, the people will be described as; White Americans, White Canadians, White Australians, White South African, White Spaniards, White Arabs, White Egyptians, and so on.

The role Esau-Edom plays in the history of the earth is a corrupt and base one, and one reason they have tried to murky the waters about their identity. The Highest, YAHUAH, predetermined the role that every nation and people he created would play for his purpose and Esau-Edom-Rome and their descendants are no different. All seeds from the tribes of the sons of Noah remain on the earth today, and there are no extinct people. Scripture shows the genealogy of all people living today begins with Noah and his three sons. Therefore, it is possible to trace where the descendants of Noah settled based on Hebrew Scriptures and true secular history when it is not influenced by the lies and distortions of Esau-Edom, "And these are the generations of Esau the father of the Edomites in mount Seir: These are the names of Esau's sons; Eliphaz, the son of Adah, the wife of Esau, Reuel, the son of Bashemath, the wife of Esau. The sons of Eliphaz were Teman, Omar, Zepho, and Gatam, and Kenaz. And Thimnathah was a concubine to Eliphaz Esau's son; she bore to Eliphaz, Amalek: these were the sons of Adah Esau's wife. And these are the sons of Reuel; Nahath, and Zerah, Shammah, the Mizzah; these were the sons of Bashemath or

Mahalath Esau's wife, and these were the sons of Aholibamah, the daughter of Anah the daughter of Zibeon, Esau's wife. She bore to Esau Jeush, and Jaalam, and Korah" (Genesis 36). Although Esau-Edom has tried to alter the names of these descendants and misidentify many of them, it is possible to trace the descendants of Esau back to these original names written in Scripture. When we translate the words back to its original, it is possible to determine the identity of the true people in history. Esau-Edom has mingled with many nations, particularly the sons of Japheth, who they claim as their forefathers. But they only assume the identity of the sons of Japheth as this is the will of YAHUAH who said that he would enlarge the tribes of Japheth, and YAHUAH used Esau-Edom to fulfill this purpose.

HOW TO IDENTIFY THE OFFSPRING OF ESAU-EDOM

Though Esau-Edom has added and subtracted names to the annals of history, the Highest YAHUAH has made it possible for Israel in these "last days" to identify still the people descended from Esau. Scripture described Esau at birth as red and hairy all over. He married the women of Canaan, the son of Ham and one of Ishmael's daughters. Scripture also lists the names of Esau's sons and daughters, but history does not always present them in their original form. The Hittites, for example, known as the white Edomite inhabitants of Turkey, are the progeny of Heth, a son of Canaan, the son of Ham, the father of the black races, not the Negroes. The Hittites are the descendants of Esau and Canaan, through the Canaanite wives Esau married. It is this name, used on the maps to describe the Hittite kingdom and the progenitors of the Turkish people. They moved into the area occupied by the sons of Japheth, changed the names to reflect that of the Hittites. These Hittites settled in these lands much later in history as the area was also a vassal state of king Angeas of Carthage Africa, who descended from Phut, the son of Ham. The Aegean Sea is named for this king. And, those who call themselves the "Jews" living in Palestine today came from the Caucasus Mountains in Eastern Europe known as the land of Gog, another descendant of Japheth. These Jewish converts also determine their children's ancestry through their Jewish mothers. However, this is not a Hebrew custom as Jacob's twelve sons and their children identified with the name of their father, Israel. Likewise, his twelve sons' children identified with their fathers and grandfather. For example, the sons of Judah, Levi, and Benjamin identified as the Judeans in later years, the northern ten tribes identified as Ephraim or Israel, "Of the children of Judah, by their generations, after their families, by the house of their fathers, according to the number of names, from twenty years old and upward, all that were able to go forth to war;" (Numbers 1:26).

The two daughters that Esau fathered with Judith, his first wife, the daughter of Berriy, married the sons of the Horite and can trace their heritage through the mothers. These descendants of the Horite and Esau's daughters are believed to be the ones who joined with the Horites against the children of Edom in the war for the land of Seir. "And in the fifth year died Yahudith, the daughter of Beeriy, the woman of Esau, in the land of Kena'an, and she had no sons but daughters only. And these are the names of her daughters which she bore to Esau, the name of the elder was Marzith, and the name of the younger was Puith" (Jasher 30:21-22).

THE GENEALOGY OF ESAU-EDOM

Esau & Adah	Esau & Aholibamah	Esau & Bashemath	Esau & Judith
Eliphaz	Jeush	Reuel	Marzith
Teman	Jalaam	Nahath	(daughter)
Omar	Korah	Zerah	Puith
Zepho		Shammah	(daughter)
Gatam		Mizzah	
Kenaz			
Amalek			

These are the dukes of Esau, who reigned in various territories in Edom and the land of Japheth. "And these are the names of the dukes that came of Esau, according to their families, after their places, by their names; duke Thimnathah, duke Aliah, duke

Jetheth, Duke Aholibamah, duke Elah, duke Pinon, Duke Kenaz, duke Teman, duke Mibzar, Duke Magdiel, duke Iram; these be the dukes of Edom, according to their habitations in the land of their possession: he is Esau the father of the Edomites," (Genesis 36:40-43). These are the sons of Seir, the Horite who inhabited the land, "Lotan, and Shobal, and Zibeon, and Anah, and Dishon, and Ezer, and Dishan: these are the dukes of the Horites, the children of Seir in the land of Edom," (Genesis 36:20-21). Both the king and duke lines are Esau's posterity and a result of Esau's marriage to Canaanite women and his sons and daughters' marriages into the family of the Horites.

THE KINGS OF ESAU-EDOM

Throughout history, many kings ruled over the children of Esau, during their time in Mount Seir. After they warred with the children of Seir and had taken the land, they learned that some of their brethren had sided with the Horites, and therefore they decided they would never have any of their brothers as king over them. These events led to them choosing kings from outside. The first king they chose was Bela. "Bela, the son of Beor, who reigned in Edom, and the name of his capital city was Dinhabah. Balak died, and Jobab, the son of Zerah of Bozrah, reigned in his stead. And Jobab died, and Asam, of the land of Teman, reigned in his stead. And Asam died, and Adath, the son of Barad, who slew Midian in Moab, reigned in his stead, and the name of his city was Avith. And Adath died, and Salman, from Amaseqa, reigned, in his stead. And Salman died, and Shaul of Rehoboth by the river reigned in his stead. And Shaul died, and Baalunan, the son of Akbor, reigned in his stead. And Baalunan, the son of Akbor, died, and Adath reigned in his stead. And the name of his woman was Maitabith, the daughter of Matarat, the daughter of Metabedzaab. These are the kings who reigned in the land of Edom' (Jubilees 38:15-25).

THE RESULTS OF ESAU'S MINGLED FAMILY

Various phenotypes exist in the physical features of Esau's mingled family, though they all have white skin. The Edomites started as a mixed-race people, and this mixture continued throughout their lineage. They intermarried with the gentile nations and whited out many of them. Science and scientists show that all people descended from a single black woman. However, Scripture states YAHUAH created man from the black dirt and woman he formed from the man; therefore, they were both black people who produced black progenies. On the other hand, Esau was different and came out red though he was the product of black parents. YAHUAH made him in this way for a particular purpose. Esau, the first red man, now described as a white man mixed with the black gentile nations and produced a white mixed race of people described as white because of the color of their skin and Esau's phenotype. Scripture describes these nations as gentiles; therefore, Esau-Edom is a gentile nation. The proof of Esau-Edom's exploits of conquest and colonizing are shown in the white color of those they conquered and intermingle. During the 17th century, the German branch of the Edomites declared they were a pure white Aryan race and wanted to live in a nation that reflected this purity. The result was the genocide of the Hebrews who lived among them. They also included in this genocide the Jewish converts living in Germany and the surrounding countries. However, the record of history only reflects the destruction of the Jewish converts. It was not possible for Esau-Edom to white-out the descendants of Jacob-Israel, so they committed mass murder against them. They carried this destruction of the people into Africa, where many of the Hebrew Israelites had been dispersed. Esau-Edom was able to white-out many people because they were, in fact, gentiles. Howbeit, they could not white-out the Hebrew Israelites in the same way, so they resorted to genocide, and afterward claim that the millions who died in the Holocaust were the Jewish converts of Eastern Europe. I believe Esau-Edom couldn't destroy the Hebrew Israelites through the whitening process because they are the chosen seed of the Highest YAHUAH, "O ye seed of Israel his servant, ye children of Jacob, his chosen ones" (1Chronicles 16:13). And even when Esau tried to mix with the Negro, their offspring is still Negro. On the Continent of Africa, in the lands occupied by the sons of Ham except for Ethiopia Esau-Edom was able whiteout a great percentage of the people, including the Hamitic countries of Egypt, Phut (Phoenicia) also known as the Carthaginian Empire, now divided into three different countries known as Libya,

Algeria and Morocco and many of the inhabitants are described by the Edomites as Caucasian. These descendants of Ham inhabited the northern and eastern coasts of the continent they call Africa. The Israelites who were scattered in the diaspora starting about the 6th century BC when the Northern Tribes of Israel were dispersed settled and built communities in these lands. Some of them, however, also dispersed into the other parts of Japheth's lands they call Europe and the British Isles, where they set up kingdoms and ruled these nations for centuries before the Greek or Roman Empires were established.

The Hebrew Israelites were not whited out by Esau Edom in these countries in the same way because black people still ruled in these nations, including the Hebrew Israelites, until the 17th century. Esau-Edom's descendants lived among these black people, but the Edomites did not gain full dominance until the revised papal Roman Empire in the 1600s. Although the tribes of Israel were in exile, their fate of being whited out did not happen as Edom-Rome so hated them; they wanted to root them from off the face of the earth. When they failed at this, they resorted to enslavement and banishment to the continent called Africa, where the Hebrew Israelites have wandered in the wilderness along with their scattered brethren throughout the earth for centuries believing they are just random Africans. It was the will of YAHUAH to use Esau-Edom to punish the descendants of Jacob for their forefathers' disobedience. Still, the enforcement of the punishment was too harsh and beyond just punishment but near-complete genocide of the Israelites. Therefore, the descendants of Esau-Edom will have to reap what their forefathers have sown.

The Parable of the Sower, is a similitude of how YAHUAH sowed all the seeds (people) in the earth, with only one good seed destined to produce fruit, and this seed represents Israel, "And he spake many things unto them in parables, saying, Behold, a sower went forth to sow; And when he sowed, some seeds fell by the wayside, and the fowls came and devoured them up: Some fell upon stony places, where they had not much earth: and forthwith they sprung up because they had no deepness of earth: And when the sun was up they were scorched; because they had no root, withered away. And some fell among thorns, and the thorns sprung up and choked them: But others fell into good ground, and brought forth fruit, some a hundredfold, some sixty-fold, some thirtyfold" (Matthew 13:3-8). The good seed predestined to bring forth fruit is the pure seed of Israel. In the early fourteenth century, an unknown author described this seed as a metaphor that appears in the Sefer Nizzahan Yashan by Joseph the Zealot.[6] They contrast the seed of Israel with that of the Edomite gentile which explains why they are black and follows the formula;

> "Know what to answer" of the claim that the Jews are black and ugly, but with a new explanation: "The gentiles ask and say" 'Why are most gentiles white and beautiful and most Jews black and ugly?' "Answer them that it is like a fruit: when it begins to blossom, it is white, but

when fully ripe it becomes black like those (a dark species) plums, while fruit that is red in the beginning will have white fruit, like apples, or peaches. This proves to Israel that it is pure of menstrual blood, with no red whatever in the beginning. But the gentiles are not warned against such blood and copulate (even) when they see blood, so there is red in the beginning; hence the fruit it brings forth is white, and they are white."

The Europeans of today emphasize they are a "white race," which they say is a social construct that entered the European languages in the late seventeenth century, in racialized slavery and unequal social status in European colonies. However, other historical evidence shows this is only part of the truth as the red Edomite population as white is found in Greco-Roman ethnography and other ancient sources. The descendants of Esau used their color as a standard of superiority and white privilege. They refused to mix with the Hebrew Israelite Negro population from ancient times as they had a perpetual hatred for the Hebrew Israelites. The will of the Highest YAHUAH was to keep Israel from mixing and mingling their seed with Esau-Edom. However, if they did mix, YAHUAH made it possible in the third generation for the children of mixed Israelites to return to the House of Israel. He also used this means to separate the sheep from the goats. Though the Edomites believed their action of not wanting to mix with the Hebrew Israelites was meant to reduce, the status of Israel YAHUAH willed it for Israel's protection from the enemy. All the same, humanity including Esau-Edom, can only do what is the will of YAHUAH even when they believe they are acting on decisions they have made. YAHUAH is the one who hardens or softens the heart of Israel's enemies, and he knows that this time is not Israel's time and they will be redeemed and resurrected to a new life when they will rule upon the earth again for eternity, "What shall we say then? Is there unrighteousness with YAH? YAH forbid. For He saith to Moses, I will have mercy on whom I will have mercy, and I will have compassion on whom I will have compassion. So, then it is not of him that willeth, nor of him, that runneth but of YAH that showeth mercy... Therefore, hath he mercy on whom he will have mercy, and whom he will he hardeneth. Thou wilt say then unto me, Why doth he yet finds fault? For who hath resisted his will? Nay, but, O man, who art thou that repliest against YAH? Shall the thing form say to him that formed it, Why hast thou made me thus" (Romans 9:14-20)?

Because Esau-Edom mixed with dark skin Gentile nations, some Edomites no longer have red hair. Their hair color and skin tone now reflect this intermixture with the people of other nations. White people, when mixed with black and brown people, can cause the black skin to lighten, and when this mixture is done for three generations, they can white out the color of the black people. Based on observation alone, there is proof that two black parents can have many shades of children, but two white parents can only produce white children. The descendants of Esau-Edom are the red people created by YAHUAH to fulfill his purpose on the earth. They mixed with the other nations, which caused them to produce a white race of people with varied phenotypes, some with red hair like Esau and some different variations of brown, black, blond, or sometimes even orange or yellow hair. In most cases, their hair texture resembles the smoothness of the hair of a goat that Rebekah placed on Jacob's hands, arms and neck when he went in and received the blessings from Isaac as the firstborn. Despite this difference in hair color and texture, the descendants of Edom all see themselves as "white" people in contrast to the "black" Negro, as they define the Hebrew Israelites in their writings. Esau was the brother of Jacob, but he looked different. He not only looked different; he was different in temperament and described as cunning in all his actions. YAHUAH predestined him to be unlike any people he created before to fulfill his purpose for humankind. The twins represented the contrast of good and evil in the earth, therefore before they were born YAHUAH said that he loved Jacob and hated Esau, "And not only this; but when Rebekah also had conceived by one, even our father Isaac, (for the children being not yet born, neither having done any good or evil, that the purpose of YAHUAH according to election might stand, not of works, but him that calleth) YAHUAH said unto her, the elder shall serve the younger. As it is written, Jacob have I loved, but Esau have I hated" (Romans 9:10-13).

The changes that occurred in the people came about because the Highest YAHUAH allowed Esau-Edom to mix with the descendants of Japheth and the other gentile nations to enlarge them. The fact is YAHUAH only created one white race to fulfill his purpose. The Edomites, the white descendants of Esau, are the ones fulfilling YAHUAH'S determined will as the end of the world. History knows them as the "red" +people of antiquity. According to Wikipedia, the online Encyclopedia, the concept of a unified white race did not achieve universal acceptance in Europe when it first came into use in the seventeenth century, or in the centuries afterward. Despite what they wrote, the census of 2010 shows the white race of people in every country on earth. The article continues that before the modern age, no European peoples regarded themselves as "white," but defined their race, ancestry, or ethnicity in terms of their nationality being Greek or Roman. Nonetheless, Esau-Edom admitting their ancestry to be that of the Greeks and Romans reveals that their history is recent, as the Greeks only ruled as an empire from BC331 to 168BC, and the Roman Empire existed from BC168 to 476AD. These Empires all consisted of a mixture of black and white people with black people being the majority. It was not until the rise of the revised papal Roman Empire and the white Edomites dominated did the changes occur. Esau-Edom is the end of the world as Scripture states, although they had revised history to reflect that humanity began with the white race of people when the Greek and Roman Empires arose. Be it as it may, Biblical and secular history identifies the people of Esau-Edom as Edomites or Idumeans long before they called them Greeks, Romans, Assyrians, or Europeans.

Their purpose is so dishonorable, Esau-Edom has hidden the truth of their identity. Because they had authority over the Hebrew Scriptures for hundreds of years, they were also able to hide the Hebrew Israelites.

The knowledge of Jacob and Esau's destiny caused the descendants of Esau-Edom to have a perpetual hatred for the descendants of Jacob. Therefore, as the people with dominion over the earth and by extension Jacob-Israel, they created a narrative that supported the belief that their white skin color made them superior, and Jacob-Israel's black skin made them inferior. These actions of Esau-Edom against the descendants of Jacob-Israel happened over many centuries as Edom-Rome began their domination over the earth. The "white" Edomites, with their many Gentile mixtures, are the progeny of Esau. Their seed is mixed with many nations and shows in the diversity of "white" people throughout the earth. The white skin color became the significant identifying marker for the blended descendants of Esau-Edom, the Edomites. According to Wikipedia, although the Edomites' identity was "white," the strongest proponents of racialism came in the twentieth century in Europe when Fascist Italy and Nazi Germany regarded some European people, such as the Slavs, as racially distinct from themselves. These people they called Slavs were probably Hebrew Israelites as the word denotes slaves. The Slavs were most likely part of the blended Edomites who still showed they were racially mixed people or colored like Karl Marx, a famous German philosopher, economist, historian, sociologist, political theorist, and socialist revolutionary, who they report to have said he hated that his heritage is mixed with the black "Jews" or as we know today, the Hebrew Israelites.

The will of YAHUAH was that Esau would give up his birthright to build his future with his own toil and effort. Esau was independent and preferred to choose his way to live. He joined with the other nations and adopted their ways of living and their gods. Esau planted his seed among the Gentiles and became scattered throughout the earth. And, it does not matter which nation they live; they believe their skin color gives them the privilege and makes them superior. These nations have adopted the customs and ways of Edom-Rome, which brings them respect. In a Rabbinic commentary, it is said many great leaders of the nations of the world followed Esau's opinion and disparaged the status of birth, and upheld the natural abilities of the individual, with an emphasis on the appearances, which brings a certain measure of outward nobility (Netziv, Haamek Davar to Genesis 23, 34).[7]

ESAU-EDOM OVERSPREADS THE EARTH

The descendants of Esau, the Edomites spread across the earth after the death of Esau and therefore, Esau himself never lived in Rome and ruled nowhere else other than the land of Edom in Mount Seir. However, early in their history, the sons and grandsons of Esau relocated into different lands conquering them and mixing with the original peoples. By the time the Israelites moved into the Promised Land the Edomites were an established country in Mount Seir and had already conquered the Assyrians their neighbors to the north and sometimes held the lands of Ammon and Moab as vassal states. After the Israelites settled in the Promised Land the descendants of Esau engaged them in several wars which ended in Edom becoming a vassal state of Israel where they paid tribute in the form of taxes for many years. Howbeit, when the Babylonians took the Judeans into captivity the Edomites joined with the Babylonians in capturing and killing many of the Judeans after which they moved into and occupied the areas where the Judeans lived for the seventy years that the Judeans were in Babylonian captivity.

Esau who is Edom and Rome populated the entire earth using the sword to accomplish their goal as they solidified their hold on the people with their pagan religions and gods. They used the scripts and scrolls of the Hebrew Israelites to support their religious doctrines which deceived many of the Israelites who believed that the Edomites worshiped the same ELOHIYM as the Israelites because they used the Hebrew scripts to create a book. After Edom-Rome completed the takeover of Jerusalem in 70AD, they established the Roman Christian church and ratified this church in 325AD at the Council of Nice, when Emperor Constantine became the first pope and named Christianity the religion of the Roman Empire. Edom-Rome took full control of the Hebrew writings and determined what Scriptures would make up the contents of this book they would use called the "Holy

Bible." They canonized these writings of Scripture that supported their brand of religion and forbade the followers of HAMASHIACH who were in fact, the Hebrew Israelites from reading or owning copies of the Torah scrolls or face death. This so-called canonized version of Scripture is still in use today with many versions all claiming it is the Holy word of ELOHIYM. In fact, the words are only holy when presented and taught by the true holy people of YAHUAH. But, in the hands of Edom-Rome it is an abomination, as they are the wicked of the earth. They created doctrines and interpretations that changed the meanings of the writings to support their theories and philosophies. This is not allowed by YAHUAH the author of the scrolls, "For I testify unto every man that heareth the words of the prophecy of this book, If any man shall add unto these things, YAHUAH shall add unto him the plagues that are written in this book: and if any man shall take away from the words of the book of this prophecy, YAHUAH shall take away his part out of the book of life, and out of the holy city, and from the things which are written in this book" (Revelation 22:18-19). Edom-Rome deceived the entire earth including most of the Hebrew Israelites who are caught up in their false religions of Judaism, Christianity and Islam which were all the creation of Edom-Rome. In these religions they are call to worship in a spiritual way the wood and the stone as prophecy foretells what Israel would do while in the diaspora, "And YAHUAH shall scatter thee among all people, from the one end of the earth even unto the other; and there thou shalt serve other gods, which neither thou nor thou fathers have known, even wood and stone" (Deuteronomy 28:64).

Historical records show Edom-Rome always knew the identity of the descendants of Jacob-Israel and sought to destroy them in every way. They scattered them into the African Continent from Europe in the 13th, 14th, 15th and 16th centuries. Edom-Rome then tracked them down in the places they settled to convert them to Roman Christianity, Islam or enslavement or death for refusing to convert. They created systems and laws that placed the Israelites at a disadvantage, and they used Israel's black skin and the cultural morays to identify them wherever they settled. After warring with nations and conquering many of them by the sword or by false treaties they stole the wealth and took possession of the lands. Edom-Rome has stolen the wealth of the Israelites throughout Europe, Israel and Jerusalem and the wealth of the African Continent. After these atrocities they would classify the Israelites as less than human. For example, in American law (Article 1, Section 2, of the U.S. Constitution of 1787) they declared African Americans as individuals as three-fifths of a person, therefore, they could not mix with white people. The Israelites may not have recognized this at the time but, YAHUAH was protecting them against mixing with Esau-Edom, their enemy and the people whom YAHUAH has anger towards forever. "Whereas Edom saith, We are impoverished, but we will return and build the desolate places; thus saith YAHUAH of hosts, they shall build, but I will throw down; and they shall call them, The border of wickedness, and The people against whom YAHUAH hath indignation forever" (Malachi 1:4).

THE REASON EDOM-ROME CREATED DIFFERENT RELIGIONS

Since Edom-Rome first prompted the great dispersal of the Judeans in 70AD, they have engineered many false schemes to further their agenda to destroy the Israelites. One such creation is the Islamic religion created by them as reported by Alberto Rivera Rosero, a former Jesuit Priest of the Roman Catholic Church. He revealed before his alleged poisoning that Edom-Rome created Islam in 1100AD to destroy Christianity. However, in other historical reports there is no specific date or timeline for when Islam was created. Some historians claim that Islam started between 700AD to 900AD. However, the vagueness of these dates is suspect and probably made-up history. He claims Edom-Rome wanted to destroy Christianity. Howbeit, it was not Roman Christianity they wanted to destroy but the Christianity followed by the Hebrew Israelites who accepted the HAMASHIACH but kept the laws of YAHUAH. Historical records show they used Islam as the sword to force the Israelites to disobey the laws of the Most High YAHUAH. And, many of the Israelites living in the diaspora in Africa had to convert or die. Yet, they use this same narrative to deceive Roman Christians today that Islam is a religion that will force them to covert or be put to death. These lies have been used by Edom-Rome to mislead the Hebrew Israelites throughout their dispersal. The Eboes of Nigeria was one such tribe the Arabs failed in forcing them to convert to Islam as they refused to surrender to the Arab forces until the Arabs gave up the fight.

Once the Islamic Holy War started, the Ottoman Turks led the charge. They branded this a war against Christianity and Rome to force Christians to convert to Islam. However, historical evidence shows that the Ottoman Turks did not force Christians to convert to Islam. In fact, they report that the Turks conscripted the young men of Edomite Christians to fight alongside them against the Hebrew Israelites living in the diaspora who refused to obey Rome and disobey the laws of the Torah. The claims made by the historians is that the Turkish Empire ruled for hundreds of years, but the timeline does not fit as the Arabs would have already converted to the religion of Islam hundreds of years before the time of the Ottoman Turks who were also saide to be Muslim. It is my belief that Edom-Rome calculated these so-called wars to rewrite history and to further deceive and destroy the identity of Chosen people of YAHUAH.

In fact, Edom-Rome used the Islamic religion to deceive the Arabs who refused Christianity to adopt another brand of Christianity with and Arab Prophet called Mohammed, similar to that of the Jesus Christ of Roman Christianity. They created a book using the New Testament writings called the Koran, written in Arabic. The Koran was believed to be so holy that it could not be translated or read in any other language but Arabic, until just recently. According to Wikipedia, Islam began its spread to the African continent from the seventh to the ninth centuries when many Hebrew Israelites had dispersed into Africa. However, the "Holy" wars of Islam, started by the Ottoman Turks, did not begin until 1914 to 1918AD, when both the Ottoman Empire and Germany engaged in a propaganda campaign to foster jihad amongst the world's Muslims. Why would they want to have jihad when most of the Hebrew Israelites had already converted to the Islamic religion? There is evidence to show that this was another of Edom-Rome's abuses to destroy more of the Hebrew Israelites and revise history to support the narrative that the Muslims are against Christians and to hide Edom-Rome's true agenda. In fact, these Arab nations are all part of the diverse nation Scripture describes as ruling at the end of the age. They are the Edomite Arabs, the Edomite Turks, the Edomite Jews, the Edomite Germans, and the Edomite Romans all part of the conspiracy against the Hebrew Israelites.

This conspiracy by the nations of the earth against YAHUAH and his people, the TORAH and the TANAKH both affirms that the history of the entire earth is about bringing righteousness to the earth through one righteous people and one people only. YAHUAH has chosen this nation, Israel, to be his own special people who will live and reign with him in righteousness. In fact, when he compares Israel to the other nations, he sees these nations as nothing, "All nations before him are as nothing; and they are counted to him less than nothing, and vanity" (Isaiah 40:17). Edom-Rome, as Israel's adversary, will continue in its quest to extinguish the people of Israel until YAHUAH delivers them from Edom-Rome's hands. The false history of the Arabs was just another method Edom-Rome used to carry out the wicked attacks against the Hebrew Israelites. However, all for naught, because prophecy declares, "No weapon formed against thee shall prosper; and every tongue that shall rise against thee in judgment thou shalt condemn. This is the heritage of the servants of YAHUAH, and their righteousness is of me, saith YAHUAH," (Isaiah 54:17). Israel is righteous because their Father YAHUAH is righteous and therefore Israel will be saved no matter what Edom-Rome does to destroy their bodies as they have no power over the soul of an Israelite, "But Israel shall be saved in YAHUAH with an everlasting salvation: ye shall not be ashamed nor confounded world without end," (Isaiah 45:17).

EDOM-ROME – JACOB'S ADVERSARY

Edom-Rome is the adversary of Jacob-Israel created by YAHUAH for this purpose. YAHUAH allowed them to punish the children of Jacob so the fire of adversity refines them as gold is refined. YAHUAH declared, through his Prophet Moses what will happen to Israel by the hand of a foolish people he would send against them, when they were still in the wilderness on the way to the Promise Land. As Israel had been disobedient to the Most High YAHUAH, he declared in his anger what would happen to the children of Jacob, "They have moved me to jealousy with that which is not ELOHIYM; they have provoked me to anger with their vanities: and I will move them to jealousy with those which are not a people; I will provoke them to anger with a foolish nation... I will heap mischiefs upon them; I will spend mine arrows upon them; they shall be burnt with hunger, and devoured with burning heat, and with destruction: I will also send the teeth of beasts upon them, with the poison of serpents of the dust" (Deuteronomy 32: 21-24). And so, these curses came upon Israel by the hand of Edom-Rome and many of Israel are still experiencing these curses even today. Edom-Rome led this great deception by changing the truth about history, recasting the people and rewriting the story to support their wicked doctrines.

The Most High YAHUAH allowed Edom-Rome to take these actions against the Israelites to bring about their removal from their heritage so he would fulfill his purpose for them both, "I said, I would scatter them into corners, I would make the remembrance of them to cease from among men" (Deuteronomy 32:26). Therefore, many people are unaware that these scattered black Negroes, who are in constant dispersion, descend from Israel, and many people have a great hatred for them. However, he will not give Edom-Rome the credit for what he has allowed because they would believe their hand destroyed Israel, "Were it not that I feared the wrath of the enemy, lest their adversaries should behave themselves strangely, and lest they should say, our hand is high, and YAHUAH hath not done all this"

(Deuteronomy 32: 27). YAHUAH the ELOHIYM of Abraham, Isaac and Jacob-Israel has given the Hebrew Israelites the children of Israel into the hand of the wicked enemy, Edom-Rome but most of Israel does not know the truth of their captivity. In fact, many of them refuse to believe they are captives because they have no memory of who they are. They accept as true they are gentiles and have known the gentile way of life. YAHUAH removed them from their heritage and they are unaware that their true father is YAHUAH the ELOHIYM of their forefathers. Edom-Rome has deceived them, and they now believe the lie that this BEAST system led by Jesus, the one they call Christ, the son of God is the true Messiah.

Even though, YAHUAH allowed Edom-Rome, the adversary of Jacob-Israel, to carry out these actions against Israel he will not let them go unpunished for the evil committed against his Chosen people. So, if the question arises why YAHUAH allowed this to happen? Paul give the answer in a letter to the Israelites living in Rome, "Shall the thing formed say to him that formed it, why has thou made me thus" (Romans 9:20)? YAHUAH creates all things for his purpose and use. Therefore, "Behold, a whirlwind of YAHUAH is gone forth in fury, even a grievous whirlwind: it shall fall grievously upon the head of the wicked. The anger of YAHUAH shall not return, until he has executed, and till he has performed the thoughts of his heart: in the latter days ye shall consider it. I have not sent these prophets, yet they ran: I have not spoken to them, yet they prophesied," (Jeremiah 23:19-21).

This research shows they have discounted the truth and eliminated anything that did not support their delusions. So, at the return of the HAMASHIACH, he will fulfill the prophecy of revealing who the hidden people are and bring Israel back to their homeland, 'And say unto them, Thus saith YAHUAH ELOHIYM; Behold, I will take the children of Israel from among the heathen, whither they be gone, and will gather them on every side, and bring them into their own land: and I will make them one nation in the land upon the mountains of Israel; and one king shall be king to them all: and they shall be no more two nations, neither shall they be divided into two kingdoms any more at all," (Ezekiel 37:21-22).

Edom-Rome was always aware of the identity of Israel, and this research will prove the histories that Edom-Rome recorded in their books are not as old as they want us to believe. In fact, it is my belief that the Vatican has in its possession all the written records of Israel stored in their libraries, located under the the church at Rome. Therefore, the claim they make that there are no records to determine who the people are on the face of the earth is a lie. As Enoch prophesied they would distort the truth, "And now I know this mystery, that sinners will alter and pervert the words of righteousness in many ways, and will speak wicked words and lie, and practice great deceits, and write books concerning their words," (Enoch 104:10). For these four hundred years, they have led Israel in its slumber to believe they are gentiles and the captivity and dispersal to the West from Africa happened to the sons of Ham, a cursed race of people. They have also deceived Israel in making them believe Edom-Rome, the Edomites are the Israelites or Jacob. However, it is all a lie, disseminated by Edom-Rome, Israel's enemy and despiser of the brotherly covenant. They led the other nations in scattering and destroying Jacob-Israel. They knew that YAHUAH had turned his face away from his people and therefore, they could destroy them, "My face will I turn also from them, and they shall pollute my secret place: for the robbers shall enter it, and defile it" (Ezekiel 7:22). And, as this prophecy states Edom-Rome as the Vatican has robbed and defiled the holy people of YAHUAH. They have dishonored the holy place by sitting in the place of YAHUAH and his people on the earth pretending to be a holy nation. In fact, they have the world believing there are gaps in history and there was a time they call the dark ages when people are said to have returned to a base level. However, the truth of earth's history is continuous and the Hebrew Scriptures with all they have added and removed is still the only recorded evidence of that truth. There are no breaks in history, neither are there any accidents or calamities hidden from YAHUAH as all things are of him, "Thus saith YAHUAH, the heaven is my throne, and the earth is my footstool: where is the house he builds unto me? And where is the place of my rest? For all those things hath mine hand made, and all those things have been, saith YAHUAH: but to this man will I look, even to him that is poor and of a contrite spirit, and trembleth at my word" (Isaiah 66:1-2). And, it is Israel the poor man who fears and trembles at the word of YAHUAH.

The Edomites sought to obliterate the Israelites at every turn. It was and is their intentions to root them from off the face of the earth, just as Esau had promised Jacob he would do once their parents had died. Therefore, wherever the Israelites settled, Edom-Rome sought to bring about destruction by whatever means possible. On the day of Isaac's death, as recorded in Jubilees, Esau's sons, after finding out the inheritance that should go to the eldest went to Jacob the younger brother they became angry and encouraged their father to forget the promise he made to his parents and to destroy his brother, Jacob. Esau then declared to Jacob his plan to wipe out his descendants; "And when the raven becometh white as the Raza, then know - I have loved thee and shall make peace with thee. Thou shalt be rooted out, and I shall root your sons out, and there shall be no peace for thee" (Jubilees 37:23). Esau-Edom's descendants has carried out this promise of destroying the children of Jacob made by their fore father thousands of years ago. They have shown no mercy and have exacted many massacres hoping to fulfill the promise made by Esau to wipe out the descendants of Jacob-Israel from the earth.

The children of Edom-Rome are a people lacking in principles, and morals and the Most High YAHUAH, placed Israel in the hands of these amoral people. Though they brand themselves as a "holy," nation they have shown they are a vile and base people. They are a foolish people, the bully, the tyrant, the devil and the wicked sinner who has wreaked havoc over the earth. They have attempted, through their deception, to destroy and replace the people of Israel. Therefore, YAHUAH will destroy them, as the prophecy declared by the Prophet Ezekiel, "Son of man, set thy face against mount Seir, and prophesy against it, and say unto it, thus saith the Most High YAHUAH; Behold, O mount Seir, I am against thee, and I will stretch out mine hand against thee, and I will make thee most desolate. I will lay thy cities waste, and thou shalt be desolate, and thou shalt know I am YAHUAH. Because thou hast had a perpetual hatred, and hast shed the blood of the children of Israel by the force of the sword in the time of their calamity, in the time that their iniquity had an end: therefore, as I live, saith YAHUAH ELOHIYM, I will prepare thee unto blood, and blood shall pursue thee: since thou hast not hated blood, even blood shall pursue thee' (Ezekiel 35:2-6). The Most High, YAHUAH, will avenge in full measure all the violations that Edom-Rome has committed against Israel.

IMPACT OF ESAU-EDOM ON THE LANDS THEY OCCUPIED

Isaac, when blessing Esau-Edom told him he would inherit the wealth of the earth and live in its fatness. In fact, he told him he would get his riches by the sword, and history shows that the descendants of Esau-Edom gained the treasures of the earth as they went about killing, stealing and destroying anyone who impeded them getting what they believed was theirs. Esau-Edom's actions resulted in the nations surrendering to their tactics and joining forces in destroying the true Israelites, the chosen people of YAHUAH. In the last four hundred years they hid the truth about their identity and the identity of the Hebrew Israelites, who they led as captives into slavery. However, many of the nations they conquered had no choice but to adopt the religions and systems of government of Esau-Edom. And, these actions by Esau-Edom resulted in increasing their power and adding to their diversity. Scripture describes them as the fourth beast who would rule upon the earth, "Thus he said, The fourth beast shall be the fourth kingdom upon earth, which shall be diverse from all kingdoms, and shall devour the whole earth, and shall tread it down, and break it in pieces" (Daniel 7:23). Historical proof shows Esau-Edom as the people ruling today who have impacted every nation which is evident in the Babylonian religious practices of the people believing they are the "holy" people of the Most High YAHUAH, deceiving the entire earth. Edom-Rome colonized most of the lands on the earth or instigated wars to bring about a division among people of the same family as was done in Korea. This colonization is evident in the languages of Esau-Edom being spoken by the indigenous peoples. In fact, they also embraced the architectural style and cultural morays of Edom-Rome. The prophecies state that Esau-Edom would live at the higher elevations of the land far above the dew of heaven and earth. And, in fact, the Edomites are a people who love the outdoors with mountain climbing being one of their hobbies. They fill their landscape with structures reaching to the heavens, and they report that some of them have even gone to the moon where they have returned several times. In fact, they even claim to have a space station floating around in the vaccum of space where astronuts live and carry out experiments from space. Many of the nations have joined and copied their style and also claim of flight to the moon. But, Obadiah foresaw and identified Edom as he prophesied concerning where and how they would live, "The pride of thine heart hath deceived thee, thou that dwellest in the clefts of the rock, whose habitation is high; that saith in his heart, who shall bring me down to the ground" (Obadiah 1:3)? Both Biblical and secular historical evidence identifies Esau and his descendants as those who lived in the Mountains of Seir where Bozra was the capital and also the Caucasus Mountains of Eastern Europe during the Byzantine era. They are also the people who have built cities where they live on top of each other in high-rise buildings call skyscrapers, "Thus dwelt Esau in Mount Seir: Esau is Edom" (Genesis 36:8).

The Caucasus Mountains, in Eastern Europe, is one of the landmarks said to have been inhabited by the Edomites. These white people from the area identified themselves as Caucasians, and therefore, whether or not they are from this area they identify as Caucasian. The Edomites spread throughout Europe but one group settled in the Caucus mountainous region and it reported they lived there from the seventh to the tenth centuries. Based on this reporting these people who inhabited the Caucasus Mountains are said to be the Jewish people occupying the land of Palestine today. They are the descendants of Esau and known as Khazars. Arthur Koestler, a noted Jewish author writes about the country of the Khazars, "The country of the Khazars, a people of Turkish stock, occupied a strategic key position at the vital gateway between the Black Sea and the Caspian, where the great eastern powers of the period confronted each other." They interweave their history into the history of the Jews of Russia. And, by their own admission, they are Ashkenazi Jews; however, it is impossible for both things to be true. Scripture described Ashkenaz to be a grandson of Japheth, and a gentile therefore; he could not be from the tribe of Judah. In an online article the author states that during the mid-19th to mid-20th century, race scientists, including most physical anthropologist classified the world's populations into three, four, or five races. During this period, they named the Caucasian race after the people of the North Caucasus Mountains, extended to all Europeans, and incorporated it as a formal category. Howbeit, it is noteworthy that according to Scripture YAHUAH only recognizes two races of people; the Israelites and the other people he called Gentiles. It is Edom-Rome who constructed the races of people based on their physical appearance and where they lived.

The tribe of Judah, from which we derive the word Jew, is the fourth son of Jacob-Israel. Ashkenaz is the son of Gomer, the son of Japheth. So, the Ashkenazi Jews could never be the children of

Israel since the sons of Japheth never mixed with the sons of Jacob-Israel. The Edomites, in fact, has a Semitic heritage as they are the descendants of Shem; through Isaac and Esau. Many other nations also claim Semitic heritage as Shem had many sons. Some of these nations include the East Indians, Arabs, Asians, and Persians. In fact, because Esau-Edom is the brother of Jacob, his descendants would also be Semitic, but they could never be the descendants of Israel because their forefather would be Esau, Jacob's twin brother. Jacob had twelve sons and the fourth son was named one Judah and the descendants call Judeans who lived in Judaea. During the persecutions of the Hebrew Israelites around the 16th century Edom-Rome adopted the label Jew to identify both the people who converted to the religion and the bloodline Hebrew Israelites. This became the standard and they wrote it into the Hebrew text. Therefore, the Jewish people living in the land of Palestine may be Semitic but cannot claim ancestry with the Israelites through Judah. They are in fact, mixed with Ashkenaz as they lived among the descendants of Japheth as a mixed people. So as a mingled people they identified with the lands, they call Europe and became the Europeans, represented by the ten toes of Nebuchadnezzar's dream. They are imposter heathen Caucasian converts to the religion of Judaism; a religion not allowed by YAHUAH. The Judeans are black Negroes and their skin color is important to their identity as the birthright of Israel can only come from the seed of Jacob-Israel and his twelve sons known as the twelve tribes of Israel, "And had a wall great and high, and had twelve gates, and at the gates twelve angels, and names written thereon, which are the names of the twelve tribes of the children of Israel' (Revelation 21:12). Jacob-Israel is the chosen son of the Most High YAHUAH and despite what Edom-Rome does it will not change the facts, "I will declare the decree: YAHUAH hath said unto me, thou art my son; this day have I begotten thee. Ask of me, and I shall give thee the heathen for thine inheritance, and the uttermost parts of the earth for thy possession' (Psalm 2:7-8). It was through Esau's grandson Zepho that the Edomites became a people known as Europeans when he moved into Kittiym, known as Rome, today and mixed with the Japhetic people. In fact, the Edomites are a mixed diverse people and carry the bloodline of the three sons of Noah; Shem, Japheth and Ham.

ZEPHO'S ROLE

Zepho, the grandson of Esau, plays an important role in the descendants of Esau becoming the white Europeans. It started at the burial service of Jacob, the father of the Israelites. When Joseph was still king of Egypt, the Egyptians captured Zepho, as the sons of Esau came up to fight the children of Jacob when they tried to bury their father in the cave he inherited as part of the land of Canaan. The children of Israel captured and imprisoned him in Egypt for several years. Zepho then escaped from Egyptian prison and went into Africa where he headed the Military forces of King Angeas of Carthage. Zepho later moved into Kittiym

(Rome) where the descendants of Japheth the original people made him their king. He had experienced many victories in his military exploits and caused an increase in the territories they held. In fact, because Zepho was so important to their victories, the people of Kittiym made him a god and changed his name to Zepho Jannes, the god of Saturn. He reigned as King in Kittiym for fifty years.

Edom-Rome has hidden their identity by claiming the identity of the descendants of Japheth. This deception, however, did not take its full form until the descendants of Edom-Rome had taken control of the earth through various wars and they had dispersed and destroyed Israel. In fact, it may have been as late as World Wars I and II when the Israelites were enslaved, and Edom-Rome had full authority. Edom-Rome was then able to hide their origins since they controlled the narrative. They have omitted from history, the timeline of Esau-Edom's move into the land of Japheth so it appears they are the original descendants of the area they call Europe. And, they have removed and discredited the books of Jasher and Jubilees that has the records able to confirm the truth of their identity.

The evidence shows that Esau-Edom was not the first people to occupy Europe and Scriptures prove they had many encounters with Jacob-Israel before they moved from the land of Edom in Mount Seir. History reveals it was not until after the Byzantine era that the Edomites abandoned the area of Mount Seir. I believe they did this to claim the fulfillment of a prophecy that the land of Edom would be desolate and they would become an extinct people. However, the facts show they remained in Edom long after the HAMASHIACH returned to the Father. Many of Esau's descendants however, moved into different lands and mixed with the inhabitants, in particular, the land of Japheth. Zepho, the son of Eliphaz, the son of Esau, is the connection between Esau and Japheth and the story shows how Esau's descendants came to people Rome, Greece, and the entire European Continent. We find the story in the books of Jubilees and Jasher, the Deuterocanonical, or second books excluded from the sixty-six books of the Protestant Bible. They quote the book of Jasher in two verses of the books known as the Old Testament but, Edom-Rome did not include Jasher in the canonized version of the text, as they show in this verse "And the sun stood still, and the moon stayed until the people had avenged themselves upon their enemies. Is not this written in the Book of Jasher" (Joshua 10: 13)? Also, there is another verse in second Samuel that confirms the writings of the book and the early descendants of Israel using them, "Also he bade them teach the children of Yahudah the use of the bow: behold, it is written in the Book of Jasher" (2 Samuel 1:18). They advance that because the Book of Jasher has many contradictions the rabbis did not include it in the canonized version of Scripture. However, my research of Israel's history has found that the Scribes of Israel were meticulous in their writings as they feared YAHUAH and knew they were not writing of themselves but as the voice of YAHUAH. And, therefore, if there are contradictions those who have had power over the Hebrew scripts for these two thousand years have added the contradictions to confuse the awakened Israelites.

In fact, it is in the Book of Jubilees where it records that it was after Isaac's death that Jacob killed Esau, when Esau's sons encouraged him to go to war against Jacob because he had received the blessings as the elder son. Esau came to war with Jacob and his sons with a huge army, however Jacob and his sons were victorious as it was not the will of YAHUAH for Esau not to overcome Jacob at that time, "And after that Yahudah spoke to Ya'aqov, his father, and said unto him: 'Bend your bow, father, and send forth your arrows and cast down the adversary and slay the enemy; and may you have the power, for we shall not slay your brother, for he is such as you, and he is like you let us give him this honor.' Then Ya'aqov bent his bow and sent forth the arrow and struck Esau, his brother on his right breast and slew him" (Jubilees 38:1-2). After this Esau's descendants became subject to Jacob and his sons as servants for many years. In fact, they were subject to the children of Israel after the Israelites moved into the Promised Land.

ZEPHO GOES TO WAR WITH EGYPT AND THE SONS OF JACOB

Zepho left Africa because he could not encourage King Angeas, whose army he led, to go to war against Egypt. King Angeas had ruled the great Northern African Empire of Carthage for many years and knew that to go to war against the Egyptians, while the children of Israel still lived there, was suicide. So, Zepho gathered his family and sailed into the land of Kittiym, where he later became the leader of their army and after many great exploits, they crowned him King. However, his presence in the land did not discourage the troops of Africa from going into Kittiym and plundering it as usual. And, in the thirtieth year of Zepho's reign over Kittiym the armies of Africa returned to Kittiym to loot and plunder it as they had done in the past. But, when Zepho learned what they had done, he gave orders concerning them and went out to battle against Angeas's troops. He destroyed the army of Angeas, which made Angeas furious. When Angeas heard what Zepho had done to his army, he decided he would go to war with Kittiym to avenge his troops. However, Angeas later changed his mind after considering what the results would be fighting against Zepho which terrified him once he realized that Zepho had a stronger army than his (Jasher 62:27).

The courage Zepho displayed heartened the children of Kittiym and they sought to please him. The successes against the Carthaginians and the land of Kittiym pleased Zepho but the ultimate prize was to go to war against the Egyptians and the children of Israel. He wanted victory over them to avenge his brethren lost when they tried to break him out of Egyptian prison. Zepho continued to resent the children of Egypt and the sons of Jacob and plotted to fight against them. Therefore, once he learned that all the mighty men of Egypt and the sons of Jacob were dead, he consulted with the children of Kittiym to go to war against Egypt. The people of Kittiym agreed, and they prepared for war.

Zepho sent for Hadad, the son of Bedad, king of Edom, and for all his brethren in the land of Edom to join him in this war against Egypt. He told them that they did not have to be concern with the original league they made with Angeas because he had already subdued Angeas in battle and he was no longer a threat to them. He had to reassure his brethren that it was okay to join him in battle as they had made a league with Angeas of Africa when he helped them in their war against the Horites. However, once they learned that Zepho had subdued Angeas, they agreed to assist him in the war against the Egyptians and the sons of Jacob. Zepho also asked all the children of the east and the children of Ishmael to join him against the Egyptians and the sons of Jacob. Scripture notes that the nations assembled a huge army that stretched about a three-day journey and resembled the sand on the seashore (Jasher 64:14-18).

When the Egyptians heard that Zepho was planning to go to war against them with such a huge army, they gathered themselves together and formed an army of about three hundred thousand soldiers. They also sent to Goshen to the children of Israel and summoned them to join with them in fighting against the children of Edom and the children of Kittiym. However, by this time the relationship between the Egyptians and the children of Israel had deteriorated and only one hundred and fifty of the children of Israel decided to help the Egyptians. This was a satisfying response because the Egyptians did not trust the children of Israel because ever since Joseph and all of his brothers had died, the Egyptians had mistreated the children of Israel. They knew the relationship between the sons of Jacob and the sons of Esau and thought they could turn against them and deliver them into the hands of Esau and Ishmael. Therefore, before the battles started the Egyptians told the children of Israel to remain behind in their camp and to only join them if the fighting became too severe. The children of Israel agreed and remained stationed in their camp, determined that they would only join the fight if the Egyptians needed their help (Jasher 64:19-24).

Before the first battle ensued, Zepho, the son of Eliphaz, the son of Esau and king of Kittiym, and Hadad, the son of Bedad who was king of Edom, and all their camps, along with all the children of the east and the children of Ishmael, formed a huge multitude and camped in the valley of Thrace opposite Athens. Zepho then asked Bil'am, the soothsayer who had accompanied them, to determine by divination if the war would be a success. When Bil'am, the Arab, tried to see what would result from the war through the art of divination, he became confused and the work shattered in his hand, "And he tried it again, but it failed, and Bil'am despaired of it and left it and did not complete it, for this was from YAHUAH, to cause Zepho and his people to fall into the hand of the children of Israel, who had trusted in YAHUAH, the ELOHIYM of their ancestors, in their war"

(Jasher 64:29). Zepho lost this war because he did not acknowledged YAHUAH'S help in him winning a war against Angeas and his brother Lucas many years before.

The troops of Zepho and the other leaders readied their forces to go up against Egypt, not knowing what the outcome would be. From the beginning, the fighting was severe against Egypt causing many of the Egyptian soldiers to turn and run away. As they ran, they came to the camp of the children of Israel who had been waiting to assist them and cried out to them for help. The one hundred and fifty men of Israel went out to confront the men of Zepho, the children of Kittiym, the children of Esau, the children of Ishmael and all the other men of the east even as the Egyptians continued to run away from them. As they went forth, they cried out unto YAHUAH, their ELOHIYM, to deliver them. YAHUAH heard their cry and delivered all the kings of the children of Esau and Ishmael into their hands. YAHUAH threw a great consternation in the camp of the kings so that the fear of the children of Israel fell upon them. This caused the rest of the army to turn and run away allowing the children of Israel to chase them all the way to the border of the land of Cush, which is ancient Ethiopia, slaying many of them as they came upon them. Yet, while the children of Israel continued to fight and chase after their enemy, the Egyptians ran in the opposite direction afraid to assist hiding themselves along the roadside while leaving the children of Israel to engage with the enemy alone.

Once the children of Israel realized what the Egyptians were doing, they stopped pursuing the other armies and slew the Egyptians they met on the road. Before they killed each one, they ask, "Wherefore did you go from us and leave us, being a few people, to fight against these kings who had a great people to smite us, that you might deliver your own souls" (Jasher 64:50)? They also made up a saying when they saw an Egyptian in the way, "Smite, smite, for he is an Ishmaelite or an Edomite, or from the children of Kittiym, and they stood over him and slew him, and they knew he was an Egyptian" (Jasher 64:46). By the end of that day, the children of Israel had killed about two hundred of the men of Egypt. This terrified the Egyptians as they saw what so few of the Israelites accomplished and what they had done to so many of those in the other armies. They trembled and became very fearful of Israel. The Egyptians recognized that the Israelites had great power and a great ELOHIYM. The children of Israel returned with joy on their road to Goshen, and the rest of the Egyptians returned each man to his home. Zepho never attempted to go against Egypt again for the rest of the time the children of Israel were living in Egypt. The hatred, however, that the children of Edom had for the children of Israel grew, fiercer after that day, "But from that day forward the children of Esau hated the sons of Jacob, and the hatred and enmity were very strong between them all the days, unto this day" (Jasher 58:28).

ZEPHO DIES

In the year that Aaron, the son of Amram of the tribe of Levi was born, Zepho, the son of Eliphaz, who was the son of Esau and king of Kittiym, died and they buried him in the city of Nabna in the land of Kittym. It is said that, "The great kingdom of Rome was built by Zepho, son of Eliphaz, son of Esau. Tirtat of the land of Elisha attacked him and killed him" (Yelamdeinu, Batei Midrashos 160). It is important to note that Elisha was one the sons of Japheth. Zepho had reigned for fifty years over the children of Kittiym, and Janeas, believe to be Zepho's son, reigned in his stead over the children of Kittiym for another fifty years (Jasher 67:5-7).

EDOMITES MIGRATE INTO JAPHETH'S LAND

When Edom-Rome first entered Japheth's land through Zepho, they ruled together as one people. The offspring of Japheth were people of color, as the evidence shows in paintings and artifacts now available. Many emperors, bishops, and leaders in Greece and Rome were black people. However, Esau-Edom, in their continuous attempt to deceive and rewrite history, has made the world believe after they had conquered the Western world that "white" people were the original inhabitants of Europe. But, Scripture shows they only added to the number of descendants of Japheth by enlarging Japheth, "YAHUAH shall enlarge Japheth, and he shall dwell in the tents of Shem, and Canaan shall be his servant" (Genesis 9:27). Many of Esau's descendants followed Zepho into Kittiym and the Greek Isles, where they either conquered the lands or integrated through mixing and mingling with Japheth's descendants. The Chronicles of Jerahmeel confirm the truth about Zepho and the other Edomites, "The people of Kittiym renamed Zepho after Saturn Zepho Janus, which is the planet the inhabitants of Italy worshiped."[8] They then worshipped Zepho Janus, and he became the first king of Italy from Esau's lineage. Zepho accepted their worship because they worshiped many gods.

The Jewish writings show that Edom's chief god was 'Qaush' (also called 'Kaush,' 'Kaus,' 'Kos' or 'Qaws') since they invoked Qaus in their blessing formula in letters and because it appears in personal names found in ancient Edom (Shmuel Ahituv, 2008).[9] Cornelius Conway concurs that the original descendants of these lands were the sons of Japheth, and "the Greeks regarded Japetus to be the father of all mankind."[10] Esau, who is Edom, the red people of antiquity, was not the original inhabitants of the lands of Japheth. Still, they cause Japheth to become a more exceptional nation when the descendants of Esau mixed and integrated with them.

The Scriptures confirm that the names of the lands reflect the name of the people who first inhabited the territory. For example, the Israelites changed the name of Canaan to Israel after Jacob-Israel, their father, once they and Joshua conquered the land. YAHUAH named the Japhetic lands for the sons of Japheth, and there are ancient maps that prove this is so. The cartographers of Edom-Rome attempted to change and to cast doubt on where the actual places were on the maps to reflect the narrative of the Edomites. The claim by the Edomites that they are the descendants of Japheth is not evidenced in the original maps or Scripture. Esau-Edom was not promised any land other than what he would conquer. His dwellings would be up high in the mountainous areas. Biblical maps and Scripture show the sons of Japheth and not the sons of Esau in the areas they claim as their heritage, "The sons of Japheth; Gomer, and Magog, and Madai, and Javan, and Tubal, and Meshech, and Tiras. And the sons of Gomer; Ashkenaz, and Riphath, and Togarmah. And the sons of Javan; Elishah, and Tarshish, Kittim, and Dodanim. By these were the isles of the Gentiles divided into their lands; every one after his tongue, after their families, in their nations" (Genesis 10:2-5).

The countries known as Europe today were first settled by the sons of Japheth and Scripture identifies the location of these lands, "And for Yaphet came forth the third portion beyond the river Tina to the north of the outflow of its waters, and it extends northeasterly to the whole region of Gog, and all the country east thereof. And it extends to the north, and it extends to the

Land Areas That Fell by Lot to the Sons of Noah

mountains of Quelt towards the north, and towards the sea of Mauk, and it goes forth to the east of Gadiyar as far as the region of the waters of the sea. And it extends until it approaches the west of Fara, and it returns towards Aferag, and it extends easterly to the waters of the sea of Me'at. And it extends to the river Tina in a northeasterly direction until it approaches the boundary of its waters towards the mountain Rafa, and it turns around towards the north. The land which came forth for Japheth and his sons as the portion of his inheritance which he should possess for himself and his sons, for their generations for ever; five great islands, and a great land to the north. But it is cold, and the land of Cham is hot, and the land of Shem is neither hot nor cold, but it is of blended cold and heat" (Jubilees 8: 25-30).

Biblical records show that Mount Seir, the original home of the Edomites, became a vassal state of Rome. It was five years after the Israelites had been living in the Promised Land of Israel, and the land became tranquil throughout the cities of the Amorites and the Canaanites, that several battles arose between the children of Edom and the children of Kittiym. In the thirty-first year of Abianus, the king of Kittiym, he conquered the children of Edom to bring them under his jurisdiction. It was this war that would merge and solidify the people of Edom with Kittiym, which strengthened Rome. They then became one nation with Kittiym–Rome. At the time of this war, they captured King Hadad of Edom and brought him back to Abianus, the king. Abianus ordered his men to kill Hadad. At the time of the King's death, he had reigned in Edom for forty-eight years. This humiliation of the people of Edom caused them to hang their heads in shame. They no longer had their king, and King Abianus placed officers in Edom, and all the children of Edom became subject and tributary to the king of Kittiym-Rome. He reigned over Edom for thirty-eight years after this war (Jasher 90:10-11).

After Abianus's death, Latinus began his reign over Kittiym, which lasted for another fifty years. Latinus or Duke Lotan, as they sometimes refer to him in Scripture, followed as the next king of Kittiym-Rome. Latinus, during his reign, fought against the inhabitants of Britannia and Germania, who were the children of Elisha, son of Javan, the son of Japheth. He prevailed over them and made them tributary to Kittiym. It was during this war that Latinus learned that Edom had revolted against Kittiym, which caused him to have to return and subdue them once again. Edom continued to be tributary to Kittiym for many years afterward, and the two governments operated as one.

IDENTIFYING THE ORIGINAL FOUNDERS OF ROME

Historians often dispute who the founders of Rome were. But there is evidence to show that when Zepho, the grandson of Esau, migrated to Kittiym, he met the descendants of Japheth. This territory was settled by the sons of Kittiym, one of the sons of Japheth. The other descendants of Esau soon followed and spread throughout Italy, Greece, and Europe. There is historical evidence that shows that Idomenus went into Italy, the Temenites went into Turkey, and Timinide migrated to Macedon. These were all the descendants of Teman, one of Esau's sons. Therefore, by the early Rabbinic period, everyone recognized Esau to be the alleged founder and an ancestor of the Romans, who typify the nations. The Scriptures reveal, however, that Esau is only the ancestor and founder of the small kingdom of Edom and was first known as the Edomites because Esau is Edom. In the book, 'How the Edomites went from the Middle East to Rome, Greece etcetera,' the author confirms the accounts written in Jasher that it was after Zepho, the grandson of Esau, moved into Kittiym, many other sons of Esau settled in the lands apportioned to Japheth and his sons. Scripture confirms that Zepho moved to Kittiym from North Africa where he led the Military forces for King Angeas of Carthage after he escaped from an Egyptian prison, "And when the year came round, being the seventy-second year from Yashar'el going down to Mitsrayim, after the death of Yoseph, Tsepho, the son of Eliyphaz, the son of Esau, fled from Mitsrayim, he and his men, and they went away" (Jasher 60: 1).

The descendants of Esau, along with the descendants of Japheth, built many cities throughout Europe. Josephus credits Duke Magdiel, mentioned in Genesis, with building Rome before Romulus surrounded it with walls. They say because of the fame of this king, many Edomites came to inhabit Rome. Other historians, however, dispute these claims. Salbast believes the Trojans founded Rome.[11]   Yet, Virgil asserts that it was the people of Evander who founded Rome.[12]   Isidro, in his

Etymologies, also did not give the descendants of Esau credit for building Rome.[13] Claims of other historians state it was Janus or Zepho who built it after he came from the east to Italy about 1500 years before the Christian era, which comes to the sixth year after the burial of Jacob and the war with Joseph (Jasher, 60).

Manasseh ben Israel, in his writings, disputes the claims and assertions made by the historians about who built Rome.[14] He believed they refused to give credit to the ancient authors who postulate that the descendants of Esau built Rome because of their bias. However, based on historical and Scriptural evidence, the descendants of Edom may have constructed places in Kittiym-Rome, once Zepho went into Kittiym, but the people of Kittiym already had established cities. Zepho, along with the armies of Angeas, used to go into Kittiym to steal and pillage from the people who lived in those lands before he made his permanent move to Kittiym.

Duke Lotan, another descendant of Esau, had a significant impact on the culture of Rome. According to Isaac Abarbanel, a Jewish statesman and philosopher, they attribute Duke Lotan or Latinus as they sometimes call him with finding the Latin language.[15] He argues the verse, "Her nobles, and no kingdom is there, because the head of Rome has not the title of a king. In that court are many Nobles, including the Cardinals." As the Edomites became the dominant people of the Japhetic lands, they changed the form of government, and the king became the Emperor who led the representatives in the Senate. This

Republican form of government used by the Greeks decided law based on the number of votes of the assembly. Most nations on the earth have adopted this form of government, which shows the impact Rome still has over the nations even today. Therefore, once Edom-Rome became the dominant empire, any nation classified as a kingdom with a king, the system replaced with a form of the Papal Roman government. The king's role became ceremonial, as evidenced in the Kingdom of Thailand and Japan.

Another of Esau's descendants was Idomeneus, who also settled in Italy. It is reported he built the city of Petilia near Salentum and, according to historians, he also built Salentum, itself (Bells New Pantheon Vol. 2, p. 5). An account from history reveals that on finding that his life was in danger, Idomeneus sailed for Italy, where he built the city Petilia, near Salentum, soon after his arrival. In this record, it states that Idomeneus and Merion, his wife, died in their own country, and the people erected a magnificent tomb for them, to which they received divine honors. The Cretans sacrificed to them as heroes, and when they went to war, they believed them to be their protectors. This tomb is an artifact that was still visible at Gnossus in the time of Diodorus, and it held an inscription that gave testimony to its validity.[16] The inscription read, "Here lies Merion, by the side of Idomeneus, went into Italy Rome or Eutrustian."

The Temenites and Temenidae are descendants of Teman. Teman was the second son of Esau and his wife, Adah. History shows that the Temenites settled in Turkey, and Timinide (or

Temenidae) settled in Macedon, a country by the sea, now known as Macedonia. Alexander the Great descended from Temenidae and was the first absolute ruler over all of Greece. They trace his lineage to the people of Thucydides. "And it happened, after that Alexander son of Philip, the Macedonian, who came out of the land of Kittiym, had smitten Daryavesh king of the Persians and Madai, that he reigned in his stead, the first over Javan (Greece), And made many wars, and won many strongholds, and slew the kings of the earth, and went through to the ends of the earth, and took spoils of many nations, so much so that the earth was quiet before him; after which they exalted him, and it lifted his heart' (1 Maccabees1:1-3). The History of Macedonia shows that "Alexander is also the father of the Perdiccas, and his forefathers who were Temenidae came from Argos" (Thucydides 2-99.3).[17] It is essential to note the word Argos relates to Agag, the title of the kings of Amalek, a son of Eliphaz, the son of Esau.

Moreover, evidence of Esau's lineage in the lands of Japheth is noted by Davidy, in his discussions about the Hittites. He states that the Temenu of Edom, who was in Gozan near northern Syria, is the same entity as the neighboring Tummana in northern Turkey. He furthers that Assyrian records from 1000BC mention Temanaye, Temans, Temeni, and Taiman. These names, he adds, were different groups descended from the same people. Teman was Esau's son and uncle of Zepho. He was the progenitor of these tribes that the prophecy of Obadiah includes for slaughter, "And thy mighty men, O Teman, shall be dismayed, to the end that every one of the mounts of Esau may be cut off by slaughter' (Obadiah 1:9). Davidy continues, and evidence shows these all to be the same people and is a common occurrence with Assyrian inscriptions. Later in 800 BC, they found more of these same people near Assyria, between Nineveh and Calah, with another group of the Temans occupying a suburb of Babylonia. This evidence confirms that the Assyrians also mixed with the descendants of Esau just as Scripture shows and why even the first scattering of the Northern Tribes of Israel was by the Assyrians who were the mixed descendants of Esau who is Edom.

Although the ancient Romans identified with Esau, historical records show Esau himself did not establish Rome, nor did he ever travel to the area. And, history shows that neither Esau nor his grandson is the founder of Rome. They are usurpers who moved into the land and replaced the people. And, without regard to the facts, Edom has revised history where they can claim ancestry as the Romans and founders of Rome. But Japheth and his seven sons are indeed the original inhabitors of these lands and had built and established cities. The book of Jasher noted that it was sons of Ham who had conquered and occupied many of these areas hundreds of years before the birth of Esau and Jacob. The Edomites have appropriated the identity of the sons of Japheth and refer to Kittiym Rome and its descendants by various titles including "kingdom of Esau," "son of Esau," "Esau," "kingdom of Edom," and "Edom" "tout court." Dionysus, a Greek writer and one who they believed was a god, writes that the people of Rome came into being without a Creator. This belief came out of the pagan culture of the sons of Japheth as they were worshipers of their ancestors and the wandering stars, they call planets.

Japheth, the second son of Noah, is described in scripture as the Gentiles, "And the sons of Javan; Elishah, and Tarshish, Kittim, and Dodanim. By these were the isles of the Gentiles divided into their lands; every one after his tongue, after their families, in their nations' (Genesis 10:4-5). All people are descendants of Noah's three sons, and there are no people who just evolved into existence. The descendants of Esau-Edom mixed his seed with the Japhetic people and became Edome-Rome. These myths have been introduced by Edom-Rome to obscure the truth about their identity. Despite the claim made by some Biblical historians, Esau, who is Edom, is not a Neanderthal but the twin brother created by YAHUAH as the antithesis of Jacob.

Although the descendants of Japheth were polytheists, they also knew they descended from Noah. Scripture shows that every nation on the earth after the flood became worshipers of other gods, and all of the families lived together in a place called Shinar, where Nimrod led the empire into building a tower that would reach heaven, which became synonymous with the Babylonian mystery religions. YAHUAH destroyed this tower, known as the Tower of Babel, by confusing the language of the people. He then scattered the people into the land areas that came to them by lot. "For this reason, the whole land of Shinar is called Babel because YAHUAH did there confound all the language of the children of men, and from thence they were dispersed into their cities, each according to his language and his nation," (Jubilees 10:25). Every nation continued to practice the worship of their Babylonian gods in the lands they settled.

Biblical history shows there were no mythical people on earth, only people who worshipped the sun, moon, and stars as their gods while they also worshiped their dead ancestors and the living and dead leaders of their nations. It was YAHUAH who gave these objects of worship to the Gentile nations and warned Israel not to do what they did, "And lest thou lift thine eyes unto heaven, and when thou seest the sun, and the moon, and the stars, even all the host of heaven, shouldest be driven to worship them, and serve them, which YAHUAH thy ELOHIYM hath divided unto all the nations under the whole heaven. But YAHUAH has taken you, and brought you forth out of the Iron furnace, even out of Mitsrayim, to be unto him a people of inheritance, as ye are this day' (Deuteronomy 4:19-20).

There is no mystery about the identity of the ELOHIYM of Israel. He is the Most High YAHUAH the ELOHIYM above all Elohim. He revealed himself through the TORAH and the Tanakh and taught Israel through his servants, the Prophets. The mystery religions are those of Babylon and Edom–Rome, which philosophies they mixed with Hebrew Scriptures to form other Babylonian mystery religions that many in Israel follow. They have spiritualized the teachings of the Torah, which now resemble the religions of Judaism, Christianity, and Islam, the religions of Esau-Edom.

HOW EDOM-ROME IMPACTED THE LANDS AND PEOPLE OF JAPHETH

Edom-Rome had its greatest impact on the land of Kittiym, which became Rome. Their influence was so all-encompassing that the indigenous people of these lands were replaced by being whited out. Edom-Rome then changed the territories and renamed them for their descendants. The descendants of Japheth's son Javan became known as the Greeks, and the descendants of Kittiym renamed the Romans. The landmass to the north of Africa was then renamed for the goddess Europa. In Hebrew, they call the Greeks bene Yawan, or "the sons of Yawan," a name identical to Ion the alleged mythical ancestor of the Ionians. Scripture identifies Yawan (Javan) as a son of Japheth, the son of Noah, who settled the Greek isles. The story they were mythical people is what Edom-Rome has used to hide the identity of Japheth and claim the lands and history for themselves.

Valerian: Publius Licinius Valerianus Augustis (193-260), also known as Valerian the Elder, was Roman Emperor from 253 to 260. He was taken captive by Persian king Shapur I after the Battle of Edessa, becoming the only Roman Emperor who was captured as a prisoner of war, resulting in wide-ranging instability across the Empire.

129

It is my belief they created these stories of mythical people to discredit the accounts about Japheth in scripture and to deceive and confuse awakened Israel. These myths help to support their narrative of there being a creation without the Creator as a means of denying the existence of the Highest ELOHIYM. They support this theory with mythical people such as the Vandals, who they say would appear from out of the swamps and vandalized beautiful things. Their account of history also claims these same people founded a kingdom in North Africa that existed for about one century. Also, the Ostrogoths, Visigoths, and Vikings some historians assert are the major German tribes. Others claim they were mythical people that appeared and fought with the Romans, which aided the fragmentation and collapse of the Western Roman Empire.

This mythology, combined with the history of the original Greeks and Romans, is meant to support the theories and lies perpetuated by Edom-Rome that they were the first of YAHUAH'S creation and everyone else resulted from something else. This myth is created by Edom-Rome to deny that the true sons of Japheth were beautiful black people, according to the book of Jasher, "And it happened in those days there was in the land of Kittiym a man in the city of Puzimna, named Uzu, and he became revered by the children of Kittiym, and the man died and had no son, only one daughter named Jania. And the damsel was beautiful, comely and intelligent; there was none seen like unto her for beauty and wisdom throughout the land. And the people of Angeas king of Africa saw her, and they came and praised her unto him, and Angeas sent to the children of Kittiym. He requested to take her unto himself for a woman, and the people of Kittiym consented to give her unto him for a woman" (Jasher 60:7-9).

Sir Thomas Browne, in his writings, stresses that the names found throughout Europe are all the same, and all belong to Edom.[18] History shows that since the Empire of Edom-Rome ruled the earth for the past two thousand years, they were able to enlarge and replace the descendants of Japheth. But Scripture also shows the names of the sons of Japheth and the sons of Edom differed. The Edomites replaced the names of the sons of Japheth through marriage and conquest. Still, it is possible to trace the names of the sons of Esau and Japheth to the Europeans. In the Works of Sir Thomas Browne, it states that Erythrae, or Erytheria, was one of the twelve Ionian cities of the Ionian League on the coast opposite the island of Chios in Asia Minor. They said the Cretan settlers, under the leadership of Erythrus ('Red'), son of Rhadamanthus, founded it, and the Lycians, Carians, and Pamphylians inhabited the area. Because of what we know of the history of the sons of Japheth, we can conclude that this is the area where Javan (Yawan) settled before the "red" descendants of Esau followed. The artifacts found throughout Europe proves that black people ruled alongside the Edomites throughout the history of the Greek and Roman Empires. Historical evidence shows that they both ruled up to the Second World War. Socrates, a Greek philosopher, lived from 470-399BC, was described as a black man who fought in the Athenian army. They describe his phenotype as a pug-nosed, thick-lipped, and rotund; his eyes though quick, were bulbous. In the writings of Herodotus, a black Greek, it notes that during the 7th century BC, Erythrae fought a war against the neighboring island Chios. Then later still, in 450 BC, Ionia came under Lydia and then Persia, and then became part of the Delian League (Sir Thomas Browne, p.177). Browne furthers that Erythrae also enjoyed an immune status under Alexander the Great and the Seleucids in 334BC, and under the Principate, it belonged to the coventus of Smyrna. Based on historical facts, Edom-Rome occupied and ruled the land of Japheth for a much shorter period than the records of their history show. They were intellectually influenced by the descendants of Japheth.

When we trace the timeline of Edom-Rome's history recorded in Scripture and secular accounts, it appears their claim of being the first and original inhabitants of Europe is false. Edom-Rome eliminated or undermined much of the history of the original people on the earth so that they could

Greek Head of Silenos - 400BC

assert dominance. When research is done on Edom-Rome's claims of being the first and superior people on the earth, it is so outrageous and sad to think that people believed them. Edom-Rome's white supremacy privilege had to be supported by many theories which they created branches of science to sustain. For example, the science of anthropology was designed to support them digging to pretend to find evidence of people having lived in a particular place and period in history. In recent times, however, cultural objects have been made available, and many artifacts show the original Greeks and Romans were black people. And Biblical history also shows there were other Empires that ruled the world before the Greeks and the Romans. The Babylonian and Medes and Persian Empires ruled before the Greek and Roman Empires, who also held the Israelites in captivity for many years.

Alexander the Great did not conquer the Persians and the known world until the second century BC. In an account given of Alexander the Great during this time, which was hundreds of years after Israel entered Canaan. They report that when Alexander returned to Memphis in April 331 BC, the envoys from Greece were waiting for him. Alexander the Great was a descendant of Esau of the Temen-idea, the people of Thucydides, and they told him that the oracles at Didyma and Erythrae, which had been silent for a long time, had spoken and confirmed that Alexander was the son of Zeus. Erythrae was renowned for its wine, goats, timber, and millstones, and the prophetic sibyls, Herophile and Athenais.

During the time the ancient Roman Empire ruled, they associated Erythrae with Pergamum and with Rome. After the death of Attalos III in 133 BC, the Pergamene kingdom, bequeathed to the Romans, flourished as a free city attached to the Roman province of Asia (Wikipedia). Scripture confirms that Pergamum, associated with Erythrae, is the place where Satan's seat is and where many of the Israelites were being persecuted at that time, "And to the angel of the church in Pergamos write; These things saith he which hath the sharp sword with two edges; I know thy works, and where thou dwellest, even where Satan's seat is: and thou holdest fast my name, and hast not denied my faith, even in those days wherein Antipas was my faithful martyr,

The Agrippine Sibyl: by Abraham Janssens, Netherlands (c. 1575). Agrippine refers to Julia Agrippina, who was a Roman Empress. She was a great-granddaughter of the Emperor Augustus, great-niece and adoptive granddaughter of the Emperor Tiberious, sister of the Emperor Caligula, niece and fourth wife of the Emperir Claudius, and mother of the Emperor Nero. She was born in what is now Cologne, Germany. Sibyl comes from the Greek word Sibylla, meaning Prophetess. It is said that medieval monks reckoned twelve Sibyls, and gave to each a separate prophecy and distinct emblem. For the Agrippine Sibyl: Jesus Christ shall be outraged and scourged. Emblem, a whip.

slain among you, where Satan dwelleth" (Revelation 2:12-13). This reference to Satan's seat, in Pergamos, now modern-day Turkey, was one of the most influential cities in the Roman Empire and was most likely the first city where the gods of Greece and Rome resided.

In the history of the Byzantine Jews, Eli Cohen writes about the Isaurian kings, descendants of Esau.[19] He recalls how Emperor Zeno visited Sichem, a city in Palestine because there was a great conflict brewing between the Samaritans and the Byzantine Empire, which first came to a head during the reign of Zeno (474-491AD). According to the Samaritan Chronicles (43), in the twelfth year of the Pontificate of the High Priest Nathaniel, Zait (Zeno) the King of Edom summoned the elders, the scholars and the priests and told them, "If you do not convert, I shall put you to death." They answered, "We are resigned to death by the will of God; we shall prostrate ourselves in front of none but him." At this, the Emperor ordered the death of many Samaritans. Cohen furthers that this happened one hundred and twenty-three years after the erection of the synagogue by the High Priest, Aschon, which shows Edom itself still existed as a kingdom under Rome during the Byzantine era and had control over Jerusalem at that time. The Byzantine era lasted from 330 to 1453AD. Emperor Zeno then took the synagogue from the Samaritans and established it as a monastery for his saints."[20] Therefore, the Muslim Arabs who are said to have taken possession of the land of Israel and conquered the Byzantine empire occupying the area for hundreds of years did not happen. Edom-Rome added the Muslim take-over of this area to history to deceive and hide their identity as the fourth beast power of Nebuchadnezzar's dream.

IMPACT OF EDOM-ROME ON PRESENT DAY PALESTINE

In 1948 AD, the Zionist Khazar Jews petitioned the United Nations for a homeland for the Jewish people living in Eastern Europe. Thus, the United Nations granted them permission to move into and occupy the land of Palestine. These Khazar Jews said to be a people of Turkish origin and descendants of Esau, converted to the religion of Judaism in the 9th century. Historians believed they had had the most significant impact on the land of Palestine since the Crusades. George Vernadsky (1943) notes that in the first millennium of the Christian era, the Slavic people of several kindred tribes occupied the land, which became known later as the north-central portion of European Russia. He furthers that to the South of them, between the Don and Volga Rivers and north of the lofty Caucasus Mountains lived a people known to history as Khazar. An Arab chronicler further describes the area where the Khazars lived.[21] "They are to the north of the inhabited earth towards the seventh clime, having over their heads the constellation of the Plow. Their land is cold and wet. Their complexions are white, their eyes blue, their hair flowing and reddish, their bodies large and their nature's cold. They have a wild disposition." A Georgian chronicle, echoing an ancient tradition, identifies them with the hosts of Gog and Magog – "wild men with hideous faces and the manners of wild beasts, eaters of blood."

It is said they established the Kingdom of the Khazars in most of South Russia long before they founded the Russian monarchy by the Varangians. Historians believe that these Khazars had blocked the advances of the Muslim conquest of Eastern Europe (Dunlop, 1954).[22] But, in 737AD, the Khazars had lost a battle with the Arabs, and by then, the Muslim "Holy" War was ending.

According to other sources, including records by the Arabs, Byzantine Russian, and Hebrew, concur that a few years later, in 741AD and perhaps as late as 865AD, the King of the Khazars, his court, and the military ruling class embraced the Jewish faith, and Judaism became the state religion of the Khazars. The Universal Jewish Encyclopedia (Vol. VI, PP. 375-377) notes that the chieftain, Bulan, "called upon the representatives of Judaism, Christianity, and Mohammedanism to expound their doctrines before him. This discussion convinced him that the Jewish faith was the most preferable, and he, along with his court, embraced it. They circumcised, thereupon, him and about four thousand; however, some historians believe it was only by degrees that the Jewish teachings gained a foothold among the population.

According to Professor H. Graetz, the successor of the Chieftain Bulan, of the Khazars, bore the Hebrew name Obadiah.[23] He notes that Obadiah was the first to make serious efforts to further the Jewish religion in the Caucus Mountains.

He invited Jewish sages to settle in his dominions, rewarded them, founded synagogues and schools, and caused Rabbis to teach and instruct the Torah and the Talmud to him and his people. They then introduced a divine service modeled on the ancient pagan communities. After Obadiah's death, there followed a series of Jewish chagans who permitted no one who did not have a fundamental understanding of the law, based on the Torah, to ascend to the throne.

There has been much speculation as to the reason the Khazars converted to the religion of the Jews, seeing they were non-Jewish people (Anthal Bartha,1968). They differed from those known as Jews because they were white. So why would they want to convert to this religion? I believe the actions taken by the Khazars are a design of Edom-Rome to replace the actual people of Israel. It is said the Khazars converted to a religion of outcasts because, at the time, all people hated the bloodline descendants of Jacob-Israel for their beliefs. The Khazars, occupying Palestine today, are descendants of the Caucasian people of the Caucus Mountains and still are ethnically different from the Judeans. They are white Edomites and not the black descendants of Jacob-Israel from the tribe of Judah. This ethnic difference was always apparent throughout history. Thus, the Khazar Zionist Jewish people from Soviet Russia could not descend from the real bloodline Hebrews, ancient or modern. They were, in fact, not the Old Testament descendants of Israel and had no Biblical claim to Palestine (Allen H. Godbey, 1930).[24]   The late former President of Egypt, Gamal

Abdel Nasir, concurs. When asked about peace in the Middle East with the Israeli Jewish people, he responded, "The Jews can never live here in peace because they left here black and came back white."[25]

To get a clearer picture of what ethnicity means, the Cambridge English Dictionary defines ethnicity as a large group of people who have the same nationality, racial, or cultural origins of the state of belonging to such a group. Based on the evidence, the Jewish people in Palestine could not be the Israelites because they are Edomites, descendants of Esau who is Edom. Edom-Rome used the knowledge they had of Israel's dispersal and removal from their heritage to steal their identity and form a religion they called Judaism for Jews when Israel did not have a religion, but laws and statutes to guide them in their lives. Therefore, when YAHUAH returns, he will identify the real people of Israel, who would be Negro having different shades of black and brown, "And I will be found of you, saith YAHUAH: and I will turn away your captivity, and I will gather you from all the nations, and from all the places whither I have driven you, saith YAHUAH; and I will bring you again into the place whence I caused you to be carried away captive" (Jeremiah 29:14).

A DIFFERENT FORM OF JUDAISM

The Khazarian Jews converted and practiced a form of Judaism, which had its roots in Babylon. According to Nigosian (2000), the period between the seventh and fourteenth centuries, there was a rise of several new Jewish groups and parties, namely the Karaites, the Cabbalists, and the Hasidic, which came about around the same time the Khazars converted to the religion. This form of Judaism was all created centuries after the dispersal of the Hebrew Israelites and did not have its origins in the truth of the Torah and the Prophets. This Babylonian mystery religion, known as Judaism, is rooted in the pagan philosophies and ideas of the Babylonian Talmud influenced by the rabbis. The Karaites, another Jewish sect, is said to have adhered only to the Bible and repudiated the Talmud.

The cabalistic movement, using the Talmud, formed another religion that had nothing to do with the Highest YAHUAH or the Hebrew Israelites. The term kabel means "to receive," and the name Kabbalist described any Jewish mystic who was a teacher of secret or inward revelation. Thus, the Kabbalist became associated with Jews who believed in the philosophical mystic lore of Judaism, based on an occult interpretation of the Bible handed down as a secret doctrine (Nigosian, 2000). It is these three pagan sects of Judaism that the Khazars follow, which is one of the Babylonian mystery religions, like Christianity and Islam.

After the Hebrew Israelites were in exile and captivity, and unaware of their heritage, Edom-Rome, under the guise of converting to the religion of the Jews, stole their identity and claimed to be the people of YAHUAH. They then took possession of the land of Palestine with the aid of Great Britain and the United Nations and moved the Edomite Jews from across the earth into the land. However, they failed to invite the true Hebrew Israelites living in the diaspora throughout Africa and the four corners of the earth to share in this return, "Therefore, ye mountains of Israel, hear the word of YAHUAH ELOHIYM; thus saith YAHUAH to the hills, to the rivers, and the valleys, to the desolate wastes and to the cities that are forsaken, which became a prey and derision to the residue of the heathen round about; therefore, thus saith YAHUAH; Surely, in the fire of my jealousy have I spoken against the residue of the heathen, and against all Idumea, which have appointed my land into their possession with the joy of all their heart, with despiteful minds, to cast it out for a prey," (Ezekiel 36:4-5).

In 1948 the Israeli Jews used the United Nations General Assembly to bring about the partitioning of Palestine so they could claim a homeland. The document signed became known as the Balfour Declaration, created by the British, Lord Albert Balfour, and signed by the Jews of Germany.[26]   The Jews of Germany promised the British, who had lost the First World War to Germany, that if they could encourage America to get involved with the second World War and fight on the side of the British, in exchange for the land of Palestine so that the Jews could form a Jewish state. The Americans agreed and joined with the British in the war, and the Germans lost the Second World War. After the war, according to John Beaty, "In the post-war years (1945 and after), Jewish immigrants from the Soviet Union or satellite states poured into the land once known as "Holy."

NO CLAIM TO THE LAND OF PALESTINE

History shows that neither the Jews nor Palestinians have any claim to the land of Palestine. Still, in 1948AD, the Khazarian Jewish people, under the banner of the Zionists, moved there, pretending to return to their homeland. Once they began the occupation of Palestine, they carried out many atrocities against the people of Arab and Palestinian descent. They seized most of the land and possessions of the people. They committed a long series of outrageous terrorists acts, including the bombings of the British Officers' Club in Jerusalem, the Acre Prison, the Arab Higher Command Headquarters in Jaffa, the Semiramis Hotel and many others followed this. The World Almanac reported the acts, and reminded us that, "Jewish terrorists carried out these bombings."[27]

Today, the Israeli Jewish people, the Edomite imposters living in the land of Palestine, continue to act as terrorists against the former inhabitants of the land, just as they did to the Judeans in the past. They have forced the Palestinians to leave their homes and move into camps, called occupied territories, where some Palestinians have lived for over fifty years, in sub-human conditions. Despite the schemes of the Edomite heathens to replace the people of YAHUAH and to delude the people of the world into believing they are the "chosen" race, their plans will fail. They knew the true Israelites were in exile and dispersed throughout the earth. They were the ones who engineered their dispersal. History has shown that Esau-Edom has had the desire to replace Jacob-Israel and reclaim the position as the first-born. However, it is not the will of YAHUAH for his ways are not our ways, and he planned it to be so, "YAHUAH hath made all things for himself: yea, even the wicked for the day of evil" (Proverbs 16:4).

YAHUAH created the Edomite heathens, including the Khazarian Jews, to fulfill his purpose on the earth. Edom-Rome, in their position of power, believes they have control over Israel, but my research shows that YAHUAH has only given them a season to accomplish his will. And, that is why he asks, "Why do the heathen rage and the people imagine a vain thing' (Psalm 2:1)? Edom-Rome has imagined that they could exterminate and replace YAHUAH'S Chosen people, but he says he sits in the heavens and laughs and holds them in derision. He plans to once again choose Jacob, "For YAHUAH will have mercy on Jacob, and will yet choose Israel, and set them in their land: and the strangers shall be joined with them, and they shall cleave to the house of Jacob' (Isaiah 14:1). And, the stranger he includes is the Northern Ten tribes of Israel, both the Judeans and Israel, he will save.

The Zionist Khazarian Jews have combined Judaism with the Christian religion, now call Judeo-Christianity. They have incorporated the universal Christian teachings of Rome, both of them using the Hebrew Scriptures to steal the land and replace true Israel. The doctrine of Christianity teaches they are now "spiritual" Israel, through Jesus the Christ. They believe YAHUAH cut Israel off when they refused to accept the

HAMASHIACH. But the Northern ten tribes known as Israel had been cut off, and the Highest YAHUAH sent the HAMASHIACH to show them the way back to him. Why would he then cut off the Judeans who had remained faithful in keeping the TORAH? This deception, driven by Edom-Rome, has blinded the eyes of many people because they do not understand that they can never replace Israel nor ever become "spiritual" Israel. The Jewish people are Edomite Jews who follow the religion of Judaism and are aware that the Zionists are wrong in their assertions. Rabbi Yaakov Shapiro notes that Zionist Jewish leaders do not speak for all the religious Jewish people because the Zionist do not believe the Bible is YAHUAH'S word. They do not believe YAHUAH spoke through his Prophets.[28] Shapiro adds that when the Zionists speak of the Bible, they are not speaking from a Judaic perspective, but from the Christian's interpretation of Scripture. Ben Gurion, the first Prime Minister of the Israeli's, was an atheist who stated, "The mandate is not the Bible, but the Bible is our mandate."[29] Which in his mind, they could use the Bible as a means to their wicked ends.

Ben Gurion was an Edomite, a bloodline descendant of Esau, who led the way in this deception of the Jews returning to their homeland in these "end" times. They wanted the land of Palestine and stole it, in the legacy of Esau, who is Edom, prophesied to live in the earth's fatness and would get wealth by the sword. They knew the land did not belong to the Palestinians because it was Rome who, after they had killed or expelled all the Judeans, changed the name to Palestine in 135AD to wipe the memory of Israel off the map and from the minds of people on the earth. No Scripture supports this false doctrine of Christians becoming "spiritual" Israel. But, they will continue the charade until YAHUAH sends his angels to gather Israel to take them into the land when he returns, "And he shall send his angels with a great sound of a trumpet, and they shall gather his elect from the four winds, from one end of heaven to the other" (Matthew 24:31). His elect is still the Twelve Tribes of Jacob-Israel, living in the diaspora as captives of Edom-Rome under the curses of Deuteronomy chapter twenty-eight.

HISTORICAL EVIDENCE RELATIVE TO EDOM AND ISRAEL

Biblical and secular historical sources have found the nations of Edom and Israel to have existed. Though, it shows that the nation of Edom had been established hundreds of years before Israel. Once Israel became a nation, the accounts in history reveal they were involved in many conflicts with other nations, including Edom. The research of K.A. Kitchen shows that Esau, who is Edom, was a substantial nation along with the nations of Moab and Ammon when Israel was just moving into the land of Canaan from Egypt. Based on Egyptian sources about ancient Jordan, there is evidence that the Pharaoh, Merenptah, knew Edom to be a nation as early as 1206BC. And, there is an account of Sinuhe, written on an extant papyrus dated 1900BC that names the

Edomite chief Jeush of Genesis 36:15-18. This Papyrus, found in the Berlin Museum, translates the Biography of Sinuhe, the 1900 BC Edomite chief, Jeush (Esau's son). The translation reveals, "Your majesty is the conquering Horus; your arms conquer all lands. May then your Majesty command to have brought to you the prince of Meki from Qedem (literal: sons of the east), Jeush the mountain chiefs of Edom and prince of Menus from the lands of the Fenkhu (Phoenicians)." This evidence illustrates that Edom was already an organized and recognized nation in 1900BC. Moses also referred to Edom when he wrote the first five books of the TORAH in 1446BC.

The Edomites also mixed with the Assyrians, and history shows that YAHUAH used them to punish the Northern tribes of Israel for their disobedience. This family lineage still exists in Syria as the house of Hal Assad today. The names found in Assyria and Saudi Arabia are traced to Esau. Edom-Rome has misled the world into believing the Arabs are Edom or the Edomites, and so they are. But this is not the entire truth because Esau, who is Edom mixed with all the neighbors that surrounded him and whited out many of them. They then identified as Edom because of their white color. Some accounts show that many Edomites migrated from Assyria into the land of Japheth. In the Arabic literature, it states that some tribes that joined the Romans became literal branches and carry the names TANUKH, NIHD, SULAYM, and GHASSAN. It is said when the Muslims drove the Edomites out of Assyria, they entered the lands of the Romans and mingled and multiplied with them and became recognized as Romans by descent. However, they are not Romans, and the Roman genealogies know the facts. Esau mixed with all people and became the ruling class of all nations on Earth today.

---

[1] Eber was a great-grandson of Noah's son Shem and the progenitor of the Hebrew people. According to the Hebrew Bible, Eber died at the age of 464 years old. (Genesis 11:14-17)

[2] The Nabateans are a people who are said to be of ancient Arabia whose settlements lay in the borderlands between Syria and Arabia, from the Euphrates River to the Red Sea. Little is known about them before 312 B.C.E.

[3] Henry Clay Trumbull was an American clergyman and author. He popularized the idea that Kadesh Barnea was not at Petra. He became a world-famous editor, author, and pioneer of the Sunday school Movement.

[4] Kadesh barnea is important to correctly locating Transjordan on the border of Edom at Petra or just north at El Beidha. Kadesh Barnea is on the border of Edom and this refutes locating Kadesh at Ein Qudeirat.

[5] Steve Rudd is a church of Christ Pastor whose views are controversial as it relates to various denominations and some Biblical accounts of history.

[6] Joseph the Zealot was a leading polemicist of Franco-German Jewry of the 13th century. He was known as Joseph the Zealot because he was zealous in defense of Judaism.

[7] Netziv, Haamek Davar to Genesis 23, 34 A commentary on the Torah. It is mostly based on the Netziv Parashat Hashavua shiur in the Volozhin Yeshiva.

[8] The Chronicles of Jerahmeel or the Hebrew Bible Historiale is a collection of Apocryphal and Pseudo-Epigraphical books dealing with the history of the world from the creation to the death of Judah Maccabeus.

[9] Shmuel Ahituv is an Israeli Professor of history at the Hebrew University of Jerusalem and the University of Ben Gurion in the Negev.

[10] Cornelius Conway was an American educator. He was regent of theSmithsonian Institution, as well as professor of Greek literature and president of Harvard University.

[11] Salbast was an ancient Greek writer who supported the idea that the Trojans founded Rome.

[12] Virgil (Publius Virgilius Maro) was an ancient Roman poet of the Augustinian period. He is ranked as one of Rome's greatest poets.

[13] Isidro (Isidore of Seville) was a Bishop of Seville (c 560-638). He was widely regarded in the Catholic Church as the last of the church fathers, "The last scholar of the ancient world."

[14] Manasseh ben Israel also Menasheh ben Yosef ben Yisrael, also known with the Hebrew acronym, MB'Y, was a Portuguese rabbi, Cabbalist, writer, diplomat, printer and publisher, founder of the first Hebrew printing press in Amsterdam in 1626.

[15] Isaac ben Judah Abarbanel, commonly referred to as Abarbanel also spelled Abravanel, Avravanel or Abrabanel, was a Portuguese Jewish statesman, philosopher, Bible commentator, and financier.

[16] Gnossus or Knossos (also Cnossos) is the largest Bronze Age archaeological site p n Crete and has been called Europe's oldest city. The name Knossos survives from ancient Greek references to the major city of Crete. The palace of Knossos eventually became the ceremonial and political center of the Minoan civilization and culture.

[17] Thucydides lived c.460-400BC. He was an Athenian historian and general. His History of the Peloponnesian War recounts the fifth-century BC war between Sparta and Athens until the year 411BC. He has been called the father of "scientific history" by those who accept his claims to have applied strict standards of impartiality and evidence-gathering and analysis of cause and effect.

[18] Sir Thomas Browne was an English polymath and author of varied works which reveal his wide learning in diverse fields including science and medicine, religion and the esoteric.

[19] Eli Cohen or Eliyahu Ben-Shaul Cohen commonly known as Eli Cohen was an Israeli spy. He is best known for his espionage work in 1961 to 1965 in Syria, where he developed relationships with the political and military hierarchy and became the chief Adviser to the Minister of Defense.

[20] Emperor Zeno the Isaurian, originally named Tarasis Kodisa Rousombladadiotes, was Eastern Roman Emperor from 474 to 475 AD and again from 476 to 491 AD. Domestic revolts and religious dissension plagued his reign; however, he succeeded to some extent in foreign issues.

[21] Arab chronicler -Ibn-Said al-Maghribi. Bodeleian MS quoted by Dunlop (1954), p. 11

[22] Dunlop a professor was born in 1909, is the son of a Scottish divine, and his hobbies are listed in Who's Who as "hill-walking and Scottish history."

[23] Professor H. Graetz was amongst the first historians to write a comprehensive history of the Jewish people from a Jewish perspective.

[24] Allen H. Godbey the author of Lost Tribes a Myth- Suggestions Toward Rewriting Hebrew History, a professor of the Old Testament at Duke University. Later he became an archeologist and historian.

[25] Gamal Abdel Nasir was the second President of Egypt, serving from 1954 until his death in 1970. Nasir led the 1952 overthrow of the monarchy and introduced far-reaching land reforms the following year.

[26] Balfour Declaration was a public statement issued by the British government in 1917 during World War 1 announcing support for the establishment of a "national home for the Jewish people" in Palestine, then an Ottoman region with a small minority Jewish population.

[27] World Almanac debuted in 1868 and is considered the most useful reference book known to modern man. It is the source for essential and authorities' facts for entertainment, reference and learning. The book contains thousands of facts and statistics that are not publicly available.

[28] Rabbi Yaakov Shapiro is a rabbi of congregation Bais Medrash of Bayswater in Far rockaway, New York, and a spokesperson for True Torah Jews a non-profit organization founded in 2001 in Brooklyn, New York that do media outreach on issues pertaining to Zionism and Orthodox Judaism.

[29] David Ben Gurion was the primary national founder of the state of Israel and the first Prime Minister of Israel. He became a major Zionist leader and Executive Head of the World Zionist Organization in 1946.

CHAPTER 4

Biblical Accounts of Wars Fought by the Edomites

ISAAC PREDICTED ESAU-EDOM would be a people of war, and Biblical history bears this out as many wars are linked to them. Scripture describes Esau as being a designing and crafty man who insisted on having the upper hand. His descendants continued in his footsteps, and the Books of Jasher and Jubilees have recorded many Edomite encounters with various nations. Zepho, the grandson of Esau, and Amalek, another of Esau's sons, facilitated many wars. One of the wars Zepho incited was the war between the children of Kittiym and Egyptians, where the children of Israel lived in Goshen. Zepho had after he could not encourage King Angeas of Carthage to engage in war with the Egyptians. So after he moved into Kittiym and ruled there for many years, he was able to entice them to go to war against Egypt. Zepho had migrated to the land of Kittiym, where the people welcomed him and hired him to lead their military forces and fight their wars. Because of Zepho's role, the Rabbinic writings describe Esau as the alleged ancestor of the Romans.

The history of Esau-Edom and Zepho's identity and what he did after the people of Kittiym welcomed him is confirmed in the Chronicles of Jerahmeel (p.96). It states, "When this Sefo, (Zepho) the son of Eliphaz traveled from Africa to Kittiym, the inhabitants received him with great honor, and presented him with many gifts, so he became rich." This account supports what is written in the book of Jasher as it relates to the events of Zepho and his move to Kittiym-Rome. What history shows are that Esau, who is Edom, never actually lived in Rome, but his offspring inhabited the lands of Japheth. It was not until the seventeenth century AD when the Edomites as the Europeans began to dominate Europe after World Wars one and two. What began with one descendant of Esau moving into the land of the Japhetic people ended with Esau, who is Edom, the Edomites supplanting the people, altering and claiming their heritage. In their desire to be above all people, Edom-Rome decided the members of their family of Germany were a pure white Aryan race superior to all people. With dominion over Europe, they went about conquering the earth using deceptive tactics of religions, money, politics, and wars. According to 'A History of Arabs in Sudan' the descendants of Esau-Edom identified as "The Romans (el Rum) descended from el Rum, son of Esau (Isa), son of Isaac (Ishāk), son of Ibrahim, the friend of God, and they are named after their ancestor."

KITTIYM-ROME GOES TO WAR WITH AFRICA

Both Biblical and secular history record the many wars of Esau and his descendants. After and during Zepho's rule in Kittiym for fifty years, other descendants of Esau followed him and gained the respect of the people, "And Angeas king of Africa died in those days, and Azdrubal his son reigned in his stead. And in those days, Janeas king of the children of Kittiym died, and they buried him in his temple which he had built for himself in the plain of Canopia for a residence, and Latinus reigned in his stead" (Jasher 74: 5-6). Latinus, another descendant of Esau, had completed three years of his reigned in Kittiym when he declared war on the king of North Africa, the land of Phut, known as Carthage. Latinus hired all the skillful men of Kittiym to build a fleet of ships to use in these battles. And, Latinus directed the children of Kittiym to go into Africa and engage Azdrubal and his army. During this war, Kittiym prevailed over the strong men of Africa, who fought hard, some even courting death but could not overcome the strength of the warriors of Kittiym. Latinus killed King Azdrubal in the last battle, which destroyed the entire army of Africa. After the death of Azdrubal, Latinus and his army declared victory and returned to the land of Kittiym (Jasher: 74).

HANNIBAL, KING OF CARTHAGE GOES TO WAR WITH KITTIYM

Once the war was over, the people of Africa never forgot how they had been humiliated. After many years had gone by, the inhabitants of Africa arose and took Hannibal, the youngest son of Angeas, the brother of Azdrubal, and made him king over the entire land of Africa. The Northern coast called the Carthaginian Empire. "And when he reined, he resolved to go to Kittiym to fight with the children of Kittiym, to avenge the cause of Azdrubal, his brother, and the cause of the inhabitants of Africa, and he did so" (Jasher 74:18). Hannibal, who was known as a warrior who fought in wars while on the back of an elephant, built many ships and sailed to Kittiym accompanied by a vast army. During this encounter, many of the people of Kittiym lay wounded or dead. Therefore, everyone learned that Hannibal avenged his brother's cause. Hannibal continued the war with the children of Kittiym for eighteen years and camped in their land for a long time after. He killed many of the children of Kittiym

Hannibal - King of Carthage

and devastated their great men and princes. By the time the war was over, Scripture records that Hannibal had killed an additional eighty thousand more of Kittym's citizens. He then returned to Carthage, in Africa, and reined in the place of Azdrubal, his brother (Jasher 74: 21-23). The victory he had over the children of Kittiym brought many years of peace for the inhabitants of Africa.

Triumph Coin of Hannibal (203BC)

Note: There are no known authentic images of Hannibal, and there is no proof that Carthaginian coins show his likeness. However, these coins do exist, and logically who else but the great Hannibal would they put on a coin? Certainly not an ordinary elephant rider.

ISRAEL ENCOUNTERS EDOM ON THE WAY TO CANAAN

Many of the Edomites migrated from Edom into Kittiym and the lands of Japheth while the children of Israel were still living in the land of Goshen in Egypt. For four hundred years, the Hebrews had lived in Egypt, and for about a hundred years, the Egyptians enslaved them. YAHUAH then raised Moses to lead them out of slavery. While being led out of Egyptian captivity, the children of Israel complained about the difficulties they were having as they traveled through the wilderness. This rebellion against Moses caused YAHUAH to punish them by having the children of Israel wander in the wilderness for forty years. The children of Israel had arrived in the wilderness of Sin in the first month of the fortieth year from their departure from Egypt, and they dwelt therein Kadesh, of the wilderness of Sin. It is here that Miriam, Moses' sister, died, and they buried her.

In the first month of the fortieth year from their departure from Egypt, Moses sent to the king of Edom to ask permission for the children of Israel to pass through Edomite land. "Moses sent messengers to the king of Edom saying, 'Thus says your brother Israel. Let me pass. I pray you through your land; we will not pass through field or vineyard. We will not drink the water of the well; we will walk in the king's road. And Edom said to him, 'You shall not pass through my country, and Edom went forth to meet the children of Israel with a mighty people. And the children of Esau refused to let the children of Israel pass through their land, so Israel removed from them and fought not against them, because, YAHUAH had commanded the children of Israel not to fight against the children of Esau" (Jasher 84:25-26). They avoided going to war with them and took the long way around Edom. YAHUAH admonished them not to provoke the children of Esau since he gave the land of Mount Seir to Edom as an inheritance and because they were brethren. The children of Israel passed the boundary of the children of Esau. They then passed the road of the wilderness of Moab, and, from there, they returned and surrounded the wilderness of Edom.

AMALEK GOES TO WAR WITH ISRAEL

Although the children of Israel tried to avoid going to war with the Edomites, because they were brethren, they did not stop Amalek, the grandson of Esau, and the people known as the Amalekites, from waging war with them on their way to Canaan. Amalek was a duke of Edom, "duke Korah, duke Gatam, and duke Amalek: these are the dukes that came of Eliphaz in the land of Edom: these are the sons of Adah" (Genesis 36:16). Just before Israel entered Canaan, the Amalekites fought with Israel in Rephidim. Before the battles started, Moses told Joshua to choose men that were strong enough to fight with Amalek. Moses then took Aaron and Hur to the top of a hill to observe the battles and to signal to Joshua when they seemed to prevail or not, "And it happened, when Moses held up his hand, that Israel prevailed: and when he let down his hand, Amalek prevailed" (Exodus 17:11). The Israelites fought against Amalek's army, which numbered about 180,000 men, and Joshua overcame Amalek and his people with the edge of the sword. After the encounter with Amalek, YAHUAH told Moses to write what had happened as a memorial to remind Joshua and Israel that, because Amalek came against them, he would destroy Amalek's memory from off the face of the earth, "And Moses built an altar, and called the name of it Jehovah-Nissi: for he said, Because YAHUAH hath sworn that YAHUAH will have war with Amalek from generation to generation" (Exodus 17:15-16).

History records, countless wars between Israel and Amalek. The records show the first war after Israel became a nation in first Samuel was with the Amalekites. Samuel had anointed Saul to be King over Israel then YAHUAH tested him. Samuel advised Saul that the Most High wanted him to go to war with Amalek and destroy them, "Thus saith YAHUAH of hosts, I remember that which Amalek did to Israel, how he laid wait for him in the way when he came up from Egypt. Now smite Amalek, and utterly destroy all that they have, and spare them not; but slay man and women, infant and suckling, ox and sheep, camel and ass" (1 Samuel 15:2-3). Saul disobeyed YAHUAH and, instead, destroyed the people but spared Agag, the king, and the best of the animals. King Saul did not heed the instructions given by Samuel to annihilate all that belonged to Amalek because of what they had done to Israel earlier. He also did not remember the promise that YAHUAH had made Moses write in a book for Israel to remember the action that Amalek did to them on their way to the Promise Land. Because Saul was disobedient, YAHUAH rejected his posterity from being King over Israel forever.

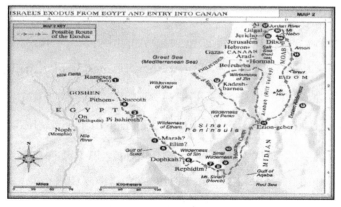

Israel's Exodus from Egypt and Entry into Canaan

Saul disobeyed YAHUAH by not destroying all the Amalekites, which resulted in one of Amalek's descendants, later in history, rising against the Judeans, who were in Persian captivity. The book of Esther records how Haman, the son of Hammedatha, the Agagite, or Macedonian, who descended from Amalek, conspired to destroy the Judeans. The story relates how Haman Agag, the king of the Amalekites' descendent, tried to have all the Judeans slaughtered. Haman, who had power in the King of Persia's court, carried a deep hatred for the Judeans and concocted a plan to destroy all of them. However, Esther, an Israelite slave chosen by the king of Persia to be his Queen, learned about this plot from her uncle Mordecai, a Judean who also lived in the King's court.

Upon learning of Haman's diabolical plan, Esther used her position as Queen and, with courage, executed a strategy to foil the vicious plot aimed at killing all the Judeans in the empire. After fasting and praying to YAHAUH ELOHIYM for three days, she told the king about what Haman had planned to do to her people. She pleaded her cause to the king for the deliverance of Israel from the fate that Haman had determined for them. King Artaxerxes's response was one of sympathy, and he sent his secretaries to rescind the decree that Haman had distributed throughout the empire. The secretaries sent letters and summoned all the provinces under Persia which stretched from India to Kush, today, known as Ethiopia, "On the twenty-third day of the first month, Nisan, in the same year; the king gave all he commanded in writing to the administrators and governors of the provinces from India to Ethiopia, one hundred and twenty-seven provinces, to each province in its own language regarding the decree of Haman" (Additions to Esther 8:9). The king added to the letters he wrote, "You will, therefore, do well not to put in execution the letters sent by Haman son of Hammedatha, since he, the one who did these things, was hanged at the gate of Susa with all his household — for God who rules over all things, has inflicted on him the punishment he deserved" (Esther addition E 17).

The letter that King Artaxerxes sent to the governors of his provinces denounced Haman and praised Mordecai, Esther's uncle, who had raised her because her parents had died. He directed his subjects to help the Judeans. King Artaxerxes allowed the Israelites in every province to kill people connected to Haman. In a footnote to the additions of the Greek version of the Septuagint, it notes that the Gentile king referred to the Judeans and their God in the most positive terms. The king praises the Judeans and their laws and confesses his indebtedness to their God. He pointed out that Haman was a Macedonian scheming to overthrow Persian rule, and an alien to the Persian blood, devoid of their kindliness. The writer of Esther reveals that this may be an allusion to the conquest of Persia by the Macedonian, later in history when Alexander the Great of Macedonia conquered Persia in 333BC.

KING SAUL SUBJUGATES EDOM

After Saul had failed the test of YAHUAH because he failed to destroy everyone and everything connected to Amalek. YAHUAH then chose the line of Judah for which the scepter would pass. However, in the 11th century, BC Saul and Israel went to war with Edom and defeated them. Afterward, Israel required Edom to pay tribute to them for many years. "Now when Saul had taken the kingdom over Israel, he fought against all his enemies on every side, against Moab, the sons of Ammon, Edom, the kings of Zobah, and the Philistines; and wherever he turned, he inflicted punishment' (1 Samuel 14:47). Isaac had told Esau that Jacob would subject him and his descendants, and this subjugation continued once the children of Israel had become an established nation. This subjugation by Jacob over Esau was described as a yoke on his neck by Isaac when he gave Esau his blessings, "And by your sword will you live, and you shall serve your brother. And it shall happen when you become great and shake his yoke from off your neck, you shall sin a complete sin unto death, and I shall root your seed out from under heaven' (Jubilees 26:34).

KING DAVID DEFEATS THE EDOMITES

After David became King, Israel engaged the Edomites and defeated them in 1001BC. They met David and his army in the Arabah valley for battle, "Moreover Abishai the son of Zeruiah slew in the Valley of Salt eighteen thousand Edomites" (1

Chronicle 18:12). David then put garrisons throughout Edom, and all the people of Edom became his servants. He dedicated unto YAHUAH, with silver and gold he brought from all the nations he had slain, including Moab, Ammon, the Philistines, and Amalek. There was no king in Edom because David had placed over the Edomites Israelite governors or prefects, and this administration continued to exist under Solomon. Joab, the son of Zeruiah, was Captain of David's army at the time and destroyed the males in Edom, "For it came about when David was in Edom, and Joab, the captain of the host, went to bury the slain after he had smitten every male in Edom. He remained in Edom for six months until he had cut off every male in Edom" (2 Samuel 8:14).

KING SOLOMON RULES OVER EDOM

When King Solomon began his rule of Israel in 960BC, he also ruled over Edom for ten years and ended up losing control in 950BC. While he had control over Edom, he also regulated the seaport of Ezion-Geber, which was a Port in Edom "And King Solomon made a navy of ships in Ezion-Geber, which is beside Elath, on the shore of the Red Sea, in the land of Edom" (1 Kings 9: 26). During his reign of Israel, King Solomon also constructed the Temple in Jerusalem.

However, King Solomon loved and married many strange women who caused his downfall and the dividing of the kingdom of Israel into two kingdoms, Judah and Israel. Solomon married the daughter of Pharaoh and dealt with women of the Moabites,

Ammonites, Edomites, Zidonites, and Hittites. All these women were from nations of which YAHUAH had instructed the children of Israel not to have any mixed children. Yet, Solomon did not obey. As a result, the Highest, YAHUAH caused Solomon's enemies to come against him "And YAHUAH stirred up an adversary unto Solomon, Hadad the Edomite: he was of the king's seed in Edom" (1 Kings 11:14).

Hadad, of the king of Edom's lineage, rose against King Solomon. He was a small child when the Edomites of his father's servants escaped into Egypt with him. He grew up with the Pharaoh in Egypt and found great favor; Pharaoh gave him in marriage to the sister of his wife, Tahpenes, the queen. Hadad remained in Egypt until after David and Joab, the commander of David's army, were dead, after which he returned to Edom. However, according to Josephus, Hadad could not make the people forsake Solomon, because he kept Edom under many garrisons. Hadad then left Edom and went into Syria. There he met Rezon, the son of Eliadah, who had fled from his lord Hadadezer, king of Zobah.

These names all connect to Esau, who is Edom. They are his posterity and continued to impact the descendants of Israel negatively. Hadad met Rezon in Syria and joined forces to fight against Israel and Syria. Hadad had success in seizing a part of Syria, where the inhabitants made him king. He also made incursions into the land of Israel and caused the citizens much stress because of this insurgency. He attacked Israel and destroyed much of the area, "And he was an adversary to Israel all the days of Solomon, besides the mischief that Hadad did: and he abhorred Israel and reigned over Syria' (1 Kings 11:25).

EDOM REBELS AGAINST JUDAH

After YAHUAH divided Israel into two kingdoms, the northern Ten Tribes identified as Israel or Ephraim, and the southern tribes became Judah. Edom then became a dependency of the Kingdom of Judah. During the time of Jehoshaphat and Jehoram, kings of Israel and Judah, scriptures record that the king of Edom went to war against the Moabites and destroyed them. However, before the battle, the kings of Judaea, Israel, and Edom went before Elisha, the prophet, to ask him about how to get water for themselves and their men and animals on their way to the battle against the Moabites. Elisha refused to address the king of Judah at first because the king of Israel and Edom were present, and he disdained them both. He considered these two kings, the enemy of Judah. He was, in fact, beneath him, "And Elisha said, As YAHUAH TSEVAOTH lives before whom I stand, were it not that I regard Jehoshaphat the king of Yehudah, I would not look toward you, nor see you" (2 Kings 3:14). However, he answered and predicted that they would have victory over Moab.

It was after the death of Jehoshaphat, however, that Edom rebelled against King Jehoram of Judah and elected a king of its own. Later in history, King Amaziah made expeditions against the Edomites and defeated them, but they continued to rebel. So, for about one hundred years, Judah and Edom fought battles, and Judah could not overcome them. Nelson Glueck (1947), noted that Amaziah of Judah waged a successful war against Edom when he captured Selah, whose name he changed to Joktheel, "He slew of Edom in the Valley of Salt ten thousand, and took Selah by war, and called the name of it Joktheel unto this day" (2 Kings 14:7). The book of 2 Chronicles also confirms this war, "And Amaziah strengthened himself, and led forth his people, and went to the Valley of Salt, and smote of the children of Seir ten thousand' (2 Chronicles 25:11-12). After Amaziah defeated Edom, however, he sought guidance from the gods of Edom about whether he would defeat Joash, the king of Israel, if he went to war with them. What he did, by consulting the false gods of Edom, went against YAHUAH, and Joash defeated Amaziah at Beth-Chemosh. After the war, Joash did not kill Amaziah but took him to Jerusalem in shame.

Following this victory over Amaziah, Joash, king of Israel, tore down part of the wall of Jerusalem, looted the temple of Solomon, and took hostages back to Samaria. Amaziah then lived for fifteen years after the death of Joash, king of Israel and these misdeeds by the King of Israel was part of the reason they became scattered, "And the people of Judah took Azariah, sixteen years old and made him king instead of his father Amaziah' (2 Kings 14:21). As king, he rebuilt Elath and restored it to Judah.

In 780BC, Judah overcame Edom, but Edom struck back at Judah and recaptured the territory from them after Azariah died.

Edom destroyed Judaea and took over their territory, which led to the prophet Amos condemning them, "Thus saith YAHUAH; For three transgressions of Edom, and four, I will not turn away the punishment thereof; because he pursued his brother with the sword and cast off all pity, and his anger tore perpetually, and he kept his wrath for ever: But I will send a fire upon Teman, which shall devour the palaces of Bozrah' (Amos 1: 11-12). This future prophecy included not just the original land areas of Edom and its capital Bozrah, but wherever the Edomites are located.

At Azariah's death, Ahaz became king and sent to the kings of Assyria for help in a war against the Edomites because Edom had again attacked Judah and carried its people captive back to Edom into the Transjordan area. During this time, the Philistines also invaded the cities of the lowland and the Negev of Judah and taken Beth-Chemosh, Aijalon, Gederoth, and Shocho and their villages, and Timnah and its villages, and Gimzo and its villages and the Philistines settled in those areas of Judaea. In 732BC, some fifty years later, Israel, which comprised the Northern kingdom, along with the Syrians, also known as the Assyrians, attacked Jerusalem. They also raided the Judean Negev and took captives back to Edom in the Transjordan area of Mount Seir (2 Chronicles 28:16-18). For this reason, the Judeans had a great dislike for the northern tribes of Israel, whom they called gentiles.

During the time of King Ahaz, the Edomites were capturing and deporting Judeans back to Edom from the Negev. So, Ahaz, king of Judah, petitioned Tiglath-Pileser III, king of Assyria, to assist him. Ahaz sought to bribe the king of Assyria with gifts and took many valuable items from the Temple and from his citizens to give to him. However, instead of this helping, his actions backfired, and the Assyrian army placed king Ahaz in submission to Assyria. "For YAHUAH brought Judah low because of Ahaz king of Israel; for he made Judah naked and transgressed sore against YAHUAH. And Tilgath-pilneser king of Assyria came unto him, and distressed him, but strengthened him not. For Ahaz took away a portion out of the house of YAHUAH, and out of the house of the king, and the princes, and gave it unto the king of Assyria: but he helped him not. And in the time of his distress did he trespass yet more against YAHUAH: this is that king Ahaz" (2 Chron. 28: 19-22). As a result, of these events, Assyria will also pay, "YAHUAH of hosts hath sworn, saying, as I have thought, so shall it happen; and as I have purposed, so shall it stand: that I will break the Assyrian in my land, and upon my mountains tread him under foot: then shall his yoke depart from off them, and his burden depart from off their shoulders," (Isaiah 14:24-25).

CHAPTER 5

Edom Moves into Judean Territory

B Y the time the Judeans had gone into the Babylonian captivity, the Edomites had moved into the Southern Negev. However, some historians contradict this timeline and claim that the Edomites still lived in Petra and did not move into the Negev for the first time until after they deported Judah to Babylon (Rudd, 2017). The Biblical account states, however, that the Edomites were living to the south of Judaea before, during, and after the Babylonian captivity, because it was they whom Scripture records assisted in the war with the Babylonian king against the Judeans, and it was them who helped burn Solomon's Temple. Therefore, Obadiah prophesies against them, "And thy mighty men, O Teman, shall be dismayed, to the end that every mount of Esau may be cut off by slaughter. For thy violence against thy brother, Jacob shame shall cover thee, and thou shalt be cut off forever. Thou shouldest not have entered the gate of my people in the day of their calamity; yea, thou shouldest not have looked on their affliction in the day of their calamity, nor have laid hands on their substance in the day of their calamity; neither shouldest thou have stood in the crossway, to cut off those of his that

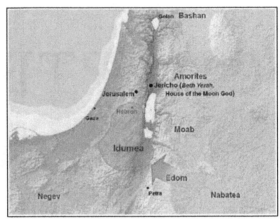

escaped; neither shouldest thou have delivered up those of his that escaped; neither shouldest thou have delivered up those of his that remained in the day of distress' (Obadiah 1:9 -10,13 -14). And, it was after the Judeans left and went into Babylonian captivity that some of the Edomites moved into Judaea where they took up residence for seventy years.

Before these events, the Edomites had lived in the land of Edom, in Mount Seir, in the Transjordan territory. By the time Israel went into Babylonian captivity, they were occupying areas south of Judaea. Rudd (2017) notes that during this time, when the Judeans were being captured and taken into captivity by the Babylonians, it delighted them to take revenge on Judah for the past grievances and because of the perpetual hatred Edom had for them. However, in trying to make the case that the Edomites were supporters of the Judeans. Rudd (2017) asserts that, during the late 600BC, gripped by fear because of the aggressive might of Babylonia, the Edomites supported the Judeans. He added that this super-power, at the head of the Persian Gulf, had threatened all the smaller kingdoms of the Middle East. King Nebuchadnezzar, the sovereign in power at the start of the Judean captivity, led the offensive. And, because of the mutual threat of the Babylonians, they say the Triad worshippers of Petra became allies with the Judeans for a brief time. But, this alliance was only superficial, and when Jerusalem fell to Babylon in 586BC, after a two-year siege, the Edomites could not resist their glee as the city burned and everything reduced to rubble. At last, they saw their revenge for the ancient hardships they had experienced at the hands of Israel.

This account contradicts the facts of Scripture as the Edomites from the start had encouraged the demolition of the Temple and the city. They also hunted the Judeans down who had fled from the city and shown them no mercy. The lamentations of the Judeans went up to YAHUAH and contained a warning to the triumphant Edomites. They abetted the Babylonians in the city's decimation and destruction of the people of Judaea, "They hunt the steps we cannot go in our streets: our end is near, our days are fulfilled; for our end is come. Our persecutors are swifter than the eagles of the heaven: they pursued us upon the mountains, they laid wait for us in the wilderness. Rejoice and be glad, O daughter of Edom, that dwellest in the land of Uz; the cup also shall pass through unto thee: thou shalt be drunken, and shalt make thyself naked' (Lamentations 4:18-21). It was the Edomites who helped to destroy the Temple by fire, and they chanted as it was burning, "Down with it! Even to the foundation" as the Babylonians destroyed Jerusalem. Therefore, it is said Edom burned Solomon's Temple at the hands of the Babylonians because Nebuzaradan, the head of Nebuchadnezzar's army, wanted it destroyed. It is also said, the Edomites volunteered to light the fire as delegated agents of destruction. "Now on the tenth day of the fifth month, which was the nineteenth year of King Nebuchadnezzar, king of Babylon, Nebuzaradan, the captain of the bodyguard was in the king's service of Babylon, came to Jerusalem. He burned the house of the Lord, the king's house, and all the houses of Jerusalem; even every large house he burned with fire' (Jeremiah 52:12-13).

The cry of the aggrieved Judeans went forth against the children of Edom and Babylon as they compared Edom to Babylon and reminded YAHUAH, "Remember, O YAHUAH, the children of Edom in the day of Jerusalem; who said, Rase it, rase it, even to the foundation thereof. O daughter of Babylon, who art to be destroyed; happy shall he be that rewardeth thee as thou hast served us. Happy shall he be that taketh and dasheth thy little ones against the stones" (Psalm 137:7-9). These verses confirm Edom-Rome to be Babylon, which would come to rule as the fourth beast power on the earth. However, Solomon's Temple would not be the only Temple that the Edomites would destroy. History shows that Edom had a role in putting fire and tearing down the Temple known as Herod's Temple in Jerusalem in 70AD while under Roman occupation. Therefore, because of the egregious acts committed by Edom against the Judeans, there is a future curse of destruction prepared for them. Another reason Edom-Rome has misled people about their identity and tried to wipe out the identity of Jacob-Israel, "And the house of Jacob shall be a fire, and the house of Joseph a flame, and the house of Esau for stubble, and they shall kindle in them, and devour them; and there shall not be any remaining of the house of Esau; for YAHUAH hath spoken it' (Obadiah 1:18).

JUDEANS RETURN HOME

After seventy years of captivity, the people returned from Babylon to their home in Judaea. Upon their return, Darius, the king of the Babylonians, had committed to allowing them to go to Jerusalem to rebuild the temple that the Edomites had burned when Judaea became desolate by the Chaldees (1 Esdras 4: 45). Darius wrote letters to all the nations that were tributaries to him including the Edomites, "Then Darius the king stood up, and kissed him, and wrote letters for him unto all the treasures and the lieutenants and captains and governors, that they should convey on their way both him and all those that go up with him to build Jerusalem... And that all the country which they hold should be free without tribute; and that the Edomites should give over the villages of the Jews which they held: Yea, that there should give a yearly tribute of twenty talents to rebuild the temple until they built it; And other ten talents yearly, to maintain the burnt offerings upon the altar every day, as they had a commandment to offer seventeen: And that all they that went from Babylon to build the city should have free liberty, and their posterity, and all the priests that went away' (1 Esdras 4: 47; 50-53). Darius made the Edomites move out of the Judean territories once they had returned. He also required the Edomites to pay taxes to assist in the rebuilding of the Temple, just as the other nations who had to pay tribute to the Babylonian Empire.

After the Edomites vacated the areas that belonged to the Judeans, they moved back into the Negev Valley, which lay south of Judaea, and stayed there for over four hundred years. The Edomites used the Greek form of their name and renamed the area they occupied Idumea, and they became the Idumeans. The Catholic Encyclopedia confirms that Idumea is the country inhabited by the descendants of Edom, and the word 'Idumea' is the Graecized form of the Hebrew name Edom, which appears to apply to the region. There, they continued to prosper until they infiltrated the borders of Judaea again. They moved into the northern Negev during the Greek Hellenistic age, which began when Alexander the Great in 333BC conquered the Persians. The hostilities held by both the Judeans and Edomites never abated throughout the time they lived in the Negev as their borders were always disputed. Their new capital became Hebron, and other towns were Marisa and Beth-Sur. During the time of the Maccabean revolt, many battles between the Judeans and Idumeans took place. Historical evidence shows that Hebron remained under Edomite control until Judas Maccabeus retook the city under Jewish control in 164BC.

IDUMEA IS EDOM

The Babylonians had taken the Judeans into captivity in 597BC, and Nebuchadnezzar, the Babylonian king, ceded portions of Judaea to the Edomites. The Edomites then took this opportunity to move into many of the towns and villages that belonged to the Judeans. At this time, the Edomites took control of the territories and lands to the east and south of the Dead Sea. The Edomites built settlements in the region comprising the southern hills of Judaea down to the area north of Beersheba. It is here where they appeared under the Graecized Idumeans, a term used in New Testament times. Biblical history continues to show that the Edomites always coveted the lands that Israel inhabited because of the abhorrence they felt for them, "Because thou hast said, These two nations and these two countries shall be mine, and we will own it; while YAHUAH was there:' (Ezekiel 35:10). This move by the Edomites caused the people of Judaea to have great contempt, which resulted in continued animosity between them. This enmity remains today between the Edomites and the Hebrew Israelites even though many are unaware of the history of these two brothers as Esau, who is Edom, has obscured the identities of both by using deflection and a revised and deceptive history.

HEBRON CONTROLLED BY EDOMITES

The Edomites controlled Hebron, and after the Greeks and the Seleucid Kingdom began their rule over Judaea, they brought great wrath upon the Judeans. The Greeks had tried to force them to turn away from the laws, statutes, and commandments of the Highest YAHUAH. The Greek king Antiochus implemented many corrupt practices and expected the Judeans to forsake their laws and do as the Greeks did. And, some of the immoral men of Judaea not wanting to be different even made themselves uncircumcised as they forsook the holy covenant (1 Maccabees). Antiochus had also taken control of the Temple and sacrificed swine on the altar. Antiochus, himself, had entered the holy sanctuary and taken away the golden altar, the candlestick of light and all the vessels, and the other valuable treasures. This action vexed Mattathias and his five sons, and they stood up against the king and fought for their lives and their laws.

Mattathias, the son of John, the son of Simeon, a priest of the sons of Joarib from Jerusalem, and his five sons, came together in this fight with other Judean warriors. The initial encounter brought success, and these men led many revolts against the Greeks. After the death of Mattathias, some of his other sons replaced him, but in the early second century BC, Simeon's son

Judas Maccabeus took up the charge. The Maccabees recovered the temple and the city, pulling down all the altars that the heathens had erected. In the TORAH, the Greeks had changed the image of the people to look like them as recorded in first Maccabees. "And laid open the Cepher of the Torah, wherein the heathen had sought to paint the likeness of their images" (1 Maccabees 3:48). After two years of fighting the Greeks, the Judeans cleansed the temple and made another altar where they offered a sacrifice to YAHUAH.

However, when the surrounding nations found out about the altar being rebuilt and the sanctuary renewed as before, they were not pleased and determined to destroy the people of Jacob-Israel that lived among them. They all set upon them, killing, stealing, and destroying all the people of Judah (1 Maccabees 5:2). However, the Judeans were not deterred, and the Maccabees continued with great exploits against Antiochus and his generals. And Antiochus could not win any of the battles against Judas and the brave men of Judah. The Judeans rebuilt the walls of mount Zion and erected tall towers all around it, setting up garrisons to keep it from being infiltrated by their enemies. They also fortified Bethsura to preserve it; that the people might have a defense against Idumea.

There were provocations by the Idumeans living in the Negev, which resulted in Judas Maccabeus and his men having to hold vigil in their defense of the city of Jerusalem and the Temple. Thus, at Arabattine, they inundated Gael: and overthrew them when they took their courage and took their spoils (1 Maccabees

5:3). Judas and his men then went into Bozrah, the capital city of Mount Seir, where the Edomites had imprisoned many of the Judeans along with the Nabateans, who came to Judas as allies informed them of what the Idumeans had done (The Antiquities of the Jews 12.8.3). "Yahudah Makkabiy also and his brother Yonathan went over the Yardan, and traveled three days' journey in the wilderness. Where they met with the Nabathiym, who peaceably came unto them, and told them everything that had happened to their brethren in the land of Gilead: And how that many of them were shut up in Bosora, and Beor, and Alema, Kasphor, Maged, and Ashteroth Qarnayim; all these cities are strong and great' (1 Maccabees 5:24-26). According to Josephus, the Nabateans were not a warlike people. Howbeit, Edom-Rome described the Nabateans in their revisionist history as a mysterious people who conquered the nation of Edom in Mount Seir.

According to this history, the Nabateans were Bedouins who traveled by caravans but occupied Edom for about two hundred years, where they built the structures that remain in Mount Seir to this day. Some years before the birth of YAHUSHA, it is believed they moved out and resumed their nomadic lifestyle. In fact, according to reports with all the sophistication, they appeared to have had the Nabatean kingdom left only a few surviving documents. This narrative supports Edom-Rome in misleading and obscuring their identity as the descendants of Esau, who is Edom, the people who lived in Mount Seir up to the time of the HAMASHIACH'S birth.

The Governor Gorgias, a Seleucid general of Idumea, hired soldiers and continued to promote war with the Judeans, "And therewithal the Idumeans, having gotten into their hands the most commodious holds, kept the Jews occupied, and receiving those that had been banished from Jerusalem, they went about nourishing war' (2 Maccabees 10: 14-15). Judas and his men proved they could hold the Greeks and Idumeans at bay. They penetrated the forces of the Edomites and went into all the cities of Mount Seir, slaughtered the Edomites, and burned their towers. Howbeit, this did not assuage Judas and his men's desire to destroy the Edomites fully, so he went with his brethren again and fought against the children of Esau in the land toward the south, where he smote the Idumeans in Hebron, and the other towns, and pulled down the fortresses and burned their towers. He retook Hebron and placed it under Judaea's control. These events all transpired through the year 164BC. It is important to note that, after Judah Maccabeus' death, his brothers, Jonathan and Simon, became High Priests in Judaea, and for many years, they clashed with the Edomites in Idumea and Mount Seir. Simon ruled in Judaea for eight years and then died. During his time in power, he had serious battles with the Edomite enemies. His son, John Hyrcanus, then became a prince and High Priest and leader of the Judean army. John and his army then recaptured the territory of Hebron in 126BC, which the Idumeans had again taken over and occupied for thirty-eight years (The Antiquities of the Jews 12.11. 2, 13.1.1-2).

It was sometime later that John Hyrcanus, High Priest of Judaea and a Sadducee-influenced Hasmonean leader, later subjugated the Idumeans to the south of Judaea, after his war with the Syrians. According to Josephus, he took the other territories, including Dora and Marissa cities of Idumea, and subdued all the Idumeans. But, he permitted them to stay in the country, if they agreed to circumcise their genitals and use the laws of the Jews. Most of the Pharisees opposed John for forcing the Idumeans to become circumcised to become part of the society of the Judeans. But, many of the Idumeans submitted to the use of circumcision and the rest of the traditions of the Judeans because they were desirous of living in the land (The Antiquities of the Jews 13.9.1). The dominant Pharisaic traditions, however, did not recognize this forcible conversion and did not accept the Idumeans or acknowledge their conversion. Therefore many of the Judeans never accepted them as part of their assembly. The blood-line descendants knew what the Highest YAHUAH thought of this action by John Hyrcanus as Scripture speaks against giving Israel's honor to another, "Give not thine honor to another, nor the things profitable unto thee to a strange nation' (Baruch 4:3).

The truth was the Idumeans worshiped many gods, and their habits were singular. They lived with the Horites, who first lived in Mount Seir, and adopted their gods. The Horites were, as their name implies, troglodytes, or cave dwellers. The Edomites had adopted their country and their gods and continued to do so after they moved into the land called Idumea, where they shared a border with the Judeans. They pretended to become Jews, yet they were not Jews. Many of them also moved into other nations. Still, those who stayed continued to practice the Jewish religion and submitted to the Jewish authority, but they could not hide from the Highest. "I know thy works, and tribulation and poverty, (but thou art rich) and I know the blasphemy of them which say they are Jews, and are not, but are the synagogue of Satan" (Revelation 2:9).

With the Edomites' assimilation into the Judean, culture began the infiltration and takeover of not just the land of Judaea but also the entire social order of the Judeans, including the Priesthood. The Edomites pretended to be Jews and soon replaced the descendants of Jacob. Like the boar, as Rabbi Meir Levin notes, Esau will even adopt certain tenets of Judaism for him to say he is a Jew.[1] The Edomites are imposters who converted to the practices of the Judeans about one hundred years before YAHUSHA was born. By the time of his birth, the Edomites, along with the Romans, had great influence over the Sanhedrin Council. And, one could conclude that it was these converted Idumeans who instigated and called for the HAMASHIACH'S death as it is known that the true bloodline descendants of Judah were afraid of the Council and the Romans and would do what they wanted. The actual blood-line Judeans had no power of their own to kill the HAMASHIACH. Before his crucifixion, the HAMASHIACH had told the leaders that if they were of the Father YAHUAH, they would love him and understand his words.

But because they could not understand what he said they were of the devil, "Ye are of your father, the devil, and the lusts of your father ye will do. He was a murderer from the beginning, and abode not in the truth, because there is no truth in him. When he speaketh a lie, he speaketh of his own: for he is a liar and the father of it' (John 8:44). It was the Edomites pretending to be Jews who killed the HAMASHIACH. YAHUAH confirms their identity and ancestry in Revelation, as the Highest YAHUAH says that he would make Edom-Rome bow to Israel when he returns, "Behold, I will make them of the synagogue of Satan, which say they are Jews, and are not, but do lie; behold, I will make them come and worship before thy feet, and know I have loved thee' (Revelation 3:9).

ANTIPATER THE IDUMEAN TAKES DOWN THE HOUSE OF JUDAH

According to the Jewish Encyclopedia, Antipater, an Idumean, was from an influential family who converted to Judaism while John Hyrcanus reigned in Judaea. Hyrcanus, according to Josephus, began his rule as the high priest on the third year of the hundred and seventy-seventh Olympiad, when Quintus Hortensius and Quintus Metellus called Metellus of Crete, were consuls at Rome. His brother Aristobulus came to make war with him, and not wanting to fight agreed to retire from the high priesthood position and turn it over to him. But, a certain friend of Hyrcanus, an Idumean, called Antipater, who was rich with a rebellious nature that held animosity against Aristobulus, because of some differences he had with him on account of his goodwill to Hyrcanus, his brother. Antipater did not agree that Hyrcanus should give in to his brother Aristobulus. Therefore, after Hyrcanus stepped down from the leadership of Judaea, Antipater persuaded him to contend against his brother for his rightful position and even convinced the unsuspecting and reluctant Hyrcanus that his younger brother intended to kill him (The Antiquities of the Jews 14.1. 2).

Antipater, an Idumean, had served under King Alexander Jannaeus and Queen Salome Alexandra, as governor of Idumea. Antipater had been a powerful official under the Hasmonean princes Aristobulus and Hyrcanus. And the King and Queen were the parents of the feuding heirs, Hyrcanus II and Aristobulus II. Antipater's scheming and trickery positioned him to become a client of the Roman general, Pompey the Great. They laid the foundation for Herod, his son's ascension to the throne of Judaea through his devious activities in the court of the Hasmoneans. The Hasmoneans were the heirs of the Maccabees, the hereditary leaders of the Judeans (The Antiquities of the Jews 14.1.2-3). Josephus notes Antipater I was the son of Antipas I and held the same name. He was a native of Idumea, located southeast of Judaea between the Dead Sea and the Gulf of Aqaba. It is said he was the founder of the Herodian Dynasty.

Antipater, a conniving and deceitful man, knew of his kinship to the Romans and recognized Rome's growing dominance in the region, therefore, exploited it to his advantage. When Julius Caesar defeated Pompey, Antipater, in 47BC, shifted his allegiance to Caesar and ingratiated himself to him. While the besieged of Caesar in Alexandria was taking place, Antipater rescued him with three thousand men and the aid of numerous friends. For his bravery, Caesar elevated Antipater to the Roman citizenry, freed him from taxes, and showered him with honors and declarations of friendship (The Antiquities of the Jews 14.8.1). Julius Caesar promoted the Idumean, Antipater I, as procurator over Judaea with the right to collect taxes. Antipater then made his sons, Phasaelus and Herod, the governors of Jerusalem and Galilee.

However, after Caesar's enemies assassinated him, it forced Antipater to side with Gaius Cassius Longinus against Mark Antony. Antipater then married Cypros, an Edomite noblewoman, which helped to merge his and the Edomites' power over the land of Judaea and Idumea. Their marriage brought about a close friendship between him and King Aretas, called by Josephus "Aretas the Arabian," a relative of Cypros. Josephus reports that Antipater and the king Aretas had such a close relationship that Antipater entrusted his children to this friend when he went to war with the Hasmonean Aristobulus II. Although Josephus describes Aretas as a friend of Antipater, because he cared for his children, I believe they were more than just friends more likely to be close family or inlaws as his wife descended from Edomite nobility. Both Antipater and Aretas were of Edomite ancestry, and Aretas remained in the land of Edom, where he ruled as the king. Antipater and his Edomite wife had four sons: Phasael, Herod, Joseph, and Pheroas, and a daughter, Salome, one of several Salomes among the Herodians who became the rulers over the Judeans under the Roman Empire (The Antiquities of the Jews).

Josephus continues that Antipater was a man of great authority among the Idumeans, both wealthy and born into a dignified family. He showed this by providing help to Hyrcanus II, brother of Aristobulus. The Romans saw he had great resources and brilliant military and political capabilities. But Antipater exploited the weak-willed Hyrcanus II, the Judean of the Hasmonean Dynasty, for the sake of his ambition once he had gotten rid of Aristobulus. With the support of Hyrcanus II, Antipater set out to conspire with the King Aretas of Edom against Aristobulus, the brother of Hyrcanus II. Together they attacked Aristobulus in Jerusalem, where there was a great disturbance. During that time, Pompey the Great had conquered Judaea in the name of the Roman Republic, and Antipater used the same cunning and designing tactics of his forefather Esau to gain his way into the good graces of Rome. Which gave him control over the Judeans and its Society (The Antiquities of the Jews 14. 2.1).

Antipater's diplomacy and artful politics gained him entrance into the Hasmonean court and paved the way for the rise of his son, Herod the Great. Herod then used this position to marry the Hasmonean princess, Mariamne, endear himself to Rome and become King of Judaea under Roman influence. This decision by Rome did not sit well with many of the Judeans, and they never accepted him as a true bloodline descendant of Israel. However, he claimed his ancestors were among the old elite in Jerusalem taken by King Nebuchadnezzar into Babylonian captivity in the sixth century BC. The facts did not concern Rome, and the assertion, by Antipater, provided enough credibility for him to lead the Jews (The Antiquities of the Jews 14.8.3-5).

Josephus notes that Nicolaus of Damascus, the court historian for Herod, wrote fabrications to support that Herod's ancestors were among the old elite in Jerusalem and taken by King Nebuchadnezzar into Babylonian captivity. Josephus furthers that Nicolaus said this to please Herod. And, he believed that Nicolaus of Damascus would say what Herod wanted him to say at the cost of truthfulness as Herod was the king. This account by Nicolaus of Herod being of the families that returned from Babylonian captivity served two purposes. First, when the Persian King Cyrus sent the captives in Babylon back to Judaea, likely, some settled elsewhere. And, a legitimate dispersion such as this would hide that Herod's ancestry is undocumented in the meticulous records of returned Judean families. Second, claiming heritage among the Jews from as early as the Babylonian captivity provided credibility for this pro-Roman and Hellenized Herod to become King over the Judeans (The Antiquities of the Jews 14.1.3).

The knowledge that Herod was not of the bloodline Judeans did not endear him to the Judeans; in fact, they despised Herod and showed him little respect. They disliked him being over them because they knew he lied about his heritage since they knew he was an Edomite. Thus, Josephus settles the truth about Antipater's family; and noted that they might have converted to Judaism during the forced conversions by the Sadducee-influenced Hasmonean leader, John Hyrcanus. So, even though Antipater and Herod the Great may have considered themselves to be of the Jewish faith, the observant and nationalist bloodline Judeans did not consider them genuine bloodline descendants of Judaea. Therefore, the Judeans resented this influential family because of their Edomite ancestry, their Hellenistic incursions upon Jewish tradition, and their cooperation with the Roman invaders (The Antiquities of the Jews 14.8.1, 20.8.7).

HOW ANTIPATER DIVIDED THE HASMONEAN BROTHERS

Antipater instigated the rift between the Hasmonean brothers, which resulted in them having to take their differences before Pompey the Great of Rome and his lieutenant, Scaurus, for adjudication. At first, Pompey ruled in Aristobulus' favor as they considered him to be the stronger one of the two although he was younger. However, on the third intervention, Pompey ordered the brothers to wait for his decision. Aristobulus, being impatient, provoked a political offense that caused Pompey to appoint

Hyrcanus the ethnarch of Judaea. However, this proved to be a mistake because Hyrcanus was ineffective as an administrator and as a tax collector. Antipater thrived on the division he caused between the Hasmonean brothers and laid the foundation for his family's success. He navigated conflicts of loyalty and power-shifting within the Roman elite to achieve his aims. These events allowed Antipater to intimate himself into a position where he had influence. They soon exercised the authority that belonged to Hyrcanus as the High priest (The Antiquities of the Jews 14.9.2).

When Antigonus, Aristobulus' son who had been imprisoned in Rome, returned from Roman bondage, he contested for power, and he accused Antipater of trying to usurp authority over the Judeans. Antipater made a great scene of the scars he earned while fighting for Caesar's life in Egypt. He defended himself with the history of unfailing loyalty to the Romans. This appeal persuaded Caesar, who then appointed Antipater, the first Roman Procurator of Judaea. This goodwill allowed the Jews special protection and freedom to govern themselves and enjoy Rome's benevolence. Josephus records that with his newfound rights and honors, Antipater rebuilt the wall of Jerusalem that Pompey had destroyed while subduing Aristobulus. He established order by tempering civil disturbances in Judaea and threatening to become a "severe master instead of a gentle governor" should the people grow lawless and unruly. During this time, civil matters in Judaea became peaceful (The Antiquities of the Jews 14.8.4-5).

186

Antipater, wanting to create a name for himself, strived to define his legacy, whereby he made his son, Phasael, governor of Jerusalem, and Herod, the governor of Galilee, to the north of Samaria between the Sea of Galilee and the Mediterranean. From the beginning, Herod set about ridding Galilee of what his court historian called 'robbers,' although they may have been people resisting Roman rule. His activities resulted in complaints raised by the Sanhedrin. And, based on evidence which confirms the historical events of this period, Antipater's work as a powerbroker between the Hasmoneans, the 'Arabians,' and the Romans, inaugurated dramatic dynamics and great changes in the history of the Judean nation. The diplomacy and shrewd politics of Antipater produced the Herodian dynasty. He paved the way for the rise of his son, Herod the Great, who married the Hasmonean princess, Mariamne, endeared himself to Rome, and usurped the Judean throne to become king of Judaea under the Roman Empire (The Antiquities of the Jews 14. 9. 2).

---

[1] Rabbi Meir Levin was a Haredi politician in Poland and Israel. He studied at yeshiva and was certified as a rabbi. He was one of thirty-seven people to sign the Israeli declaration of independence. He served in several Israeli cabinets and was a longtime leader and Knesset minister for Agudat Yisrael and related parties.

CHAPTER 6

The Herodian Dynasty

EROD WAS THE FIRST TO LEAD the Herodian Dynasty. He was the son of Antipater and was first made governor of Galilee when he was only fifteen years old, according to Josephus (The Antiquities of the Jews 14.9.2). Antipater, his father, was a friend and deputy of King Hyrcanus of the Judeans. In 63BC, the Roman general Pompey conquered Jerusalem and made the Jewish kingdom a client state of Rome. In 37BC, the Roman Senate appointed Herod 'King of the Jews.' It was this Herod the Great who enlisted the wise men to reveal the whereabouts of the baby YAHUSHA when he was born. It was this Herod, also called

Herod Ascalonite, whom the Roman Senate made king in place of Hyrcanus, his master. After Herod died in 4BC, Rome divided the kingdom among his sons into the Herodian Tetrarchy. These Tetrarchies lasted for about 100 years, and the Romans incorporated most of these kingdoms, including Judaea proper, into Judaea Province in 6AD when Emperor Augustus deposed the last ethnarch of Judaea. He combined the territories of Edom and Samaria with Idumea and annexed it as Judaea Province under direct Roman administration. However, some historians claim Rome restricted the Herodian kingship, and it only continued in Northern Levant until 92AD when the last Herodian monarch, Agrippa II, died. The name Judaea became obsolete after the revolt of Simon Bar Kochba in 135AD, at which time the Romans renamed the area Syria Palaestina.

THE HERODIAN DYNASTY

Before Rome appointed Herod as king, he and his wife, Cyprus, had escaped to Rome after the Judeans restored the Hasmonean dynasty under king Antigonus. But Mark Antony resolved to have Herod named King of the Jews by telling the Senate that it would be to their advantage during the Parthian war to have Herod as king. The Senate voted for this decision, and, once they had ended and separated from the Senate, Mark Antony and Caesar Augustus received a procession with Herod between them. This action confirmed that Herod was their choice for a king, and both Antony and Caesar Augustus, along with the other magistrates, set off before him to sacrifice to the Roman god Jupiter. Antony also made a great feast for Herod on this first day of his reign.

Thus, the Herodian Dynasty began its rule over Judaea with Herod, as the king of the Jews. The people of this dynasty were of Idumaean-Edomite descent. Herod assumed possession of his kingdom as a client ruler under Roman protection in 37BC after the Parthians had tried and were unsuccessful in taking back Syria and the Judean territories. Herod and his army had captured Jerusalem, and they carried Antigonus of the Hasmonean dynasty in bonds to Rome. However, being fearful that Antony, the Roman Emperor, would have kept Antigonus in prison, Herod gave Antony a great deal of money to persuade him to have Antigonus killed. Herod's instigation resulted in his death and the Romans' successful removal of the last Hasmonean (The Antiquities of the Jews 14.16.4). Herod's appointment as the king did not sit well with the Judeans as they considered Herod to be a foreigner. According to Josephus, they knew he was the son of Antipater, who was of a vulgar family, and of no eminent extraction, but one subject to other kings who had no love for the Jews (The Antiquities of the Jews 14.16.4). Likewise, Herod made no secret that his sympathies lay with the non-Jewish inhabitants of his kingdom, which included the Idumeans and Herodians. The Idumeans and Herodians were the descendants of Esau-Edom, who both had the same common heritage. But, to prevent a revolt of the Judeans and to protect himself from a national uprising, Herod devised and set moderate policies for the different Jewish sects who included the Scribes, Sadducees, Essenes, and Pharisees.

Herod assumed the throne of Judaea, with Roman support that had elected him "King of the Jews." He was effective in causing the century-long Hasmonean Kingdom of the Maccabean era to fall. Herod was, in fact, not of Judean stock; and only given the right to be king of Judaea because Rome wanted him in the position. Josephus confirms that Herod was an Edomite whose parents converted to the practices of the Judeans during the forced conversion by the Hasmonean ruler John Hyrcanus.

THE FATE OF THE HASMONEAN DYNASTY

The Hasmonean Dynasty was the last of the bloodline descendants of Jacob to reign over the Judeans and Jerusalem. During King Herod's rule, he eliminated many of the representatives of the Hasmoneans. After he had Antigonus killed, the fate of the remaining male members of the family was not a happy one. Aristobulus III, the grandson of Aristobulus II, through his elder son Alexander,

The Hasmonaean Dynasty

Mattathias Asamoneus	?—166 B.C.
Judas Maccabeus	165—160 B.C.
Jonathan Apphus	160—142 B.C.
Simon Matthes	142—135 B.C.
John Hyrcanus I	135—104 B.C.
Judah Aristobulus I	104—103 B.C.
Alexander Jannaeus	103—76 B.C.
Alexandra Shlomziyyon	76—67 B.C.
John II Hyrcanus	76—67 B.C.
Judah II Aristobulus	67—63 B.C.
John II Hyrcanus	63—40 B.C.
Mattathias II Antigonus	40—37 B.C.

Ασαμωνευς: 165—37 B.C.
The Maccabean victory over the Greeks makes the Hasmonean principality (not the Roman Empire); the fourth kingdom of Bible prophecy (Daniel 2:40; 7:7;11:32-35 cf. 1 Maccabees 13:41)

became a High priest, but because of Herod's jealousy, he also had him executed. Although Herod married Aristobulus' sister, Mariamne, she too was a victim to his notorious jealousy. He had her executed because she had suspected him in the murder of her father, Alexander, and her brother Aristobulus. Josephus describes her as a woman of an excellent character, both for goodness and greatness of soul. In his final attempt to destroy the blood-line descendants of Jacob-Israel, Herod even killed the sons Mariamne bore for him, Aristobulus IV and Alexander, once they reached adulthood (The Antiquities of the Jews 15.7.5-6).

After Herod had murdered or caused to be killed all the family members related to the Hasmonean dynasty, except John Hyrcanus II, the last member of the Hasmonean bloodline, he set out to satisfy his need to destroy John Hyrcanus II the only bloodline family member left. John Hyrcanus II, an older man by this time, lived in Babylon, and Herod could not rest until he had eliminated him. He plotted against Hyrcanus II, who the Parthians held for four years from 40BC until 36BC as a prisoner. He was over the age of eighty years old and had lived among the Babylonian Jews who paid him great respect. But Herod feared that Hyrcanus II might induce the Parthians to help him regain the throne, so he invited Hyrcanus to return to Jerusalem. The Babylonian Jews tried to encourage Hyrcanus not to go, but he returned anyway, hoping that all would be well. When Hyrcanus II first arrived, Herod received him with every mark of respect, including assigning him the first place at his table and positioned him as president of the State Council. However, as part of his scheme, he waited for an opportunity to get rid of Hyrcanus. In the year 30BC, Herod made up charges against Hyrcanus of bribery and treason with the King of Arabia to take back the kingdom from him. He went before the Sanhedrin and initiated Hyrcanus' execution immediately before they could appeal to Rome. In his mind, the last remaining Hasmonean was too dangerous a rival for him (The Antiquities of the Jews 15.6.3-4).

HEROD THE GREAT, THE IDUMEAN KING OF JUDEA

Upon Herod's removal of all his rivals and threats to his position as king of the Jews, he ruled the Herodian kingdom as a vassal king of Rome. He squashed any opposition to his rulership while starting huge building projects, including the Caesarea harbor, the Temple Mount, the Masada, and the Herodium. Besides, he continued the rebuilding and expansion of the second Temple in Jerusalem damaged during the war fought with the Parthians before he gained control. He repaired many of the destroyed areas of the Temple and built many additions to it.

Herod instituted countless practices against the Judeans and their customs and observances while increasing the prestige of the Sadducees priestly class. He was, however, still able to remain on good terms with the Pharisees considered the "freedom fighters" during the Maccabean era. According to Frend (1984), Herod ruled like a Hellenistic monarch, and the Hebrew language disappeared from the coinage. In 26BC, he built a Greek city named Sebaste (meaning royal city) near the city of Sepphoris in Galilee. He gave it the trappings of Greco-Roman civilization, including baths, arcades, fountains, and temples. Because Herod's activities went against the Judean culture, they appealed to the Roman Senate about what Herod had introduced into their nation. This appeal by the Judeans granted relief as the Roman Senate believed their request reasonable. However, this did not change Herod's attitude, and he continued to violate the laws and practices of the Judeans.

Herod the Great was on the throne at the time YAHUSHA was born and sought to kill him because he feared for his position as King of the Jews. "When Herod, the king had heard these things, he was troubled, and all Jerusalem with him. When he had gathered all the chief priests and scribes of the people together, he demanded of them where HAMASHIACH should be born. And they said unto him, In Bethlehem of Judaea: for thus the prophet writes it. Thou Bethlehem, in the land of Judah, art not the least among the princes of Judah: for out of thee shall come a Governor that shall rule my people Israel" (Matthew 2:3-6). Herod then sent the wise men from the east to look for the birthplace of the HAMASHIACH on the pretense he wanted to worship him. Howbeit, after the wise men found the location, an angel appeared to them and told them not to return to Herod because of his plan to kill the baby. In retaliation to the wise men not returning, Herod had the entire population of Judean baby boys two years old and under slaughtered. Therefore, the cry went out, "In Rama was there a voice heard, lamentation, and weeping, and great mourning, Rachel weeping for her children, and would not be comforted, because they are not" (Matthew 2:18).

Herod and the Herodians never embraced the practices of the Judeans. Instead, they replaced parts of the religion of the Jews with practices of pagan origin. Herod had appointed Costobarus to be governor of Idumea and Gaza. He was a descendant from the priest of the KOZE, whom the Idumeans served as a god (The Antiquities of the Jews 15.7.9). Samuel Ahituv confirms that the nature of the Edomite religion was unknown before their conversion to Judaism by the Hasmoneans. However, evidence suggests that the national god of Edom was Qaus (also known as Qaush, Kaush, Kaus, Kos, or Qaws) since they invoked Qaus in the blessing formula in letters. They also determined that because they were close relatives of other Levantine Semites, they may have worshiped such gods as El, Baal, Qaus, and Asherah. The Herodians, Idumeans, and the Edomites were idolaters, their habit was singular, and they dwelt in caves. They had usurped authority and replaced the Judeans, the chosen people of YAHUAH. Therefore, YAHUSHA, when he was in Jerusalem, told them, "Ye are of your father, the devil, and the lusts of your father ye will do. He was a murderer from the beginning, and abode not in the truth, because there is no truth in him. When he speaketh a lie, he speaketh of his own: for he is a liar and the father of it" (John 8:49).

FORMATION OF THE HERODIAN TETRARCHY

After the death of Herod in 4BC, Rome divided Herod's remaining kingdom between his sons, who became tetrarchs. As tetrarchs, each son was made ruler over a quarter of their father's kingdom. One of these quarters was Judaea, which corresponded to the region of the ancient Kingdom of Judah. The Romans gave Herod Archelaus, son of Herod and Malthace the Samaritan, the main part of the kingdom. Herod Archelaus ruled Judaea proper, Edom, and Samaria. However, he was such a poor leader that the Roman Emperor Augustus soon dismissed him. By 6AD, he had ruled for ten years when the Roman Emperor appointed Quirinius to exercise direct Roman rule over Archelaus' territory after the Judean population appealed to his poor rulership. As a result, Rome formed the separate Province of Judaea.

Rome gave Herod's other son, Philip I, who they called Herod Philip II, jurisdiction over the northeast part of his father's kingdom, which included Iturea, Trachonitis, Gaulantis, and Paneas. Philip I's mother was Cleopatra of Jerusalem, Herod's fifth wife, and according to Josephus, he ruled those areas until he died in 34AD.

Herod Antipater was born before 20BC and died after 39AD. They knew him by his nickname, Antipas, the son of Malthace. Antipas was a first-century ruler of Galilee and Perea. It was a client state of the Roman Empire. He built projects at Sepphoris and Betharamphtha, and he also constructed the capital, Tiberius, on the western shore of the Sea of Galilee. Herod Antipater named this place in honor of his patron, Emperor Tiberius, and the city later became a center of Rabbinic learning. Rome referred to him as both Herod the Tetrarch and King Herod in the New Testament. The New Testament accounts also speak of Herod's role in the events leading to the executions of John the Baptist and the crucifixion of YAHUSHA. Herod Antipater ruled Galilee until Emperor Caligula exiled him to Gaul in 39AD.

Herod Agrippa, also known as Herod Agrippa I, was a King of Judaea from 41 to 44AD. He was the father of Herod Agrippa II, known to be the last King of the Herodian dynasty. Herod Agrippa was the grandson of Herod the Great and son of Aristobulus IV and Berenice. He was the king named in the Acts of the Apostles, and Josephus antiquities notes they also knew him as Agrippa the Great. Herod Agrippa's territory included most of Israel, including Judaea, Galilee, Batanaea, and Perea. From Galilee, his territory extended east to Trachonitis. Rome then gave Agrippa the territories of Herod Antipas after they exiled him. In 41AD, Emperor Claudius added to his territory the parts of the Idumean province that belonged to Herod Archelaus. These appointments by Rome resulted in Agrippa I ruling over the reunified kingdom of his grandfather, Herod the Great. History records that Agrippa I died in 44AD.

Herod Agrippa II was the son of the first, and more well-known, Herod Agrippa, the brother of Berenice, Mariamne, and Drusilla. Rome educated him at the court of Emperor Claudius. At the time of his father's death, he was only seventeen years old;

therefore, Claudius kept him in Rome. Following the death of Herod of Chalcis in 48AD, Rome gave the Syrian kingdom to Herod Agrippa II with the right to administer the Temple in Jerusalem and appointing its High priest. However, Rome only gave this area a tetrarchy. In 53AD, Rome forced Herod Agrippa II to give up the tetrarchy of Chalis. In exchange, Claudius made Herod Agrippa II ruler with the title of the king over the territories governed by Philip. According to Josephus, Agrippa lived in an incestuous relationship with his sister, Berenice. The New Testament shows that it was before Agrippa and Berenice that Paul the Apostle pleaded his case at Caesarea Maritima in 59AD. "And after certain days king, Agrippa and Bernice came unto Caesarea to salute Festus. And when they had been there many days, Festus declared Paul's cause unto the king, saying, there is a certain man left in bonds by Felix" (Acts 25:13-14). Records show that Herod Agrippa II died in 92AD.

These accounts of the Herodian dynasty and its kings help to identify the descendants of Esau-Edom and their relationship with Rome. According to the historical documentation of the Edomites, before the Herodian Dynasty ended, it had already united with Rome. The result was more tensions between the Idumeans who were, in fact, Edomites who lived in the Negev and also in Judaea. Because there was such a large Roman presence in Judaea and the changes Rome made to the administrative life of the nation added further to the stress. These suppressive conditions caused the Judeans to rebel against the Roman Empire, which later led to three wars and the final expulsion of the Judeans from the land of Israel.

MAP OF PALESTINE UNDER THE HERODIAN DYNASTY

ROMAN WARS WITH THE JUDEANS

The history provides the backdrop for Roman-Jewish tensions, which resulted in several Roman-Jewish wars from 66 to 135AD. The Roman Empire was often callous and brutal in its treatment of the Judeans, and they continued to deal with them in a harsh manner, which led the Judeans to revolt. At the time of the fall

of Jerusalem, there was civil turmoil among the Zealots, the Idumeans, and the Judeans. This great revolt, which started in

66AD, was the first of three major rebellions by the Judeans against the Empire. It was the Roman Emperor, Vespasian, and Titus who destroyed the Second Temple. After this first war, they instituted a Jewish tax, which made the Judeans' circumstances worse. According to Josephus, twenty thousand Idumean infantry slaughtered thousands of the Judeans (The Wars of the Jews 6. 6. 1-4). When the war was over, they sold those who survived into slavery. However, because the Herodians identified with Caesar, they gave some 40,000 Idumeans their freedom. This historical account further proves the Idumeans were Edomites and the kin of many of the Romans who they supported.

THE WARS OF 70 – 117AD

Before YAHUSHA returned to his Father, he prophesied about the wars that would take place in Jerusalem when his disciples asked him when the kingdom would come, and he told them of things that would happen before he returned. "And YAHUSHA answered and said unto them, take heed that no man deceives you. For many shall come in my name, saying, I am HAMASHIACH; and shall deceive many. And ye shall hear of wars and rumors of wars: see that ye be not troubled: for all these things must happen, but the end is not yet" (Matthew 24:4-5). The first war the Judeans engaged with Rome began in 66AD. At the end of this war, the Romans destroyed and plundered the Temple at Jerusalem and the people. The victors took artifacts, such as the Menorah, along with all the silver and gold the fire had not destroyed when the Temple burned. Josephus states, "While the holy house was on fire, everything the Romans plundered that came to hand, and ten thousand of those caught they slew; nor was there a commiseration of any age or any reverence of gravity; but children and old men, and profane persons and priests, were all slain in the same manner" (The Wars of the Jews 6.5.1). They reported that some Judeans who they did not kill could remain in Jerusalem but could only live as Jews and practice the religion if they paid the taxes instituted by Rome. The Romans sold thousands of Judeans into slavery while those who escaped settled in other provinces of the Roman Empire and other Israelite communities throughout the African Continent.

There was great tribulation during these times, and those who heard YAHUSHA'S warning remembered his appeal to them, "When ye, therefore, shall see the abomination of desolation, spoken of by Daniel the prophet, stand in the holy place, (whoso readeth, let him understand) then let them which be in Judaea flee into the mountains: Let him which is on the housetop not come down to take anything out of his house: Neither let him which is in the field return to take his clothes... for then shall be the great tribulation, such as was not since the beginning of the world to this time, no, nor ever shall be" (Matthew 24:15-17, 21). YAHUAH predetermined this tribulation, and the people who did not take YAHUSHA'S warning to leave the first time would experience many more atrocities at the hand of Edom-Rome. Rome instituted heavier taxes, and food was scarce because they could not farm. These circumstances led to the Judeans feeling more desperate, which caused more revolts in other parts of the empire where many of the Hebrews lived. The Kitos Wars, which lasted from 115 to 117AD, where the Israelites revolted throughout the Roman Empire. The Jews that lived in the diaspora in places such as Cyprus, Egypt, Mesopotamia, and also Judaea rose and fought against the conditions when they learned how their brethren had been living in such dire straits in Judaea and Jerusalem. However, these revolts only lasted for two years before Edom-Rome crushed them and scattered more Israelites into the Continent of Africa, Spain, Portugal, and the British Isles.

THE JUDEAN WAR OF 133AD

The third and final rebellion took place in Judaea from 132 to 136AD. Simon Bar Kokhba, a militant and nationalist Jew, led this revolt. He was thought to be by some of the Judeans, a Messiah. It was the last of three major revolts of the Judeans against Roman suppression. This uprising erupted because of ongoing religious and political tensions in Judaea and because of the failure of the other two revolts that did not result in any change in the way the Romans treated the Judeans. They remained living under oppressive conditions enforced by the Romans. This revolt began as a result of a new city constructed by the Romans called Aelia Capitolina, over the ruins of Jerusalem. They also erected a temple to Jupiter on the Temple Mount. To the Judeans, these actions by the Romans were the highest form of blasphemy that anyone could commit against the ELOHIYM YAHUAH. However, the Romans believed they had a right to this most sacred place. They believed in many gods, and their chief god was Jupiter, who was the ancient Indo-European Dyaus Pitar (or Diovis Pater or Zeus Pater). Pater was another word for Peter whose exalted title was Optimus Maximus. He was the god of light, lightning, thunder, rain, and storm. And, was also the god who prescribed and ordered human affairs, which soothsayers could predict by using the signs in the heavens or the flight of birds. Jupiter was also the guardian of laws and oaths (Nigosian, 2000).

Jupiter, the Roman god, was fashioned and believed by them to the Elohim of Abraham, Isaac, and Jacob. He was and is a god; however, Jupiter is the Elohiym of the Edomites and not the god of Israel. As the Rabbis of old tells how that Esau will even pretend to adopt the practices of Jacob-Israel like being monotheistic, a worshiper of one god. However, scripture shows the Elohiym of the Edomites is not the same Elohiym of the Israelites. Nigosian, (2000) noted that the Romans built Jupiter's sanctuary, or temple, on the Capitoline Hill, and called it Jupiter Capitolinus. They associated Jupiter with the imperial glories of Rome. Jupiter gained various titles, including Victor, Invictus, and Imperator. It was after the Romans encountered the Greeks that they equated the Roman god Jupiter with the Greek god Zeus. His consort was Juno, whom the Greeks identified as Hera.

The erection of the temple dedicated to Jupiter by Edom-Rome so enraged the Judeans that they had no choice but to fight for their laws and their land. I believe it was Jupiter's Temple being constructed on the Temple Mount that YAHUSHA referred to in Matthew as an abominable act of desolation, "When ye, therefore, shall see the abomination of desolation, spoken of by Daniel the prophet, stand in the holy place, whoso readeth, let him understand" (Matthew 24:15). They knew the temple that Edom-Rome built to honor Jupiter was on the Temple Mount, the Holy place of YAHUAH. This abomination was unbearable in the eyes of the Judeans and YAHUAH. And, YAHUSHA prophesied that these actions would be taken by Rome when he lived in Judaea. However, the Roman Christian Church has chosen the narrative and prophecy to teach that it refers to some future event that includes the fake Jewish people living in Palestine. But, YAHUSHA told them it would happen in their generation, "Verily I say unto you, This generation shall not pass, till all these things are fulfilled' (Matthew 24:34). YAHUSHA spoke these words to the generation still living in the land of Israel and not to the Christian pagan church created by Rome. They have deceived the world into believing that the Highest YAHUAH was or is speaking through them and the imposter Jewish people living in Palestine. But, the word YAHUAH wrote is to his Chosen people, Israel. The book made by Rome and call the Holy Bible is Israel's historical past, present, and future. The prophecies tell what would happen to them throughout the ages before YAHUAH comes to gather them and return them to the Land of Promise.

At the end of the war in 135AD, the Hebrew Israelites who survived were exiled and not allowed to even go into Jerusalem for the Feast days. The Christian Church fathers and Rabbinic literature emphasize the role that Rufus, the governor of Judaea, played in provoking the people to rise against Rome. He was Quintus Tineius Rufus, a name associated and given to a red person of Edomite ancestry. In the early phase of the uprising, the Romans blamed him for adopting a policy to stay out of the revolt and not do anything to subdue the rebellion before it escalated and got out of hand. Therefore, despite significant Roman reinforcements from Syria, Egypt, and Arabia, the Judean rebels had significant victories and established an independent state that lasted for over two years.

The Romans, under Emperor Hadrian, did not take this sitting down and was determined to put down the insurgency of the rebels. He committed to stamping out nationalism among the Judeans as he believed they would continue to rise if they stayed together. Therefore, traditions such as circumcision, keeping the Sabbath, and reading the TORAH became forbidden under penalty of death throughout the Empire. He also resolved to rename the region to obliterate any memory of Judaea or Ancient Israel. Then he wiped the name from the map and replaced it with Syria Palaestina, which is Latin for Philistia. This revolt resulted in the extensive depopulation of Judaea and much persecution of the followers of YAHUSHA and those who followed the ancient Mosaic Laws throughout the Empire. The actions of Edom-Rome resulted in a near-complete genocide of the Hebrew Israelites.

The sages and Rabbi Yohanan both note that in many historical writings they used the word 'myriad' to describe the number of Judeans killed at the time of the wars because the number was so great it was uncountable, and, in fact, much more than the reported 800,000 the original number given.[1] Rabbi Yohanan added that the number of Judeans killed could be closer to 800 million. In the Gospel of Matthew, YAHUSHA told his disciples of these horrible events to come, "For in those days shall be affliction, such as was not from the beginning of the creation which YAHUAH created unto this time, neither shall be. And except those days should be shortened, there should no flesh be saved (alive):, but for the elect's sake, I shall shorten those days" (Matthew 24:21-22). Edom-Rome also teaches that this prophecy refers to the last days of the Roman Christian Church; however, YAHUAH only spoke to his people through his Prophets and to no one else. They scattered the real people of YAHUAH throughout the earth living in the wilderness of the people not aware of whom or whose they are. The Roman Christian Catholic church is not Israel but has tried to replace the actual people of YAHUAH. They are imposters, and at no time do the prophecies refer to them as the elect but only as of the enemy of YAHUAH and real Israelites.

There is evidence that shows that YAHUAH shortened the days because there is still a remnant of the Hebrew Israelites alive and being awakened to the truth. Since the Great Tribulation of those days, the descendants of Israel have experienced many other slaughters throughout the diaspora. None of these atrocities can compare to what happened during those early wars in Jerusalem and Judaea. Historical records describe them as dreadful and the time when the Israelites ate their children as one woman did during the siege of Jerusalem in the War of 70AD. Josephus writes that this woman attempted a most unnatural thing when she was angry by the seditious rogues who took the food she had preserved for her and her child. In her anger, she took the child from her breast and said, "Come on; be thou my food, and be thou a fury to these seditious varlets and a byword to the world, which is all that now wants to complete the calamities of us Jews." She killed the child and ate half. When the rebellious men came again to her for food, she offered the other half of the child to them. They were so appalled by what they saw; left the house trembling and frightened because they had never seen anything like it in the history of Israel. The entire city realized what the mother did, and this unheard-of action so frightened and distressed those going through the famine they desired to die (The Wars of the Jews 6. 3. 4).

These wars led to the end of Israel as a nation, and the remnant of the Judeans that remained lost their permanent homeland and was scattered to the four corners of the earth. Upon

Emperor Hadrian's death in 138AD, Rome prohibited all Judeans and Israelites from coming back to Jerusalem, except for attendance at Tisha B'Av, which Rome chose as one day designated for them to lament the loss of their homeland. YAHUAH told Israel they would become few and, in every nation, that the Israelites have lived they are among the minority. The Judeans and Hellenized Israelites were no longer permitted to teach about the coming HAMASHIACH. Still, Edom-Rome allowed them to teach an abstracted and spiritualized form of their universal religion of Christianity. Rome crushed Hebrew nationalism, and, according to some historians, these events separated Christianity as a religion from Judaism and its people, which made Christianity the religion of the Edomites (Frend, 1984).

JACOB'S TROUBLE – THE IMPACT OF EDOM-ROME ON ISRAEL

The Edomites fomented wars against the Israelites and plotted to blot out the Nation of Israel and destroy its people either by physical death or through the religions they created. It was Edom-Rome that brought on the great tribulation referred to as Jacob's Trouble in Scripture. The tribulation included pestilence, famine, and the sword, and these events were to happen to Israel over a time that YAHUAH designated according to his purpose and will. Scripture describes the nation that would cause Israel to experience these troubles, and Daniel and Nebuchadnezzar's dreams predicted the outcome. The Targums of Onkelos also showed this kingdom.[2] The prophecy expressed that Jacob-Israel would have trouble until the return of the HAMASHIACH when he would gather them from the four corners of the earth. Edom-Rome via the Christian Church has deceived the world into believing this trouble would occur at the end of this age and would include them. But, YAHUSHA outlined many things that would ensue as a part of Jacob's trouble before the end. Scripture declares that day would be great, which could mean a great amount of time, "Alas! For that day is great, so that none is like it: it is even the time of Jacob's trouble, but I shall save him out of it' (Jeremiah 30:7). The prophecy describes the time as great and does not give the specific number of days or years as the ladder that Jacob saw in his dream depicted and represents Edom-Rome's rule as the fourth kingdom to have dominion over Israel. In the dream, Jacob saw ladders that represented Babylon, Madai, Greece, and Rome. Babylon's angel climbed up 70 rungs and went down, Madai went up and down 52 rungs, then Greece went up and down 180, and Rome's went up and up and up, and Jacob did not know how many rungs it would ascend. However, YAHUAH said even if it reached heaven, he would bring them down. The number of rungs showed the number of years the Babylonian nations held the Israelites in captivity, and Edom-Rome's number appeared endless.

The Roman Christian church took control of the Scripture and scrolls of Israel, made a doctrine for the universal church, and interpreted the time of trouble to be within a specific period. They teach a deception that the Christian Church would experience seven years of trouble. However, the prophecy stated that the enemy of Israel, known to be Rome, would destroy Jerusalem and that it would be during the time of the greatest tribulation that Israel would experience as a nation. YAHUSHA was responding to the disciples' question of when the Highest would return to set up the kingdom. He told them a series of events would happen before and did not direct this prophecy to the entire world. Neither did he address the Edomite Christian church. The Christian church appropriated the scriptures and claimed that he was speaking to a universal audience.

The prophecies of Jacob's trouble pertain to Jacob-Israel, and the wars with Rome started Jacob's Trouble. However, the replacement theology of the Roman Christian church teaches that the trouble that YAHUSHA spoke of in Matthew pertains to the Christian church because they have replaced Israel and are now "spiritual" Israel. But, the prophecies about Israel included the entire dispensation of days and the impact the trouble will have on the children of Jacob. In fact, according to Rabbinic literature, the time amounts to about two thousand years that Israel would be under Edom-Rome's control. Howbeit, because Edom-Rome has changed the calendar several times throughout history and has instituted times that do not match with the times of the Highest YAHUAH, it is difficult to tell when the two thousand years begins or ends. While the calendar in use today reflects two thousand nineteen years, we know that YAHUAH created

Mankind based on Biblical history about six thousand years ago and not based on a fixed Greco-Roman calendar.

Scripture shows the Most High YAHUAH uses the sun, moon, and stars as his timepiece, which includes days, months, and seasons to determine the number of years. Therefore, we base YAHUSHA'S return on the time of YAHUAH and not information supplied by Edom-Rome. The Highest gave his oracles to one nation, "who are Israelites; to whom pertains the adoption, and the glory, and the covenants, and the giving of the law, and the service of YAHUAH, and the promises" (Roman 9:4). YAHUAH gave the knowledge and understanding of his plan of salvation to the nation of Israel only. Since Israel is no longer a nation in their land, the other nations do not understand the things about YAHUAH. Edom-Rome has a counterfeit knowledge based on numerology, which includes gematria and so-called science. Therefore, Edom-Rome does not know the time or how YAHUAH determines the time, "But, beloved, be not ignorant of this one thing, that one day is with YAHUAH as a thousand years, and a thousand years as one day" (2 Peter 3:8).

The world, including the descendants of Israel, has been deceived by Edom-Rome. They based the coming of their Messiah on knowledge of the terrestrial bodies in the sky. However, YAHUSHA said there would be no signs other than the wickedness as in days of Noah and Sodom and Gomorrah. In Paul's letter to the Thessalonians, he confirms that in the last days the man of sin will appear with lying signs and wonders and will deceive the nations, "And then shall that Wicked be revealed, whom YAHUAH shall consume with the spirit of his mouth, and shall destroy with the brightness of his coming: Even him, whose coming is after the working of Satan with all power and signs and lying wonders' (2 Thessalonians 2:8-9). Thus, the signs that are seen in the "end" times will be those of the man of sin. Scripture bases the time of YAHUSHA'S return on his time and not on-time determined by Edom-Rome. The prophecy states Israel would go through troubles starting while still in the land, and two-thirds of Israel would die by famine, pestilence, and the sword throughout history. "A third part of thee shall die with the pestilence, and with famine shall they be consumed amid thee: and a third part shall fall by the sword round about thee, and I will scatter a third part into all the winds, and I will draw out a sword after them' (Ezekiel 5:12).

Historical data and current events show that these calamities have followed the remnant of Israel throughout their exile on the Continent of Africa, where many Israelites still live and have experienced many famines, pestilences, and the sword even today. And, the scattered of Judah to the four corners of the earth. The Greatest Tribulation, however, occurred during the time Israel was a nation when they warred with Edom-Rome from 66 to 135AD. Most of Israel's descendants today do not connect the struggle they are going through with events in Judaea when Edom-Rome almost carried out the complete extermination of their ancestors. The Israelites do not know this because

YAHUAH removed Israel from their inheritance, and therefore, they have lost their memory of who they are. They do not know, nor do they consider, that their struggles relate to the curses outlined in Deuteronomy chapter twenty-eight. But, Edom-Rome has known the truth and has deceived Israel by making them believe they are Negroes from Africa who are Christians and Muslims. All of this Edom-Rome did to replace Israel and to keep them from inheriting the Kingdom of the Highest YAHUAH.

History shows Jacob has endured trouble for over two thousand years based on the Roman calendar. These troubles include the sword, famine, and pestilence. YAHUAH stated that the wicked would bring death and destruction to the people of Israel, not to everyone on the earth because he sent YAHUSHA to the lost sheep of the house of Israel. The trouble that will come on the heathen will be that of the magnified plagues of Egypt, but the plagues will not affect Israel if they come out from among them and be separate, "A thousand shall fall at thy side, and ten thousand at thy right hand; but it shall not come nigh thee. Only with thine eyes shall thou behold and see the reward of the wicked" (Psalm 91:7-8). In the Targums of Onkelos (Genesis 15:12-14 pg. 202) it confirms these plagues are to come, "And he said to Abram Knowing, thou must know thy sons shall dwell in a land not their own because thou has not believed and they will subjugate and afflict them four hundred years, and also that the people whom they shall serve I will judge with two hundred and fifty plagues, and afterward they shall go forth into liberty with great riches."[3]

THE ROLE OF THE ARABS IN JACOB'S TROUBLE

The Muslim Arabs played an important role in helping Edom-Rome to enslave and destroy many of the people descended from Israel. The Muslim Arabs were used throughout the continent of Africa to force Israel to turn away from obeying the Highest YAHUAH's laws. Mohammad tried to construct his religion as carefully as he could after the   Israelite religion. They wanted them to go into idolatry and worship Allah and the Arab gods of the Kabah stone. Christianity used similar tactics to convert the Israelites to Roman Christianity. The Arabs used the sword to force Israel to convert and to turn to the false god of the Kabah stone. Prophesies show that the wood and stone of these Babylonian Mystery religions would play a significant role in the curse on Israel and would serve as an identifying mark, "And YAHUAH shall scatter thee among all people, from the one end of the earth even unto the other; and there thou shalt serve other gods, which neither thou nor thy fathers have known, even wood and stone' (Deuteronomy 28:64). The descendants of Jacob-Israel have worshiped the false gods introduced by Edom-Rome, the wood of the Cross in Christianity, and the Kabah stone of Islam. "For it shall happen in that day, saith YAHUAH of hosts, that I will break his yoke from off thy neck and will burst thy bonds, and the strangers shall no more serve themselves of him: But they shall serve the ELOHIYM YAHUAH, and David their king, whom I will raise unto them. Therefore fear thou not, O My servant Jacob, saith YAHUAH; neither be dismayed, O Israel: for, lo, I will save thee from afar, and thy seed from the land of their captivity; and Jacob shall return, and shall be in rest, and be quiet, and none shall make him afraid," (Jeremiah 30:8-10).

OBSCURE LABELING

The move into the Judean territory began the obscuring of the Edomites' history. It is here that they changed their name to the Greek form Idumea. Other influences that concealed their identity included the artful politics of Antipater. He established himself as a friend of John Hyrcanus because he had ulterior motives for this friendship. These effects paved the way for the rise of his son Herod the Great. Herod used his position to marry the Hasmonean princess, Mariamne. Then he endeared himself to Rome and became king in Judaea under Roman power. The Herodians were all Edomites and considered being almost Jews, according to the Roman mindset. The Romans liked the Edomites and preferred dealing with them rather than actual bloodline Judeans. They favored them because the Edomites and Romans descended from Esau, who is Edom.

According to Meir Levin, in an article, 'Do West and Christianity Represent Esau and Edom?' he reveals that although voluminous Roman chronicles do not appear to contain any awareness of descent from Esau, there are traditions preserved and handed down from Esau that they accept. He notes that the Edomites have the knowledge and sometimes appear to be proud of the fact Zepho built Rome. In a Midrash, it records that "Zepho, son of Eliphaz, son of Esau, built the great kingdom of Rome. Tartan (Tartar) of the land of Elisha attacked him and killed him."

Levin adds that because Esau's descent was such a disgraceful and shameful one, the Edomites hid and suppressed the data of their identity via Rome. And, in a Malbim commentary of Obadiah chapter one, it suggests that besides genealogical descent, the Edomites also based their identity of both Rome and Esau on the "founding of their faith by the children of Edom."[4] These accounts help in piecing together parts of the puzzle as it relates to Esau, who is Edom and Rome. In another commentary on Isaiah 34, R. Isaac Abarbanel concurs with proof of who Edom-Rome is. The Great wise men, Rabbis Kimchi, Ibn-Ezra, Maimonides, and Abarbanel, speak with one voice as to the genealogical descent of Esau. Their previous testimony claims all Gentile Christians are the seed or children of Esau or Edom and that the prophets prophesied not only against the land of Edom, which is near Israel but also against the seed of Rome or Edom.

ROME INCORPORATES EDOM

The Biblical history last recognizes Esau-Edom as the Idumeans and Herodians. These labels identified them before the Romans fully incorporated the land of Edom and the people of Idumea. Chuck Missler explains that after the 135AD Bar Kokhba revolt, the Edomites, known as Idumeans, became assimilated into the area known as Palestine today and are the current orthodox Jews. These Jews, he furthers, continue to view the international globalists as Edomites, which is a term they used to refer to Rome. Based on historical evidence, however, after the last war of the Judeans with Rome, the Israelites who remained and were able to escape Roman captivity scattered into other places outside of the empire, which meant the wilderness and deserts of the African Continent. The entire population of the Hebrew Israelites who refused to obey the dictates of Rome went into exile. Jerusalem and Judaea were replete of the Israelites other than those captured and sold into slavery where they became Gladiators and food for the lions and other animals in the Roman Coliseums. The Edomite converts to Judaism, and the Roman Christians could stay in the land when they renamed it Palestine. Therefore, the people known as orthodox Jews were not the true Israelites, but descendants of Edom-Rome. These two religions of Rome became what we know today as the Judeo-Christian religion.

Although current history recognizes that the people of Edom became one with Rome after the death of the MASHIACH, older accounts of History tell a different tale. The book of Jasher and other historical accounts show that the people of Edom became one with Kittiym, which is Rome, thousands of years before the birth of YAHUSHA. What we know is that the present-day Zionist Jewish people from Eastern Europe are converts to the religion of Judaism and have no links to the land of Palestine other than usurpers. The converted Jews who remained in the land of Palestine and, the Druze a sect of Muslim Edomites, were also

Edomite Romans allowed to stay in the land after the Crusades. Missler is correct in his insistence that the globalists are Edomite Romans, but so are all white Europeans, including the Jewish converts. The orthodox Jews are Edomite Romans who created a sect called orthodox but are the same Edomite imposters. And, history shows there are several branches of the Edomites who have tried to replace the Hebrew Israelites with different sects of the religion using the Hebrew Scriptures. Therefore, Missler's conclusion that the people left behind in the land were the orthodox Jews is only correct in part. Because the true Hebrew Israelites were Negroes, this distinction barred them from staying or reentering the land after they expelled them. In fact, throughout history, some may have attempted to return, but Rome sent the Crusades who destroyed them and forced them into exile again. The children of Jacob-Israel are currently scattered on the African continent and the four corners of the earth in the diaspora. The land of Palestine has been trodden down by the Gentiles, "And they shall fall by the edge of the sword, and shall be led away captive into all nations: and Jerusalem shall be trodden down of the Gentiles until the times of the Gentiles be fulfilled' (Luke 21:24).

As the Jewish tradition that stems from the Talmud states, the descendants of Esau would become the Romans, and to a large extent, all Europeans. They have caused Israel to err. YAHUAH used Edom-Rome, the wicked and personified devil, to punish his chosen people for their fore-fathers' disobedience. YAHUAH cast out Israel, the Northern tribes, first, "Therefore YAHUAH was furious with Israel, and removed them out of his sight: there was none left but the tribe of Judah only," (2 Kings 17:18). It was after HAMASHIACH's death that YAHUAH cut off some Judeans because they did not accept the MASHIACH making it possible for YAHUAH to have mercy on both Israel and Judah, "For YAHUAH hath concluded them all in unbelief, that he might have mercy upon all," (Romans 11: 32). Paul here was reminding the Hellenized Israelites known as Gentiles about the Jews who did not accept the HAMASHIACH. It was the leaders who did not accept the MASHIACH. Therefore, Paul compares their fall to making Israel rich, "Now if the fall of them be the riches of the world, (Israel) and the diminishing of them the riches of the Gentiles (Hellenize Israelites); how much more their fullness," (Romans 11:12). YAHUAH will find Edom-Rome, the descendants of Esau, Jacob's elder brother guilty of being the destroyer of Jacob-Israel, "Therefore I shall devour them that devour you; and all thine adversaries, every one of them, shall go into captivity; and they that spoil thee shall be spoil and all that prey upon thee will I give for a prey," (Jeremiah 30:16).

The historians who recorded the revised history omit important information about Esau to mislead and deceive the masses, particularly those of the Christian faith. Many of them believed the prophecies of YAHUAH'S destruction of Esau-Edom apply to the Arab nations today. However, Edom-Rome as the diverse Papal Roman Christian Empire which has arisen and has deceived the entire world is a mixture of these nations of white people, "And he shall speak great words against the Highest, and shall wear out the saints of the Highest, and think to change times and laws: and they shall be given into his hand until a time and times and the dividing of time. But the judgment shall sit, and they shall take away his dominion, to consume and have to destroy it unto the end. And, the kingdom and dominion, and the greatness of the kingdom under the whole heaven, shall be given to the people of the saints of the Highest, whose kingdom is an everlasting kingdom, and all dominions shall serve and obey him' (Daniel 7:25-27).

Daniel's dream of the Four Beasts in the Book, known by that name, chapter seven, refers to Edom- Rome as one of four diverse great beasts that emerged from the sea. Biblical scholars have interpreted this fourth beast to be the Roman Empire. The empire reported to have ruled the earth from 168BC to 476AD then separated into East and West. However, the Empire did not end but, transformed from the pagan Roman Empire to the Papal Roman Empire. Scriptures show this revised empire as diverse nations that signify the ten toes of Nebuchadnezzar's dream. This Empire, led by the Vatican and Rome is where the Pope sits in Caesar's seat as King. They have altered the history relabeled the characters and have changed the times and laws to support their narrative that Rome's dominion ended in 476AD. However, Edom-Rome continues to have dominion over the entire world today as the United Nations symbol depicts the laurel wreath of

Rome, which is a Greco-Roman symbol worn by the victors of the military conquest and the victors of the ancient Olympic Games.

The Prophecies in Scripture are true, and history recalls the rise of the revised papal Roman Empire who changed the events and replaced the white Edomites

Rome Rules the Flat Earth as the United Nations

at the genesis of humanity and as a superior people with the divine right to rule over all nations on earth including the children of Israel, "After this, I saw in the night visions, and behold a fourth beast, dreadful and terrible, strong exceedingly; and it had great iron teeth: it devoured and brakes in pieces and stamped the residue with the feet of it: and it was diverse from all the beasts that were before it, and it had ten horns' (Daniel 7:7). Daniel's vision was symbolic of the nations that would rule on the earth in the "end" times. It showed their interactions with and how they would impact the descendants of Jacob-Israel. This fourth kingdom would be an inferior kingdom made of iron, but it would dominate the earth longer than the previous empires and would shower destruction upon the people of the Most High YAHUAH.

We find the truth about the events of history in the Hebrew Scriptures, and I believe it to be one of the few factual sources

George Augustus Polgreen Bridgetower (1778-1860), was born in Galicia Poland; where he was baptized Hieronimo Hyppolito de Augusto. He was a virtuoso violinist, who lived in England for much of his life. In 1791, the British Prince Regent (later George IV) took an interest in him and oversaw his cntinuing musical education.

that tell the truth of history. Edom-Rome has declared a false chronicle and changed much of the facts to hide their identity and the identity of the true Israelites. They have deleted information about places and people. They have even replaced paintings and artifacts to reflect the image of the Edomites, as shown in the image of YAHUSHA, who they call Jesus. Despite evidence to the contrary, some Jewish historians still claim there is no difference between the Jews (Israel) and Edomite Gentiles. Cohen (1999) asserts that the Jews and Gentiles in antiquity were indistinguishable corporeal, when observed through the senses, of sight, language, and their social practices. He adds that even the sages of the Rabbinic academy could not discern Romans in their midst. However, this is not the entire story because history shows Israelites were living in the diaspora as Romans, and Greeks, some practicing their Jewish culture while living in separated communities. In contrast, others lived among the Romans and Greeks as Gentiles. History shows that the Hebrew Israelites, though scattered, lived in groups set apart from the people of the countries they occupied. They lived in similar societies of the so-called Jewish people today, where they had their schools, shops, and synagogues like those in England, Australia, and Brooklyn, New York.

Before the final dispersal out of Israel, the Judeans who lived in Judaea considered these Hebrew Israelites scattered throughout Europe and Africa to be Gentiles or Greeks because they spoke the language of the countries where they lived. However, the Jews were black people, living among a mixture of black Romans and white Edomite Romans and Greeks. Like Paul the Apostle, a Hebrew of the tribe of Benjamin and also a citizen of Rome reminded the centurion of his identity before they were about to scourged him and found out he was not an Egyptian, "And as they bound him with thongs, Paul said unto the centurion that stood by, Is it lawful for you to scourge a man that is a Roman, and uncondemned' (Acts 22:25)?. Being Roman meant that he had Roman citizenship and not Roman by nationality.

A Black Dutchman by Alber Eckhout, circa mid 1600s. Invariably all Blacks in European paintings are declared Servants, descendants of Slaves, or Ambassadors/Emissaries of the king of Kongo. This particular Black man is called Don Miguel de Castro, Emissary of Kongo, who was painted by Eckhout while on a visit to Dutch Brazil. That convoluted tale is necessary because Eckhout was in Dutch Brazil (which existed from 1630-1654) painting local people and flora from 1636-1644. However, this tale might not work anymore, as these paintings are also said to be by Jasper Becx, c. 1643 – died: 1647: of Middelburg, Zeeland, Netherlands. Becx is not known to have gone to Brazil.

In the book 'Shakespeare and the Jews' (pg. 171), John Shapiro wrote an account of the collective experiences of years of travel and conquest that had convinced the Europeans that some of the accepted stereotypes of Jewish racial otherness including the belief that the Jews were black needed to be qualified. "When William Brereton jotted down his impressions of the Jews in the synagogue in Amsterdam in 1635AD, he noted that the Jewish 'Men are most black' and when the Scottish Minister Robert Kirk

Russian General Abram Petrovich (1696-1781) Gannibal

toured London in January 1690AD, he also paid a visit to the synagogue there, where he observed over two hundred Jews worshipping. He noted in his journal, 'They were all very black men.' Francis Maximilien Mission's, 'A new voyage of Italy' clarifies that, 'it is 'a vulgar error that the Jews are all Black is only true of the Portuguese Jews.' 'The Swarthiness of their complexion is entailed upon their whole race even in the Northern regions, but the Jews who are from Germany, those, for example, I have seen at Prague, are not blacker than the rest of their countrymen.'" These eye-witness accounts show that the black Hebrew Israelite Jews were prominent people who lived scattered among all nations, not only in Africa, as the revised history of Edom-Rome would have the world believe. The

Israelites are in Africa because they were dispersed into Africa by Edom-Rome. Therefore, they too are in diaspora.

---

[1] Sages were the active leaders and teachers of the Jewish religion from the beginning of the second Temple period until the Arabian conquest of the East. They are also known as Hazal, and acronym for Hakhameynu zikhronam li-berakhah, 'our sages of blessed memory.'

[2] Targums Onkelos (or Onqelos), is the Jewish Babylonian Aramaic Targums ("translation") of the Torah.

[3] Targum Onkelos (or Onqelos), תרגום אונקלוס, is the Jewish Babylonian Aramaic targum ("translation") of the Torah. However, its early origins may have been Western, in Israel.

[4] Malbim is an analysis of the pasha, or the simple straight forward meaning of the text, the author of Midrash Haggadah, the formal title of the Malbim Haggadah.

CHAPTER 7

How Christianity Impacted Israel

THE NEW TESTAMENT WRITINGS of the Acts of the Apostles reveals Christianity begun on the Day of Pentecost or Feast of Weeks (Leviticus 23:15; Deuteronomy 16:9). This event is reported to have occurred after YAHUSHA ascended to heaven around the early first century AD. The word Pentecost is a Greek word meaning 'count fifty.' It refers to the fifty days after the wave sheaf offering of Passover. In the Acts of the Apostles, it tells us that YAHUAH poured out his RUACH HaKodesh on the believers in HAMASHIACH in the form of fire similar to the cloud and fire that led the children of Israel when they came out of the land of

Egypt. The disciples had gathered in the Upper Room on the Day of Pentecost to wait as YAHUSHA had instructed them. "When they, therefore, were come together, they asked of him, saying, ADONAI YAHUSHA will you restore the Kingdom again to Israel? And he said unto them; it is not for you to know the times or the seasons, which the Father has put in his own power. But ye shall receive power, after that, the RUACH HaKodesh comes upon you: and ye shall be witnesses unto me both in Yerushalayim, and in all Yahud, and Shomeron, and unto the uttermost part of the earth" (Act 1:6-8).

Biblical history records that the Highest YAHUAH sent YAHUSHA HAMASHIACH to the lost sheep of the house of Israel through the tribe of Judah, to prepare the way for the redemption of the ten tribes of Israel who had been separated and in the diaspora. However, the Edomite Romans usurped authority over the Hebrew texts and the renewal movent and formed another religion that taught a variation of the Babylonian Mystery religions. This religion added pagan ideas and philosophies to the teachings of YAHUSHA. The fundamental change in the doctrine was that the HAMASHIACH made it possible for his coming to include all nations, when in fact, he came to redeem Israel who was scattered in all nations. This doctrine formed the bases for the Roman Christian Church known as Catholic, a word meaning universal. Therefore, all Christian churches that follow this universal teaching are catholic. The religion of the Israelites then became the religion of Edom-Rome and the Edomites.

Some accounts describe what occurred when the assembly of the HAMASHIACH transformed into the Christian church led by the Edomites. Historians believed Rome impacted the religion of the Israelites as early as 70AD after the fall of the Temple in Jerusalem. Others say it occurred about 100AD when the Edomite Roman Christians decided they no longer needed to identify with Israel to attain salvation. Still, others assert that the greatest impact Rome had on the people and religion of Israel occurred in 325AD at the Council of Nicaea. It was at the end of the council when they concluded and penned and adopted twenty canons that made it possible for the Roman Emperor Constantine to incorporate the church and govern it from Rome. Constantine had accepted the Christian god after revealing a vision he experienced while on the battlefield. He then called for a Synod with all the churches in the Roman Empire, where they ratified the doctrines and dogma of the Christian church.

ISRAELITES – FOLLOWERS OF YAHUSHA, NOT CHRIST

When the Set-apart Assembly started on Pentecost, they did not call themselves Christians but Saints, set apart believers in MASHIACH or Nazarites because it was the MASHIACH they followed. It was the Edomite Greeks of Antioch who first branded the followers Christians because of their dislike of the Hebrew Israelites. The Antiochians so hated the Israelite Jews who lived among them that after the War of 70AD, and the Romans had destroyed Jerusalem and the Temple. They petitioned Titus Caesar to expel the Jews from their city. They had only tolerated HAMASHIACH's followers because of the Hebrew Israelites' relationship they enjoyed with Rome. The Israelite Jews were wealthy, prominent, and provided many taxes to Rome; therefore, Titus rejected the calls for their expulsion (Wars of the Jews 7. 5. 2). Josephus describes the relationship the Hebrew Israelites enjoyed as "equality with the Greeks." The Greeks hated that the Romans saw them as equal. And, this favor granted by Rome to the Jews provoked deep antipathy between the Jews and Greeks in the cities of Asia (Frend, 1984).

Therefore, people of Antioch attached the name Christian to the Israelites as a derogatory by-word that meant "poor fellow." Because the Antiochians were pagans and they knew the Edomites were also pagans and connected to the Israelites by Roman Christianity, they taunted them with this description. Edom-Rome had attached itself to the Israelites by falsely claiming that since the HAMASHIACH came, he offered salvation to the Edomites and all other nations through his death, burial and resurrection. During this time, the Hebrew Israelites under the rule of Edom-Rome held little power to prevent them from adding the pagan doctrines that pushed an alternative narrative from that of the Israelites. Edom-Rome was a mighty Empire and did what was politically expedient. They had the authority of the scripts and scrolls of Israel and formed the Christian religion that included everyone. The Antiochians knew the Israelite Jews resented being described as Christians because they did not believe the Christians Elohiym was the same as the Highest YAHUAH, the ELOHIYM of the Israelites. Edom-Rome, like the Greeks, worshiped pagan gods. The Greeks were also the descendants of the mingled people of Esau-Edom and Japheth, and the sworn enemies of the Hebrew Israelites. The Hebrews, who accepted the HAMASHACH, despised any association with the Christians because of who they worshiped and because they did not keep the laws of the Most High. Those who followed the teachings of YAHUSHA preferred the label Nazarites because the MASHIACH came out of Nazareth. Some Historians described the followers as the sect of the Nazarene. "And he came and dwelt in a city called Nazareth: that it might be fulfilled which is spoken by the prophets; He shall be called a Nazarene' (Matthew 2:23). Records show they translated the name Nazareth into many languages to describe the followers of YAHUSHA throughout the Empire (Wikipedia).

CHRISTIANITY, THE RELIGION OF THE EDOMITES

The Hebrew Israelite Jews recognized Christianity as an Edomite religion after 100AD because there was then less of a tendency for Christians to claim to be Israel. Christians contrasted Christianity and Judaism as separate religions (Frend, 1984). But, separate not because they did not accept the HAMASHIACH, but because the Hebrew Israelites did not accept the pagan practices introduced into the religion by Edom-Rome.

Christianity advanced that they would be heir to the Universalist claims of Judaism. Records show they applied the word 'catholic" to the church for the first time (as done by Ignatius in the Letter to the Smyrnaeans).[1] Edom-Rome believed and put forth the idea that YAHUAH sent YAHUSHA to save the entire world and not just the "Lost Sheep," of the House of Israel as he said to the woman from Canaan, "But he answered and said, I am not sent but unto the lost sheep of the house of Israel (Matthew 15:24). The Edomite Christians took the teachings of the HAMASHIACH and applied it to another god, one they called Iesus (Jesus) as their savior god who they believed came to save them and the whole world. The savior-god had similar characteristics of the Christ of the mystery religions of Babylon that shared common attributes to YAHUSHA, the HAMASHIACH of Israel. The Letter is written to the believers in Smyrna by St. Ignatius in 107AD confirmed that the Hebrew Israelites did not take part in the Eucharist and prayer because they did not believe the Eucharist to be the flesh of the Savior Jesus Christ (YAHUSHA) who came in the flesh, died and raised again to a new life in the spirit. It was doctrines such as these that separated the true believers in HAMASHIACH from those who believed in Iesus (Jesus) the Christ.

The ideas and philosophies that the Christians used came from the mystery religious cults' belief in a "savior god" who had died and rose from the dead. Those who would attain immortality would share as a symbol in the death and resurrection of the savior god, whether he was Mithras or Osiris, Adonis, Orpheus, or Dionysus (Nigosian, 2000). Partaking in the Eucharist meant all persons became one with the savior Christ; therefore, the Gospel of Christianity revealed the passion of Christ as the savior for the entire world. These added ideas were of the Babylonian Mystery cults. Therefore, the religion came to be another Babylonian mystery cult religion of the Edomite Romans using the Hebrew scripts and scrolls to support and promote loyalty to the Roman Empire (Nigosian, 2000). The Universalist religion of Christianity teaches that Jesus' death, burial, and resurrection saved humanity, and therefore, obedience to the Laws of the Torah is no longer necessary. Hence, Warder Cresson concludes, in the article titled, "Origin of Edom, Babylon, and Rome, or Christianity," as to the origin of Edom, that Rome, Edom, and Christianity are synonymous with Babylon which is the mystery religion described in the book of Revelation.

The Christian Synagogue dominated the sub-apostolic era with a love-hate relationship between the members of the two Israels (Frend, 1984). These groups comprised the Hebrew Israelites and the Edomites of the Greco-Roman Empire, which also included Edomites who were proselytes converted to the religion of the Jews and took part in Jewish practices. The Romans who became Christians adopted the Jewish MASHIACH as their god with the philosophies of St Ignatius and other Hellenized Jewish philosophers. They named their god Iesus the Christ, who they later renamed Jesus after they added the letter

"J" to the English alphabet in the 17th century. This name is also a translation of the Greco-Roman god Serapis Christus or Jesus Christus. Therefore, the Talmud, the source of Jewish laws, believed and presented Jesus the god of the Edomite Romans as an imposter and a bastard, and it claims he possessed the soul of Esau.

Christ became the foundation on which Edom-Rome based Christianity and its name and title credited to Jesus, or Christ, which also stemmed from the Greek word Christos. The word meant 'anointed' as in the word Mashiach, hence the English word Messiah (Nigosian, 2000). Christ was the Christian Messiah of a religion that began in Rome. The Roman Empire assumed authority over the religion and its practices comprised a mixture of pagan Greco-Roman beliefs along with the teachings of Hebrew Scriptures and other writings. This new religion combined the ideas and philosophies of Gnosticism, Manichaeism, and the Hebrew teachings of the followers of HAMASHIACH. These things happened in the Roman church because the Roman Empire was pluralistic as it tolerated Greek religions from the earliest times. They also encouraged its citizens to worship the emperor to promote loyalty to the empire (Nigosian, 2000).

Frend (1984) further notes that the religion of Christianity shared the same political views as Rome, and during the time of Philo, an Alexandrian Jew and supporter of Rome derived his concepts from contemporary Stoic beliefs. They believed him to have been the father of Christian political thought, which included many aspects of Greek theology. His ideas proved to be of immense importance in the Christian religion's history (Philo).[2] Philo wanted to show the harmony and rationality of the universe, and it is from this mixture of Babylonian mystical ideas, practices, and Greek philosophies that Christianity was born and became the religion of the Edomites. Today, we find these religious beliefs in the Christian religions of Catholicism and Protestantism.

However, in the Hebrew's mindset, there was a distinction between YAHUSHA, the true HAMASHIACH, and Jesus, the imposter; therefore, they did not accept the Christian's idea of Jesus as the Messiah. One doctrine they refused to accept was the belief that the HAMASHIACH was part of a trinity of gods, and for this reason, Edom-Rome instigated fierce persecutions against them. They tortured and destroyed the followers of YAHUSHA and made up horrific charges against them, which included lies that they sacrificed their children. Between the years 57 to 68AD during the reign of Emperor Nero, they used the accused Israelite victims for the bloody Roman arenas where they fed them to the lions. According to Nigosian, other emperors, such as Decius from (249 to 251AD) and Diocletian from (264 to 395AD), used ruthless measures to stamp out Christianity as followed by the Hebrew Israelites. They were not inclined to destroy the Roman supported Christianity because it was the religion of Edom-Rome and the Edomites. So, when we hear the narrative that Rome persecuted Christians, it was to hide the fact that they persecuted the Hebrew Israelites. The latter refused Rome's pagan teachings or the false doctrine that the Edomites were now eligible and could be grafted into Israel. Edom-Rome oppressed both the Hebrew Israelites who followed the HAMASHIACH and those who did not accept the HAMASHIACH. They also persecuted them because they refused to disobey the Laws of the Most High YAHUAH and follow the laws instituted by Edom-Rome in the Christian Church. Edom-Rome wanted to replace the Most High YAHUAH and, therefore, saw the Hebrew Israelites as having a divided loyalty between the Roman Empire and the Highest YAHUAH.

As Isaac Abrabanel, a philosopher and Jewish commentator postulate, "the wise accept as a tradition that the soul of Esau reappeared as the soul of Jesus, the Christian, and that is why they called him Yeshua."[3] He furthers that this name, Yeshua, in Hebrew is an anagram of Esau, and all those who adhere to this religion and Christian beliefs and worship should also call themselves the children of Edom, for Yeshua (Jesus), is Esau is Edom. He adds that "This religion began in Rome and this is also where his, Yeshua's, (Jesus) roots are. The Roman Caesars and Christian kings were the first to accept it as all Christians who adhere to the religion of Yeshua (Jesus) are; they, without a doubt, are people of Edom, the descendants of Esau." There is much confusion among the Hebrew Israelite sects awakening today, about whether to believe that the HAMASHIACH was born and was sent to the lost sheep of Israel scattered in the diaspora. He was sent to prepare the way for Israel's redemption. Some of the awakened accept Jesus as the Messiah, while others reject him. I believe, and this research will prove that the HAMASHIACH was born and came to his people. However, Edom-Rome created another form of the HAMASHIACH who they call Jesus who those of the Christian Church believe is a God and have put great faith in this belief, which has caused chaos among the Hebrew Israelites.

Once Edom-Rome took authority over the Hebrew writings and created a Universalist doctrine, those who followed the true teachings of the HAMASHIACH could not accept the additions. Thus, Edom-Rome victimized and destroyed them. Edom-Rome then controlled the narrative and wrote the history where they claim that the Hebrew Israelites did not accept the HAMASHIACH, and it was they who crucified him. This false teaching of the Christian church continues today while the imposter Edomite Jews living in Palestine and throughout the world claim the HAMASHIACH did not come so, they await the coming of their false Messiah. In reality, many of the Hebrew Israelites accepted the HAMASHIACH. Still, they refused Jesus the Christ of Edom-Rome, which was another HAMASHIACH.

YAHUSHA warned his followers that this would happen when he told the Pharisees, "I have come in my Father's name, and ye receive me not: if another shall come in his own name, him ye will receive' (John 5:43). So, history shows Hebrew Israelites who joined Edom-Rome and accepted this Jesus. Many of them accepted Jesus by force, and the edge of the sword. There is evidence that also shows that many black Hebrew Israelites even rose to be popes and cardinals in the Roman Christian church. The Jacobites of Britain also accepted the Roman Christian religion, which was reformed in the 16th century by Martin Luther and other reformers forming the Protestant Church. There are many artifacts available today which show the popes and other high officials of the church to be black people in Europe. Israel's surrender to Rome caused the Hebrew Israelites today to have taken the mark of this beast system, and why, as we awaken to the truth, the Highest YAHUAH has called the Israelites to come out from among them.

The Pope Speaking to Saint Maurice

As the commentator Abrabanel shows, he knew the difference between YAHUSHA and Jesus even while he was a Hebrew living in the diaspora in Portugal and Spain during the 13th and 14th centuries. He believed in the HAMASHIACH, but he refused to break the commandments of the Highest and accept the pagan doctrines the Romans taught. One of them is that Jesus or the Messiah was the god of the Universe who came to die to save all humankind, including the Edomites. Abrabanel knew Jesus was the god of Esau, who is Edom, and not YAHUSHA of Israel. And, because he knew this teaching was false, he refused to accept Edom-Rome's Universalist religion and god. He became one of the many hundreds of thousands expelled from Spain and Portugal. He dispersed onto the West Coast of Africa where their children and grandchildren after being forced baptism into Christianity by Edom-Rome went on ships into slavery via the transatlantic slave trade.

WHEAT AND TARES REPRESENT JACOB AND ESAU

What Edom-Rome has done by usurping authority over Israel is expressed in the Parable of the Wheat and Tares told by YAHUSHA and repeated by Matthew. Edom-Rome represents the seed being planted by the enemy among the good, righteous seed of YAHUAH in the earth. The parable expounds how Edom-Rome could invade the Kingdom of YAHUAH by pretending to be the good seed, a "holy" people using the Hebrew Scriptures to look like the people of the Most High, "... the kingdom of heaven is likened unto a man which sowed good seed in his field: But while men slept, his enemy came and sowed tares among the wheat, and went his way. But when the blade was sprung up and brought forth fruit, then appeared the tares. So, the servants of the householder came and said unto him, sir, didn't thou sow good seed in thy field? From whence then hath it tares? He said unto them, An enemy hath done this. The servants said unto him, wilt thou then we gather them up" (Matthew 13: 24-28)? The Highest told them not to gather them up because, in doing so, they may destroy some of the good wheat.

Later, when YAHUSHA was alone with his disciples, they asked him to explain what the parable meant and how it applied to himself and the enemy of Israel, "He answered and said unto them, He that soweth the good seed is the Son of man; the field is the world; the good seed are the children of the kingdom, but the tares are the children of the wicked one; The enemy that sowed them is the devil; the harvest is the end of the world, and the reapers are the angels. As therefore the tares are gathered and burned in the fire; so, shall it be at the end of this world. The Son of man shall send forth his angels, and they shall gather out of his kingdom all things that offend, and them which do iniquity; And shall cast them into a furnace of fire: there shall be wailing and gnashing of teeth," (Matthew 13:37-42). Therefore, Edom-Rome, the brother of Jacob-Israel, is the enemy of Israel, and Scriptures identify them as the devil that would pretend to be what they are not.

Origen, considered a father of the Christian Church, describes the tare sown among the wheat as darnel. In one of his homilies on Genesis and Exodus, he cautioned followers of the Messiah to make sure that their fruit had no darnel or no tares. Origen characterized darnel as a weed able to grow among the wheat but is false wheat. It resembles the wheat from the outside and not recognized by the unsuspecting until the harvest. Such is the case of Edom-Rome, who resembles the good wheat, as they speak piously wearing long robes and priestly garments but, they are hypocrites and liars. They are imposters of true Israel and have replaced the kingdom of Israel with the false religions of Judaism, Christianity, and the "Nation of Islam." These all represent the darnel or false wheat. Therefore, YAHUAH will reveal the true identity of Edom-Rome before YAHUSHA'S return and why Paul in his letter to the Thessalonians admonished the followers of the HAMASHIACH, "Let no man deceive you by any means; for that day shall not come, except there comes a falling away first, and that man of sin be revealed, the son of perdition" (2 Thessalonians 2:3). The Latin word for this tare means 'drunken,' and if eaten, it can be fatal. Edom-Rome is the darnel planted on the earth among the holy people of YAHUAH. It is poison, and Israel must avoid it. The tares appear to be the real thing and have deceived the unsuspecting Israelites. Edom-Rome has done this by misrepresenting themselves to the world using the Hebrew scripts and scrolls to create a version of YAHUAH's kingdom that includes everyone they now call "Spiritual Israel."

Scripture shows the descendants of Edom-Rome to be frauds, who bow to the wood and stone, which YAHUAH says is idolatry. But, they know the truth and introduced these false gods to deceive and remove the Israelites from their heritage and the hope of inheriting the Kingdom prepared for them. "Their gods of wood, and which are overlaid with gold and silver, are like the stones that be hewn out of the mountain: they that worship them shall be confounded" (Baruch 6:39). YAHUAH warned Israel against worshiping these idols, and today they are confused worshiping in vain what they know not. Edom-Rome pretends to worship the one true ELOHIYM, but they know that the god they serve in secret and not so secret is another god, as shown at the Easter Vigil service at the Vatican where they praise Lucifer. The Exultant sings during the vigil, "Flaming Lucifer finds mankind, I say: Oh Lucifer who will never be defeated, Christ is your son!" Edom-Rome's god is Lucifer, and in plain sight, they have deceived the entire world about the role they have played in destroying YAHUAH'S Chosen people. However, YAHUAH will reveal the false gods of Christianity and those of the other religions of Edom-Rome as the darnel planted among the true wheat, "... for ADONAI YAHUAH Seeth not as man Seeth; for man looketh on the outward appearance, but YAHUAH looketh on the heart" (1 Samuel 16:7).

THE MESSIANIC SYNAGOGUE

The Messianic synagogue of Israelite believers first assembled in the homes of the brethren to receive instructions. But, after entire synagogues came to believe in the HAMASHIACH, they still regarded the assemblies as synagogues, and its members prayed three times a day and fasted twice a week like Hebrews. Those of the Edomite Christians fasted on Wednesday and Friday to commemorate the arrest and crucifixion, and the Hebrews who followed YAHUSHA chose Monday and Thursday. The Christians professed monotheism in the same terms as did the Hebrews, with the exception that Jesus Christ was also God in the flesh, and they also used Hebrew Scriptures. Like the Hebrews, they claimed to be "saints," although the Hebrew Israelites (Jews) still denied them the privilege of calling themselves Israel (Jervell).[4]

After the fall of Jerusalem in 70AD, the Assembly experienced several changes. The Hebrews, who were followers of YAHUSHA that remained in Judaea and throughout the Empire, rallied to the Pharisees, who were the traditional upholders of religion and nationality (Frend, 1984). Perhaps, it was because Edom-Rome had destroyed the Temple, along with the fact that the Hebrew people were so wounded by the Romans who claimed to be Christians, that they cut their association with the Christian religion of Rome. So then, between 70 and 135AD, Christianity became a religion based on the geography and organization of the Hellenistic synagogue united into the Greco-Roman world (Frend, 1984). The Temple's destruction also meant that the followers of HAMASHIACH no longer had a central point of reference because, throughout Israel's dispersions, Jerusalem had remained the focus of the Hebrew's allegiance no matter where they were. It was the capital, as Philo declared, of the disseminated Israelites. And, even more than just being their capital, it was their homeland. Therefore, the question they asked during this period of Israel and the Temple's destruction sought to determine whether the Christians were true Israel bearers of the new covenant, the Holy Remnant, or rebels and outsiders (Frend, 1984).

The bloodline descendants of Israel did not consider the Christian outsiders who assumed the religion of the Hebrew Israelites part of Israel. The Christians supported the claim that Jesus the MASHIACH came to bring a universal gospel. This gospel was inclusive of the Edomite Romans and all other people who accepted the MASHIACH as their savior alongside the Israelites, the chosen people of YAHUAH. The Hellenistic leaders of both the Jews and Edomites inserted pagan philosophies and doctrines into the original teachings of Israel out of jealousy that YAHUAH had favored Israel and because it was they who were the bloodline descendants of Jacob-Israel. Edom-Rome offered the Christian's Jesus to everyone and then used the sword against them to force those who did not accept him. Therefore, around 395AD Edom-Rome issued the Edict of Theodosius, where they prohibited, on pain of death, the right of any other religion to exist except Christianity:

> We forbid all persons of criminal pagan mind from the accursed immolation of victims, from damnable sacrifices, and from all other such practices prohibited by the authority of the more ancient sanctions. We command that all their fanes, temples, and shrines if even now any remain entire, shall be destroyed by the command of the

magistrates and shall be purified by the erection of the sign of the venerable Christian religion. All men shall know if it should appear, by suitable proof before a competent judge, that any person has mocked this law, he shall be punished with death (Nigosian, 2000).[5]

It was Edom-Rome and the Christian church who convinced those who joined Christianity and accepted the belief that Jesus died to save humanity from their sins, they too, could embrace the covenant which they labeled the "new" covenant. And, those who joined did not need to keep the laws, statutes, and commandments of YAHUAH because the laws were for the Israelites and the grace and love of Jesus negated the law for Gentiles and made it of no effect. As a result, many pagans joined hoping to take part in the life that YAHUAH only promised to the Chosen line of Abraham and Isaac through Jacob, the younger son and not Esau. The book of Revelation confirms the persecution that would come upon those who accepted YAHUSHA and kept the commandments of YAHUAH. Scripture describes Israel as the woman who would experience such atrocities, "And the earth helped the woman, and the earth opened her mouth and swallowed up the flood which the dragon cast out of his mouth, 'And the dragon was wroth with the woman, and went to make war with the remnant of her seed, which keeps the commandments of YAHUAH, and have the testimony of YAHUSHA," (Revelation 12:16-17).

As the Christian church expanded, the controversy grew between the Orthodox Jews and the pro-Jewish party, and they counterattacked. They left it to Marcion, an agnostic Christian in the 140s AD, to cut the Gordian knot. He denied the relevance of the Old Testament to Jesus' saving work. He held the belief like the Hebrews that the earthly life of Jesus was an apparition in human form, but he did not believe he was the incarnation of the Supreme Being. The Israelites also believed YAHUSHA was the HAMASHIACH, but they did not believe him to be God. However, it was the Gnostics who claimed Jesus did not take on material existence but appeared as a Redeemer from the realm of the spirit (Nigosian, 2000). Therefore, it is believed that these attacks left a mark on the later books of the New Testament as they addressed only the scattered tribes of Israel and the rivalry between the Hebrews who followed YAHUSHA and the Christians who followed Jesus ensued. The Hebrews wanted to remain faithful to YAHUAH by keeping the laws, statutes, and commandments, while the loyalty of Edomite Christians lay with Rome and the gods of Rome. The Edomite Christians did not believe it was necessary to obey the laws. However, YAHUSHA said he came to fulfill the law, "Think not that I am come to destroy the law or the prophets: I am not come to destroy, but to fulfill. For verily, I say unto you, till heaven and earth pass, one jot or one tittle shall in no wise pass from the law, till all be fulfilled' (Matthew 5:17-18). This rivalry between the Hebrews and Edomites caused the authorities of the Roman Empire to notice and embrace the Edomite Christians (Frend, 1984). Thus, Edom-Rome then incorporated the Christians into Roman political society embracing it as an important institution of their empire. They omitted the laws of the Highest because Esau, who is Edom, and Rome are lawless people.

HEBREW ISRAELITES LIVE BY THE LAWS

The Hebrew Israelites who embraced YAHUSHA also followed the laws, and circumcision remained an essential part of the Law. Howbeit, Gentile Christians also believed they had a pathway to YAHUAH through accepting the older covenant of Noah, which guaranteed them salvation. They believed the covenant of Noah allowed them to associate with Israel, while the Hebrew assembly remained as Israel and addressed their Epistles to the synagogues in the dispersion (Frend, 1984). In the debate of whether the church was a form of 'Judeo' or 'Jewish' Christianity, J. Danielou answered that to some extent, the question is a misconception since all Christianity, at that stage, was, in fact,, 'Jewish Christianity.'[6] It was Israel that could not have accepted Jesus Christ "as God." To do so meant breaking the first commandment that says Israel shall have no other gods before YAHUAH their ELOHIYM. However, some of the Hellenized church fathers, after adopting the pagan beliefs accepted Jesus as God and, in 2 Clement and Pliny's report on the Christians in Bithynia in 112AD wrote to the Christians and told them Jesus Christ was God in their teachings. Clement and Ignatius both wrote in their letters, "Brethren, we must think of Jesus Christ as God, as of the Judge of the living and the dead" (2 Clement 1, and Pliny Letters X.96.7).[7] This doctrine caused many Hebrew Israelites to remove themselves from the Roman Edomite Christians and become scattered Israel hidden among the heathens throughout the earth.

EFFECTS OF JUDAISM AND CHRISTIANITY ON YAHUSHA'S FOLLOWERS

The changes made to both Judaism and Christianity had a detrimental impact on the followers of YAHUSHA, including those who succumbed to the old sectarian ways of the Scribes and Pharisees, and those who ascribed to YAHUSHA but fell into the pagan Roman trap of Christianity. False teachings destroyed these followers through the deceptive philosophies added to Judaism and Christianity. Social strife and sectarian rivalries blunted the consciences of the groups, although every Jew accepted the Law (Torah). In the New Testament, it names the rival Jewish groups as; Herodians, Sadducees, and Pharisees. However, Josephus does not list the Herodians but adds the Essenes, because, in his opinion, the Herodians were not Jews but, in fact, Idumeans, from the Herodian dynasty of Herod the Great. According to Josephus, the Herodians were Edomites converted to the religion and were also supporters of Rome and its leaders (Frend, 1984).

After Simon Bar Kochba tried to liberate the Judean people following the last war in the fall of 135AD, the hopes of the

Judeans faltered, and the results had lasting effects on those who followed the HAMASHIACH. It resulted in Roman Christianity growing away from Judaism, and Messianic hopes became less urgent, and there was less emphasis on the church as Israel (Frend, 1984). Thus, from 135AD until the end of the century, the Edomite Christians attained self-identity based on their sacred literature, the New Testament, their distinctive liturgy, their rule of faith, and their wide-ranging organization became more prevalent. As a result, they became the 'third race' which, in terms of religion, they claimed themselves to be (Eusebius HE VI2.14).[8] The Christian church then assumed and replaced true Israel by becoming "spiritual Israel." These developments continued within the Christian church, and the Israelite legacy persisted in the background. However, Judaism remained the singular continuous theme throughout all different variations of Gnosticism. Also, historical evidence confirms that Babylonian influenced Jewish rabbis played a role in the canonization of the Torah, portions of the Prophets, and the New Testament, which, today, typifies the Christian Bible (Frend, 1984).

EARLY LATIN BECOMES NEW TESTAMENT

The Muratorian Canon, a new document written in Latin, the language of the Roman Christian church, included a list of the books of scripture allowed and read by the church whereas, they rejected the other books of scripture. This list of books became the New Testament and is similar to the New Testament used today (Eusebius, pp. 144-147). Lactantius, a 4th century Christian, confirms that both Old and New Testament writings were in existence in the early church, although the contents were not as they are today. The Testament included the Wisdom of Solomon and the Apocalypse of Peter. But, it omitted the first and second books of Peter, the letter to the Hebrews and third John. The Christian Church also allowed followers to read The Shepherd of Hermas, but not as Scripture, as they did not consider it to be an apostolic document (Frend, 1984). Rome intended to have the believers use this canon as a guide to Christendom. Although this document may have been correct in its content, because they interpreted the teachings from the perspective of Edom-Rome and the Hellenized Israelites, the doctrines misled those who followed the teachings. They made the letters the Apostle Paul wrote to the Hellenized Israelites living in the diaspora to apply to all people living in the nations that Edom-Rome ruled. However, we now understand that when Paul addressed the Hellenized Israelites, he referred to them as Greeks and Gentiles and even strangers. He identified the Judeans as Hebrews or Jews, but his letters were always addressed to the descendants of Jacob-Israel. At no time was he writing to the Edomites or Idumeans, Syrians, Arabs, etcetera as they were not part of the covenant. He was the Apostle to the dispersed Israelites living as Gentiles in nations throughout the Roman Empire.

The letters that Paul wrote to the Hebrew Gentiles living in the diaspora formed the basis for Edom-Rome to create a universal Christian Church. They believed Paul opened citizenship by "adoption" of anyone without ties to the bloodline descendants of Israel. They used this means to recruit many men and women, which made it possible for the religion of Jesus to become the religion of the nations. However, today we understand Paul sent letters to Hebrew Israelites living in the diaspora and considered Gentiles because they spoke the language of the countries where they were born and lived. Paul's letters must, therefore, be understood through the lens of the TORAH and Hebrew customs. The names used by Paul to identify the Israelites; Edom-Rome used to muddy the truth about who Paul was addressing in his letters. They took these letters and claimed they did not have to obey the Laws of the TORAH because the blood of Jesus covered the sins of the world. When in fact, Paul explained in his letters how the Israelites returning to the ways of Israel should act as YAHUAH had cut them off for hundreds of years, and they needed to know what YAHUSHA'S coming meant for their salvation and return to the Father whom they disobeyed. Edom-Rome took these letters and applied the instructions to the members of the pagan Christian Church. And, the New Testament became the book designated for Christians.

However, we find without the TORAH, which is the word of the Most High YAHUAH, there is no truth. We can only understand the New Testament concerning Hebrew Scriptures and culture as Paul himself wrote, "For I am not ashamed of the Besorah of HAMASHIACH: for it is the power of YAH unto salvation to everyone that believes; to the Yahudiy first, and also to the Yavaniy. For therein is the righteousness of YAH revealed from belief to belief: as it is written, the just shall live by belief' (Romans 1:16-17). The New Testament only fulfills what YAHUAH has written in the TORAH and Prophets; therefore, YAHUSHA could not bring a new doctrine to give to the Roman Empire. Paul wrote to his brethren living in the diaspora because YAHUAH called him to be an Apostle to them. But, because Edom-Rome has been the authority and administrators of the Hebrew Scriptures for thousands of years, they have been able to continue their use of these writings in the propagation of their false religions. Therefore, it is incumbent on all Hebrew Israelites who say these writings are not valid to do the research and draw the correct conclusions based on the facts of both Biblical and secular history. The Hebrew Israelites are the bloodline descendants of Israel, the true people of YAHUAH. Edom-Rome may have had authority over them for a long time. Still, they could not change the outcome of Israel's awakening, or the purpose YAHUAH allowed Edom-Rome to create the religions of Judaism, Christianity, and Islam. These all work together for the good of Israel. The TORAH is the foundation, "All Scripture is given by inspiration of YAHUAH, and is profitable for doctrine, for reproof, for correction, for instruction in righteousness: That the man of YAH may be perfect, thoroughly furnished unto all good works' (2 Timothy 3: 16-17).

DOCTRINES OF THE NEW TESTAMENT

The doctrine espoused by the Edomite Christians implies that YAHUAH disinherited Israel and replaced them with the descendants of Edom-Rome and the people of other nations that follow the teachings of Jesus. This canon established that those who receive Jesus Christ and follow His example of love could become part of the new Israel and be grafted into the family of YAHUAH. Edom-Rome established and spread this false gospel using the Hebrew Scriptures, which reveals only the history of the Hebrew people, and the writings only speak to these people.

For over 2000 years, Edom-Rome has committed untold violence against Israel to accomplish their goal of destroying Israel both physically and spiritually. And, in a public article published in 2000AD, Pope John Paul II of the Christian Roman Catholic Church recognized and admitted to atrocities committed by the Roman church and asked: "the children of the church" for forgiveness. The article stated, "... For the first time in history, John Paul II will confess the sins committed... in the service of truth, intolerance, and violence against dissidents, religious wars: violence and abuse of the Crusades: and violent methods of the Inquisition" (The Vatican Information Services, March 12, 2000). This apology, however, did not name nor address the specific people that Edom-Rome has had a perpetual hatred and has committed untold violence against them. The article did not explain that they directed their viciousness against the Negro Hebrew Israelites, the chosen people of YAHUAH. In another recent article of April 2019, written by Giada Zampano of the Associated Press, and recoded in a video presentation. Pope Francis at the Vatican kneeled and kissed the feet of South Sudan's African rival leaders in a show of humility. He stated, "I express my heartfelt hope that the hostilities will finally cease, that the armistice will be respected, that political and ethnic divisions will be surmounted and that there will be a lasting peace for the common good of all those citizens who dream of building the nation." As an unaware observer, it may appear that the Pope is bowing because he wants peace between these rival brothers. Still, he is bowing and kissing the feet of the Hebrew Israelites whom Edom-Rome has tried to destroy these many centuries. It was in Sudan where Edom-Rome forced many Hebrew Israelites to convert to Christianity and Islam or compelled into slavery or murdered if they did not convert. He kissed their feet because he was compelled to do so by the Highest YAHUAH as he said they would, "The sons also of them that afflicted thee shall come bending unto thee; and all they that despised thee shall bow themselves down at the soles of thy feet; and they shall call thee, The city of YAHUAH, The Zion of the Holy One of Israel," (Isaiah 60:14). I am sure he kissed their feet to pretend to apologize, but he did not identify the atrocities Rome committed against the fore-parents of these Hebrews in the past. As Scripture says, they hold themselves not guilty. Because they believe what they did the Highest sanctioned, and they will not be held responsible for their actions. "Thus saith YAHUAH my

ELOHIYM; Feed the flock of the slaughter; whose possessors slay them, and hold themselves not guilty: and they that sell them say, Blessed be YAHUAH; for I am rich: and their shepherds pity them not" (Zechariah 11:4-5).

ROME, A CHRISTIAN CENTER

Along with the seven churches in Asia, Rome emerged as a leading Christian center from 100AD (Frend, 1984). During this period, the Christian Church had presbyter-bishops rather than a solitary monarchical bishop, Greek was the church's language, and they based the underlying social message on woes with famine and pestilence among them. Many Christians denounced the merchants who traded between the East and Rome, and Christianity opposed many of the values the rulers of the Roman Empire had accepted (Frend, 1984). As severe Hellenization intensified, different teachings and beliefs caused many divisions among the body of believers.

One leader to influence the Christian teachings was Marcion, whom Roman leaders considered being a prominent believer and teacher. He developed a dualist belief system and wrote his thoughts about YAHUAH, the ELOHIYM of Abraham, Isaac, and Jacob in a book title, 'The Contradictions.' Marcion hypothesized that there were many contradictions between the Old and New Testaments. He contrasted every point of the 'judicial god' with the god of goodness. He concluded that YAHUAH'S dealings with His Chosen people, the Jews, had nothing to do with Christianity, which proclaimed his wonder, majesty, might, and an amazing promise of the gospel. Marcion believed Jesus was the savior sent by God and that Paul the Apostle was his chief apostle to the Gentiles. Marcion equated YAHUAH with God as a judge and ruler. He described Jesus as a God of love and mercy. He ascribed these aspects and characteristics in two separate principles-the righteous and wrathful God of the Old Testament who created the world versus a god of the gospel of Jesus, who is only love and mercy. Marcion understood what the prophets wrote was not allegorical and must be accepted or rejected on its merits (Frend, 1984). However, scripture proves that he was wrong. It was not only Paul who was called to preach to the Israelite Gentiles, but YAHUAH also called Peter to preach to the Israelites identified as gentiles in the diaspora, "And when there had been much disputing, Peter rose, and said unto them, Men and brethren, ye know how that a good while ago YAHUAH chose among us, that the Gentiles by my mouth should hear the word of the gospel, and believe' (Acts 15:7).

The contradictions that Marcion advocated came about because of the Hellenized Greco-Roman mindset of the people living in the Empire who believed in two gods, a terrible and vengeful god and the other loving and kind. They wanted a pathway to eternal life without the laws and instructions, as proclaimed by YAHUAH to Israel. Therefore they incorporated the teachings of the mystery religions. In Marcion's view, Jesus saved the entire world when He came to redeem the scattered tribes of Israel back to YAHUAH ELOHIYM. The attempts of teachers, like Marcion, to change the course of history by espousing a replacement theology, confused Israel and, today, many continue to follow the beast system of Edom-Rome identified in Revelation, "And they worshipped the dragon which gave power unto the beast: and they worshiped the beast, saying who is like unto the beast? Who is able to make war with him' (Revelation 13:4)?

Rome's influence over Judaea and the Judeans began over a hundred years before YAHUSHA was born. Judaea was a vassal state of Rome which earlier had existed under the Greek Empire. It was this reason the disciples worried and wanted to know if YAHUSHA would set up the kingdom at that time. Because, by the time he appeared with the ministry of redemption for Israel, the Greco-Roman culture had already entrenched itself into the mindset of the people. The dispersed of Israel had been in the diaspora for over six hundred years living as Greek and Roman citizens throughout Asia, Africa, and what later became known as Europe. These cultures had impacted the way the Hebrews conducted their lives, and while they still knew they were Hebrew, the culture of the Gentiles they lived among had influenced their attitude. Most of them kept the laws and returned to Jerusalem for the Feast Days, and they continued to support the Temple with their finances. And, around 40AD, Philo, the Alexandrian philosopher, noted that although the passionate convictions that inspired and directed the Hebrews' life had diminished, they still believed they were the people who alone saw YAHUAH. Philo added that they accepted the discipline imposed upon them to result from divine ordinances and were ready to face the consequences when they refused to break YAHUAH'S laws as instructed by Edom-Rome.

Josephus, the Jewish historian, concurs as he described to his pagan opponents of the convictions the Hebrew Israelites held, which attested to their faith. "There should be nothing astonishing in our facing death on behalf of our laws with courage; no other nation can equal," he said. "It is an instinct with every Hebrew, from the day of his birth, to regard (the books of the Law) as decrees of God, to abide by them, and, if need be, cheerfully to die for them." Edom-Rome knew it would be difficult to dislodge the Hebrews from their beliefs, so they used every form of physical torture and terrorism to destroy them physically, spiritually, then by mixing the religion of the Hebrew Israelites with the pagan religions of Babylon, Greece, and Rome, and later Islam. Many Hebrews surrendered to martyrdom rather than submit to the dictates of Edom-Rome.

EMPEROR CONSTANTINE CONVERTS TO CHRISTIANITY

The era of the martyrs ended with Emperor Constantine as he entered Rome in triumph over Maxentius, who he defeated in a battle across the Milvain Bridge. This victory resulted in the Roman Senate declaring Constantine senior Augustus on 29th

October. They believed his success resulted from a heavenly protector. However, for Constantine, it was a question of which one? Because as early as 320 to 322AD, Christians in Rome believed that Constantine had seen this vision of a cross of light, and he used that experience to influence the Roman Christian Church. According to Frend (1984), the Romans knew him as a sun worshiper influenced by Christian teachings. The church leaders believed that Constantine's decision to join the Church came about as he realized the powerful influence of the Christian church on the citizens of Rome. He deduced that it would be best if he merged his political power with the power of the already-influential church. These things happened after three hundred years of persecution by many of the Emperors of Rome, including Constantine's father. He joined the Christian Church then announced that he would hold the first Ecumenical Council for the churches spread throughout the Empire at Nicaea in 325AD. Constantine convened this council of churches to bring the believers together to discuss the many schisms in the body. Historians too, believed Constantine's strategy was less of a conviction and more about bringing the churches under the control of the Roman government (Frend, 1984)

After declaring his conversion to the Christian faith, he described the vision he saw of Jesus, the Christ of God, who appeared to him. They say he saw a cross of light. Eusebius recounts Constantine's story that the symbol represented the cross ☧ (Chi-Rho), which was yet unused by the Christians. The light had an inscription that said, 'In Hoc Signo Vinces!" It meant, 'Under this sign thou shalt conquer!' Constantine told Eusebius that the voice he heard told him to go forth with this cross as a symbol and banner and conquer nations. He then ordered the artificers to make the symbol according to the instructions he gave them. They made the standard cross in the likeness of that sign. The artificers designed and formed it as a spear a safeguard in engagements with his enemies. It took shape and form of a long spear overlaid with gold, crossed by a piece laid over it. On the top was a crown formed of gold and jewels interweaved on which they placed two letters showing the name of Christ - the Greek letter P being intersected by X in its center. The Romans then called this the Labarum (Dean Dudley, 1880).

Constantine claimed the vision he saw was of Jesus telling him

to conquer using that sign. However, Hebrew Scriptures prove the sign did not originate in Hebrew practices. YAHUSHA, the son of YAHUAH, did not believe in the cross's symbol as it was of Greco-Roman pagan origin and would be idolatry in the eyes of YAHUAH. Eusebius and Lactantius reported that Jesus, whom Constantine saw in this vision, became known as the Christ, the god of the Edomite Christians (Frend, 1984). They also interpreted the vision in a solar context because Constantine was a sun worshipper, and he reformed it to fit the Christian beliefs. George Latura did not believe the description given by Eusebius and Lactantius. He advanced an alternate explanation of the Labarum symbol as Plato's visible god, Timaeus, which represented the intersection of the Milky Way and the Zodiacal Light. He confirms it signified a rare apparition important to pagan beliefs that the Christian bishops used and reinvented as a Christian symbol. Therefore, many of the Hebrew Israelites who believed in the HAMASHIACH never accepted neither the symbol nor Emperor Constantine.

THE COUNCIL OF NICEA, 325AD

The participants of the Council convened from all churches throughout Africa, Asia, and Europe. These included Syrians and Cilicians, Phoenicians, Arabs, and Palestinians. Besides these, there were also the Libyans, Thebans, and those from Mesopotamia and Persia, Pontus, Galatia, Pamphylia, Cappadocia, and many other countries throughout the Empire (Dean Dudley, 1880).

According to Dean Dudley, the principal object of this Synod was to discuss and settle, upon a firm basis, the true Christian doctrine respecting the Divine nature of Christ, and his precise relation to the Almighty Deity of the material Universe, because there was a controversy regarding the belief that Jesus was part of a trinity of gods along with the Holy Spirit and was equal with the Most High YAHUAH. What they also needed to establish was a formula of faith in the god (Jesus the Christ). The Bishops sought to divide YAHUAH'S divinity into three different gods, even creating a god out of the Holy Spirit. According to Ibn Ezra, when this teaching about Jesus started, "few believed in the man (Jesus) of whom they made a God. However, when Rome believed, in the days of Constantine, who changed the whole religion, and put an image of that man (Jesus) upon his standard, only the Edomites observed the New Law. Therefore, they called Rome, the Kingdom of Edom."[9] At the end of the meeting, the Council concluded agreeing with the Emperor that, "Jesus was the Christ, the divine, the Word of God, God of God, Light of Light, Life of life, the only begotten Son, the first-born of all creatures begotten of the Father before all ages; by whom all things were made, and they were one being with the Father, etcetera, etcetera" (Dean Dudley, 1880).

Regarding the final deliberations and decisions of the Council the Canons and Decrees supported by Constantine the recorder of the events summarized the results;

> I think the best time for the Easter festival would have been the ancient, honored day of the Jewish Passover. On a whim of Constantine, he opposed it because, as a Roman, he hated the nation of the Jews, which his country had long detested and persecuted. The truth forced him to admit, however, that God had ever preferred them before all other people. His change in the day of rest arose from the same unjust prejudice. The Sabbath was as good for Gentiles as it had been for Israel; and, although Christ did

not regard it as holy, he appointed no other in its stead (Dean Dudley, 1880). [10]

The results brought about by this council confirm the official start of Christianity as the faith of Edom-Rome the religion of the Edomites. And, the teachings and ideas have little to do with the truth brought by the HAMASHIACH of being sent to redeem Israel back to the Father. In the Rabbinic literature an account by MARC Saperstein tells how the Israelites responded in Christian Europe when the Crusaders, Israel's enemy sought to destroy them for not accepting the teachings of the Roman Christian church although they accepted the HAMASHIACH;

> The foe Encío proclaimed in the community's hearing the enemy be driven from the city and be put to flight. Panic was great in the town. Each Jew (Israelite) in the bishop's court girded on his weapons, and all moved towards the palace gate to fight the Crusaders and the Burghers. They fought each other up to the gate, but the sins of the Jews (Israelites) brought it about that the enemy overcame them and took the gate. The hand of the LORD was heavy against his people. All the Gentiles were gathered together against the Jews (Israelites) in the courtyard to blot out their name, and the strength of our people weakened when they saw the wicked Edomites overpowering them. [11]

YAHUSHA'S word rings clear in his warnings to the Hebrew Israelites that there will come a time when those who kill them would think they are doing the Most High a favor. "True" Christians are Edomites, the descendants of Esau, who is Edom-Rome, and they despise the descendants of Jacob-Israel. They continue to carry out hateful acts against them to this day. Edom-Rome is a hypocrite and knows how to hide behind the trappings of religion. The Hebrew Israelites who they labeled "Jews" were not the white Edomites known as Christians or the Edomite Jewish people. It was Edom-Rome the white Edomites who persecuted the Hebrew Israelites even when they were in the Christian faith but refused to accept the Pantheon gods and practices of the Romans.

When the Synod concluded, they adopted twenty canons, which gave no reference to the TORAH. These synodical decrees copied and translated sought to settle inevitable schisms, including; "In the first place the impiety," as the Synod termed it of Arius, who they condemned for his blasphemous sentiments, his belief that Jesus was not equal to God the Father. The council settled the coalition question, and then, that of the Paschal Festival, and that of the Novatian schism.

It was Edom-Rome who changed what the followers of YAHUSHA learned and then excommunicated those who opposed the teachings of the Roman church. These men tried to show why Rome's doctrine was an error. In the rabbinical writings they explained why YAHUSHA could not be ELOHIYM;

> The Divine Attributes, or Perfections, cannot be personified or made personal, without idolatry. Therefore,

this other gospel was the embodiment of the Divine perfection, attributes, powers, or virtues, which laid the foundation, and upon which was built the whole system of the heathen mythology, or worship of the 'fabulous deities,' or 'false gods.' Thus, we see that all heathen or pagan Rome (of which Christian Rome or Daniel's "four (gentile) beasts" or kingdoms were but the high image. Which was set up and established upon the significant error of dividing the divine unity into separate and distinct gods, or attributes, or perfections or virtues, personified or made substantive. This we can see from Saturn, Vesta, Jupiter, Mercury, Diana, of Ephesus, down to the statue of the Virgin Mary, which succeeded Diana, and then came Jesus Christ, of whom they made a god, as they had done of all the rest of their extraordinary men, under the heathen mythology, whom they declared were all begotten, and sons, (as they declared he was,) by some of their gods having cohabitation with women.[12]

Constantine used his conversion to Christianity as motivation to call for the Ecumenical Council of Nicaea. At this Synod, the god of the empire colluded with the God of the Christian church. The Mighty Catholic (Christian) church became little more than a baptized Roman Empire, which meant that they had transformed and converted Rome. The capital of the Old Empire became the capital of the Christian Empire, and they continued the office of the Pontifex Maximus in the form of the Pope

(Alexander C. Flick).[13] Christianity had become an institute of the government, which was no better than the old religion of Paganism. And the church soon became transformed, so that Christ would have been ashamed of its name because as soon as people could make their fortunes in the church, it became a fruitful field of ambition (Dean Dudley, 1880).

PAPAL ROME

Edom-Rome replaced by Papal Rome attempted to change the Highest YAHUAH with the man, Jesus Christ. The leaders of Edom-Rome appointed popes whose titles described them as substitutes of God, and Constantine became the first one with this title. The popes identified with the titles Dyaus Peter or Divis Pater or Zeus Pater, whose exalted title was Optimus Maximus (Nigosian, 2000). Other names that mean the same thing are; VICARIUS, meaning substitute of Christ, FILII DEI meaning Vica of the son of God, which is the official title of the pope inscribed in his MITRE. Also, LUDOVICUS, which means Vica of the Court, DVX CLERI meaning Captain of the Clergy, and REX LATIN VS SACER DOS, which means King of the Romans Priest. The followers of the religion know the Vatican as SANCTA LVX DEI, which they define as the Holy light of God. These Latin titles are all synonymous with Antichrist, who assumes the power of God on the earth.

The Roman Empire with the Church became the imposter "holy nation" of Israel. They used a false religion, a false god and image, and false people and nations to replace the actual people of YAHUAH. Warder Cresson made the connection between Babylon, Rome, Edom, and Christianity under Constantine after 325AD. They sought to be leaders of a people without laws that gave rights and privileges, and he noted the similarities described in 'Religions of Manarchies':

> A government tolerating freedom of opinion in religion must tolerate freedom of opinion in politics, for as religion comprehends duties to society and God and as rights and duties in society are correlative, freedom in religion leads to freedom in everything else. All great despots have understood this, and have, therefore, always tried to surround themselves with an "odor of sanctity," by courting a connection between religion and politics. For this purpose, Constantine the Great professed Christianity, made it the religion of the Roman Empire; and to counteract its free tendencies, he corrupted it with the old State religion, that Heathen Mythology in which they had educated him. He, therefore, converted the Pantheon into a church, gave to all its statue of Jupiter an image of St. Peter, and changed all the fast days to the gods in the Calendar to Saint's Days. Diana became the Virgin Mary, Venus, Mary Magdalene, and they metamorphosed Minerva, so handy with her needle into Saint Dorcas, the patroness of sewing societies. Thus Christianity, which is spiritual, (they say,) which tolerates no idolatry, which

places no human intermediaries (except Jesus) between God and man, was defiled with the grossness of the superstitions which it was sent to dispel, to enable a crafty politician to stupefy humankind to govern them absolutely.

The destiny for Rome reveals it is unashamed of having subjected itself to a "holy nation" status an undeserved fate, which fits into the context of messianic apocalyptic (Warder Cresson). Rome believes that papal authority is the ultimate power which Peter the Apostle passed down to the popes. Although based on historical evidence, Peter was just another name for Jupiter, Rome's chief god. Christopher B. Coleman translated the Latin document into English that describes this authority:

> As the blessed Peter saw to have made up vicar of the Son of God on earth, so are the Pontiffs who are the representatives of that same chief of the apostles, should get from us and our empire the power of supremacy more magnificent than the clemency of our earthly imperial serenity seems to have conceded to it, choosing that same chief of the apostles and his vicars to be our constant intercessors with God. To the extent of our earthly Imperial power, we have decreed that his holy Roman Church shall be honored with veneration and that more than our empire and the earthly throne the most sacred seat of the Blessed Peter shall be gloriously exalted, we giving to it power, and dignity of glory, and vigor, and

honor imperial. And we ordain and decree he shall have the supremacy as well over the four principal seats, Alexandria, Antioch, Jerusalem, and Constantinople, as also over all the churches of God in the whole earth. And the Pontiff, who at the time shall be at the head of the Holy Roman church itself, shall be more exalted than, the chief over, all the priests of the entire world, and according to his judgment everything which is provided for the service of God and the stability of the faith of Christians is to be administered.

This papal authority is represented by the Dragon worshiped in Jesus Christ, the deity that Rome established in place of the true HAMASHIACH. The Rabbinic literature confirms that the Christian Church represents Rome. Kimchi, Ibn-Ezra, Maimonides, and Abarbanel, all sages of ancient Israel agree with the preceding scripture testimony that all Gentile Christians are the seed or children of Esau, who is Edom.[14] Modern rabbinical writers concur that the people of Rome and the West are the descendants of Esau and have come together with the Jews, under the banner labeled Judeo-Christian. The rabbis state, "One day they will say, here was his palace, theater, his court. One look at the site, and there will be nothing." The Christian church is guilty first of the "inexorable sin of schism, in separating herself from the first and only true Church of God, which was the Jewish Church (Warder Cresson). Edom-Rome created another religion, then joined with those who say they are Jews and formed the

Judeo-Christian church. Ibn Ezra, an Israelite Jew, Biblical commentator, and philosopher, expounds what the fate of Rome would be because of their actions, "Rome, which led us away captive, is of the seed of Kittiym and so the Targumist has said, in Numbers 24:24 "And ships shall come from the coast of Kittiym and shall afflict Asshur, and shall afflict Eber, and he also shall perish forever." This Kittiym, Edom-Rome, YAHUAH will root them from off the face of the earth because they made a god of one of their deities who deceived the entire world of Israel and called him "the saving spirit" Jesus Christ who replaced YAHUSHA the "warrior Messiah" of the contemporary Jewish model" (Frend, 1984).

THE IMPACT OF MYSTERY RELIGIONS ON JUDAISM AND CHRISTIANITY

During the period of Roman rule, the pervasive influence of the Hellenistic culture and the Mystery religions had a great impact on Judaism and Christianity. The universal ideas and philosophies of Christianity evolved from the teachings of the Babylonians, Egyptians, Greeks, and Romans, who were polytheistic and worshiped many gods. Edom-Rome added Jesus Christ, who became one of their chief gods. In their belief system, the Edomite Christians described Jesus as the son of God and Mary as the Mother of God. This belief placed Mary above God as she is the mother, and he the child similar to the religions of the pagans. Alexander Hislop (2012), believes the image of the beast to be Mary, the Mother of God. He notes this as a common theme among the pagan religions, and the attributes all refer to the Babylonian Madonna and not the mother of YAHUSHA. Thus, Christianity became another mystery of religion. Nigosian (2000), notes that all Mystery religions included deities, gods, goddesses, oracles, seasonal festivals, Emperor Worship, and secret rites made available to people seeking a personal and satisfying religious experience. They termed the experience mysterious rather than mystical because they kept the rites secret from all others. The Roman Christians incorporated many of these forms and practices of worship into Christianity, which solidified its pagan roots. The Roman Christians teach that Jesus the Christ, along with GOD the father, and the Holy Spirit, made up a Trinity of gods yet, one God. Hebrew Scriptures, however, does not support this theory as Scripture shows the Father sent YAHUSHA (Jesus) his son to redeem Israel, back to him. But, Edom-Rome took authority and twisted the teachings to reflect that the Most High YAHUAH, the son YAHUSHA and the Ruach HaKodesh (Holy Spirit) are three persons in one like the gods of the Babylonian mystery religions.

The Hellenized teachers and philosophers of Christianity taught the doctrine that Jesus (YAHUSHA) was equal to the Highest YAHUAH. These early Gnostic Christians who advanced this belief are regarded as the fathers of the Christian Church. These fathers included Basilides, Cerinthus, and they credit Clement of Alexandria, Valentinus, and Marcion as being the root of Christian beliefs (Nigosian, 2000). Such dogmas ranged from astrology and complex mythology to beliefs that elaborated in contemplative and philosophical terms. And, despite the many differences in teachings and practices, the overarching gnostic teaching accounted for human nature as being compounded of a mortal material body and an immortal ethereal soul. The Christian church today continues to expand these lessons, as most people who believe in God believe YAHUAH made them with three parts, comprising a spirit, soul, and body, like the three parts they say make up the Highest YAHUAH, the Father, Son, and Holy Spirit. However, YAHUAH created humanity in his image and likeness. He formed them from the dust of the ground and then breathed into them, and they became living souls. His breath gave life to their bodies.

The Israelites knew these truths before YAHUAH dispersed them into the many captivities. They knew and believed that everything, both good and evil, came from YAHUAH, and they also knew things could not possess them, but they could possess things. Yet, after the Judeans returned from Babylonian captivity and being influenced by the Babylonian religious thought, they began to perceive YAHUAH as only good and Satan as the author and representative of evil (Nigosian, 2000). These new thoughts led certain sects of the Hebrews to adopt the belief that Satan was YAHUAH'S antagonist, called the adversary. But, Scripture shows that YAHUAH has no opposite and equal adversary because he is the Creator of all things, both good and evil. He is the Alpha and the Omega, the beginning and the end, and the author and finisher of our faith as he says, "I form the light, and create darkness: I make peace, and create evil: I YAHUAH do all these things" (Isaiah 45:7).

Most of the early believers did not accept the teachings of the Roman Christian Church because they understood YAHUAH, not as a mystical, ethereal spirit and experience, but their Father, the Highest ELOHIYM the ELOHIYM above all. He had direct contact with Israel through the Law and Tanakh, and he spoke to them through His Prophets. The nations which surrounded them knew this to be so. And, after the destructive anti-Judean riot in Alexandria in 138AD, Philo noted that "the Jews living in Judaea are many, physically strong, and mentally courageous, and prefer to die for the traditions in a spirit which some of their traducers would call barbaric but which is free and noble." He believed and added that "A glorious death met in defense of the Law is a kind of life" (Frend, 1984). They label them Barbarians because of these acts.

ESAU-EDOM REPRESENTS ROME

Mireille Hadas-Lebel, a modern French historian who specializes in the history of Judaism, comments on the relationship of Esau and Jacob as it relates to Rome in Babylon and states, "Esau-Edom chosen to represent Rome in Babylon because Edom appears as an enemy who has harassed Israel throughout its history." However, we need to ask which Israel?

Because they have hidden true Israel in the "wilderness of the people" for about four hundred years, and most of true Israel do not understand or even believe they are the children of Jacob-Israel. She appears to base her observation on the imposter Jewish people living in Palestine today and not the Negro descendants of Jacob-Israel. They have suffered much more than mere harassment by Edom-Rome. Edom-Rome has attempted to carry out a complete genocide of the Hebrew Israelites over the centuries.

As a historian, Lebel knows that the Jewish people occupying the land of Palestine are not the true Israelites. They are the imposters harassed by their brethren to make it appear they are the enemies; Jacob and Esau. She describes the acts against the Jewish people as mere harassment because to be harsh on those who committed these acts against them would be biting the hand that feeds it. Lebel is aware that what has happened to the Jewish people now living in Palestine does not compare to the myriad atrocities carried out by Edom-Rome against the true people of YAHUAH. It is apparent they never thought the true Israelites would awaken and come into the knowledge of the truth about Jacob and Esau's identity. Anyone teaching Jewish history knows the truth about this world's history, so they are better able to write false accounts. She would know that the Jewish people in Palestine are not the descendants of Jacob-Israel. The Holocaust event is one version of persecution created by Edom-Rome against the Jewish people to hide the atrocities they have committed, and at the same time, still committing against the Israelites. The Hebrew Israelites are the Negroes found throughout most of the African Continent and those scattered to the four corners of the earth and the isles of the sea via the transatlantic slave trade. These are the people whom YAHUSHA will gather when he returns, "And I will bring you out from the people, and will gather you out from the people, and will gather you out of the countries wherein ye are scattered, with a mighty hand, and with a stretched out arm, and with fury poured out" (Ezekiel 20:34).

Esau-Edom wanted not only to destroy the physical descendants of Jacob, but they wanted to lead them to eternal death. They attempted to do this by having them join in religious practices that caused them to break the commandments of the Highest YAHUAH. In Esau-Edom's mind, these actions by Israel would prevent them from attaining the kingdom to come. However, just like YAHUAH created Esau for wickedness, YAHUAH has also created Jacob as his righteous seed. Therefore, it is not Jacob's choice to be righteous, YAHUAH chose him for that purpose, and there is nothing Edom-Rome can do to change the outcome. And why Shem, the progenitor of Abraham and his descendants, explained to Rebekah while she was still pregnant, "Two nations are in your womb, two nations with each its own universe, a Torah, the other sin" (Berachot 57b).[15] Esau, who is Edom, represents the nation of sin in the earth, which is his universe, and Scripture describes him as the man of sin. The TORAH portrays Jacob-Israel as the man of righteousness, who will rule when YAHUAH'S kingdom comes on the earth based on the covenant He made with Abraham and his seed forever. Thus, this covenant stands, and it is not based on any actions taken by the descendants of Jacob, "All these things are the book of the covenant of the Highest YAHUAH, even the law which

Moses commanded for a heritage unto the congregations of Jacob" (Ecclesiasticus 24:23).

The covenant YAHUAH made with Abraham, Isaac, and Jacob gave righteousness to Jacob

Mystery Babylon The Great

and his descendants before they were born, just like he assigned Esau and his descendants' sin before they had committed any sin. They were both created for YAHUAH's purpose to fulfill his plan. Scripture further confirms that after YAHUAH reveals the man of sin, He shall return. Edom-Rome, the man of sin, is a diverse "white" people occupying and leading the nations of the earth today. They are play-actors who have deceived the world. Because they are in disguise, YAHUAH will have to make known their identity. Therefore, YAHUSHA reminded his followers they should guard against being deceived, "Let no man deceive you by any means: for that day shall not come, except there comes a falling away first, and that man of sin be revealed, the son of perdition" (2 Thessalonians 2:3).

All Christian churches today, along with Islam and Judaism, come out of Edom-Rome and form the mysterious Babylonian religion. Edom-Rome, the Mother church, describes the other churches that came out of her as her daughters. And, they have adopted all her ways. Historical evidence shows that "Rome is the last empire in history and will have no successor from their family lineage. They will return the rulership of the earth to its rightful owner, the people of YAHUAH, Jacob-Israel, a crown they usurped" (Warder Cresson).

Therefore, YAHUSHA came to Jerusalem to redeem the Northern tribes of Israel cut off by the Father YAHUAH for disobedience to His TORAH. But, because Edom-Rome ruled, they seized authority over the assembly and Scriptures and created another religion. This universal religion became dominant and, in 1825AD, on the occasion of the jubilee of Pope Leo XII, The Roman Christian church struck a medal bearing the image of the pope on one side and, on the other side, the church of Rome symbolized as a woman holding a cross in her left hand and a cup in her right hand with the surrounding legend 'Sedet super Universum' which means "The entire world is her seat" (Hislop, 2012). This act by Edom-Rome shows that they know their place in history and have embraced their role. Although most people today do not acknowledge Rome's influence over the earth, the Pope who sits as king in Caesar's seat knows they rule the entire world, and the nations' governments must surrender to them.

Pope Leo XII confirmed the revelation that the Apostle John saw and recorded in Revelation as YAHUAH carried him away in the spirit. He saw the Roman Empire being represented as

Babylon established in the book of Daniel. The mystery religion he saw was the woman symbolic of the false church (nation). Edom-Rome, as a usurper, has power over the nations and Israel in the wilderness of the people where there is no life or light. "So he carried me away in the spirit into the wilderness: and I saw a woman sit upon a scarlet-colored beast full of names of blasphemy, having seven heads and ten horns. and the woman was arrayed in purple and scarlet color, and decked with gold and precious stones and pearls, having a golden cup in her hand full of abominations and filthiness of her fornication: and upon her forehead was a name written, Mystery, Babylon the great, the mother of harlots and abominations of the earth," (Revelation 17:3-5).

ISRAEL'S LIFE BEFORE THE INFLUENCE OF PAGAN RELIGIONS

The early records of the religious history of the Israelites date from Abraham, the father of Isaac and grandfather of Jacob and his twelve sons. Biblical history shows that the twelve tribes of Jacob-Israel went into Egyptian slavery when an Assyrian king conquered Egypt and enslaved the children of Israel. Moses delivered them from this bondage in Egypt in the thirteenth century BC after about one hundred and twenty years of slavery (Nigosian, 2000). They moved into the Promised Land and lived in peace for many years as the people whom YAHUAH the Highest had chosen. Before the religions of Babylon and its surrounding neighbors influenced the Israelites, the Israelites lived in a theocratic state in which YAHUAH vested power in the priesthood and the High Priest ruled overall, even after there were secular Kings. The laws, statutes, and commandments guided them in how they lived. They fulfilled their way of living by obeying the covenant that YAHUAH wrote and gave to Moses for them.

However, after the Judeans returned to Judaea, from Babylonian captivity, many of their ideas and practices reflected the Zoroastrian religious thought of the Persians. Some leaders adopted the concept and belief that the Spirit or the Holy Spirit was an ethical principle that permeated the world and held it together. They believed it to be a divine force that taught human beings God's will (Nigosian, 2000). This idea led to some Hebrews adopting the belief that the Holy Spirit was another god separate and apart from YAHUAH, and to which they assigned the feminine attributes. Later, they added it as a mediator of divine revelation in the New Testament scriptures. However, many Judeans disagreed with this thought, which resulted in several sects forming all holding differing beliefs. Some Judeans remained true to the teachings of the TORAH and rejected the ideas and concepts of the Mystery religions of Babylon. The Judeans knew YAHUAH to be the Highest ELOHIYM of Israel, and the Spirit he gave to Israel was His Spirit, which is his temperament, not a separate entity. "But over Israel, he appointed none angel of ruach (spirit), for He alone is their ruler, and He will guard them and require them at the hand of His angels and His ruachoth (Spirit), and at the hand of all His powers so that He may guard them and bless them, and that they may be His and He may be theirs from henceforth forever" (Jubilees 15:32). The Highest YAHUAH's Spirit is in Israel and leads and guides them, not a separate god-like being the Christian Church depicts as a dove.   The Hebrew Israelites lived by the traditions and guiding principles of their faith, written in the TORAH. They understood who they were and sacrificed their lives rather than live in the face of breaking the Covenant Laws. Knowledge of their identity in YAHUAH caused them to have extreme national pride. They knew the Highest YAHUAH, not through a mystical experience, but direct participation. No other nation had this kind of relationship with the ELOHIYM of Israel. YAHUAH chose them, and they committed to maintaining a special sense of responsibility toward YAHUAH and his commandments. Edom-Rome could not define Israel in terms of the Christian catechism, the Jewish cabbalistic teachings, or the teachings of the Koran. The truth about their identity created a sense of jealousy and hatred unmatched in history by the descendants of Edom-Rome. The relationship the Father YAHUAH had with the Israelites was supreme above all the other people on the earth. Therefore, Edom-Rome sought to change the bond of their relationship with YAHUAH by spiritualizing the natural connection the Israelites had with the Father by adding the pagan Zoroastrian teachings of Babylon.

Edom-Rome wanted to wipe out the National pride the Hebrews expressed as the Chosen people of the Highest YAHUAH. This spiritualized version of Israel's religion made it possible for Edom-Rome to offer all nations the opportunity to come under the umbrella of Israel by converting to Judaism and Christianity. Later, they added a forced conversion to Islam. All who believed in Christianity had to receive and accept the teachings of the Messiah Jesus, and he would save them from their sins, and it would assure them of eternal life with him in heaven. Edom-Rome wanted an alternate route to enter the kingdom but, YAHUSHA warned, "Verily, verily, I say unto you, He that entereth not by the door into the sheepfold, but climbeth up some other way, the same is a thief and a robber" (John 10:1). The Edomite Jews living in Palestine and the Edomite Christians all ruling the earth today as converted Rome is a thief and robber of Israel's identity and heritage

The two main religions created by Edom-Rome are Christianity and Islam. These religions have become the largest on earth, with over two billion people. The Israelites and people of other nations converted to Christianity by force when Edom-Rome conquered their territories. They report Christianity to cover all of Europe, Britain, Canada, and the Americas and has an estimated following of over 1.78 billion people worldwide. They say Islam is the second largest after Christianity and has about 950,000,000 followers (Nigosian, 2000). The Hebrew Israelites, in its destroyed state, make up many of the members of these

Babylonian religions. Because they have lost their true heritage, they have not just joined the religions, but have become one with Babylon. They follow the man of sin, Esau, who is Edom, whom YAHUAH will soon uncover as he reveals the true identity of the descendants of Jacob-Israel, "Then shall the righteous man stand in great boldness before the face of such as have afflicted him, and made no account of his labors. When they see it, they shall be troubled with terrible fear, and shall be amazed at the strangeness of his salvation, so far beyond all they looked for" (Wisdom of Solomon 5:1-2).

Israel's history confirms the truth of YAHUAH's existence and his continual activity among the people of the earth. The Highest YAHUAH allowed Edom-Rome to place Israel under harsh bondage just as they were in Egypt. He then sent his servant Moses to deliver them out of Egyptian slavery. Based on today's Gregorian calendar, the Hebrew Israelites have experienced over two thousand years of persecution and destruction, including four hundred years of slavery and bondage at the hands of Edom-Rome. As YAHUAH sent Moses to deliver the children of Israel out of Egypt, he will send YAHUSHA to deliver them out of the captivity of Edom-Rome, also described in scripture as Egypt. Millions of Hebrew Israelites have died throughout the ages at the hand of Edom-Rome, and the catacombs of Europe and Rome have kept the evidence. In the catacombs of Rome, there are millions of Hebrew Israelite skulls and bones. As the prophecy predicted, YAHUAH will give power to his two witnesses, Judah and Israel, to do miracles, and Edom-Rome, the fourth beast, would kill them. Their bodies will lay in the streets of Jerusalem, the same place where they crucified the HAMASHIACH. This prophecy is symbolic of what occurred to Israel in Jerusalem and throughout the earth. Although the Christian Church believes two other witnesses will come and fulfill this prophecy. But the fact shows that the Highest has chosen his two witnesses. They are getting ready to rise and stand upon their feet again as the dry bones come together, and YAHUAH breathes life into them. Their rising will bring fear to the nations of the earth. "And their dead bodies shall lie in the street of the great city which spiritually is called Sodom and Egypt, where also our HAMASHIACH was crucified... And after three days and a half, the RUACH CHAYIYM from YAHUAH entered them, and they stood on their feet; and great fear fell upon them which saw them. And they heard a great voice from heaven saying unto them, Come up hither. And they ascended to heaven in a cloud; and their enemies beheld them" (Revelation 11:8, 11-12).

Today, Israel is a Nation of people scattered among the nations of this world and not established in terms of Christian theological categories or has its roots in the cabbalistic teachings of Judaism or even those of the Koran. YAHUAH chose them as the righteous and to be above all people upon the earth. While in captivity, Edom-Rome forced Israel to submit to the Babylonian religions where they have worshiped other gods. Nevertheless, YAHUAH has secured the faith of the Hebrew Israelites on divine-human actions for a specific purpose, "For the gifts and calling of YAHUAH are without repentance" (Romans 11:29). As they are his righteous people, they will desire to keep the laws of YAHUAH once He gives them the right mind. They will not keep the laws to become righteous. He created two vessels from one lump of clay to fulfill His purpose and His will on the earth, and His word will not return void. Therefore, the revised history of events or the change of the identity of the people will not prevent the Highest YAHUAH from accomplishing his determined will in Jacob-Israel and Esau-Edom.

---

[1] Ignatius Letter to the Smyrnaeans was written by Saint Ignatius of Antioch around 107AD to the early Christians in Smyrna. The letter contained among other doctrines the earliest recorded evidence of the use of the term "Catholic Church."

[2] Philo of Alexandria was a Hellenized Jew who lived in Alexandria Egypt. He was one of the first philosophers to interpret the Old Testament as an allegory. He mixed the Jewish religion with Plato's philosophy. He had a great influenced on the Judeans who accepted this Jewish Gnosticism.

[3] Isaac Abrabanel was born in Lisbon, Portugal, into one of the oldest and most distinguished Iberian Jewish families, who escaped massacre in Castile in 1391. He became well versed in rabbinic literature and devoted his early years to the study of Jewish philosophy.

[4] Jacob Jervell was a professor of theology at the University of Oslo. He commented on Law the gospel of Luke and Acts and states, "He (Luke) fights the Jews who charge Christian-Jews with apostasy and treachery to Israel, thus not be entitled to salvation."

[5] Edict of Theodosius a Roman Emperor signed this edict on February 27, 381, which commanded everyone to be a Christian or die. They had to accept that the Father, Son and Holy Spirit as one Godhead equal in majesty.

[6] Jean-Guenolé Daniélou was French member of the Jesuit order and a Roman Catholic cardinal. He was also a theologian and historian and a member of the Académie française.

[7] Clement, was bishop of Rome from 88 to 99AD. And, Pliny known as the younger, was the governor of Bithynia in northern Turkey.

[8] Eusebius of Nicomedia was the man who baptized Constantine the Great. He was a bishop of Berytus (modern –day Beirut. He was later made the Bishop of Nicomedia where the imperial court resided. He died in 341AD.

[9] Ibn Ezra was a medieval Jewish polymath; a mathematician, astronomer, astrologer, Biblical commentator, poet and grammarian.

[10] The First Council of Nicaea was a council of Christian bishops convened in the Bithynian city of Nicaea, now Bursa province, Turkey by Roman Emperor Constantine I in AD 325.

[11] MARC Saperstein is a Professor of Jewish History and Homiletics. He has held positions at three American Universities and teaches Worlds of Medieval Judaism.

[12] Rabbinic literature/writings, in its broadest sense, can mean the entire spectrum of rabbinic writings throughout Israel's history. The term refers to literature from the Talmudic era, as opposed to medieval and modern rabbinic writing and corresponds with the term "Literature of our sages."

[13] Alexander C. Flick was a historian and university professor who taught history and political science at Syracuse University from 1899 to 1923. A specialist in European history, he also wrote on New York history, American Revolution and church history.

[14] Kimchi, Ibn-Ezra, Maimonides, and Abarbanel are Jewish sages who wrote about Esau-Edom's role in history as it relates to Christianity.

[15] Berachot is "Blessings" is the first tractate a collection of the Mishnah that primarily deals with laws relating to plants and farming. The Berachot 57b has to do with the two nations in Rebekah's womb being the proud ones.

CHAPTER 8

How Esau Is Recognized Today

ACCORDING TO MEIR LEVIN, the Rabbinic identification of Rome with the Biblical figure of Esau is basic to the deep-rooted understanding of much of the pertinent sections of the Chumash Bereishis.[1] Levin furthers that Esau's faults and shortcomings, along with his complex and tortured relationship with his brother, Jacob is seen by the Rabbis of old through the lens of his identification. The conflict between these two brothers typifies the struggle for spiritual and moral supremacy between Rome and Jerusalem. This spiritual and moral supremacy, however, belongs to Jacob only. YAHUAH created these twin brothers to bring about specific goals in the earth's history. YAHUAH called Esau, the elder brother, to rule in this age. However, Esau would like to change the outcome and rule in this world and the next. As the ruler of this world, he has used his cunning and crafty character to impersonate Jacob pretending to be righteous while wreaking havoc against the descendants of Jacob, his righteous brother, destined to rule in the kingdom to come.

The descendants of Esau are the people with dominion over the earth, today. They are the conquerors and have colonized most of the nations on the earth. They are the red people of antiquity and identify as Europeans. The Jewish Khazarian, Ashkenazi, and Sephardic Jews occupying the land of Palestine and scattered throughout the earth, are all descendants of Esau and make up the members of the religion called Judaism. These same people have created the religions of Christianity and Islam that are used to deceive Jacob's descendants. The Edomites are described as hypocrites who love to engage in wars while at the same time speaking as if they are peacemakers. They speak with a fork-tongue pretending to love with their words, but their actions reveal utter hatred towards the descendants of Jacob-Israel and the Highest YAHUAH. They are incapable of loving anything other than money, which they have used as a measurement of their success. They have designed thousands of malevolent acts intended to crush the Chosen people of YAHUAH. Despite all Edom-Rome's efforts to hide their identity, what they have done to the children of Jacob-Israel reveals who they are. They are, as the Scripture says, wicked and prepared for this purpose.

EDOMITES DOMINATE THE EARTH

Edom-Rome, as an Empire, has dominated the earth and its peoples for thousands of years. However, the white Edomites who lived among the original descendants of Japheth and mixed with them have only had complete dominion as the revised papal Roman Empire for about four hundred years. The white Edomite descendants of Esau took full control of the governments of the earth in the late seventeenth century. The original rulers of Greece and Rome were mixed people comprising the descendants of Japheth, Ham, and Esau. Later in history, Esau-Edom replaced the original descendants of Japheth through conquest and by whitening out the people of color. Which has resulted in the people known as Europeans being mingled people of Edom, Japheth, Arabs, Assyrians, and Canaanites? They are the white Europeans, the descendants of Esau, whom YAHUAH has allowed having authority over the earth today.

The nations that make up Edom-Rome appear to be separate and independent, but in fact, they are all the seed of Esau, who is Edom. And, they have joined forces as a League of Nations, which later evolved into the United Nations General Assembly in 1945 after World War II. In March 1957, the Treaty of Rome established the European Common Market, where it began with six charter countries of Europe. This Common Market, according to Wikipedia, is a regional organization whose aim was to bring economic integration among its member states. The original countries that make up this European Community include Belgium, The Netherlands, Italy, West Germany, Luxembourg, France, England, Denmark, and Ireland, with Greece being accepted in 1979. The ten toes of Nebuchadnezzar's dream are symbolic of these ten nations of the revised Roman Empire. Some modern-day prophets claim that one nation will drop out of this Common Market, making it possible for the United States to join. However, the United States doesn't have to join as they are included, being a colony of Great Britain. Isaac, the father of Jacob and Esau, blessed Esau with the earth's wealth and told him he would live by the sword. Isaac further blessed Esau's sons at the time of his death and told them how they would act among the nations. Esau, who is Edom, has lived in the earth's riches and has gotten all their wealth by the edge of the sword while being a terror to the nations. Therefore, confirming the blessing and the purpose for which YAHUAH created them.

Since Edom-Rome took dominion over the earth, they have been a force that other nations respect. We know them in history as the conquerors of the entire world. However, all of Edom-Rome's modern-day wars have been against nations they perceive as different with a desire to possess the wealth of these nations. Once they take dominion of the land, Edom-Rome sets up their system of government known as a democracy, which they say provides the most just form of governance. They advertise this system as being a government by the people, for the people, and of the people. Edom-Rome emphasizes that the entire voting population should vote to choose their representatives, based on the puppets Edom-Rome has set in place. Once the people make a choice, the true powers set about manipulating behind the scenes to bring the desired results in economics and policy based on Edom-Rome's agenda. Edom-Rome calls this system a parliamentary democracy that begins with the war they force on those who refuse to accept their interference.

After conquering and possessing the lands and people, Edom-Rome then sets up its democratic form of government with white Edomite descendants as the authority. This form of the governmental system keeps the black descendants of Jacob-Israel in the place of servitude. And, though many of the Nations have declared independence from their colonizers, Britain still claims to possess fifty-three nations as part of a commonwealth of nations. Howbeit, as the blessing, shows Esau-Edom was only told he would live in the earth's fatness but never to possess it. Because it is Jacob's inheritance, and he will own all the earth. But, Edom-Rome having this knowledge did not prevent them from taking the land from the people they met in the lands. They will never relinquish their power over the nations and to believe that any nation they colonized is free of their oppressors is a fallacy. History shows that most of the conflicts within nations Edom-Rome, the colonizers start. During World War II, the military historian and critic, Major Hoffman Nickerson, confirmed that, when the leaders of Edom-Rome have some "undisclosed purpose of their own, if they foresee war, they intend that war to begin either with a disaster or a helter-skelter retreat." They have labeled these actions the Hegelian dialectic, which refers to a problem created, followed by the reaction of the people. Edom-Rome responds by solving the crisis via war or some other form of military action.[2] It was this tactic Edom-Rome first used in the Spanish American War of 1898 and continues to provoke wars in this manner even to this day. However, Edom-Rome has used this method to ferment wars centuries before 1898. In fact, during the war with the Judeans, Rome created a crisis in 133AD when they built a temple to their god, Jupiter, on the Temple Mount in Jerusalem. The Judeans still living in Jerusalem revolted as well as those scattered throughout the diaspora. Edom-Rome took this opportunity to complete the total decimation of the descendants of Jacob-Israel and bring about the final removal of the Israelites from the land known as Israel. Edom-Rome then renamed Jerusalem Aelia Capitolina and changed the name from Israel to Palestine after the Philistines, Israel's sworn enemy.

History further shows that the descendants of Edom-Rome are warmongers, and they go about agitating wars because blood is the only thing that satisfies them. They are the only people on earth that have created a sport out of killing animals as a sporting activity and not for food. They also create this conflict and wreak havoc on the earth to keep the descendants of Israel in perpetual dispersal. Although the antics of Edom-Rome affect the other nations, the intended consequences of their actions are to impact the descendants of Israel. Enoch shows the distinction between Jacob and Esau as he describes Esau-Edom as the boar who is wild by nature and Jacob as the sheep with good intentions, "But that bull born from him begat a black wild boar and a white sheep, and the former begat many boars, but that sheep begat twelve sheep" (Enoch 89:12). In the Rabbinic writings of Rabbi Simon, he analyses this scripture. It describes Esau as the black boar as his heart is dark, while Jacob being the black people, has a pure heart they describe as white. The analogy shows that just as the pig Edom-Rome sets and presents its first claims to establish courts of justice, even though it is the one who commits the violence and looting. The Rabbi compares the parallel to be between the hypocrisy of the Romans, who hide their atrocities under the guise of justice, compared to the pig, who hides his impurity, only highlighting its cloven hooves. "And the swine, though he divides the hoof, and be cloven-footed, yet he cheweth not the cud; he is unclean to you" (Leviticus 11:7).

RED PEOPLE OF ANTIQUITY

How can we be sure that the white man ruling today is Esau, who is Edom? A significant identifying mark of Esau, who is Edom, is his skin color. He is the first and only character in Scripture identified by his color. "And the first came out red, all over like a hairy garment; and they called his name Esau" (Genesis

25:25). Later in his life, Esau sold his birthright to his brother

Roman Edomites

Jacob for a mess of red lentil pottage "Then Jacob gave Esau bread and pottage of lentils, and he ate and drink, and rose, and went his way. Thus, Esau despised his birthright" (Genesis 25:34). Esau was a man of the field who hunted animals, which suggests that he liked to draw blood, which is red, therefore tying him to the name Edom.

In a classical baby names book, they classify the name Esau as Hebrew, meaning hair, and add that, according to some commentaries on Hebrew culture, they consider Esau to be a significant character in world history and as the forefather of the Roman Empire. Despite Esau being qualified as necessary in history, why is his identity hidden? Why, when told, "they" rule the earth, people would ask who they are? Esau-Edom has hidden

Trumphet and Palm of Victory. Villa del Cassale Sicilia, Italy. Roman circa 300AD

his identity in plain sight, which has led to the classic dispute about the identity of Esau. However, this research confirms that Esau is the "red man" known today by his alias, the "white man" who has dominion over the earth. And, a familiar name associated with Roman culture is Rufus which designates red. In Latin Rufus, also means red with Pompeius Rufus being an example of how they use it.

Red was significant in Roman use and Servius's commentary on Virgil, (Eclogue X. 27)[3] He explains the use of red in Rome. While commenting on the word vermillion, red, Servius explains that the color red the Romans associated with the Roman chief god Jupiter. He adds that when Romans celebrated triumphs, those who had all the symbols of Jupiter, including the scepter, palm branch, tunic, and Juvenal wore the tunic of Jupiter and even colored their faces with red paint. The color, red, was a significant indicator of Roman identity.

The change in skin color of the Japhetic people of Javan who became the Greeks and Kittiym, now known as Rome, occurred over many generations. When Greece and Rome first became empires, there were both black and white Caesars. There are Frescoes available that depict Constantine as having Negroid features, and there are statutes that show Herodotus a Greek philosopher as a black man with Negro phenotype. This mixture of the descendants of Esau with Japheth has resulted in Europeans having a diverse phenotype, but still

Bust of Antonio Emanuele Ne Vunda, called "il Nigrita". Basil-ica od Santa Maria Mag-giore, Rome. The nickname "'il Nigrita" suggests that he is of Greek origin from the region of Nigrita.

considered white because of their skin color. We can see the results in white people with blonde and yellow hair, black and brown hair, and red and orange color hair. Recent historical evidence also confirmed by Edom-Rome based on their DNA science alleges that all people, including white people, are descendants of a single black woman. My research, however, shows that DNA science was never necessary to determine the origins of people on the earth since Hebrew Scriptures and the fact that the color black cannot ever come from, which is not a color. Therefore, white people also have their genesis in the same black ancestor. Esau-Edom is the child of Isaac and Rebekah, two black parents who had twin boys born to carry out the purpose of the Highest YAHUAH in these "end times."

Very early in Esau-Edom history, they identified as white Edomites, and they have always been able to identify the descendants of Jacob-Israel as black Negroes because this is how they identified them in history. Rabbi Isaac, in the book, 'Haven of Ships: Israel was in Carthage,' Karta states, "From Tyre to Carthage the nations know Israel and their Father who is in heaven, but from Tyre westward and Carthage eastward the nations know neither."[4] However, for over three to four hundred years, Esau-Edom has tried to wipe out the truth about Israel's heritage as the Hebrew Israelites lived in the diaspora and had lost their identity. The Edomites always knew the identity of the descendants of Jacob-Israel, which made it easier for them to hunt them down for destruction. Though today, Esau-Edom says the skin color of the Israelites does not matter to the truth of their identity because they have been mixed in with all people. Yet, Edom-Rome has embraced all white people regardless of the mixture and their phenotypes and has treated them with benevolence as the white family of Esau-Edom.

Edom-Rome declares that there are many gaps in history; therefore, it is difficult to tell the origins of the people on the earth. Despite this claim, Hebrew Scriptures contain the genealogy of the descendants of Noah since the flood, and it shows that none of the descendants of Noah have become extinct, although some

Bigio Morata - Greek Man in Anatolia - 200BC

have mixed with Esau, who is Edom. Scripture states all people from the beginning are still on the earth. But, Edom-Rome has sought to cast doubt on the validity of Scriptures claiming them to be a myth or poetry written as allegories, and metaphors or just out-right false. They then give the writing of the Greek philosophers who mix their writings with mythology credit as the great historians and philosophers of the past. Edom-Rome had tried to claim their history began when YAHUAH first created humanity with the white people of Egypt being its foundation. However, there is historical evidence that proves this is false. Edom-Rome revised history and disseminated the version of events to support their theories and a narrative that helped to hide their identity. Artifacts are now available to the public that exposes the truth about the identity of the original people who lived in Europe and worldwide during the time of the Ancient Roman Empire and before. The white Edomite descendants have used their power and influence to change history by whiting out paintings and artifacts of the original people of the earth.

The facts show that there has never been a time in history that Edom-Rome did not know they were the red people, and descendants of Esau. They also always knew the identity of the descendants of Jacob-Israel as there are many written accounts by people who claimed to have searched for and encountered the tribes of Israel living on the

Revising Ancient Art

Continent of Africa. When these missionaries would find the Hebrew Israelites, they would seek them out to convert them to Roman Christianity by force or influence. Edom-Rome knew the Israelites were black Negro people as they described them using the Spanish word that means black. The area that they settled they named in Sub-Saharan Africa, Negro-land, which included Sudan, which means when translated, a foreigner of Judah.

KHAZARIAN AND SEPHARDIC JEWS LIVING IN PALESTINE

The descendants of Esau are the Jewish converts living in the land of Palestine. They have appropriated the name Jew claiming to be descendants of Judah. However, they did not use this name to identify Hebrew Israelites until much later in history, which they then added to the New Testament. Edom-Rome took the name Jew as a label to identify the people of Judaea. It is said they applied this name to all Jews, whether they converted or were born into the bloodline during the expulsion of the Hebrew Israelites out of Europe. Edom-Rome used this as a means to blot out the memory of the Hebrew Israelites from history. They then called the Edomite-Khazarian converted Jews of Eastern Europe and the converted Spanish-Sephardic Jewish people of Spain Jews or Jewish which only meant they were something like the original.

However, to make these Jews fit the people spoken of in prophecy, Edom-Rome substituted a made-up history and events to support the story that all nations hate the Jews. All nations do hate the black Israelites on the earth, but outside of the Middle East, few people have any hatred for the so-called Jews because most people have no contact with them, and those who hate them have a reason to do so. They are imposters who have only assumed the identity of the Judeans by labeling themselves Jews. To claim this title of "hated" Edom-Rome destroyed many of the Eastern European Jewish people along with many more of the Hebrew Israelites in Germany during World Wars I and II through the holocaust designed by the German Nazis. They allowed this to support the story of hatred for the Jews. Moreover, they used this event to claim the land of Palestine as a homeland for the Eastern European Jewish people. They also used this to cover up the truth about the black Negro Hebrew Israelite holocaust that Edom-Rome had carried out for hundreds of years. Edom-Rome used this war to replace the Hebrew Israelites in the land of Palestine in 1948. They are frauds, and, as Hitler describes them in the book Mein Comp, bastard Jews.

According to Firpo Carr (2003), there is evidence that proves Germany's hand in a black holocaust, not only in Germany but throughout Africa. Much of the violence cited by Jewish Germans are similar, although they have hidden the evidence of this additional holocaust event that took place on the African continent. Reports show that Africans were the victims of one of the worst atrocities ever committed in human history. Still, they have hidden the records of these killings and only mentioned as a footnote to history. The Edomite Germans, who are also part of Edom-Rome, carried out this African holocaust from 1890 to 1945 in Namibia, Africa, where it is said they first established concentration camps.

The Edomites used the so-called Africans in their concentration camps as guinea pigs for medical experiments. This holocaust involved not only the Germans, as evidence shows the participation by the French, British, and Americans. They routinely carried out abusive acts against the Africans well into the latter part of the 19th century (Carr, 2003). One researcher states, "The files of the Imperial Colonial Office revealed that the official policy of the German government was to deport and destroy the Nama people. Until mid-1906, they held the Witbooi and Bethanie people in Concentration Camps at Windhoek and Karibib." These were all the descendants of Israel living in the diaspora in West Africa because they selected the people they wanted for extinction. The record shows that the Germans killed 80 percent of the Herero people, and more than half of the Nama and Damara people died at the hands of the German colonial forces. They hung those they did not kill in the wars from trees in mass executions in the form of group hangings (Firpo Carr, 2003).

However, the fate of the white Jewish people in Germany and other Eastern European countries was different because, on November 29, 1947, led by the United Nations General Assembly and with the support of the United States, the Jewish Khazarian, and Sephardic Zionists seized the land of Palestine. They created a State of Israel (John Beatty, 1954). The United States and the United Nations pledged to support Zionist aggression in Palestine. However, everyone did not agree with the moves made by the Zionist Jews. Professor W.T. Stace, one who did not approve of the takeover, declared, "The Soviet-supplied Jewish troops, which seized Palestine, had no rights ever before recognized in law or custom except the right of triumphant tooth and claw." Allen H. Godbey concluded that "In the first place the Khazar Zionists from Soviet Russia did not descend from the people of Hebrew religion in Palestine, ancient or modern, and thus not descended from Old Testament People." Yet, the United States and the United Nations General Assembly gave the Khazar permission to expel the Palestinians. The latter had inhabited the land for hundreds of years after Edom-Rome had banished the Hebrew Israelites in 135AD. Therefore, most of the people the Khazar Jews expelled during the takeover in 1947 were a mingled people of Arab and Canaanite descent. But they allowed a small community of white Edomites called the Druze, who were Arabic-speaking to remain in the land and become citizens by the Israeli government. They say the Israeli Druzes are not Muslims, although they follow the Islamic faith. But, because they are Edomites, the Israelis designated them with a distinct ethnic community status where they have citizenship and serve in Israel's Defense Forces (Wikipedia).

The Khazars are descendants of Esau, and I believe they are the descendants of Amalek, a grandson of Esau. Historians reported they acted as a buffer to the Byzantium offense against invasions. They blocked the Arabs in its most devastating early stages, and, thus, prevented the Muslim conquest of Eastern Europe. According to Professor Dunlop, the Khazarian country's location was important to Byzantium. It was the bulwark of European civilization in the east, and it would have found itself outflanked by the Arabs had it not been for the Khazars. Their position was important to the events that occurred and, if not for them, would have changed the history of Christendom and Islam might have differed from what we know, today. Therefore, it is not surprising, however, that given these circumstances, in 732AD, after a huge Khazar victory over the Arabs, the future Emperor Constantine V married a Khazar princess. Later, they produced a son who became Emperor Leo IV, known as Leo the Khazar (Koestler, 1976).

According to the certified written story of the Jews living in Palestine and throughout the earth today, they claim that the Jewish nation existed ever since Moses received the tablets of the law on Mount Sinai. The Israelis assert that they are its direct and exclusive descendants except for the ten tribes that they have not located. Rendering this version of history, they recall that YAHUAH had exiled the Jews from Israel two times - after the fall of the First Temple in the sixth century and again after the fall of the Second Temple in 70AD. Yet, even before the second exile, this unique nation had created the Hebrew Hasmonean kingdom, which revolted against the wicked influence of Hellenization during the Maccabean period. Based on the Jewish account of history, they believed their nation is the most ancient because they wandered in exile for two thousand years. However, despite this prolonged stay among the Gentiles, the Jewish people said they avoided integrating with or assimilating into them. These Jewish converts also claim that the nation scattered far and wide into Yemen, Morocco, Spain, Germany, Poland, and distant Russia, but it always maintained close blood relations among far-flung communities to preserve its distinctiveness (Sands, 2009).

The Jewish people, however, have many variations of their history written by Jewish historians. Most of them write from a perspective not based on Torah and the Prophets, and they too cast doubt on Hebrew sources because they do not align with the narrative of Edom-Rome. What they use, however, is the evidence they found written on Egyptian papyrus and steles and the Talmud. The stories written by the imposter Jewish people are vague and do not reflect the truth written in the Torah and the Prophets with their version beginning hundreds of years later during the time of the Maccabees. I believe this is also done, so they are better able to control the narrative. Most Jewish people living in Palestine today admit they are descendants of the Khazar converts who lived in the Caucasus Mountains. And, the Edomite Sephardic Jews of Spain also admit they replaced the Hebrew Israelite Sephardic Jews of Spain after Edom-Rome expelled the Hebrews into Africa in the thirteenth, fourteenth, and fifteenth centuries.

However, some Jewish historians hold to the belief they are the original people of Israel. Sands (2009) noted that between Flavius Josephus and the modern era, there were no attempts by Jewish authors to write a general history of their past. Therefore there is no written history during the long period called the Middle Ages. What is true is that when they show the true Israelite history, the imposter Zionist Jewish people could not write a true account because they have no history if they are not willing to use the accounts written in Hebrew Scriptures. Starting in the early eighteenth and nineteenth centuries after Edom-Rome had replaced the Hebrew Israelites, historians, including Jacques Basnage, a Normandy born Huguenot theologian wrote a book titled; 'The History of the Jews from Jesus Christ to the Present Time, Being a Supplement and Continuation of the History of Josephus.' He wrote this account from the Christian's perspective, which does not begin with the Genesis account but with the New Testament. And, he did not draw an unbroken line from the ancient Hebrew Israelites to the Jewish communities of his time because he thought the Old Testament belonged to the offspring of Jacob-Israel who he believed YAHUAH cut off. He used the term "Children of Israel," a term that embraced the Christians more than the Jews because, in his mind, Christendom was the "true Israel" (Sands, 2009).

This account of Basnage that alleges that the converts to Judaism are the original Israelites is false, and there is no evidence for this claim. The Edomites of Christianity and Judaism are both imposters. They cannot be Israel because they have not experienced any of the curses written in the prophecies other than the ones they created. Scripture declares that the Israelites, the Chosen people of YAHUAH, would be a poor, broken, imprisoned, and persecuted people hated above all nations on the earth and facing much destruction. There is no proof that the Jewish people experienced any of the atrocities prophesied in Scripture to happen to the Hebrew Israelites as the Prophet Jeremiah states, "And I will deliver them to be removed into all the kingdoms of the earth for their hurt, to be a reproach and a proverb, a taunt, and a curse; in all places whither I shall drive them. And I will send the sword, the famine, and the pestilence, among them; till they are consumed from off the land, I gave unto them and to their fathers" (Jeremiah 24:9-10).

YAHUAH promised these curses would come upon Israel because their fore-parents did not keep his laws. These conditions would be upon Israel as a sign of who they are. Instead, the Jewish historians omit much of the Biblical facts because it does not apply to them. Evidence shows they are the riches people living on the earth today, and it is clear they are the descendants of Esau living in the earth's fatness, accomplishing it all by the power of the sword or the barrel of a gun. The Jewish converts, too, like Edom-Rome cast doubt on the Scriptures and choose those things helpful in putting forth the false narrative they are the chosen people of YAHUAH. These Jewish converts who call themselves Israelis have created an entire organization to address what they label anti-Semitism or hatred of the Jews. But the Scripture never describes Israel as Semitic because they were, in fact, the direct descendants of Jacob-Israel and known as Israelites or Hebrews and in Africa Igbos or some other derivation of their Hebrew name. Semitic people are descendants of Shem. And, Shem's offspring could be anyone, including the Arabs, the Persians, the Chinese, and the East Indians.

The present-day Zionist Khazarian Jewish people have taken authority and moved into the land. They have set up a government pretending to be the descendants of Israel with the right to return to their "homeland." They believe in their continued success of this hoax, but YAHUAH ELOHIYM said it is all in vain and asks, "Why do the heathen rage, and the people imagine a vain thing" (Psalms 2:1? Edom-Rome hoped the descendants of Jacob-Israel would not awaken and uncover the truth because they thought YAHUAH had forgotten. The fourth beast power, as Edom-Rome would continue to rule forever. But, YAHUAH told Jacob that if their ladder reaches to the heavens, he will still bring them down as prophecy says Rome will fall just like the other empires.

This prediction that the Gentiles would be in the land of Israel and will tread it down until YAHUSHA returns is what should be happening at this time, "Therefore thus saith YAHUAH ELOHIYM; Surely in the fire of my jealousy have I spoken against the residue of the heathen, and against all Edom, which has appointed my land into their possession with the joy of all their heart, with despiteful minds, to cast it out for a prey" (Ezekiel 36: 5). Prophecy does not predict the Hebrew Israelites to be in the land before YAHUSHA HAMASHIACH returns. However, the Gentiles would be there, and when he comes, he will gather Israel and take them to the land. The Jewish occupiers are not the Israelites, as the evidence shows because the Israelites are still in the diaspora where they will be held until the HAMASHIACH returns. "Therefore, say, thus saith YAHUAH ELOHIYM; I will even gather you from the people, and assemble you out of the countries where ye have been scattered, and I will give you the land of Israel" (Ezekiel 11:17).

TEACHERS OF JUDAISM

Based on early church history, the leaders of the orthodox Jews of the sect of the Pharisees and Sadducees practiced Judaism and adhered to the Laws of YAHUAH. However, they did not accept the HAMASHIACH. Still, many of them later accepted the truth. They admonished those of Israel being grafted back into the congregation of the righteous what they should do, "But there arose certain of the sect of the Pharisees which believed, saying, That it was needful to circumcise them, and to command them to keep the law of Moses" (Acts 15:5).

What I have found through this research is that the orthodox Jewish Edomite supporters of Rome were allowed to practice their religion still as it shows that in the eighth century the entire nation of the Khazar a people of Turkish stock living in the Caucasus Mountains converted to Judaism (Koestler, 1976). While at the same time, many of the scattered Hebrew Israelite followers of HAMASHIACH were being persecuted by Edom-Rome for wanting to obey the laws of the Torah even though they had accepted the HAMASHIACH. This form of Edomite Judaism continues to be a religion supported by Rome and the Edomite Christians but have eliminated any history that includes the true bloodline descendants of Jacob-Israel. They removed the true Israelites from participating in any form of TORAH practices and allied with the Jewish religion known today as Judaism when combined forms Judeo-Christianity, a religion of the revised papal Roman Empire.

The name, Judeo-Christian, explains the revisionist history that has permeated modern biblical history. In these "last days," Edom-Rome has reunited the Protestant Christians with the Roman Christian Catholic Church and Judaism with a visit of the Pope to the land of Palestine. In 2019, Pope Francis visited the United Arab Emirates, where he and the Muslim Imam signed an agreement to come together as a one-world religion. However, this was just optics because the Muslim has its genesis in the Roman Catholic Christian Church. By doing this, Edom-Rome hopes to bring about a false return of their Messiah to replace Israel as a one-world government with a one-world religion. But, the Babylonian system of Edom-Rome has had its time and recognizes its end. The Highest YAHUAH will never recognize or accept any worship of these religions. Therefore it is vain worship, just like that of the Pharisees, "Howbeit in vain do they worship me, teaching for doctrines the commandments of men' (Mark 7:7). Edom-Rome will continue to sow their lying signs and wonders to make the world believe these events will bring Armageddon and the coming of the HAMASHIACH. The Hebrew Midrash gives an account that typifies the personalization of Rome and the west as Esau while not sparing his hypocrisy.[5] And, it describes the actions of Edom in these end times:

Esau will wrap himself in a tallis, sit down next to Yakov, and say to him, 'You are my brother'... Yakov will say to him, 'My brother, you will not be like me. I will lead you to death. I will be the pestilence that leads you to Sheol' (Hosea 13:14). Had I upheld the decrees you promulgated against me, I would have been guilty in the eyes of Heaven. Had I violated them, you would have killed me?' (Yalkut Shimoni, Yirmiahu 333). This was Esau's intention when he told Yakov, 'Let us travel together, and I will go before you' (Genesis 33:12). In effect, Esau wanted them to join together in both this world and the world to come, to meet each other halfway, with each changing his conduct until they were alike (Yalkut Shimoni Genesis 1:33). It is said Esau will even adopt certain tenets of Judaism, such as monotheism, the Divinity of the Torah, and reward and punishment—but only if Yakov-Israel will give up some of its heritage.

This Midrash reveals that Edom-Rome has indeed taken the place of Jacob on the earth, pretending to be the holy set-apart people of YAHAUH in the religions of Judaism and Christianity. As Edom-Rome, they are papal Christian Rome, and like Jacob, they are the Israeli Jewish synagogue. The allegory describes Jacob's response when he gets the opportunity to say these words to Esau, who is Edom and Rome. The truth is shown in Biblical and secular history that Edom-Rome's desire has always been to replace Jacob-Israel and would do anything to have his inheritance.

Many modern-day Rabbis have commented on this deception, which proves that Jacob-Israel is not at this time enjoying this world. For example, Tanna D' Bei Eliahu Zuta (19)[6] Describes Esau's proposal to Jacob, "Give up mitzvah that divides us. You will enjoy this world and still have half the world to come. Isn't that enough?" (Bais Halevy, Vayishlach).[7]

Esau would like to have it both ways, to be the unrighteous bully while pretending to be morally superior and above all others. Nonetheless, YAHUAH has chosen Jacob-Israel, and his twelve sons that make up the tribes to be His royal priesthood and a holy nation and Edom-Rome will not share it with Jacob-Israel, "But ye are a chosen generation, a royal priesthood, a holy nation, a peculiar people; that ye should shew forth the praises of him who hath called you out of darkness into his marvelous light" (1 Peter 2:9). Thus, Jacob cannot be part of this world and still rule in the next. The Highest requires total obedience to his laws, statutes, and commandments that Israel will obey after they are born again. The commentary made in the Midrash refers to the imposter Edomite Jewish people posing as Jacob and Esau acting like there is a relationship between them. But Scripture shows the only relationship that Esau has had with Jacob has been an adversarial one of perpetual hatred. And, at no time has Edom-Rome ever reached out to Jacob-Israel other than to betray and destroy them. The commentary sums up the ancient writings by asking one to reflect on what we have observed. "Do we not see the pinnacle of Esau's civilization, the country that is the utmost embodiment of his values of individualism and superficiality, image, offering this bargain to the sons of Yakov and most of them have taken it? Indeed, the imposter Jews have taken the offer because they are both descendants of Esau playing different roles. They both crave the material gains this life offers as they live by the sword in the fatness of the earth. They are all hypocrites. YAHUAH'S will is to keep Israel for his holy use, and therefore they are still in the diaspora being refined, so they become like pure gold. The narrative that Jacob accepted some of Esau's mitzvah is false. The pretenders say Esau has placed his political and military might in the service of common goals, to support the so-called 'Judeo-Christian' values." Esau, who is Edom, has gone to great lengths to hide the true identity of Israel, even writing Midrashic commentary to support the theory that the Jewish people living in Palestine are the true Israelites so they could feel secure in their lie.

TEACHERS OF CHRISTIANITY

The Edomite Romans, and the Idumeans or Jews who ruled Israel, influenced and created the religion of Christianity as an Edomite religion. It differed from the religion of the Hebrew Israelites, and this difference caused the Hebrew Israelites to experience many persecutions at the hands of Edom-Rome and the Sadducean high priesthood, which Rome supported because the Edomite Jews had already infected the council. Therefore, in

70AD, after the fall of Jerusalem, Christian church history began (Frend, 1984).

Frend (1984), noted that it was two years after Paul arrived in Rome, the Sadducean high priesthood murdered James, his superior in 62AD. After this, Titus and Vespasian destroyed the Temple of Jerusalem, which caused the further scattering of the Judeans and the Hellenized Jews the people YAHUSHA came to redeem. Therefore, many of the followers of YAHUSHA HAMASHIACH rallied to the Pharisees, who were the traditional upholders of religion and nationality (Frend, 1984).

During this same time, the Christians still regarded the churches as synagogues. Its members prayed three times a day and fasted twice a week, just like the Hebrews. Yet, those who labeled themselves Christian chose Wednesday and Friday to commemorate Christ's arrest and crucifixion and not the usual Hebrew Monday and Thursday. These Edomite Christians used the Hebrew Scriptures and claimed to be "saints" (James 3; 1 Tim. 5:10; Heb. 6:10), "the people of God" (Heb. 4:9), "a royal priesthood," and a "holy nation" (1 Peter 2:9) (Frend, 1984). The Christians followed a different Hebrew model, and there was much debate over how vital Jewish Christianity was to salvation. Christianity had accepted Jesus Christ as God, but the Hebrews did not. Therefore, they labeled Christianity as Israel with a difference, because no Israelite would have ever accepted Jesus Christ as God (Frend, 1984).

In 2 Clement and Pliny's report on the Christians in Bithynia in 112AD, they admonished the Christians; "Brethren, we must think of Jesus Christ as God, as of the judge of the living and the dead" (C. Mohlberg, 1937).[8] The Christian church and religion, Hellenized Jews and Pagan Rome, influenced and changed the religion of the Hebrew Israelites and preached a different gospel from the one YAHUSHA brought and established by the word of YAHUAH. And, when Hadrian, the successor to Trajan, the Roman Emperor who ruled from 117 to 138AD, made a distinction between the Christians and the Israelites who had taken part in the uprisings of 135AD in Jerusalem he put laws in place that favored Christians (Frend, 1984).

Christianity may have begun as a Jewish religion, but it did not remain so once Edom-Rome decided that the laws of the Torah were no longer binding. The Israelites then expelled those Christians from their assemblies who refused to adhere to the laws of the Christian Synagogues. Those expelled moved into the Roman pagan Pantheons that became churches. The issues and differences between Jew and Christian became more clear-cut, and, after 100AD, there was less of a tendency for Christians to claim to be Israel and, instead, more of a tendency to contrast Christianity and Judaism (Israel) as separate religions.

Within Christianity, various ideas and teachings emerged that claimed Jesus as Lord and God. They were looking forward to his return, and when the hope of his soon return faded, the people turned to other concepts, including the direct sovereignty of the spirit. During this time, spiritual power, prophets, and apocalyptic events had to compete with the ideas of the morality of the enlightened and Pharisaic teachings that had a strong influence on the Hellenistic-Jewish communities (Frend, 1984). The keeping of YAHUAH'S laws, according to Frend (1984), was the biggest trial of Judaism and was a last great effort to proselytize the Greco-Roman world when it collapsed. The fall of Judaism saw Christianity emerge and progress because many Hellenized Israelites joining wanted to be in the church but also be part of the Greco-Roman world, which the Christian church afforded them.

The teachings of Christianity declared that Christians were the heirs to the Universalist claims of Judaism. They also added the word Catholic or universal to the church for the first time after AD100. The Romans continued to persecute the Hebrew Israelites because they feared the hope that Israel had in HAMASHIACH threatened their rulership. They dreaded that the HAMASHIACH would return to replace the Roman rule. Many of the followers of YAHUSHA never compromised with Christianity and suffered because of it. The Judeans and the Hellenized Jews who had been grafted back into Israel had no power and were both persecuted by Edom-Rome because they refused to separate themselves from the Law of YAHUAH.

ARAB MUSLIMS AND OTTOMAN TURKS

The Arabs never accepted Christianity or converted to religion. Therefore, Edom-Rome created another religion called Islam into their culture with a Prophet like the Christian Messiah. They then used the Hebrew Scriptures to design a book called the Koran. They furthered the deception by insisting that the Koran should never be translated from the Arabic language to English or any other language. The Arabs who converted to Islam were forced to memorize the teachings in the Arabic language, whether they spoke this language or not. Edom-Rome then used the Arabs to force the Hebrew Israelites living in Africa in the diaspora to convert to the religion by the pain of death. According to an account written about the Sephardic Jews of Mali, they described what happened to these Jews when the Muslims came;

> According to Zakhor, some of the Jewish survivors of Touat, following the routes of the caravans, took refuge with other Jews settled along the Niger, but their safety was only temporary. Soon after 1493, under the influence of the same Meghili, Askia Muhammad the Great, the ruler of this region introduced a proclamation for the eviction of the Jews of Songhai. They found themselves in the position of choosing to renounce their faith or die. Haidara, the leader of Zakhor, noted that "the Jews could not go further, in front was the great Nile and behind the Arabs. They stopped facing the Koran and the sword. They converted." They concluded that this is the way the black Jews became Muslims. Today, the members of the Zakhor portray themselves as a small early

Jewish population, which is said to have been superseded by the subsequent Islamic community, with only tiny remnants of Judaism surviving. The heads of the families who founded Zakhor relates that the three families constituting their community from the 16th century, the Levite Kehaths, now named Kati, the Cohens and the Ababas were not the first Jewish inhabitants of these regions.

Later in history, it is reported that Edom-Rome tried to convince the Ottoman Turkish Empire to begin an Islamic "holy war" against Christians so that Edom-Rome could claim that the Muslims were against Christians. However, the facts show that the Christians the Muslims destroyed and forced to convert were the Hebrews who refused to follow the doctrines of Edom-Rome. The Arab Muslims were used as a deflection to hide the real destroyers of Israel. Historical accounts show that the Muslims never forced Edomite Christians to convert to the Islamic religion. Instead, their goal was to force those of the Hebrew Israelites living in the diaspora on the African continent who had remained faithful to the TORAH to convert to Islam. It is this account of their history that Edom-Rome has used today to deceive those of the Christian faith to believe that those of the Islamic faith are enemies of Christianity. Christianity and Islam are two sides of the same coin used by Edom-Rome against the Hebrew Israelites.

PEOPLE OF HYPOCRITICAL LOVE

The Edomites have no love for the Highest YAHUAH, his people, or his Laws. Edom-Rome threw away the commandments of YAHUAH and established their laws and required everyone to obey them or face death. As a lawless people, they constructed a justice system with two standards - one for the Edomite and the other for the descendants of Israel. According to Christian church history from the first century, one schism that developed among the body of the early believers who followed YAHUSHA was that the Edomite Christians did not see the need to continue keeping the Laws of the TORAH if they accepted Jesus as their Messiah. To keep their standing in the church, many of the Hellenized Israelites agreed with this teaching. Yet, this brought about heresies that caused confusion and went against the teachings of the Highest YAHUAH.

Edom-Rome has shown that they are hypocrites who speak with both sides of their tongue. They say they love all people, yet they shed the innocent blood of the Hebrew Israelites. They have gone into many lands bearing the cross of Jesus Christ, their savior, in one hand and wielding a gun or sword in the other. Then, with fury poured out, they force inhabitants to bow to their cross and accept their Jesus and form of worship. Edom-Rome loves money, their god above all else in heaven and on the earth. They have shown this in their system, which measures the amount of money as the determining factor of peoples' success. Therefore, they have designed a system to keep those of Israel from ever attaining success without first stripping them of their moral character.

Edom-Rome believes that by having Israel engage in immoral acts to attain success will prevent them from attaining the kingdom of the Highest YAHUAH.

Today, the Israelites live in this Greco-Roman influenced world and have accepted this pathway to success, which has destroyed them. But, YAHUAH knew this would happen because Israel lacks knowledge of whom and whose they are. However, all these things work together for the good of Israel as Scripture says Israel is blessed when they are meek, poor in spirit, and the persecuted and not when they are rich with the money god of this world. The Christians of Edom-Rome believe they are blessed when they have obtained the money of this world. They also believe the laws given by YAHUAH to Israel do not apply to them. They say YAHUAH covers them under the covenant he made with Noah. They call this the Noahide covenant. They were certain YAHUAH only gave the laws to the Jews or the Hebrew Israelites, and Gentiles were exempted and did not have to obey these laws. Yet, they believe they can receive the redemption of Israel.

It is said the Noahide covenant makes it possible for Gentiles to be part of Israel's covenant. However, the covenant that YAHUAH made with Noah had nothing to do with saving his chosen seed. Noah's covenant was about flooding the earth and destroying it with water, "And I will establish my covenant with you; neither shall all flesh be cut off any more by the waters of a flood; neither shall there any more be a flood to destroy the earth.

And ELOHIYM said, this is the token of the covenant which I make between me and you and every living creature with you, for perpetual generations: I set my bow in the cloud, and it shall be for a token of a covenant between me and the earth," (Genesis 9:11-13). Therefore, the covenant made with Noah says he will not use a flood to destroy the earth or humanity again. However, he will use the fire of his indignation, "Therefore wait ye upon me saith YAHUAH, until the day that I rise to the prey: for my determination is to gather the nations, that I may assemble the kingdoms, to pour upon them mine indignation, even all my fierce anger: for all the earth shall be devoured with the fire of my jealousy," (Zephaniah 3:8).

Chief Rabbi Alain Goodman notes what the sages observed about Edom-Rome and how they were the example of all the misfortunes of Israel:

> Our sages see in Rome, Ancient Rome, which refers to Esau, and all those who live according to his way of being. This illustration let us know that Rome had no respect for law and humanity, never ceasing to use all the means of violence and cunning. It thus had strength unequaled. Such as Esau, the implacable enemy of his brother, and it was Rome who had no mercy for Israel, while what drives Jacob-Israel is a deep sense of justice and love of neighbor."

Esau, who is Edom-Rome, has none of the traits that Israel displays even when they hunt them down and destroy them, Israel will forgive the injustice. Those pretending to be Jews living in the land of Palestine would prefer to kill, steal and destroy the Palestinians before they allow them to have a small piece of the land in Israel when they know for a fact that the land does not belong to either of them. Edom-Rome loves to shed innocent blood. It is on record that the Judeo-Christians lead a genocidal slaughter of innocent people throughout the earth in the name of their religion while claiming to serve a God who epitomizes love for all humankind. Maurice Samuel, a modern Jew, declares, "We Jews, we are the destroyers and will remain the destroyers. Nothing you can do will meet our demands and needs. We will forever destroy because we want a world of our own." Samuel's statement is accurate, not only for Jewish people but for all Edomites who are descendants of Esau, who is Edom. They are greedy people who want more and find it necessary to enact destruction in this pursuit. Even the Highest YAHUAH cannot satisfy their unquenchable thirst for more blood, more money, more of everything. And the pages of the real history of the earth are abounding with accounts that show the vicious actions taken by Edom-Rome against the Hebrew Israelites in their quest to destroy them and to gain more.

The Roman Christian Church forced hundreds of thousands maybe millions of Hebrew Israelites to baptize into Christianity against their will as John Ogilby records the methods they used when giving the Israelites the mark of the Beast; [9]

> When any Jew or other infidel, will embrace the Roman
> Religion, they put the Solemnity of his Baptism off to the

Saturday of Holy Week, unless some urgent Confederation requires greater haste. They perform this ceremony in a little building called at Rome, Baptisterio joining to the Church of St John de Lateran, where they believe they baptized Constantine the Great. We saw six Turks baptized in that place: they wore a Cloak of white Damask, and a Sawn Band, with a Silver Cross hanging at their neck. The Cardinal that was to officiate being come with the Canons of that church, they began the Ceremony with blessing the water; after which the Proselytes presented by their Godfathers advanced everyone in his turn, and declared their desire to be baptized. Then they leaned over the font, and the Cardinal baptized them by pouring water on their heads out of a large silver spoon and gave them their names. Afterward, taking Wax Tapers in their hands, it confirmed them in the Chapel of the Baptistery, and from thence went to hear Mass in the same Church.

This pouring of water over the head and the wax tapers in hand is the mark of the Beast that John spoke about in Revelation. As late as the 17th century, the Hebrew Israelites still identified as Israel, and the enemy was Edom-Rome. Therefore, John was writing about the future of Israel and what they would experience at the hand of this Beast system of Edom-Rome. The Christian Church of today has tried to appropriate the prophecies of the end time to refer to the believers of the Babylonian Christian church.

However, prophecy signifies that the Roman Church is the harlot recorded in Revelations. And, true Israel is the woman who was led into the wilderness by the Beast of Edom-Rome, "And he causeth all, both small and great, rich and poor, free and bond to receive a mark in their right hand, or their foreheads: and that no man might buy or sell, save he that had the mark or the name of the beast or the number of his name. Here is wisdom. Let him that hath understanding count the number of the beast: for it is the number of a man; and his number is Six hundred threescore and six" (Revelation 13:16-18).

Moreover, the revelation does not pertain to the universal religion that Edom-Rome created. John prophesied these persecutions to transpire among the Israelites, the true people of YAHUAH, not the Roman Christians who claim they are "spiritual" Israel, neither does it apply to the Israelites. The latter believe they are Gentiles living in the land of their captivity. Edom-Rome has created a narrative that states the Arabs or Muslims will rise and rule after they have persecuted and beheaded many believers in Christ. But there is no scriptural evidence of Ishmael's rule as a people over the earth. Prophecy names one set of people who would be persecuted at the hand of Edom-Rome. And, they are for the "end times" but not just the end of Esau's reign on the earth but the "end times" for Israel as a nation of people who knew who they were and willing to die for the Highest YAHUAH and his Laws. The Israelites were persecuted because they kept the Laws of the Most High. There is no system or religion in place today, keeping the laws, statutes, and commandments of YAHUAH. All the religions follow the Beast power and believe Jesus will return to save and take them to heaven. This false doctrine invented by Edom-Rome is a great part of the deception. Today, the Israelites are dispersed and unaware of their identity, and YAHUAH has not changed his mind about who his people are, "Therefore, thus saith YAHUAH ELOHIYM; Now will I bring the captivity of Jacob again, and have mercy upon the whole house of Israel, and will be jealous for my holy name; ... When I have brought them again from the people, and gathered them out of their enemies' lands, and am sanctified in them in the sight of many nations; then shall they know I am YAHUAH their ELOHIYM, which caused them to be led into captivity among the heathen: but I have gathered them unto their land. I have left none of them any more there" (Ezekiel 39:25, 27-28).

INQUISITORS OF ROMAN INQUISITION

According to Krauskopf (1886), the Inquisition started in the city of Seville, with Thomas de Torquemada as Inquisitor General of Castile and Aragon. For 600 years, it waged a cruelest reign of terror in the southern province of France, where the Albigenses, a sect of the Hebrew Israelites lived and where the Moorish and Jewish civilization from across the Pyrenees had made themselves felt. The terror stopped with the extermination of almost the entire population. Krauskopf (1886) noted that a few years later, the Inquisition found its way into every town in Spain and confined itself almost only to the Israelite Jews. Edom-Rome enforced and encouraged these horrific acts of violence and hatred against the Israelites in the name of Christianity. The author believes these deeds of cruelty are recorded upon the annals of history in letters of blood and fire, and they cannot conceal them by the combined cruelties of all humanity.

There were a series of brutalities visited upon the Israelite Jews in Spain. And, according to Krauskopf (1886), it was not a rare sight to see the populace of Spain fueled by the fanatical clergy make a fierce assault upon the Jews guilty of no other crime than that of promoting Spain's prosperity and of adhering to their inherited belief. These Christians broke into their houses, violating their most private sanctuaries, and consigning them by the thousands to an indiscriminate massacre, without regard to sex or age. They enacted cruel laws against them which prohibited them from mingling with the Christians, and from following the trades and professions for which they were best suited because of their high intelligence and thrift.

As the Inquisition persisted Edom-Rome executed the Israelite Jew Antonio Joseph, a celebrated author and dramatist of Portugal who made a statement at the time of his death;

> I own I belong to a faith that you yourselves acknowledge to be of Divine origin. God loved this religion, and He, according to my belief, is still attached to it, while you think He has ceased to be so; and because your belief

differs from mine, you condemn those who are of the opinion that God continues to love what he loved. You demand we should become Christians, and yet you are far from being Christians yourselves. Be at least men, and act towards us as reasonable as if you had no religion at all to guide you and no revelation for your enlightenment. 'Some spectators shouted, "Osseitaro Barbaro" ("clip his beard"), and immediately one executioner besmears his venerable beard, with a long brush, with pitch and turpentine, and sets fire to it. One more cry, "Sh'ma, Yisrael, Adonay Elahenu, Adonay Echad" (Hear, O Israel, the Eternal, Our God is One"), and the flames have done their work, amidst the rapturous applause of the spectators, and amidst the pious ejaculations: "Blessed be forever the goodness and mercy of the Holy Inquisition. Blessed be the Holy Trinity, the sister of the Virgin Mary." Not a tear among the spectators, Father, mother, husband, wife, child, relatives, friends, all are eye-witnesses to this bloody sacrifice, and yet from them, not a sigh, of regret, nor dare they be absent, nor dare they abstain from applauding, that would fasten suspicion upon them, and condemn them to a similar fate. Confiscation of the

convicted possessions ended the mournful tragedy'
(Krauskopf, 1886).

Historians have written many accounts of the destruction of
the Hebrew Israelites at the hands of Edom-Rome throughout
history as they sought to obey the Most High's Laws, statutes,
and commandments and reject the laws of Roman Christianity.
In the book, 'The Jews and Moors in Spain,' there are examples
of extreme brutal acts committed by Pope Innocent III and the
"Dominican Monks" against the Israelites when they refused
baptism and conversion to the religion of Christianity. They
massacred the Hebrew Israelites even after they converted to
Christianity for the slightest accusation brought against them by
anyone. From 1481 to 1808, based on figures given by Edom-
Rome, the number of Hebrew Israelites killed by the Roman
Christian church amounted to about 340,000 persons (Joseph
Krauskopf, 1886). They report that the Pope, along with the king,
expelled the Israelites from Spain and Portugal in the 1300s, and
when they hesitated to leave, they snatched their children and
babies and placed them on ships
bound for West Africa. Although
there are reports they sailed into
North Africa, there is evidence that
shows the ships took them to Guinea
on the West African coast. They were
all black Hebrew Israelites and not
the white imposter Jews who claim

A black Saint John Ogilvie
being hanged

Sephardic ancestry who remained in Spain and Portugal when Edom-Rome banished and persecuted the faithful Israelite Jews scattering them into Africa. John Ogilvie reports on one of the appalling acts and horrendous treatment Edom-Rome committed against the Hebrew Israelite Jews in Spain when they were being expelled;

> The Jews have experienced the unmatched skill of the church in administering pain. Mothers cast themselves at the feet of the tyrants and pitifully begged to be taken with their babies; they were heartlessly thrust aside. Hundreds of mothers mad with despair ran behind the ships as they carried off the idols of their heart, and perished in the waves. The serene fortitude with which the exile people had borne so many grievous calamities gave way at last and replaced by the wildest paroxysms of despair; piercing shrieks of anguish filled the land. Childless and broken-hearted, they now sought to leave the land, but they told them they had given up their right, and they gave them a choice between baptism and slavery.

There is much historical evidence that shows both Edom-Rome and the Christian Church's commitment to destroy thousands upon tens of thousands of the Chosen people of YAHUAH. And, if these same atrocities happened to the fake Jews in the eyes of the world, it would be wrong. As I read these accounts, it is incomprehensible that people should continue to believe that the god of Edom-Rome is the same Elohiym as the

Most High YAHUAH, the ELOHIYM of Abraham, Isaac, and Jacob-Israel. The god, the Edomites, serve is Satan, the devil a deceiver, liar, and murderer the fourth beast of Daniel's dream. Edom-Rome indeed is the man of sin, YAHUAH created to be wicked on the earth. The Hebrew Israelites, after they learn the truth, need to come out from among them and be separate so that they would not experience the plagues prophesied to come upon the wicked heathens of Babylon.

Death and destruction such as these mentioned never happened to the white Ashkenazi or Sephardic Jews, or they would still memorialize them to this day because they claim they never lost their heritage and, in fact, always remember to observe the events of the Holocaust of World War Two. If the people of YAHUAH knew the truth about the religions of Rome that includes Judaism, Christianity, and Islam, they would leave these institutions in droves and return to the POWER of the Highest, who will give them the power to resist the evil both in the natural and spiritual realm. YAHUAH ELOHIYM is not using the Christian church or any form of this Harlot to bring salvation to Israel or any other people. They are frauds, and no truth is in them. They are of their father, the devil. Edom-Rome is Babylon with its mystery religions, it is the mother of harlots who will soon fall, "And there followed another angel, saying Babylon is fallen, is fallen, that great city, because she made all nations drink of the wine of the wrath of her fornication" (Revelation 14:8).

TRANSATLANTIC SLAVE TRADERS

The transatlantic and Arab slave trades caused the Israelites to become servants to all nations. Edom-Rome via the papacy went about to destroy all the Hebrew Israelites who had settled in the area known as Negroland. They instituted a slave-trade where the Hebrew Israelites were traded to the Western side of the world on slave ships during the transatlantic slave trade. This great massacre began when Edom-Rome established via a papal Bull the perpetual slavery of the descendants of Israel. Pope Nicholas V of Portugal signed this document on January 8th, 1455. The legal right was granted to Portugal to enslave all people they encountered south of Cape Bojador, which is on the coast of Western Sahara. It was this Pope who declared perpetual slavery for the Israelites. And, as the prophecy foretold, they would trade the children of Israel for

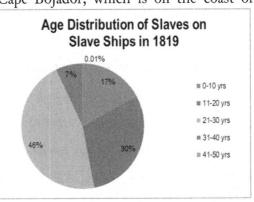

Age Distribution of Slaves on Slave Ships in 1819

- 0-10 yrs
- 11-20 yrs
- 21-30 yrs
- 31-40 yrs
- 41-50 yrs

wine and other commodities, "And they cast lots for my people; and have given a boy for a harlot, and sold a girl for wine, that they might drink' (Joel 3:3). They captured and dispersed them to the four corners of the earth. Millions of Hebrew Israelite boys and girls were captured and sold into slavery to the Americas. This slave trade lasted for three hundred years, which removed the Hebrews far away from their borders.

Most of the slaves were children and young people when captured. Many Hebrew Israelites still knew their identity, but because they trafficked in children, the children did not remember their identity. And, once they removed the children of Israel from their borders and history, they had no

Children of the Slave Trade

way of keeping their identity. These young people and children had no grounding in their Hebrew culture, coupled with the trauma of being stolen from their homeland and taken far from away resulted in a complete loss of the memory of who they were. Therefore, the transatlantic slave trade is believed to have had the most significant impact on the lives of the Hebrew Israelites in these "last days." When Edom-Rome captured the slaves, they would baptize them into the Christian faith and give them Christian names once they arrived at their destination, which further removed them from their heritage. Statistics compiled from the Manifest of slave ships show the average age of slaves captured and carried on these ships to the West in 1819. The results reveal that over three-quarters of the slaves were below age 30, with half between the ages of 21 and 30. The evidence confirms the prophecy that it would be the children of Israel who go into captivity, "Thou shalt beget sons and daughters, but thou shalt not enjoy them; for they shall go into captivity" (Deuteronomy 28:41).

Edom-Rome has continued to carry out the systematic destruction of the children of Israel since they took them from the shores of West Africa to the Americas. This captivity in various forms has lasted for about four hundred years, and its effects are seen in the lives of the descendants of the slaves even today. The Hebrew Israelites who remained on the African Continent suffered no less as the same colonizers of Edom-Rome sliced up the African Continent into sections based on the resources they wanted. They enslaved those who remained and caused continuous havoc among the

Hebrew Israelite Slaves

Hebrew Israelite Children on a Slave Ship

tribes. In dividing the land, they divide families and tribes, which brought much hardship to the people. And, today many of the Hebrew Israelites living in Africa cannot imagine they are the children of Israel. Because of Edom-Rome's impact on the Continent of Africa, many of the countries continue to experience adverse effects. However, they have declared their independence from Edom-Rome their oppressors.

HATERS OF TRUE ISRAEL

Edom-Rome is identified in history by their intense hatred for the black people known as Negroes. This hatred did not emerge based on color alone because Edom-Rome always knew Israel's identity, and they knew what their role was in subjecting Israel to the punishment allowed by YAHUAH. However, they were brutal in delivering the chastisement and went far beyond what was necessary to punish Israel. They knew Israel was YAHUAH'S Chosen people, and that knowledge increased the hatred for Jacob a hundred-fold. Edom-Rome used the color of Jacob-Israel as a by-word and the identity marker they could not hide. Therefore, they contrasted the color of their white skin, a claim that made them superior to Jacob-Israel's black skin, which made them inferior and less than human.

This hatred that Edom-Rome has for Jacob-Israel intensified once the Judeans went into Babylonian captivity in 605BC. The Edomites were living in the Negev valley, south of Judea. Because of their envy and resentment toward Jacob, they delighted in the Babylonian captivity of the Judeans, taking part when they burned Solomon's Temple and captured those who had escaped. And, since that time, they have pursued Jacob-Israel carrying this ancient hatred and loathing of Israel fo more than two thousand years. As a result, YAHUAH reminds us who rules the earth, "The earth is given into the hand of the wicked: he covereth the faces of the judges thereof; if not where, and who is he" (Job 9:24)? Although they have recorded and allowed individual accounts of the history of the persecution and destruction of Israel, they have replaced the actual Israelites in later years with the imposter Jewish Edomites living in Palestine and scattered throughout Europe and other parts of the earth. Edom-Rome has used the Jewish converts to replace Israel in Europe and claim the atrocities that happened to the Israelites either happened to the fake Jews or Protestant Christians. Edom-Rome expelled the Black Hebrew Israelites from Europe onto the African continent and revised history to reflect that all black people they enslaved are just random people and have their origins in Sub-Saharan Africa. They have deceived even the Israelites into believing Africa is the "Motherland" of the black population. They are fraudsters, and Scripture describes them as people who are wicked and are born with the desire to lie, "The wicked are estranged from the womb: they go astray as soon as they are born, speaking lies' (Psalm 58:3).

---

[1] Chumash Bereishis – The book of Genesis

[2] Hegelian dialectic is the framework for guiding our thoughts and actions into conflicts that lead us to a predetermined solution.

[3] Virgil Eclogue X. 27 also called the Bucolics, is the first three works of the Latin poet Virgil.

[4] Karta means manager of joint family and joint family properties. He is the person

who takes care of day to day expenses of the family, looks after the family and protects the joint family properties.

[5] Midrash is the biblical exegesis by ancient Judaic authorities, using a mode of interpretation of hermeneutics, comparative and homiletics, which makes great use of parables, allegories, metaphors, puns, etc.

[6] Tanna D' Bei Eliahu Zuta (19) alternate transliterations include Tana D'vei Eliahu is the composite name of a Midrash, consisting of two parts, whose final redaction took place at the end of the 10th century AD. The first part is called "Seder Eliyahu Rabbah" (31 chapters); the second, "Seder Eliyahu Zuta" (15 chapters).

[7] Mitzvah in its primary meaning "commandment" refers to precepts and commandments commanded by ELOHIYM, with the additional connotation of one's religious duty.

[8] C. Mohlberg, "Bibliographia L. Cuniberti Mohlberg," was called to work at the Vatican Library in 1924 from 1927 to 1939 he devoted himself to his first great series of liturgical editions, and in 1931 he was named professor for early church history of liturgy at the Pontifical Institute for Christian Archeology.

[9] John Ogilvie, (1579-10 March 1615) was a Scottish Catholic martyr. A Catholic priest, he is the only post-Reformation Scottish saint.

CHAPTER 9

How Jacob and Esau Impacted the Earth

I N THE BEGINNING, YAHUAH created the heavens and
the earth. And the earth was without form and void, and
darkness was upon the face of the deep. And the RUACH
HA KODESH moved upon the face of the waters. And
YAHUAH said, let there be light: and there was light. And
YAHUAH saw that it was good: And YAHUAH divided the light
from the darkness. And YAHUAH called the light Day, and the
darkness he called Night. And the evening and the morning were
the first days" (Genesis 1:1-5). These first five verses of Genesis
are analogous to the concept that YAHUAH had for Jacob and
Esau's creation on the earth as he made them have rulership over

two different worlds. Jacob and Esau represent night and day, black and white, darkness and light, good and evil, which signify righteousness and sin. YAHUAH created both, so the ultimate result is righteousness on the earth, "I form the light, and create darkness: I make peace, and create evil: I YAHUAH do all these things" (Isaiah 45:7).

YAHUAH never called the darkness good, and he ended the day in the evening so that darkness could never be part of the day. However, Edom-Rome sought to change the time the day began and decided that night-time was the start of a new day, which implies that sin is the beginning of something new. Scripture states that the morning and evening were the first days, not night. Before YAHUAH created the day, darkness was upon the face of the deep and not considered part of the day just as YAHUSHA confirmed what period makes up the day, "YAHUSHA answered, Are there not twelve hours in the day? If any man walks in the day, he stumbleth not, because he seeth the light of this world" (John 11:9). Jacob represents the day and Esau the night. According to YAHUAH, the twelve-hour period was a day, and he separated it from the night. They measure the nighttime in watches with the day ending in the evening, followed by night. Scripture also supports the idea that, in the Kingdom of YAHUAH, there will be no darkness no night, which means no sin, "And the gates of it shall not be shut at all by day: for there shall be no night there" (Revelation 21:25).

The purpose of Jacob and Esau's existence on the earth is to fulfill the plan that YAHUAH set in motion from the foundation of the earth to bring about righteousness in the people he chose to be his own on the earth as well those who will become the servants in the kingdom. "For the children being not yet born, neither having done any good or evil, that the purpose of YAHUAH according to election might stand, not of works, but him that calleth; It was said unto her, The elder shall serve the younger, As it is written, Jacob have I loved, but Esau have I hated" (Romans 9:11-13). YAHUAH selected Jacob for righteousness and Esau for wickedness. Therefore, YAHUAH used Esau as the chastening rod to punish the descendants of Jacob for their fore-parents disobedience to his laws, statutes, and commandments and they are reminded, "Now no chastening for the present seemeth to be joyous, but grievous: nevertheless, afterward it yieldeth the peaceable fruit of righteousness unto them which are exercised thereby" (Hebrews 12:11). Edom-Rome could rule over Jacob-Israel but, Jacob-Israel will overcome Edom-Rome and rule in the kingdom to come. In 2 Maccabees 6:12, Israel is therefore admonished, "Now I beseech those that read this book, that they are not discouraged for these calamities, but that they judge those punishments not to be for destruction, but a chastening of our nation."

Because Esau and his descendants went far beyond what YAHUAH required them to do in implementing the punishment YAHUAH will bring his vengeance upon them in the form of plagues and pestilences, "And I saw another sign in heaven, great and marvelous, seven angels having seven last plagues; for in them is filled up the wrath of YAHUAH" (Revelation 15:1). YAHUAH made Esau live and rule in this age while Jacob had to overcome this adversary in righteousness, which will result in Israel ruling in the kingdom of YAHUAH where no evil may exist. The Hebrew Sages confirm the dichotomy between Jacob, who they described as good and one who stayed near to the home, and Esau, who they described as wicked and a bestial man for the field (Genesis 25:27). It is these important differences that describe the purpose of YAHUAH'S creation, which shows in the distinction between light and darkness, "...and YAHUAH called the light Day, which is Jacob, and the darkness he called Night which is Esau" (Bereshit Rabbah 2:4). Abarbanel also translated this distinction to include the differences in the skin color between Esau and Jacob.

DECEPTION IN THE GARDEN OF EDEN

When YAHUAH created Adam and Eve, he instructed them to eat from the tree that brought life. He also warned them not to eat the fruit of the tree of knowledge of good and evil because eating it would bring death. However, Hashatan deceived Eve. That is the lust for what she saw enticed her into wanting what she should not have. She, therefore, ate of the forbidden fruit, which she believed would make her and Adam both be like the Highest. Hashatan is her lust, which is an evil inclination that convinced her that by eating the fruit, she would have the right to choose between good and evil for herself. The Highest YAHUAH never intended for humankind to choose good and evil for themselves. He had instructed both Adam and Eve, the tree from which they should eat and the one which they should not eat because, in doing so, they would die. Therefore, YAHUAH did not tempt them as some teachings imply, "Let no man say when he is tempted, I am tempted of YAH for YAHUAH cannot be tempted with evil, neither tempts he any man: But every man is tempted, when he is drawn away of his lust, and enticed. Then when lust hath conceived, it bringeth forth sin: and sin, when it is finished, bringeth forth death" (James 1:13-15). It is the perpetuation of this lie that has caused humanity to believe they have a right to make choices. Eve lusted after the fruit, and from that time, man has been deciding what is good and evil for them based on their lust. The result is that none of their choices were good because it is rooted in disobedience to the Highest, "For all that is in the world, the lust of the flesh, and the lust of the eyes, and the pride of life, is not of the Father, but is of the world" (1 John: 2:16).

Eve's disobedience brought sin to the entire human race because the eye of lust was open. Humankind has no capacity without the Creator to know what is moral and just and good. YAHUAH, as the Creator of the Universe, is the only one who knows what it is to be noble. Man sees the good as only what appeals to his senses and is pleasing to his flesh. However, in the wisdom of YAHUAH there is a time for every purpose under heaven and what is right and just may not always be pleasing to the flesh, therefore, "To everything, there is a season, and a time to every purpose under heaven: A time to be born, and a time to die; a time to plant, and a time to pluck up that which is planted; a time to kill, and a time to heal; a time to break down, and a time to build up" (Ecclesiastes 3:1-3).

In the face of the lust of Eve wanting to choose between good and evil for herself, in the hope of her becoming like the Most High there is no good remaining outside of obeying the Most High Creator ELOHIYM. All of Eve's choices from there on are in disobedience, which is evil and brings death. YAHUAH'S original creation, Adam and Eve, chose not to obey Him, and they rejected life for all of humanity. YAHUAH, therefore, threw them out of the Garden of Eden, "And YAHUAH ELOHIYM said, Behold, the man is become as one of us, to know good and evil: and now, lest he put forth his hand, and also take of the tree of life, and eat, and live forever: therefore YAHUAH ELOHIYM sent him forth from the garden of Eden, to till the ground from whence he was taken" (Genesis 3:22-23). Thus, YAHUAH had in his plan another way to bring righteousness and life on the earth, "For as by one man's disobedience many were made sinners, so by the obedience of one shall many be made righteous" (Romans 5: 19). YAHUAH in wisdom made it possible to redeem humanity, and his redemption for humankind would come through one seed of Abraham, Isaac, and Jacob-Israel.

YAHUAH created all things for his purpose, including evil that all people on the earth will know he is the ELOHIYM above all Elohiym, knowing the end from the beginning. He makes the choices, and he chose Israel, the carriers of his righteous seed. He chose them to be his children before he created anything, "The portion of Ya'aqov is not like them: for he is the former of all things; and Yashar'el is the rod of his inheritance: YAHUAH TSEVA'OTH is his name" (Jeremiah 10:16). Through them would righteousness be brought to the earth, and in them will righteousness be found. Then every knee shall bow, and every tongue shall confess and worship YAHUAH, just as the twenty-four elders, who continuously say in YAHUAH'S presence, "You are worthy, O YAHUAH ELOHAYNU, to receive glory and honor and power: for you have created all things, and for your pleasure they are and were created" (Revelation 4:11).

TWO NATIONS

YAHUAH created the competing personalities of Jacob and Esau as two different people who would become two separate nations on Earth. However, they would not rule at the same time. Esau would have dominion as the wicked first, and Jacob would follow to rule in righteousness for eternity. Therefore, Esau was promised to live in the fatness of the earth and Jacob to own the earth. YAHUAH determined that Esau, the eldest, would rule the earth as sin, and Jacob would have to overcome many difficulties because sin prevails. This sinful world has to be overcome through adversity. Hence, Scripture describes Jacob as clay that can be molded into the shape needed, then fired, so it remains in shape formed to reach its full potential. On the contrary, Scripture characterizes Esau as iron, which is not pliable with a form that is unbendable. YAHUAH would use this iron to bring hardship upon Jacob's descendants and perform as the fire. In the end, this firing of the clay of Jacob would produce a vessel fitted for holy use. Therefore, Israel is encouraged by the Father, "My son, despise not the chastening of YAHUAH; neither be weary of his correction" (Proverbs 3:11).

The Most High YAHUAH is righteous, good, and just, however, because of sin, humankind has experienced adversity and death. At the beginning, when YAHUAH made the earth, and before the borders of the world stood, or ever the winds blew, and he had made anything, YAHUAH decided what his plan would be as it related to Jacob and Esau, "Then did I consider these things, and they all were made through me alone, and through none other: by me also they shall be ended, and by none other" (2 Esdras 6:6). YAHUAH chose Jacob-Israel to bring a holy and just nation that would lead the people in righteousness upon the earth where YAHUAH would come and live among the righteous. However, for righteousness to prevail, Israel would first have to endure much difficulty throughout their generations. Esdras, curious about what would happen in the end, asked the Highest what would bring about this end, "And he said unto me, From Abraham unto Isaac, when Jacob and Esau were born of him,

Jacob's hand held first the heel of Esau. For Esau is the end of the world, and Jacob is the beginning of it that followeth" (2 Esdras 6:8-9). Esau brought about harsh conditions for Jacob to kill the pride that sin brings. Therefore, Israel, being chosen for such a role, must have light-hearted ease of mind and spirit and wait with patience to change from his low estate "For gold is tried in the fire, and acceptable men in the furnace of adversity" (Ecclesiasticus 2:5).

YAHUAH allowed Esau-Edom to bring evil against Israel however because YAHUAH is a just ELOHIYM he must also repay Esau for the wickedness they heaped upon Israel, "Behold, saith YAHUAH, I will bring plagues upon the world; the sword, famine, death, and destruction" (2 Esdras 15:5). YAHUAH caused Esau to fulfill his will so that Israel would desire the characteristics of the Father and the Kingdom of the Highest when the refiner returns. "But who may abide the day of his coming? And who shall stand when he appeareth? For he is like a refiner's fire, and like fuller's soap: and he shall sit as a refiner and purifier of silver: and he shall purify the sons of Levi, and purge them as gold and silver, that they may offer unto YAHUAH an offering in righteousness" (Malachi 3: 2-3). YAHUAH uses fire to purify and destroy the evil brought about by pride. He must stamp out this pride of those who call themselves good and righteous. YAHUAH needs a righteous people to live with him for all eternity, and he confirmed to Esdras how he would bring this about, "I will tell thee a similitude, Esdras; As when thou askest the earth, it shall say unto thee, that it giveth much mold of which you make earthen vessels, but little dust that gold cometh of even so is the course of this present world. There are many created, but I shall save a few" (Esdras 8:2-3). YAHUAH created the earth for the people he chose before he created its foundation. "And therefore, be thou not curious how the ungodly shall punish, and when: but enquire how the righteous shall be saved, whose the world is, and for whom the world is created" (2 Esdras 9:13).

PREDESTINATION

Eber is a progeny of Shem, who was the choice bloodline from which YAHUAH chose Israel as his peculiar people. YAHUAH had a blueprint for separating and dividing the earth, and Israel was foreordained to come through Abraham, and Isaac his predetermined choice. The Highest purposed to establish his righteous kingdom through Abraham's son Isaac the father of Jacob-Israel, the patriarch of the twelve tribes, "The earth is YAHUAH'S, and the fullness thereof; the world, and they that dwell therein" (Psalm 24:1). And, although humanity is free to operate in the Highest ELOHIYM'S system, He is the ultimate ruler. Everyone will act according to his will on earth as He so chooses, "For the potter, tempering soft earth, fashioneth every vessel with much labor for our service: yea, of the same clay he maketh both the vessels that serve for clean uses, and likewise also all such as serve to the contrary: but what is the use of either sort, the potter himself is the judge" (Wisdom of Solomon 15:7). Therefore, humanity can only accomplish what He has preordained. YAHUAH chose a people, Israel, of all the people he created, to be his own and said they were righteous before they did anything righteous. "For you are a holy people unto YAHUAH ELOHAYKA, and YAHUAH has chosen you to be a peculiar people unto himself, above all the nations upon the earth" (Deuteronomy 14:2).

YAHUAH covenanted with his people and gave them laws which he expected them to obey, but he knew they would not; "For he established a testimony in Jacob, and appointed a law in Israel, which he commanded our fathers, that they should make them known to their children: that the generation to come might know them, even the children which should be born; who should arise and declare them to their children: that they might set their hope in YAHUAH, and not forget the works of YAHUAH, but keep his commandments," (Psalm 78:5-7). However, YAHUAH planned for their disobedience, and when sin also became clear in his people, the Highest cut them off for disobedience to the covenantal laws he had made with their fathers. "And I saw when for all the causes whereby backsliding Israel committed adultery, I had put her away, and given her a bill of divorce yet her treacherous sister Judah feared not but went and played the harlot also," (Jeremiah 3:8). YAHUAH chose Israel to be his bride, whom he married under the cloud on Mount Sinai, and she became his wife. But Israel disobeyed, so he divorced the Ten Northern tribes because of their rebellion.

However, after divorcing Israel and because his word does not return void as to them being his children forever, he made it possible for him to remarry Israel. In, Hebrew culture a man who has given his wife a bill of divorcement could never marry her again. She may marry other husbands, but she could never return to the first. Therefore, YAHUAH from the beginning made it possible to marry Israel and renew his covenant. He sent YAHUSHA as his servant to prepare the way for Israel's redemption back to him after the order of Melchizedek, "YAHUAH hath sworn and will not repent, Thou art a priest forever after the order of Melchizedek" (Psalm 110:4). Israel will be born again as a new bride when YAHUAH returns. The new birth of Israel will take place at the coming of YAHUSHA as he said to Nicodemus, "YAHUSHA answered and said unto him, Verily, verily, I say unto thee, Except a man be born again, he cannot see the kingdom of YAHUAH" (John 3:3).

Both the male and female had to symbolically die and become a new person so YAHUAH could make a New Covenant. The marriage in the New Covenant has not occurred yet but will take place at Mount Zion at the coming of the kingdom. "But this shall be the covenant that I shall make with the house of Israel; After those days, saith YAHUAH, I will put my law in their inward parts, and write it in their hearts; and will be their ELOHIYM, and they shall be my people," (Jeremiah 31:33). He made it possible for Israel to return and become righteous through this new covenant and in Hebrews Paul confirms this word written by the Prophet Jeremiah, "For finding fault with them, he saith, Behold, the days come, saith YAHUAH, when I will make a new covenant with the house of Yashar'el and with the house of Judah not according to the covenant I made with their fathers, in the day when I took them by the hand to lead them out of the land of Egypt; because they continued not in my covenant, and I regarded them not, saith YAHUAH. For this is the covenant I will cut with the house of Yashar'el after those days, saith YAHUAH; I will put my Torah into their mind, and write it in their hearts: and I will be their ELOHIYM, and they shall be to me a people. And they shall not teach every man his neighbor, and every man his brother, saying Know YAHUAH: for all shall know me, from the least to the greatest" (Hebrews 8:8-11). YAHUAH will renew this covenant with the same bloodline descendants of Jacob-Israel, who came out of Egypt and covenanted with YAHUAH in the wilderness of Sinai. YAHUAH never gave the other nations on earth the laws, and therefore he did not make a covenant with them so they could not break the covenant. In fact, at this marriage, the children's hearts will return to the fathers and the fathers to the children. These fathers are; Abraham, Isaac, and Jacob, "And he shall turn the heart of the fathers to the children, and the heart of the children to their fathers, lest I come and smite the earth with a curse," (Malachi 4:6).

As the Creator of humanity, YAHUAH knew Israel would disobey, and he also knew that both good and evil could never exist in the same universe in peace. Therefore, he put a plan in motion to redeem humankind before he created anything. He chose a people from earth's foundation for which this plan would be automatic, and he chose the twin brothers Jacob and Esau to represent these two worlds to bring about the righteousness he needs to dwell among his chosen people on the earth. "And I have chosen the seed of Ya'aqov from amongst all that I have seen, and have written him down as my firstborn son, and have sanctified him unto myself forever and ever; and I will teach them the Sabbath, that they may guard the Sabbath thereon from all work" (Jubilees 2:21). Esau has lived in this age in rebellion to the Highest, which will end in the death of him and his descendants. Jacob's rule will follow, and they will live in righteousness in the kingdom to come for eternity, "But Israel shall be saved in YAHUAH with an everlasting salvation: ye shall not be ashamed nor confounded world without end" (Isaiah 45:17). YAHUAH knows the end from the beginning, and he allows every action by humanity to produce his purpose within his creation. So, when YAHUAH shaped Jacob and Esau from the same lump of clay, he fashioned one for His honor and one for dishonor. The Highest chose Jacob to love, and He hated Esau as he represented sin. He chose this means to bring righteousness to the earth. Thus, YAHUAH predestined Jacob for salvation, and he destined Esau for destruction.

Esdras noted that YAHUAH created everything on earth. Still, he only chose one people as his children, "All this have I spoken before thee, O YAHUAH, because thou madest the world for our sakes, as for the other people, which also come of Adam, thou hast said they are nothing, but be like unto spittle: and hast likened the abundance of them unto a drop that falleth from a vessel" (2 Esdras 6:55-56). Paul, in his epistle to the Hellenized Hebrew Israelites living in Rome, reminded them of the Most High's plan and purpose for Esau and Jacob. He implored that as the creation made by the Highest Creator, they had no right to question why YAHUAH created differences and each one for a specific purpose, "Nay but O man, who art thou that repliest against YAHUAH? Shall the thing form say to him that formed it, Why hast thou made me thus? Hath not the potter power over the clay, of the same lump to make one vessel unto honor, and another unto dishonor" (Romans 9:20-21).

In truth, YAHUAH is also the Husbandman who sows the seed upon the earth, that may or may not bring forth fruit, "For as the husbandman soweth much seed upon the ground, and planteth many trees, and yet the thing that is sown well in his season cometh not up, neither doth all that is planted take root: even so is it of them that are sown in the world; they shall not all be saved" (2 Esdras 8: 41). It has never been YAHUAH'S plan to save all people. He created all things and corruptible people for its purpose and chose a particular people from his creation because he did not create all people equally. He has also chosen servants of the other nations who will work for his people in the Kingdom to come, so; it is YAHUAH'S choice. And, YAHUSHA reminded his disciples it was he who chose them, "Ye have not chosen me, but I have chosen you and ordained you, that ye should go and bring forth fruit, and that your fruit should remain: that whatsoever ye shall ask of the Father in my name, he may give it to you" (John 15:16).

All things, including all men, are subject to the Creator and made to fulfill his will on the earth. Humankind must realize the purpose for which YAHUAH calls them to, "Let us hear the conclusion of the whole matter: Fear ELOHIYM and keep his commandments: for this is the whole duty of man. For ELOHIYM shall bring every work into judgment, with every secret thing, whether it be good, or whether it be evil" (Ecclesiastes 12:13-14). YAHUAH predestined the descendants of Jacob-Israel to experience certain destructions at the hand of Esau-Edom, which is a sign that identifies the children of the Most High and intended to distinguish the people of YAHUAH from the other Gentile nations. Then, at the end of Edom-Rome's rule over Jacob, the kingdom of heaven will come to earth. Therefore, we pray, "Thy Kingdom come on earth as it is in heaven." Jacob-Israel will begin their rule with YAHUSHA under the order of Melchizedek, "And the kingdom and dominion, and the greatness of the kingdom under the whole heaven, shall be given to the people of the saints of the Highest, whose kingdom is an everlasting kingdom, and all dominions shall serve and obey him" (Daniel 7:27).

CURSES FOR DISOBEDIENCE

YAHUAH promised the Israelites blessings for obedience to the laws, but if they disobeyed, they would suffer the curses. After Moses had given Israel the laws, they obeyed them and experienced the blessings. One blessing was that once people recognize they belonged to YAUAH, this knowledge alone will make them afraid, "And Israel served YAHUAH all the days of Joshua, and all the days of the elders that overlived Joshua, and which had known all the works of YAHUAH, that he had done for Israel" (Joshua 24:31). However, after many centuries the influence of the other nations that surrounded them caused some of them to seek the gods of these nations. The curses were that YAHUAH said would come on Israel happened throughout the history of the nation of Israel. Later in history, they were taken into slavery that would take them far away from their borders, "And YAHUAH shall scatter thee among all people, from the one end of the earth even unto the other; and there thou shalt serve other gods, which neither thou nor thy fathers have known, even wood and stone" (Deuteronomy 28:64). Historical evidence shows that during the time of the Greek and Roman Empires, the Hebrew Israelites rejected the laws of YAHUAH some by force and others who just chose to disobey because they wanted to be part of the culture.

Once the Israelites had become disobedient and dispersed into the other nations, they lost their identity and experienced all the curses spoken of in the prophecies. "YAHUAH shall cause thee to be smitten before thine enemies: thou shalt go out one way against them and flee seven ways before him: and shalt be removed into all the kingdoms of the earth" (Deuteronomy 28:25). Because Edom-Rome removed the children from their parents and scattered them into the nations, they only knew themselves as slaves with roots in Africa and those who had been dispersed into Africa also lost their identity, "Thy sons and thy daughters shall be given unto another people, and thine eyes shall look, and fail with longing for them all the day long: and there shall be no might in thine hand" (Deuteronomy 28:32). There is evidence that shows this prophecy being fulfilled many times throughout the dispersion of the Israelites. And, the curse of the kings that Israel would place over themselves in the diaspora also came to pass during the rise of Edom-Rome's papal Empire in the fifteenth century, "YAHUAH shall bring thee, and thy king which thou shalt set over thee, unto a nation which neither thou nor thy fathers have known; and there shalt thou serve other gods, wood and stone" (Deuteronomy 28:36). In fact, in Britain, Ireland, Scotland, and the other European nations before the rise of the revised papal Edom-Roman Empire, the Israelites in the diaspora ruled in these nations and served the other gods of Edom-Rome. The Jacobites of Britain was one monarchy along with others in Russia, Germany, and many in Africa that Edom-Rome conquered, hid their identity, and recast the people to look like the white Edomites. They then led the children of these Israelites into slavery to the West via the transatlantic and other slave trades, even to this day.

Edom-Rome, the fourth beast power has carried out YAHUAH'S will to be against the Israelites for a much longer time than all the other nations that have held them in captivity. In the Letters of Jacob chapter 5: 1-17, in the dream, he saw a Ladder and how Edom-Rome would force the Israelites to worship idols and the dead. Jacob recalls what he saw and heard, "The Highest will raise up kings from your Brother Esau's children's, children and they will exceed all the rulers of the peoples of the earth who have done evil to your descendants and they will be given over into his power, and they will suffer him against their will. He will hold them by force and rule over them. And they cannot oppose him until the day he decrees upon them to serve idols and to offer sacrifices to the dead, and he will command that all people in his kingdom be forced to do this. There will be some who would be guilty of such offense; some of your family will serve the Highest, and some will worship idols. Know Jacob that your descendants will be exiled in a strange land, and they will afflict them with slavery and put wounds on them every day, but the Lord will judge the people whom they serve." The descendants of Edom-Rome have led the descendants of Jacob to worship idols and the dead to this day in the religions of Judaism, Christianity, and Islam. They have also kept Israel in perpetual slavery. These trials of the Israelites in history have helped to identify them as the true people of YAHUAH, "Therefore shalt thou serve thine enemies, which YAHUAH shall send against thee, in hunger, and thirst, and nakedness, and in want of all things: and he shall put a yoke of iron upon thy neck until he has destroyed thee," (Deuteronomy 28:48). "For many great miseries shall be done to them that in the latter time shall dwell in the world, because they have walked in great pride" (2 Esdras 8: 50).

Edom-Rome applied YAHUAH'S permissive will, which gave way for them to destroy the people of Israel, just as they had crucified the HAMASHIACH and blamed the Judeans for his death. However, this was the will of YAHUAH as YAHUSHA told Pilate at his trial that the only power he had over him was the power given from the Most High, "Thou couldest have no power at all against me, except it were given thee from above," (John 19:11). Pilate felt guilty which led him to commit suicide, "And Sha'ul stretched forth his hands upon the water, and prayed unto YAHUAH, saying, O ADONAI ELOHIYM, give a sign unto all nations that here Pontius Pilate, which condemned your only begotten son, plunged headlong into the pit," (Acts 29: 20). Like YAHUAH gave the HAMASHIACH over to Pilate, which represents Rome, YAHUAH handed Israel to Edom-Rome to do his will, "And it shall happen that in all the land, saith YAHUAH, I shall cut two parts off and they shall die, but I shall leave the third. And I will bring the third part through the fire and will refine them as silver is refined, and will try them as gold is tried: they shall call on my name, and I will hear them: I will say, It is my people: and they shall say, YAHUAH is my ELOHIYM," (Zechariah 13:8-9).

So whatever Edom-Rome, the descendants of Esau has done YAHUAH predetermined for it to be so against the Hebrew Israelites. Edom-Rome is that fourth beast power ruling over the earth for a long time as Daniel noted, and as Jacob also saw in his dream, "God showed Jacob, Babylon's angel climbing up 70 rungs of the ladder and going down again. Then he showed him Media's angel going up and down 52 rungs, then Greece's going up and down 180. Then Rome's went up and up and up, and Jacob did not know how many rungs it would ascend. So, Jacob took fright of this and said, 'O Lord, do you mean that this one has no descent?' God said to him, 'Even if you see him reach the very heavens, I will still cause him to go down as it is written, Though you soar aloft like an eagle, though your nest is set among the stars, from there will I bring you down,' says the Lord." (Ladder of Jacob, 5:1-17, ref. Obadiah 1:4).

WHAT IS THE DECEPTION?

The great deception led by Edom-Rome has many layers, and the fact that Esau, who is Edom no longer exists, is one. The historians claim they became extinct as a people in 550 BC. According to Steve Rudd (2017), Arab pressure on the Edomite territory, to some extent, caused them to move into the Negev. They then removed from Judah's control in 597 BC when the Babylonians handed the Negev over to the Edomites. However, by the fifth century, during the Persian period, the land of Edom had no sedentary occupation, and nomadic Arab tribes called the Nabateans displaced the Edomites in Edom. Rudd also asserts that the Nabateans are the Idumeans spoken of in Scripture. However, the Nabateans could not have taken the land of Edom and also be the Idumeans who occupied the Negev. Because history shows, the Edomites moved into the Negev after they claim the Nabateans conquered the land of Edom. Ancient history shows the name of the Edomites changed to the Greek form Idumeans and the area south of Judaea, which was the Negev they renamed Idumea. The Nabateans, according to Josephus, however, were friends of the Judeans and assisted them in battles against the Edomites in the land of Edom and Idumea during the Maccabean period, which came many centuries after the Judeans had returned to Judaea from Babylonian captivity. Therefore, this theory of the Nabateans taking the place of the Edomites is a lie, and the Edomites becoming extinct is also false. Hebrew Scripture and history do not support the theory that any group of people became extinct. If Edom-Rome could not exterminate the true Israelites after pursuing them for these past two thousand years, then no other nation or people have vanished from the face of the earth.

Historians have tried to fit this version of the Edomites becoming an extinct people from the Biblical prophecies that predict Edom's destruction. However, the prophecies are future and forecast the obliteration of the Edomites at the end, when Jacob-Israel will begin their rule, "Shall I not in that day, saith YAHUAH, even destroy the wise men out of Edom, and understanding out of the mount of Esau? And thy mighty men, O Teman, shall be dismayed, to the end that every one of the mounts of Esau may be cut off by slaughter. For thy violence against thy brother, Jacob shame shall cover thee, and thou shalt be cut off forever" (Obadiah 1:8-10). Esau, who is Edom the Edomites and Kittiym Rome, still exists today, and they continue to shed the blood of the children of Jacob-Israel. They have been the thorn in the Hebrew Israelite's flesh. They have hidden their identity and created a narrative about the Arabs occupying Mount Seir, which is the Edomite territory to support the deception.

Another aspect of the deception is the truth about the identity of the Hebrew Israelites, the bloodline descendants of Jacob-Israel. Edom-Rome claims that Israel is an ancient people who no longer exist. However, these people still exist today and have not been so mixed in with the other nations that their identity is no longer viable. However, Edom-Rome created DNA science to support the theory that the bloodline of all people is mixed. The white Edomites have replaced true Israel as the chosen people of the Highest. They are identified as the modern-day Jews living in Palestine awaiting their Messiah because they do not believe that the HAMASHIACH came as history shows. The Jewish converts, along with the Christian Church, have now replaced Israel. They claim that Jesus came to die to save the entire world. Everyone who believes and receives him has salvation. They say YAHUAH cut off the blood-line descendants of Israel for disobedience to his laws, and he also cut off the Judeans because they did not receive the HAMASHIACH as the Redeemer. Yet, I do not find this reason for disinheriting true Israel in Scripture as the HAMASHIACH came to prepare Israel for their redemption back to the Father. This teaching of Edom-Rome contradicts what they believe and preach. They teach that the laws of YAHUAH have been done away with, and Christians no longer have to obey them. However, if the Highest YAHUAH cut off true Israel because they did not accept the HAMASHIACH or because they broke his covenant laws, then why does he now choose a people, the white Edomite Jews who do not accept that the Messiah has come and still await their Messiah's coming. He now also has accepted the Edomite Christians who claim he saved them, but they too no longer have to keep the laws of YAHUAH. They do not realize that if they were righteous, they would desire to keep the laws of the Highest YAHUAH because the laws of YAHUAH are not harmful but were given to demonstrate our love for the Highest YAHUAH.

Edom-Rome has deceived the world and made them believe that YAHUAH adopted Gentile Christians who replaced the children of Israel. These Christians, they say, are a mixture of people from all nations who can be saved by the Edomite savior god Jesus by grace through faith in him. They imply there is no longer a need to obey the Laws of YAHUAH as they have been fulfilled by Jesus as he kept them perfectly. Edom-Rome also claims that YAHUAH no longer has physical blood-line descendants from the tribes of Jacob-Israel. However, in Revelation it describes how the New Jerusalem will appear, "And had a wall great and high, and twelve gates, and at the gates, twelve angels, and the names are written thereon, which are the names of the twelve tribes of the children of Israel" (Revelation 21:12). The twelve tribes of Israel will be the only people allowed through the gates of the New Jerusalem; therefore, Scripture does not support their theory of YAHUAH's salvation for all people.

Papal Edom-Rome, who sits in Caesar's seat as the head of the Roman Empire today, has stolen the Hebrew Scriptures, recast the people while at the same time sow doubt about Scriptures' validity. They claim that most of the Scripture is written in metaphors, allegories, or poetry. The Scriptures may include allegories and parables, but they all pertain to the people of Israel and their history. And all the prophecies only refer to the chosen people of YAHUAH. For example, the story of the 'Woman at the Well' is a picture of Israel's history of being divorced from the Highest and married to other gods. YAHUSHA tells the woman she had five husbands, and the one she was with was not her own. The allegory depicted the woman as Israel and her five husbands, the false gods of Baal that Israel worshiped. Yet, the one she was with was not the Most High YAHUAH. He then told her she needed the water that he had to offer to give her life as she represented Israel, who was cut off for idolatry. The Scriptures are written to the Israelites about their history and future. For this reason, those in Christianity cannot understand its content or context.

Another deception is that all black people have their origins on the African Continent and existed nowhere else on the earth until they migrated through slavery. However, Scripture and historical records show the original people of the earth were people of dark skin, and they lived throughout the earth, including the isles of the sea. They also moved from place to place, not as 'hunter-gathers' but as expert land and sea-travelers. Edom-Rome claims the slaves they brought to America on slave ships were black Negroes from Africa, the children of Ham and not the Hebrew Israelites of the twelve tribes of Israel. However, in a book titled Whence the Black Irish of Jamaica, in it, there are several accounts of Lord Henry Cromwell. A Major General in Ireland enlisted 1500 soldiers to go to Jamaica as planters and to secure 1000 young Irish girls he referred to as wenches. He wrote they did not expect a problem, but they would have to use force and suggested adding 1500 to 2000 boys from twelve to fourteen years of age to the slaves. In this same book, there are also accounts of black Irish children being taken to Barbados. There is much evidence that shows that black people ruled Europe. Yet, Edom-Rome asserts they are the original people of Europe, and humanity begins with the white race.

Edom-Rome has tried to revised history to reflect that the Highest YAHUAH, the ELOHIYM of the universe, does not exist. They have obscured the truth that YAHUAH destined Edom-Rome to rule at this time in history. And, after their rulership comes to an end, they would be destroyed because it is His will and His plan for Jacob-Israel to rule in the world to come. YAHUAH gave the Gentiles other spirits that led them to form false, pagan religions and secret societies to keep the masses unaware, "...for there are many nations and many peoples, and all are his, and overall has he placed ruachoth (spirits) in authority to lead them astray from him" (Jubilees 15: 31). The Pope of Edom-Rome and the nation's leaders recognize that they are Esau, who is Edom, and they also know the identity of Israel. They have led the other Gentile nations in a conspiracy against Israel as prophesied in the Psalm, "They have taken crafty counsel against thy people, and consulted against thy hidden ones. They have said, Come, and let us cut them off from being a nation; that the name of Israel may be no more in remembrance' (Psalm 83:3-4).

WHY THE DECEPTION?

Edom-Rome set out deceive Israel to prevent them from attaining rulership in the kingdom that is to come. To do so, they had to deceive the entire world. Scripture shows that Edom-Rome is the adversary of Israel and the only nation they fear and can stand against them with the power of Most High. Therefore, it was necessary to keep the descendants of Israel in ignorance about the identities of both Edom and Israel. Because, once Israel knows who they are and whose they are, the roles will be reversed, and Israel becomes the head above all nations, including Esau-Edom. In Israel's dispersed and uninformed state they have no power because they have rejected knowledge, "My people are destroyed for lack of knowledge: because thou hast rejected knowledge, I will also reject thee, that thou shalt be no priest to me: seeing thou has forgotten the law of thy ELOHIYM, I will also forget thy children" (Hosea 4:6). The children of Israel went into the diaspora in Africa then taken on slave ships tho the four corners of the earth where they have lost their identity. Edom-Rome wanted to replace Jacob-Israel as the righteous on the earth and regain the lost birthright he sold to his younger brother, Jacob. Therefore, they created this massive deception. They are liars and fraudsters and could only operate based on the characteristics of which they were born. Edom-Rome cannot change as noted by the prophet, "Can the Ethiopian change his skin or the leopard his spots? Then may ye also do good, that is accustomed to doing evil" (Jeremiah 13:23).

Because Esau, who is Edom, is a liar and a cheat, they did what was natural to them. Edom as Rome hoped to establish a kingdom that would deliver them from the destruction that YAHUAH purposed for them. They have created and used their religions to support the hoax. They made these religions because they hated YAHUAH and his people, and they have envied the love YAHUAH has for Israel. Throughout history, Edom-Rome sought to kill, steal, and destroy the descendants of Jacob-Israel. They are thirsty for blood, which is the only thing that satisfies their thirst. Therefore, YAHUAH says, "Because thou hast had a perpetual hatred, and hast shed the blood of the children of Israel by the force of the sword in the time of their calamity, in the time that their iniquity had an end: therefore, as I live, saith YAHUAH ELOHIYM, I will prepare thee unto blood, and blood shall pursue thee: since thou hast not hated blood, even blood shall pursue thee" (Ezekiel 35:5-6).

Edom-Rome is also a hypocrite who appears to be principled. They hide their identity behind the outward appearances of the nobility they crave and steal from the Israelites who ruled the British Isles and many countries throughout Europe and Africa. They have appropriated all of what was Israel's, the architecture, art, music, and history of the real people of Nobility on the earth. Edom-Rome believes they have been given the divine right to rule as king over the earth, and so they have. Therefore, they destroyed hundreds of millions of the truly righteous people of Israel over the centuries. It was during the American Civil War when William T. Thompson, the creator of the Confederate flag of the United States of America an Edomite, confirmed their belief of this right, "As a people, we are fighting to maintain the Heaven ordained supremacy of the white man over the inferior or colored race; A white flag would thus be emblematical of our cause. Upon a red field would stand forth our southern cross, Gemmed, preserving in beautiful contrast the red white and blue." [1] In an example of an accurate depiction of Edom-Rome written by a rabbi in the rabbinical literature compares Edom-Rome to a pig or wild boar (Leviticus Rabbah 13). He makes this comparison because the hoof of the pig splits into two nails, which makes him cloven-footed and appears suitable for food, but the pig does not chew its cud. Therefore, the pig is acceptable by appearance, but because it does not chew the cud, he is impure, which makes him a hypocrite. Edom-Rome, the white Edomites, appear to be noble but are impure and base in their actions.

Esau, like Nimrod, wanted to occupy the throne of YAHUAH and become the ELOHIYM of the Universe. Therefore, Nimrod tried to build a tower to reach heaven. Babylonian religions continue to teach that somehow in the next life, they will attain this impossible feat of reaching Heaven where the throne of YAHUAH exists. But, it is the will of YAHUAH for Esau only to live and obtain the wealth of the earth and has rulership in this world, and not in the kingdom to come. Scripture destines him for ruin because of the wickedness he has perpetrated on the earth and the destruction he has committed against the chosen people of YAHUAH. He has a finite time to rule in this dominion just as prophecy predicts, "Remember the former things of old: for I am El, and there is none else; I am ELOHIYM, and there is none like Me, Declaring the end from the beginning, and from ancient times the things that are not yet done, saying, My counsel shall stand, and I will do all my pleasure" (Isaiah 46:9-10).

WHY HIDE THE PURPOSE FOR JACOB AND ESAU?

Edom-Rome has hidden the purpose and identities of Esau and Jacob for over three hundred years. Before this time, everyone knew the identities of these two peoples and the role they would play in the earth's history. It was during the Renaissance that Edom-Rome instituted the changes in artifacts and paintings and revised the history to reflect the present narrative. Many Israelite scholars and historians scattered throughout the diaspora have known the purpose of Edom-Rome and the role they played in Christianity and the other religions to destroy Israel and therefore have written commentaries based on this knowledge. Abarbanel, one such Jewish sage in Spain, revealed in one account written in the 1300s, as it relates to Edom-Rome's identity, "From this, you may learn that the prophet Obadiah did not prophesy only against the land of Edom, which is in the land's neighborhood of Israel, but also against the people which branches off from thence, and spreads through the entire world, and is the people of the Christians for they are the children of Edom." Esau is Edom, and Edom is Kittiym and Rome. "Shall I not in that day, saith YAHUAH, even destroy the wise men out of Edom, and understanding out of the mount of Esau" (Obadiah 1:8)? Josephus, the historian of the Israelites, concurs that the descendants of Esau, who is Edom, reigned in Kittiym, which is Italy. Edom-Rome reigned in Italy and Greece hundreds of years before they had even established the Christian church. Edom-Rome became the Papal Roman system that came out of the Chaldean mysteries, which unified with the mysteries of Egypt, Greece, Phoenicia, and Rome (Hislop, 2012).

The false teachings Edom-Rome created was designed to hide their real identity and purpose and the true identity and purpose of the descendants of Israel. Edom-Rome also recognized that they could engage in this deception because they have always known what their purpose was. They also knew that YAHUAH would one day awaken the Hebrew Israelites to the truth about their identity and that they would reclaim their position as the head nation. They also knew that when this happened, the charade of them being a 'holy' nation YAHUAH would expose, and their kingdom would come to an end. There is much evidence written by historians of the experiences of black Hebrews being persecuted by Edom-Rome just because they were Israel. In one example, during the expulsion of the Israelites from Spain and Portugal, Edom-Rome forced many of them into Africa where their descendants are today. They expelled them from Europe into Africa, where they met other Israelites who had fled there in previous dispersals. The vast majority of Israelites in Europe knew their own identity well into the 17th to 19th centuries and had accepted their fate because they too knew that their ancestors had sinned against the Highest YAHUAH and that He had assigned Edom-Rome to punish them. Abraham Zacuto, one of the Israelites living in Spain at the time wrote;

> And so, too, because of our sins, we saw with our own
> eyes the expulsions from Spain, Sicily, and Sardinia in

1492 and 1497 from Portugal. For from France we had come to Spain, where we had our enemies on one side and the sea on the other; but flight was possible from France, from which my great-grandfather came so that the descendants of (my grandfather) Abraham Zacuto were in Spain and I was born there into that good name. And all of them withstood the Castilian persecutions of 1391 and remained steadfast in the Holy One's faith One, Blessed Be He, and His Torah. I, too, was given the privilege of sanctifying the Holy Name along with my son Samuel, and we came to Africa after having been prisoners twice.[2]

The descendants of Israel knew the Highest YAHUAH directed his punishment toward them, and Edom-Rome would subjugate Israel. Therefore, Paul wrote in a letter to the Hebrews, "If ye endure chastening, YAHUAH dealeth with you as with sons for what son is, he whom the father chasteneth not? But if ye be without chastisement, of which all are partakers, then are ye bastards, and not sons" (Hebrews 12:7-8). In the end, Israel will experience YAHUAH's mercy, whereas Edom will experience his wrath. He will repay them for what they have done, "For YAHUAH will not be slack, neither will the Mighty be patient toward them, till he have smitten in sunder the loins of the unmerciful, and repaid vengeance to the heathen; till he has taken away the multitude of the proud, and broken the scepter of the unrighteous; Till he have rendered to every man according to his deeds, and to the works of men according to their devices; till he has judged the cause of his people, and made them rejoice in his mercy" (Ecclesiasticus 35:18). The events of these end times are evidence that the schemes and plans prepared and executed by Edom-Rome will not have its intended effect because YAHUAH has committed to saving Israel with an everlasting salvation, "For I knew they would not hear me because it is a stiff-necked people: but in the land of their captivities, they shall remember themselves. And shall know I am YAHUAH their ELOHIYM: for I will give them a heart, and ears to hear: And they shall praise me in the land of their captivity, and think upon my name, And return from their stiff neck, and their wicked deeds: for they shall remember the way of their fathers, which sinned before YAHUAH" (Baruch 2: 30-33).

The promised salvation that Israel will receive has conditions, and Edom-Rome thought they could change the outcome of Israel's deliverance by replacing them as the Chosen people of YAHUAH. However, YAHUAH chose Israel. They did not choose him, and therefore, the conditions taught by the Roman Christian Church does not apply to Israel. YAHUAH will save Israel with everlasting salvation even though Edom-Rome seemed to have destroyed them. The false Universalist doctrines imposed by the Babylonian mystery religions of Christianity tell its followers they could choose YAHUAH. But, no one can choose the Highest YAHUAH, and it is only him who can save.

Edom-Rome has taught doctrines that contradict the Highest, which has led Israel astray from him. Coupled with persecutions by the Roman Empire and dispersions, most of Israel followed the beast system and would have had its mark. During the period from 75 to 100 AD, the Roman Edomite Christians considered themselves to be a new Israel and desired to break all links with the old Judeo Christianity (Frend, 1984). The Edomite Christians taught another gospel, which proclaimed they would receive the same redemption YAHUAH offered to the Hellenized Israelites living in the diaspora. These changes in the teachings by Edom-Rome has caused true Israel to be in the wilderness because there is no truth on the earth and every form of dogma taught by Edom-Rome is a lie, "And to the woman were given two wings of a great eagle, that she might fly into the wilderness, into her place, where she is nourished for a time, and times, and half a time, from the face of the serpent" (Revelation 12:14). This woman represents true Israel; a nation scattered who fled into the wilderness and is hidden. The dragon representative of Edom-Rome made war with the remnant throughout the earth, "And the dragon was wroth with the woman, and went to make war with the remnant of her seed, which keeps the commandments of YAHUAH, and have the testimony of HAMASHIACH" (Revelation 12:17). Therefore, it is the Israelites who are still in their dispersed and lost state being nourished by the Highest YAHUAH.

---

[1] William T. Thompson designer of the second Confederate flag was an Ohioan writer and newspaper editor during the 19th century. During the American Civil War, he worked in Georgia as a newspaper editor and supported the confederacy. After the war ended, he supported the Democratic Party and opposed the Republican Party's civil rights efforts.

[2] Abraham Zucato, a Romanized form of his name Avraham ben Shmuel Zacut, was a Spanish astronomer, astrologer, mathematician, rabbi and historian who served as Royal Astronomer to King John ii of Portugal. The crater Zagut on the Moon is named after him. He lived from 1452- 1515 AD.

CHAPTER
10

How Edom-Rome Revised History and Deceived the World

THE APPROACHES EDOM-ROME USED to delude the Israelites and the world, in general, are many and maybe too many to outline in this chapter. However, what is important to understand is that the history of the world, as they have taught it, is a lie. The narrative they base on how the earth and its people came into existence. These are false theories, and therefore if the foundation is wrong, then so are all the concepts built on these theories. This chapter looks at several of the theories and methods of deception used by Edom-Rome and compares them with Scripture to analyze and determine what is the truth. Historical data shows that the descendants of Esau-Edom, the white people, have only dominated the earth since World Wars I and II. It was after these wars they recast and revised history to reflect the worldview of Esau-Edom via the Vatican and the Roman Catholic Church. We must know, however, that before the rulership of Edom-Rome, many other nations of black and brown-skinned people ruled on the earth, not only on the continent of Africa. The revisionist history of Edom-Rome has tried to change the way people understand their environment. In the past, all people learned about the earth they lived on by observing through their five senses the natural world around them, and through the spirit gods relative to their culture. However, Edom-Rome added, the religion called science to deny that the Highest ELOHIYM of creation exists and to deceive the world into believing that humanity evolved or began with a Big Bang. Paul, the Apostle, admonished Timothy in his day to avoid the false ideas and philosophies of these so-called scientists, "O Timothy, keep that which is committed to thy trust, avoiding profane and vain babblings, and oppositions of science falsely so called: Which some professing have erred concerning the faith" (1 Timothy 6:20-21). To support their theories, Edom-Rome has used philosophies and pagan ideas to form different branches of science. They then insisted it was only necessary to believe the ideas put forth by the scientists with no other proof, not even the observations made through the senses.

CHANGES IN WAYS WE KNOW THE TRUTH

The Highest YAHUAH created human beings with the ability to gain knowledge through their five senses, unlike the animal world he created that can only know via their instinct. YAHUAH created human beings with five senses that include seeing, hearing, tasting, smelling, and feeling. The Highest expected humans to use their senses to learn about the natural world around them. These senses placed human beings at a higher level of the food chain than the animal world and gave them the ability to think and draw conclusions about their observations. However, Edom-Rome's desire to replace the Highest YAHUAH as the Creator developed subjects categorized as science, where they used mathematical calculations to determine whether something exists. And, the scientists are the only ones allowed to make these calculations. The so-called experts appeared to possess more knowledge than the average person and would be the ones to impart this knowledge to the masses. Therefore, the understanding that people would receive would be the results and interpretation of the scientists who act and stands in the place of the ELOHIYM of the universe. This use of science became Scientism, another pagan religion of Edom-Rome, and the scientist became its "high priest." In the 19th century, once Edom-Rome had established and instituted these ideas about the earth. How all things came to be as they are, they forced these ideas on the world through their religions and educational institutions.

The word science in Hebrew is madda, and its origin is yada. The word means knowledge and thought. Historian Howard Markel discusses how the word scientist first came into use in 1834 when a Cambridge University historian and philosopher of science William Whewell coined the term scientist to replace the older term cultivators of science because he noted that people sought knowledge by observation in the beginning. Many of them observed the stars and used what they saw to determine what would happen. Abraham as a young man also observed the stars before he surrendered to YAHUAH and asked him to deliver him from the hands of the evil ruachoth that made him believe he needed to know more than necessary about the future rains which caused him to walk in the deceitfulness of his heart, "And in the sixth week, in the fifth year thereof, Abram sat up throughout the night on the New Moon of the seventh month to observe the stars from the evening to the morning, to see what would be the character of the year regarding the rains, and he was alone as he sat and observed. And a word came into his heart, and he said: All the signs of the stars and the signs of the moon and the sun are all in the hand of YAHUAH. Why do I search them out" (Jubilees 12: 16-17)? Abram came to realize at that moment that this was not what the Highest YAHUAH wanted him to do if he was to learn to trust him for all things.

One theory introduced by the so-called scientists of Edom-Rome is that the earth is a ball that came into existence after a big explosion of nothing that created everything. Today, they refer to this theory as the Big Bang. They believe everything then evolved, which took about 4.53 billion years. This heliocentric model of the earth has persuaded most people to believe without observation that the earth is a sphere, despite the evidence written in Scripture that the earth is a flat plane with a foundation, four corners, and a firmament above, all created by YAHUAH, who sits above in the heavens outside of the earth with the earth as his footstool, "Thus saith YAHUAH, The heaven is my throne, and the earth is my footstool: where is the house that ye build unto me? And where is the place of my rest" (Isaiah 66:1)? The common sense of man tells him - if nothing else told him - that there is an "up" and a "down" in nature, even as regards the heavens and the earth; but the theory of modern astronomers necessitates the conclusion that there is not: therefore, the theory of the astronomers is opposed to common sense and inspiration. Which is common proof that the earth is not a globe (Carpenter, 1885)? Most people, including those who believe Hebrew Scriptures, also accept the theory of Edom-Rome that the earth is a ball with no evidence even though their senses should tell them differently. In fact, on a sphere, all land areas will have curvature, and no matter how big the sphere, all buildings will be crooked. They believe that this ball, which spins through the universe at thousands of miles per hour, keeps everything in place because it has an invisible force called gravity, which prevents things from flying off into space, except small birds, moths, flies, feathers, and so on. These same scientists insist that if the earth is flat, it would be possible to fall off if you get near the edge. But if it is a spherical ball, it is impossible to fall off the sides or the bottom because of the force of gravity that causes things to stick to the ball.

The Scriptures state that YAHUAH created the earth in six days and everything in it. However, it is the view of the scientists of Edom-Roman that the Earth had a different beginning, which they have based only on mathematical equations and unproven ideas. They illustrate these beliefs in a 2014 article that quotes the views of Pope Francis, the head of the Roman Catholic Church, and all other Christian churches. The article specified that he agreed with evolution and had rejected the creation story of Genesis. Pope Francis stated, "When we read about Creation in Genesis, we risk imagining God was a magician with a magic wand able to do everything. But that is not so." He furthers, "The Big Bang, which today we hold to be the origin of the world does not contradict the intervention of the divine Creator but requires it." Based on their thinking, the Highest YAHUAH of the Universe needed help in creating his Creation. It is theories of Edom-Rome that have led many Israelites astray from the Highest YAHUAH into false religions.

The concepts of Edom-Rome have become institutionalized despite evidence that shows they are not provable, and therefore, only theories. Paul, in his letter to the Thessalonians, however, told the Hebrew Israelites awakening to the truth in his day, "Prove all things; hold fast that which is good" (1 Thessalonians 5:21). We can prove most of Edom-Rome's ideas to be false even though they have divided these scientific theories into three major groups and sub-groups, including mathematics and logic, which uses a priori as opposed to the factual method. They made mathematics a logical science, when, in fact, numbers are just adjectives that describe the number of things that are nouns and cannot be observed without the number of objects it describes. Edom-Rome also uses natural science, which is the study of natural phenomena (including cosmological, geological, chemical, and biological factors of the universe), and social sciences, which is the study of human behavior and societies. They have further divided these groups into twenty-two sub-groups, which comprise religion, history, geography, language, art, anthropology, archeology, iconoclasm, and many others. These many branches of science make it difficult to determine the truth and confuse the ordinary person who forces them to give up on their observation and, instead, relies on what the "experts" scientists declare as the truth.

THEORY OF EVOLUTION

The spread of the theory of evolution was another idea first proposed in the 19th century by Jean-Baptiste Lamarck, and later by Charles Darwin considered the father of the philosophy of evolution who supported the theory of the creation happening without the Creator. Charles Darwin furthered evolution by challenging that all species of organisms arise and develop through the natural selection of small, inherited variations that increase the individual's ability to compete, survive, and reproduce. According to his study published in 1859, the process of natural selection enables the individuals with the most suitable characteristics in a species not only to survive but to pass these characteristics on to their offspring producing evolutionary changes in species over time, as less suitable traits disappear and more suitable traits endure. The ideas espoused by Darwin gained wide acceptance in the scientific community. As a result, science teachers have taught this theory in schools and universities, and most students have become indoctrinated and therefore believe that the ELOHIYM Creator of the Universe does not exist. Instead, they learn and believe that man evolved from a small sea creature over billions of years. This view assumes that humanity came into existence without a Creator. This theory also supports the belief that the earth evolved into its current arrangement when the continents collided before being torn apart, which resulted in ancient maps being different from those of today. But, when one thinks about this, it cannot be true as to how would scientist know what the maps looked like before this collision that occurred billions of years ago when the man himself did not experience this phenomenon or have any means of determining what happened so long ago. My belief is that because Edom-Rome changed the boundaries on the maps, they needed to have a story to support why the ancient maps would differ from the modern maps, and therefore, a created tale needs to be told. Changing the geographic history of the earth supported their theories and prevented many research scientists from speaking out against these lies. However, there scientists who did not buy into the lies and have spoken against the common views.

These scientists believe that the materialist evolutionist theories and ideas advanced by Edom-Rome are anti-YAHUAH ELOHIYM. And, papal Rome has protected these theories for over one hundred and fifty years but has failed to show proof of how these theories work. According to Harun Yahya, a scientist who wrote a book titled, "The Evolution Deceit," noted the Evolutionary theory claims that life started with a cell that formed by chance. The assertion is, "according to this scenario, four billion years ago various lifeless chemical compounds underwent a reaction in the primordial atmosphere on the earth in which the effects of thunderbolts and atmospheric pressure led to the formation of the first living cell." He challenges this claim by stating, "The first thing that must be said is that to claim inanimate materials can come together to form life is unscientific and not verified by any experiment or observation. Life only generates life from life. Each living cell is formed by the replication of another cell. No one in the world has ever formed a living cell by bringing inanimate materials together, not even in the most advanced laboratories. The theory of evolution he adds faces no greater crisis than on the point of explaining the emergence of life. The reason is that organic molecules are so complex; you cannot explain their formation as being coincidental, and the organic cell can't have been formed by chance."

The astronomer, Fred Hoyle, compare the odds of the earth evolving based on the Big Bang theory to "a tornado sweeping through a junkyard and assembling a Boeing 747 from the materials." He furthers that, "If there were a basic principle of matter which somehow drove organic systems toward life, its existence should be evident in the laboratory. One could, for instance, take a swimming bath to represent the primordial soup. Fill it with any chemicals of non-biological nature you please. Pump any gases over it, or through it, and shine any kind of radiation on it that takes your fancy. Let the experiment proceed for a year and see how many of those 2,000 enzymes (proteins produced by living cells) have appeared in the bath. He added the answer to save the time and trouble and expense of experimenting. You will find nothing at all, except for a tarry sludge composed of amino acids and other simple chemicals." The Astrobiologist, Chandra Wickramasinghe, agrees and adds that "The likelihood of the spontaneous formation of life from inanimate matter is one of a number with 40,000 zeros after it." She adds that these numbers are big enough to bury Darwin and the whole theory of evolution, and she concludes, "The beginnings of life were not random; they must have been the product of purposeful intelligence." However, in an online article titled, "How Long Have Humans Been on Earth?" The author is attempting to support the theories espoused by Edom-Rome and Darwin while still claiming a belief in creation. The article puts forth the idea that "While our ancestors have been around for about six million years, the modern form of humans only evolved about 200 thousand years ago, but civilization as we know it is only about 6,000 years old, and industrialization started only in the eighteen hundreds." But there is no evidence for most of these claims, and when observed with a critical mind, one concludes that this is not possible. It is telling that the writer wants to use the Scriptural evidence for man's time on the earth because the scientist can find no evidence to the contrary yet, claim the earth is millions of years old to support evolution. The statement that the industrial age is only about 300 years old supports the belief that modern man and more specifically the white man produced these theories as they have no proof before about 350 years ago that humanity and the earth came into being any other way than what Hebrew Scriptures and the other older cultures wrote.

OLD AGE OF THE EARTH

The scientific theories of Edom-Rome claim that the earth is older than what Scripture implies it to be. They have used the old age of the Earth theory to cast doubt on the truth written in

Hebrew Scriptures and other ancient texts. The scientist determined the old age of the earth based on archeological evidence. However, the books of Genesis and Jubilees tell when and how YAHUAH first created heaven and Earth and based on this timeline and the evidence of the oldest human skeleton they discovered according to Scripture the approximate age of the earth is 6000 years old. Science claims that the Earth came into being through evolution from a single cell prokaryotic cell, such as bacteria, and therefore, they judge the Earth to be about 4.5 billion years old.

The proponents of the old age theory of the earth may believe that it is billions of years old, but they cannot prove this hypothesis with evidence. However, they continue to use the calendar and timeline based on the Hebrew Scriptures to determine when events occurred in history. They have no other written evidence other than steles that have etchings that tell their story. The great inconsistency between Scripture and science as far as the age of the Earth makes it difficult to reconcile the two beliefs. Science cannot prove the age of the Earth and so those who believe the theories of science still must do so by faith. Like William Shatner, an actor who played the character Captain James Kirk in the Star Trek movies notes, that science and science fiction are both the same since they can prove neither.

Claiming that the earth is older aids the evolutionary theory as it is necessary to have billions of years for the earth and human beings to evolve and change. The extended time supports the theory that people and places are ancient. They have described the descendants of Jacob-Israel as ancient people who somehow became extinct. The progenitor of Edom-Rome is Esau, the twin brother of Jacob, born around 2006 BC. They are not as ancient as the descendants of Noah and his sons, Ham, Shem, Japheth, the descendants of Abraham's nephew Lot, Moab and Ammon (Asians), and Ishmael the older brother of Isaac the ancestor of the Arabs. Although Jacob and Esau were twins, the nation of Esau-Edom is older than the nation of Jacob-Israel, and based on when Edom was established as a nation; they should be considered ancient when compared with Israel.

To maintain and support this belief, Edom-Rome has created and introduced vocabulary like the word prehistoric, to mean a history that preceded the known history of the earth. The word prehistoric also supports the theory that there were animals that became extinct millions of years ago, of which they have found skeletal evidence to prove these dinosaurs existed. They have introduced words to describe people, places and periods such as a primate, primordial-soup, megalithic builders, Neolithic, Mesolithic, Miocene times, Pliocene times, the Baroque period, Christian era, Bronze Age, Stone Age, Iron Age, Ice Age, Dark Ages, Dolichocephalic and hundreds more. But the true, history of language proves that all languages spoken in ancient times have parallel pictures and meanings that use similar pictures when these words compare to other ancient pictorial-languages there are no parallel pictures to show that these words existed, or that there is even justification or the need for such words. Instead, Edom-Rome has created words with no basis or historical meaning in the attempt to make the Earth and its people appear older than they are, like the mathematical equations produced to describe things in "Space." They invoke these words to confuse and to cast doubt in the minds of those who believe in the Creator of the Universe and make it difficult to challenge the theories of Edom-Rome. But, maybe this is their way of pretending to answer the challenge by the Highest Creator for anyone to measure and tell him the height and depth of the earth which would cause him to cast Israel away, "Thus saith YAHUAH; if they can measure heaven above, and the foundations of the earth searched out beneath, I will also cast off all the seed of Israel for all they have done, saith YAHUAH" (Jeremiah 31:37).

CHANGED COSMOLOGY OF THE EARTH

In the late 16th century, Edom-Rome sought to change the cosmology of the earth. They theorized that the earth was spherical and was moving around the sun at over one thousand miles per hour. However, Edom-Rome and its science led the world to believe that the reason we could not experience this movement with our senses that were given to us by YAHUAH was that gravity held all things firm and fast to the spherical ball which is Earth. But throughout the earth's history, all cultures knew the earth to be a flat plane, and the Highest ELOHIYM lived above in the heavens. This theory was to deny further that the Creator ELOHIYM existed. While they hoped to deceive the masses, they also used it as an opportunity to place their sun god at the center of the Highest YAHUAH'S universe and claim that the earth revolves around the sun. John Calvin, of the reformation, was so incensed by this assertion that he preached a sermon about it and declared those who thought the earth moved to be insane;

> We will see some who are so deranged, not only in religion but who in all things reveal their monstrous nature that they will say that the sun does not move and that it is the earth which shifts and turns. When we see such minds, we must indeed confess that the devil possesses them and that God sets them before his mirrors, to keep us in fear.

They hypothesized that the earth came into being because of a "big bang" to deny the truth of there being the Highest Creator who chose a people as his own and connects with them as the ELOHIYM of Jacob-Israel. Edom-Rome wanted to make humankind's existence insignificant, based on the Copernican theory of the earth spinning around the sun god. They linked this theory with the others to push Scriptures out as a force of truth, therefore creating a material cosmology. However, everyone knew the earth was flat as the characters in the movie 'Men in Black' noted, "1500 years ago everybody knew the earth was the center of the universe-500 years ago everyone knew the earth was flat." According to Eric Dubay (2014), Edom-Rome has taught a falsehood so gigantic and diabolical that it has blinded people from their own experiences, separated them from common sense, and shielded them from seeing the world and the universe as they are. Edom-Rome asserted that the earth is just one of eight planets in a solar system, and the other planets are also huge, spherical Earth-like habitations or globular gas giants millions of miles away. They believe and theorize that the Earth and the seven other planets all revolve in concentric circles or ellipses around the Sun, and therefore, they have coined the term heliocentric.

Eric Dubay quoted from C. S. McGill's book; The Flat Earth that heliocentrism is the belief that the sun is the center of the universe and the solar system. However, it was Nicolaus Copernicus who first presented this theory in his book, "On the Revolution of Heavenly Spheres" in 1543. He introduced a heliocentric model of the universe similar to the way Ptolemy presented his geocentric model of the earth in the 2nd century AD. Copernicus believed that the heliocentric model most likely paid homage to the Greek god, Helios, whom they called the god of the sun. Helios was the offspring of the titans Hyperion and Theia and his sisters were Selene (the Moon) and Eos (the Dawn). These are pagan concepts and beliefs. Therefore, when Edom-Rome took dominion over the earth and its religions, they drew from these pagan ideas as they already worshiped the sun and believed their sun god to be the center of the universe. This pagan belief of the sun being the center of the universe contradicts the Most High Creator's plan and purpose for the creation of these heavenly bodies, which he created as lights in the sky. The sun he gave to rule the daytime and the moon to give forth light at night,

"And YAHUAH said, Let there be lights in the firmament of the heavens to divide the day from the night, and let them be for signs, and seasons, and for days, and years" (Genesis 1:14). These heavenly bodies he gave to be the objects of the Gentiles' worship, and he warned Israel not to worship these idols.

The fact is that YAHUAH created no planets. He created the sun, moon, and stars as written in Scripture, "And on the fourth day, he created the sun and the moon and the stars, and set them in the heaven's firmament, to give light upon the earth, and to rule over the day and the night, and divide the light from the darkness. And ELOHIYM appointed the sun to be a great sign on the earth for days and for Shabbathoth and for months and for feasts and for years and for Shabbathoth of years and jubilees and all seasons of years," (Jubilees 2:9). The book of Enoch confirms how the luminaries call stars would move concerning each other and how the sun and moon move throughout their courses. However, it also warns of the days when the wicked will rule and what would happen. Enoch states that during this time, the years would become shorter, and Edom's seed would decelerate on their lands and fields. The chief stars known as wandering stars and labeled planets by Edom-Rome would then transgress the order prescribed by the Highest YAHUAH, "And these shall alter their orbits and tasks and not appear at the seasons prescribed to them. And YAHUAH shall conceal the whole order of the stars from the sinners. And the thoughts of those on earth shall err concerning them, and it shall alter them from all their ways, yea, they shall take them to be gods. And it shall multiply evil upon them, And punishment shall come upon them to destroy all" (Enoch 80:11-17). Edom-Rome has taken the wandering stars to be their gods and changed the cosmology of the earth to fit their theory. As a result, there are changes made to the climate brought about by the chaos of the altered orbits and punishment brought on by these gods of the stars or planets that Edom-Rome worships.

Scripture further confirms that the sun could not be the center of the universe as the sun and moon moved around the Earth the day Joshua asked YAHUAH to deliver up the Amorites before Israel, "Sun, stand thou still upon Gibeon; and thou, Moon, in the valley of Ajalon. And the sun stood still, and the moon stayed until the people had avenged themselves upon their enemies. Is not this written in the book of Jasher? So the sun stood still amid heaven and hasted not to go down about a whole day" (Joshua 10:11-13). These verses show the earth is an enclosed system, and everything that YAHUAH created for humanity is within the firmament. Therefore, if one believes the word written in Scriptures, this alone should convince the doubters that the Earth is not a ball spinning around the sun, but the sun and moon move within the system and circles the flat earth.

YAHUAH created the earth and everything in it and on it. The Earth's geocentric placement positions it as the immovable center of the universe with the sun, moon, and stars revolving around it. According to Harpers Bible Dictionary, the Hebrews imagined the world as flat and round, covered by the great solid dome of the sky held up by mountain pillars (Job 25:11; 37:18). Above the firmament and under the earth was water, divided by God at creation (Gen. 1:6, 7, Ps. 24:2; 48:4). YAHUAH joined

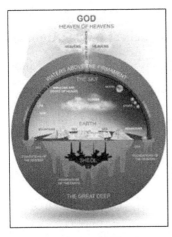

Depiction of the Earth According to Ancient Hebrews

the upper waters with the waters of the primordial deep during the Flood; they believed the rains to fall through windows in the firmament (Gen.7:11; 8:2). The sun, moon, and stars moved across and fixed in the firmament (Gen. 1:14-19; Ps. 19:4, 6). Within the earth lay Sheol, the realm of the dead (Num. 16:30-33; Isa. 14:9, 15). The model described by the Hebrews is the only true model of the Earth, as they were and are the only covenant people of the Most High, and he only reveals his truth to them and through them. YAHUAH did not give Edom-Rome power to know the truth about His creation, and therefore, they teach deception. Because Edom-Rome has an evil inclination, they have created human-made processes to explain their belief that the earth came into being without an intelligent designer to replace the one and only Creator, the Most High YAHUAH with their false god.

According to the heliocentric model, as alleged by NASA and modern astronomy, the Earth is spinning at 1,000 miles per hour around a central axis while traveling 67,000 miles per hour in circles around the Sun, spiraling 500,000 miles per hour around the Milky Way, while the entire galaxy rockets at a speed of 670,000,000 miles per hour through the universe. The heliocentric

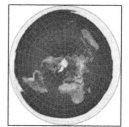

Map of the Flat Earth

model of the Earth credits these motions and the Earth's creation to an alleged big bang explosion 14 billion years ago (Eric Dubay, 2014). Dubay adds that both NASA and modern astronomy identify Polaris, the North Pole star, somewhere between 324 to 434 light-years, or about two quadrillion miles away from us. It is important to note, however, that the difference between these two numbers is 666,000,000,000,000 (over six hundred trillion miles). Because this claim is so outrageous, people find it easier to believe what the scientists tell them as it would be very difficult for them to prove otherwise. Edom-Rome knows the earth to be flat as the United Nations symbol depicts flat earth with the symbol of Rome encircling it, which shows that Rome rules the earth. They created the false globe model of earth to mislead so that the observer would not trust their natural senses but depend on the scientists that are influenced by Roman to inform them of truth. Edom-Rome, the perpetrators of this hoax, would have people believe that they could no longer trust what they saw with their own eyes or know through the sense of touch or a sensation they feel. Therefore, although the sun, moon, stars and the wandering stars they call planets, and every light in the sky above revolves around the motionless Earth beneath our feet, Edom-Rome's science insists that the earth is careening through space at 1000 miles per hour even though no one has ever felt or seen this. No one can prove this to be true (Eric Dubay, 2014).

The simultaneous awakening of the Hebrew Israelites and revelations of the truth about the Earth's cosmology is no coincidence. Instead, these occurrences are for the Highest YAHUAH'S purpose. These revelations are all part of his plan and meant to happen at the same time as a sign of confirmation to his Chosen people. YAHUAH is still on the throne and in charge despite how Edom-Rome has attempted to use the shape of the Earth and the big bang theory to deceive the world. Scripture states that the Earth is a flat plane and, although Edom-Rome has always known this to be so, they just added the letter "T" to the word plane and changed it to the planet and then changed the entire cosmology to fit this false ideology. This letter 'T' is a pagan Tau symbol with a numerical value of 300. The ancient Greeks considered the symbol to represent life and resurrection. In Egyptian paganism, the symbol represented the phallus and

How Ancient Hebrews Viewed the Earth

regarded as the marker for holy waters. In ancient Greek mythology, they associate it with the deity Attis, and the Roman god Mithras. The Christian church also connects the Tau with the crucifix. They added this letter to the flat plane of the earth to claim it for their pagan gods, who they believe rules over the earth. And, this knowledge proves that the changes made by Edom-Rome and designed to the Earth's cosmology paid homage to their gods to cause the unaware Hebrew Israelites to worship the Roman pagan gods. The change in how the world is described and viewed shows the length and depth of the deception perpetrated by Edom-Rome. They hoped to trick the mind and hide the truth about the Creator, the Highest YAHUAH, and his people, the Hebrew Israelites. It is, however, YAHUAH's plan to bring about his purpose for Jacob and Esau and to show his power among men. Therefore, the descendants of Israel must not fear Edom-Rome because their power is what YAHUAH allows them, "O YAHUAH, Lord, the King Almighty: for the whole world is in thy power, and if thou hast appointed to save Israel, there is no man that can gainsay thee: for thou hast made heaven and earth, and all the wondrous things under the heaven. Thou art Lord of all things and no man can resist thee, which art the Lord" (Esther Additions 13: 9-11).

The heliocentric model, also called the globe, moved YAHUAH as the creator and replaced him with the idea that man could evolve and become like gods. They have established these theories with ideas taken from the biblical context mixed with paganism, such as Darwinism, Scientism, Trans-humanism, and the New Age movement. However, in a biblical context, these are all forms of Satanism (Eric Dubay, 2014). In fact, "The heliocentric theory, by putting the sun at the center of the universe... made man appear to be just one of a host of wanderers drifting through a cold sky. They hoped to show that humanity was less likely to be born to live and to attain paradise upon his death. Less likely, too, was he the object of God's ministrations" (Morris, Kline). Humans, animals, and everything in nature ELOHIYM created in a matter of days, not, "evolved" over billions of years" (Eric Dubay, 2014). Therefore, the question we should reflect on noted Dubay, 2014 is that how it would be possible for the earth and all in it to come about without a Creator, when, in fact, so many things need to be inter-connected just to make an average-sized protein molecule composed of 288 amino acids of 12 varying types which combine 10 to the 300 power different ways? It takes this known formula for just one molecule that scientists could create under laboratory conditions, so how could billions of these molecules form without a Supreme Designer?

These examples are just a few of the ways Edom-Rome has misused science to deceive the entire world. They intended these ideas to remove YAHUAH and the true history of the people of Israel. They designed the entire scheme to mislead and deceive the descendants of Israel, the chosen people of YAHUAH, hoping this lie they would prevent them from taking their position as the rulers for all eternity. Because the promise is to Jacob-Israel, the Highest YAHUAH answers the question Esdras asked about what will happen at the dividing of the times and the end of the world as we know it, "And he said unto me, From Abraham unto Isaac, when Jacob and Esau were born of him, Jacob's hand held first the heel of Esau. For Esau is the end of the world, and Jacob is the beginning of it that followeth. The hand of man is betwixt the heel and the hand: other question, Esdras, ask thou not" (2 Esdras 6:8-10).

RECASTING AND RELABELING PEOPLE

Changing the history of the world and the role that Edom-Rome has played recasting and relabeling people was paramount to the deception. Edom-Rome has showcased their superior power, influence, and importance throughout this dispensation. They have been able to dominate the historical narrative for the past three hundred years. After they dispersed the children of Israel via the transatlantic slave trade and their identity became hidden, Edom-Rome set out to destabilize the lands the Israelites had been scattered into on the continent of Africa by instigating wars among the different tribes. With the scattering and murdering of the people allowed Edom-Rome the opportunity to kill, steal, and destroy more of the people, then remove them from the land and further scattering them into the wilderness. Because Edom-Rome had taken over the lands that belong to the sons of Japheth and replaced its inhabitants with themselves, they claimed to be the progeny of Japheth, and by extension, the Europeans. However, the original descendants of Japheth were all black and brown people who mixed with the black Phonecians of Africa, and many of them also became whited out by Edom-Rome, who then claim the ancestry of Japheth labeling themselves Caucasian.

Edom-Rome also appropriated the scrolls and scripts of Israel after the Council of Nice in 325AD. They then merged the ideas and philosophies of pagan Rome with papal Rome. The religion of the Judeans became the religion of Rome, and it led the Israelites into the wilderness of the people where they are to this day. They replaced the Hebrew Israelites with what they call spiritual Israel or the third race. The Christians believed that the new covenant with the house of Israel and Judah, Jeremiah had foretold already was enforced and superior to the old (Jer. 31:31-34). The Edomites and others in the Hellenistic world of Israel became the Christians, and Jesus Christ became their God. The Christians believed that the way they interpreted Jesus' teachings freed them and gave them a sense of liberation from the real shackles of the Law of the Highest YAHUAH (Frend, 1984). Therefore, they used only the Hebrew Israelite Torah and Scriptures that supported their narrative to expand their religious beliefs and, later, offered it as a universal call to all people. In doing this, they recast and replaced the faces of the original people of Israel to be that of the white Edomite.

Because Esau-Edom has hidden their identity, there is not much historical evidence available, and this should make the researcher pause and question why this is so, seeing they are the rulers of this world. Why should they have such a short history which only goes back as far as the Greek and Roman Empires? Yet, they have made themselves the center of the history of every nation and claim the identity of these other people. Today, Edom-Rome is known as the white people described in Scripture as red. They have mixed and recast themselves as the descendants of Japheth and with many of the other people in the nations on the earth. They were able to accomplish this, through war and false treaties and then mixing their seed with the people of these nations. In recent history, Edom-Rome changed the face of the people living in Israel then renamed the land in 1948. The Zionist Jewish Edomites who stole the identity of the Israelites in this region, cast themselves as Jews as they invaded the land of Palestine. They moved the inhabitants out of the areas they wanted to steal the property and the land the Palestinians had occupied for centuries. They then claimed the land as their Jewish homeland.

The people known as Jews, along with Christians who spread the religions of Christianity and Judaism, are all descendants of Esau, who is Edom-Rome. Together, they have usurped authority over the land they now call Israel. Some Hebrew Israelites appear to have joined them. They, too, have been deceived as Scripture notes that Hashatan will deceive the entire world, including the descendants of Israel. Jacob-Israel is the clay described in Nebuchadnezzar's dream that Edom-Rome, the iron, will attempt to mix his seed with, but iron and clay will not adhere to each other. "And whereas thou sawest iron mixed with miry clay, they shall mingle themselves with the seed of men: but they shall not cleave one to another, even as iron is not mixed with clay" (Daniel 2:43). The religions of Edom-Rome may have words of truth mixed in because they use elements of the Torah and the Prophets, but this is a false mixture, and YAHUAH will never accept these religions or their followers. Truth mixed with lies makes it a lie. "For every tree is known by his own fruit" (Luke 6:44). The foundation is sand on which these religions stand and bound to fall as YAHUSHA admonished, "And every one that heareth these sayings of mine and doeth them not, shall be likened unto a foolish man, which built his house upon the sand: and the rain descended, and the floods came, and the winds blew, and beat upon that house; and it fell: and great was the fall of it" (Matthew 7:26-27). Likewise, Edom-Rome will fall.

As Edom-Rome moved further north, south, east, and west, they conquered lands and peoples as they went, spreading the gospel of Christianity by the edge of the sword. They forced the inhabitants of these lands to convert to their Babylonian religions, which made them slaves to the Christian Catholic church. They then instilled fear by teaching the doctrine of hellfire for those who refused to join by baptism and adherence to the doctrines of the church. The church of Edom-Rome taught a false gospel filled with pagan ideas and a false concept of love conditioned on obedience to join them or die. They made Jesus be this god who loved all people and embraced them as his children as long as they converted to the religion. However, if they refused, he did not show this love but came down with the swift arm of the sword. When viewed through the awakened eyes of the Hebrew Israelites, we see this Jesus filled with hypocrisy, which is also a description of Esau-Edom.

Likewise, the Roman Christian church shows itself to be a hypocrite, pretending to be godly as they go about destroying the souls of men. Because Edom-Rome has done these hypocritical acts against Israel, the Highest will send YAHUSHA to destroy them because they have led the earth with deceit. Even though they have lived in the earth's fatness and owned all the money in the world with the ability to purchase whatever they wanted, they have still rejected the Highest, YAHUAH and practiced wickedness toward Israel, "And the merchants of the earth shall weep and mourn over her, for no man buyeth their merchandise any more: the merchandise of gold, and silver, and precious stones, and of pearls, and fine linen, and purple, and silk, and scarlet, and all thyine wood, and all manner vessels of ivory, and all manner vessels of most precious wood, and brass, and iron, and marble, and cinnamon, and odors, and ointments, and frankincense, and wine, and oil, and fine flour, and wheat, and beasts, and sheep, and horses, and chariots, and slaves, and souls of men" (Revelation 18:11-13).

REPLACING THE BLACK ISRAELITES WITH WHITE

EDOMITES

According to the Rabbinic literature, the ancient Semites were black people. "He blessed Shem and his sons (making them) dark and comely, and he gave them the inhabitable earth (Pirke Eliezer 24).[1] Tarikh Tabari, a Persian historian, concurs that the descendants of Shem were black. 'Born to Noah were Shem,

Portrait of a Young Swiss Woman: Unknown Swiss Artist, Switzerland (circa. 1800). Formerly thought to be by Jean Etienne Liotard.

whose descendants colors are black complexion with a slight brownish undertone (bayadh) and a dark blackish brown (udmah). Ham, whose descendants color is true black (sward) and a few are black complexions with a slight brownish undertone (bayadh). Abraham, the father of Isaac and Jacob, who became the father of the twelve Tribes of Israel, were Shemites, and they were all black people. When Joseph married an Egyptian descended from Ham, she had black skin. Japheth was also brown. They described him as fair-skinned, so he had a light brown color. However, Japheth's descendants mixed with the Phoenicians the descendants of Ham before they ever mixed with Esau, who is Edom, as Esau-Edom's descendants did not appear in Kittiym until thousands of years after the sons of Japheth. All three of Noah's sons were people with black skin. Esau was the 'red" twin to Jacob, who married the women of Gentile nations, including the Canaanites, the Arabs, and the Japhites. Esau mixed with these nations, and his color is evident in the people, as milk mixed in black coffee shows.

Therefore, Esau cannot hide as the Prophet Jeremiah noted, "But I have made Esau bare, I have uncovered his secret places, and he shall not be able to hide himself: his seed is spoiled, and his brethren, and his neighbors, and he is not (Jeremiah 49:10).

It is important to substantiate the color of the people of Israel because Edom-Rome has replaced the true people of the Highest with a white race of people called the Jews. They are imposters who have stolen the identity of the true Hebrew Israelites.

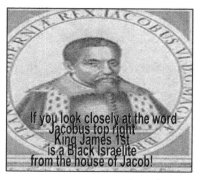

If you look closely at the word Jacobus top right King James 1st is a Black Israelite from the house of Jacob!

Because Edom-Rome knew who the Israelites were, they described them as they carried them off into slavery as Negro, which is the Spanish word meaning black. They also knew that YAHUAH had turned his face away from his people, and therefore, they could carry out these atrocities against them, and they would not have to suffer immediate consequences for their actions. The prophecy that predicted Israel's captivity at the hand of Edom-Rome stated as much. And, they also knew that YAHUAH had placed Israel into their hands to carry out the punishments. Therefore, all the prophecies about Jacob-Israel happened because Edom-Rome executed severe actions against the children of Israel and also conspired with the other nations against them, "And he will wake up against them the sinners of the other nations, who have neither mercy nor compassion, and who shall respect the person of none, neither old nor young, nor anyone for they are more wicked and strong to do evil than all the children of men. And they shall use violence against Yasharel and transgression against Yaakov, and they shall shed much blood upon the earth, and there shall be none to gather and none to bury" (Jubilees 23:23).

According to the Biblical history records the Israelites of the Northern tribes while in the diaspora hundreds of years before the birth of the HAMASHIACH moved into Spain and Portugal known in Scripture as Tarshish. It was the land of the descendants of Phut or the Phoenicians and part of the Carthaginian Empire. According to 'Empires of Medieval West Africa,' the Arabs referred to the Jews as black. Therefore, the land in Africa where

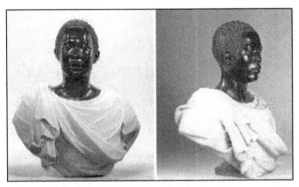

Black and White marble bust of a European Black man:
by Melchior Barthel (1625-1672)

the Israelites settled in the Savanna of the sub-Saharan Desert in West Africa was first described by Arab travelers

and geographers as Bilard al-Sudan, which means "land of the blacks." Sudan is the Arabic word for a black person. They call the land Soudan or Negroland; therefore, when we translate Soudan in Hebrew, 'So' means foreigner or of foreign origin, and 'Yudan' means Judah, which is the Southern Kingdom of Israel. Thus when the two words combine and defined in Hebrew, it means

"Foreigner of Judah." The descendants of Israel had settled in Negroland or Nigritia, a geographical term which in its widest sense embraces the vast region of Africa that stretches from the Atlantic to the Red Sea and the Abyssinian mountains, and from the Sahara and Egypt proper in the North to the Gulf of Guinea, the central equatorial regions, and the Albert and Victoria Lakes (1892 Chamber's Encyclopedia: A Dictionary of Universal Knowledge Vol.9).

If the color of Israel's skin was not important to Edom-Rome, why would they go to such lengths to hide Israel's identity and replace it with Edomite Christians, Khazarian-Ashkenazi Jews, and Sephardic Jews? Why would Esau, who is Edom, hide the identity and history of the Edomites? If it did not matter, why was the color of the MASHIACH who they call Jesus changed from black to white in the paintings found in Europe? They have used various means of deception to nurture the idea they are the descendants of Jacob-Israel when the true history when the pieces are put together tell a different story.

Map of Negroland

DNA science is another means used by Edom-Rome to refute the truth of the Hebrew Israelites identity. They claim that DNA results show people have been so mixed that it is impossible to determine the identity of any specific race of people. As a result, the outcomes they show reflect only the DNA of the people presently living in the areas once occupied by the Hebrew Israelites. Since Rome expelled the Israelites from the lands, they lived in many other countries, and their DNA would not be evident. What it reveals is that DNA science is not a good scientific indicator for determining the identity of people based on those now occupying the lands. The Hebrew Israelites have moved and been displaced as people and are not present in their original lands. DNA is not a perfect indicator because the bloodline of a person is not determined by the land borders. However, because Israel is the chosen seed of YAHUAH, DNA is not a practical gage of the true heritage of Israel, as there are other factors to consider. One of these factors is the color of the Israelites, who were black or what they describe as Negro. And, although the Israelites have mixed with the people of other nations, by force and by influence, Edom-Rome could not change the color of black Negro people. This truth is similar for Edom-Rome, for although they have mixed with people of every nation, we can still identify them as white Edomites because they continued whitening out the black or brown Gentiles for generations. We still consider them white people based on their color despite the mixture. Therefore, notwithstanding, the mixture and difference in the black skin tones, of the Negro, Scripture says YAHUAH will recognize them and cleanse their blood, "But Judah shall dwell forever and Jerusalem from generation to generation. For I will cleanse their blood I have not cleansed: for YAHUAH dwelleth in Zion" (Joel 3:20-21).

There are many written accounts and portraits of black people who lived throughout Europe up to the 19th century, which proves that the Jews (Israelites) were black. John Ogilby, a Black Cosmographer, wrote in 1674 how King John III of Portugal used to ship the Black Hebrew Israelites from Portugal to the West coast of Africa to become slaves in the Sugar Mills. Although he did not describe them as black, they had to be black because there is no evidence that any white Sephardic Jews went into Africa as slaves. Though they claim the Sephardic Jews living in Palestine today once lived in Spain and Portugal and descended from the Spanish Jews. The actual Sephardic Jews were Black, but revisionist history describes them as white. It can be concluded that the white Sephardic Jews of Spain today converted to the religion of Judaism and have stolen the identity of the original Sephardic Jews who lived in Spain and Portugal. This research reveals that the original homeland of the Jews (Israelites) was not the Continent of Africa nor Spain or Europe, but they had been dispersed into these areas. And the Israelites' homeland is indeed the land of Israel, and it was Edom-Rome who exiled them into Africa. This evidence confirms why the people of Africa always appeared to be destitute and living in sub-par conditions. They were in the diaspora, moving from place to place, and having to build many temporary shelters with little resources. These conditions also prove their identity. History shows the Hebrew Israelites lived throughout the continent of Africa as Ogilby gives more insight on how the Negro Jew moved into Africa when they came out of Portugal;

> John third King of Portugal sent a Colony thither about two hundred years before, whom though the unwholesome air destroyed, yet the place was not left desolate; for he sent new inhabitants, who first settled in Guinea, next in Angola, and on the Island St. Thomas, that so they might be the better used to the air that the said king sold all those Jews for slaves that refused to embrace the Roman Religion, and caused their children to be baptized from whom (coming thither in great numbers) most of the present inhabitants were descended.

The Hebrew Israelite Negro of the world has experienced the full wrath of Edom-Rome's tyranny no matter where they settled. They have experienced the many curses outlined in Deuteronomy 28, even to this day. Yet, the Jewish imposters claiming to be the descendants of Israel have experienced no hardship other than the holocaust they created and would not allow the world to forget. However, their current condition shows they have none of the effects of these curses. Instead, they are the wealthiest people on the earth with support from the leaders of the Edomite-Roman world. Their position on the earth proves they are not the true sons and daughters of the Highest YAHUAH, as the prophecy states that the captivity of Israel and its curses are to be a sign on the people until the Redeemer YAHUSHA returns, "Moreover all these curses shall come upon thee, and shall pursue thee, and overtake thee, till thou be destroyed; because thou harkenedst not unto the voice of YAHUAH thy ELOHIYM, to keep his commandments and his statutes which he commanded thee. And they shall be upon thee for a sign and a wonder, and upon thy seed for ever" (Deuteronomy 28:45-46).

Other firsthand accounts tell of the black Jews living in Africa. One example shared by Governor Don Francisco de Moura (Moore), who in1622 reported to the King of Portugal that, "the Guinea coastal rivers were full of Jews who were masters of the local regions and were independent of the Crown." These African areas had become populated by the Jews after Edom-Rome barred them from Europe during various expulsions beginning in the eleventh through the fifteenth centuries. Most of the Jews found themselves in Africa, where many of their kin had been dispersed by Edom-Rome during the scattering of 70AD thru 135AD.

Other sources, including the book, 'Hebrewisms of West Africa,' describe many accounts that illustrate that the Hebrew Israelites were black and lived in Africa. While criticizing a map, T. Edward Bowditch, published in 1819, states, "Beginning then at the top of the map, I find a place called Yahoodee, a country or town of non-existence." He explained that it means Jews or the tribes of Jews, which the Muslims apply to those of the Mosaic faith who inhabit the lower Atlas, and districts of Suse. They also apply the term Yahoodee to the Hebrew or Jewish tribes, if they are native Africans, who inhabit Maroa, some parts of Villainy, and the neighborhood of Timbuktu. They divided the Sudanese Jews into small and large tribes according to Dupuis' narrative. He continues; that their mode of life in some countries is pastoral, but they fill the towns with traders and artificers of that faith, who gain subsistence at their several employments, in the service of the Muslims under whose government they live as vassals.

Still, Rudolph Windsor, (2003) in his book, 'From Babylon to Timbuktu' confirms with more proof from his research that, the black Jews had an advantage over the African tribes in Africa because they carried their culture with them; their history, laws, and written records. He added that this assured them a constant precedent for developing a higher social organization. However, what is noteworthy is that because the culture of black Jews was stable, the indigenous population did not absorb the Jews. They report that the Jews absorbed some of the native tribes. However, these may not have all been native tribes of Africa that the European Jews met in the area when they arrived, but the scattered Hebrew Israelites of the Northern tribes or the Judeans scattered during the Roman wars and destruction of the Temple from 70 to 135AD. It is said the Jews used every opportunity they had and was known as a diligent and skillful people. In the Hebrew, Ghanaian states remained kings, princes, governors, generals, secretaries, treasurers, revenue agents, judges, architects, engineers, doctors, historians, language interpreters, mathematicians, jewelers, sculptors, masons, carpenters, painters of art, goldsmiths, leather-workers, potters, armorers, saddlers, blacksmiths, agriculturists, and many other artisans. He also added that the black Hebrew kings of Ghana had two titles: Kayamaga, which meant master of gold, and Ghana, which meant war chief. Another researcher confirmed that twenty-two Hebrew kings reigned in Ghana before the Hegira in 622AD, and forty-four had reigned by 790AD (Godbey, 1930).

Edom-Rome fermented wars and destabilizing events wherever the Hebrew Israelites lived, which caused perpetual dispersion and enslavement of the people on the African Continent. History shows the black people living throughout Africa are not the descendants of Ham because it was, in fact, Israel who Edom-Rome expelled out of Jerusalem and the other European countries they had settled. And, there is no evidence of Ham's descendants ever going into diaspora other than the false narrative Edom-Rome has used. Scripture shows the area of the land that Ham possessed his descendants remain in their lands to this day. These descendants include Cush (Ethiopia), Mizraim (Egypt), and Phut (Phoenicia, or Carthage), known today as Libya, Algeria, and Morocco. Ham's son Canaan inhabited the land of Canaan; the land promised to Abraham and his descendants forever, and they lived as Israel's enemy within the Promise Land. It would be them described as the Philistines or Palestinians still occupying the land today. "And for Cham came forth the second portion, beyond the Giychon towards the south to the right of the Garden, and it extends towards the south, and it extends towards the west to the sea of Atel, and it extends towards the west till it reaches the sea of Mauk that into which everything which is not destroyed descends. And it goes forth towards the north to the limits of Gadiyr, and it goes forth to the coast of the waters of the Great Sea till it draws near to the river Giychon and goes along the river Giychon till it reaches the right of the Garden of Eden. And this is the land which came forth for Cham as the portion which he was to occupy forever for himself and his sons unto their generations forever" (Jubilees 8:22-24).

The sons of Ham occupied the northern and eastern coasts of Africa and are the original Africans. But, many of them have been whited out by Esau-Edom, and no longer have the phenotype of a black son of Ham. Because, according to Esau-Edom, Ham is the father of the dark races, but this is not true as all people in history except Esau-Edom were black people. It is the Hebrew Israelites who have kept their black color and still identify as Negro because it is the will of the Highest YAHUAH that Israel maintains their natural phenotype. YAHUAH chose one peculiar people the descendants of the youngest son of Isaac and Rebekah. They can still be identified today and Scripture declares that not one of them will fall to the ground even though they may be scattered among all people, "For, lo, I will command, and I will sift the house of Israel among all nations, like as corn is sifted in a sieve, yet shall not the least grain fall upon the earth" (Amos 9:

9). YAHUAH chose Edom-Rome to be wicked on the earth, and they can be identified as the people who have inflicted much devastation upon the descendants of Israel. And, it is evident who both the children of Jacob and Esau are as Edom-Rome has attempted to destroy the Negro, the black descendants of Jacob-Israel. However, the will of the Highest YAHUAH is to save them. He reminds Israel of his promise, "But fear not thou, O My servant Jacob, and be not dismayed, O Israel: for, behold, I will save thee from afar off, and thy seed from the land of their captivity; and Jacob shall return, and be in rest and at ease, and none shall make him afraid" (Jeremiah 46:27).

ALTERING THE ICONS AND ARTIFACTS OF HISTORY

Regardless of what Edom-Rome's history depicts, more and more facts are being revealed each day, which proves the people who first occupied the lands now call Europe were the descendants of Japheth, a people of color. They later mixed with

French Icon of Mary and Jesus

Esau and the descendants of Ham. Until now, it has been difficult to ascertain that the people of Scriptures were black since Edom-Rome destroyed most of the physical evidence beginning in 730AD until the 18th century when they tried to destroy all the religious artifacts and paintings of Europe. This specific destruction of religious artifacts they call iconoclasm and the person who carried out the destruction of the artifacts an iconoclast. There were several periods in history when Edom-Rome resolved to eradicate the proof that black people lived in Europe and ruled Europe before they gained control in the late 17th century.

Wikipedia reports that the first iconoclasm took place between 726 and 787AD. The second incident took place between 814 and 842AD. The Byzantine Isaurian king, Emperor Leo III, declared that all paintings, icons, and statues in the church be destroyed, which started a ban on religious images. He claimed that he was against idol worship but was not against using idols to depict saints. Once he had destroyed or removed most of the black icons, he commissioned the recasting of the idols to resemble Edomites instead. Therefore, the same saints and apostles he destroyed they recreated and whited out to resemble the Edomites. Many of the Hebrew Israelites, in their Hellenized mindset, had adopted the pagan ways of Rome and created images that depicted YAHUSHA as a black man. However, this went against the laws of YAHUAH. They also made an image of a young baby on the lap of a black Mary, who was his mother. During the Renaissance period, the paintings of Mary and Jesus were whited out, and the icons and paintings were all replaced with the image of the white Edomite Caesar Borges, the son of Pope Alexander VI. Today, the new images and icons depiction of

Mary is the whitewashed Isis, who is the Edomite Queen of Heaven (Nigosian, 2000).

During the Classical and Renaissance periods, between the 14th and 17th centuries, in Europe, it is reported that they destroyed thousands of paintings and icons of black people. What they did not destroy the Edomites stole from their owners who became part of the wealthy Edomites' private collection. Some of the paintings and icons being found and shown today are taken from these collections. The artifacts are also displayed in museums throughout Europe. As a result, we can still find icons and paintings of the original black rulers of Europe in the back rooms of museums hidden away from public view. And, more and more of these pieces continue to make their way to the public via the world wide web on the internet.

Russian Icon of Jesus Washing the Disciples' Feet

In 2015, in a report by the Daily Telegraph Media Group, they revealed that Thomas Cromwell, an adviser to King Henry VIII, tried to destroy all evidence of the fact that black people had once ruled Britain. This report noted that no one could be sure of the exact number of artifacts they destroyed. However, they estimated that once Cromwell legalized the destruction of 97% of English art in existence met its demise. The paintings and icons they saved during this time, thanks to the internet, are now accessible for viewing and use. However, in these surviving pieces and remaining portraits of black people, it is typical for the captions to read that they were ambassadors who represented the king of the Congo. What is noteworthy is that according to the Slave Voyages database, that in 374 years, the record shows that Britain, France, and Holland, bought 456 African Slaves in total. Yet, they all have abundant Black artifacts in their national records with stupid tales to explain why they have them. The narrative they would wish to remain is that all black people came out of Africa. But the facts show that the black Hebrew Israelites were dispersed into the African Continent where they remain today in exile. And, still more evidence shows that the people in these images were wealthy black Europeans whom the Edomites stole their identity and mimicked their style of dress, pretending to a noble class of people, to this day. These paintings depict black monarchies of Hebrew Israelite heritage who ruled in Europe under the Roman Empire before the Edomite Germans conspired with papal Rome to have them removed.

Cross Pattée
"Iron Cross"
version

Cross Pattée with
Triangular Arms
version

Laughably called "Dom Nicolau, Prince of Kongo on a visit to Portugal." The
Prince also wears around his neck another tye cross of the Teutonic Knights
(The Order of Brothers of the German House of Saint Mary in Jerusalem), OR
a cross of the Portuguese Templar knights (which would be be red). The Prince
also wears a mefieval Tyrolean Jacket: (Tyrole/Tirol was a State of th Holy
Roman Empire). In the aggregate, the Prince's garb suggests that he was a
Prince of the Holy Roman Empire.

Note that the Prince wears European clothing and Icons: a Royal coronet (cap)
with two versions of the Teutonic Knights of the Holy Roman Empire's "Cross-
Pattee" on the band. The "Iron Cross" version, commonaly used by the modern
German military. And a triangular closed-tip version of the "Cross Pattee".
These types of crosss are also common on British heraidry, because the current
British Royalty are of German extraction.

SUBSTITUTING PHYSICAL ISRAEL FOR
'SPIRITUAL' ISRAEL

Edom-Rome created "spiritual" Israel for those who converted to the religion of Christianity because the Edomites believed it possible for any Gentile person living in the nations where the Hebrew Israelites lived in the diaspora, could join Israel by accepting the Messiah YAHUSHA (Jesus). This doctrine was added after Edom-Rome had persecuted many hundreds of thousands of the followers of the HAMASHIACH who Israelites were. But, Edom-Rome reconsidered and changed their tactic after they thought they were losing control of the empire as many more people began to join the church. They saw a need to merge the powers. They encouraged their Roman citizens to join the religion of the Jews through baptism with water. The Roman Catholics refer to it as baptizing into the church. Later, the Protestants called their experience being born again. Conversion to the religion of Judaism, certain sects required converts to take part in specific rituals and then to adhere to various practices and obey the letter of the law. But because there is no Scriptural precedence for this method of joining Israel, they decided the proselytes were now spiritual" Israel. These teachings they took from the mystery Babylonian religion. And, although these ideas were false, Edom-Rome taught a replacement theology that claimed that "spiritual" Israel would be a way for them to become one with the Israelites. The implication was that YAHUAH would include them in the plan he created for redeeming the scattered tribes of Israel. This falsehood deceived those who joined the Christian church, believing they could become Israel in this way. However, a Gentile cannot choose YAHUAH since YAHUAH is the one who makes a choice. He created the earth and established Israel as his chosen people, which he will not change. His choosing destines the Israelites to become Spiritual Israel, "For I will take you from among the heathen, and gather you out of all countries, and will bring you into your land" (Ezekiel 36:24).

The goal of Edom-Rome has been to undermine and replace Jacob-Israel in this world and in the kingdom to come. In fact, in a Yalkut of Yirmiahu, it shows how Jacob and Esau will interact with each other as it describes the true response of Jacob to Esau as he begs to share the kingdom to come. After all, Esau has done to remove Jacob or cause him to move from his position, Jacob will say to him, "... My brother, you will not be like me. I will lead you to death..." (Yalkut Shimoni, Yirmiahu).[2] Esau wants to have it both ways. He has lived in this world as a king, and as a king, he has tried to destroy Jacob, and at the same time, take his place. He wanted to share in the kingdom, so he used deception, murder, and the Babylonian religions to appear holy. However, Edom-Rome is full of dead men's bones as YAHUSHA told the leaders in Jerusalem in his day, "Even so ye also outwardly appear righteous unto men, but within ye are full of hypocrisy and iniquity" (Matthew 23:28).

At the coming of the HAMASHIACH, YAHUAH will bring Israel, the physical, bloodline descendants of Jacob, back to their land just as he led them out of Egyptian captivity. He has promised to take them into the wilderness of the people, and there he will teach them, "And I will bring you into the wilderness of the people, and there will I plead with you face to face. Like as I pleaded with your fathers in the wilderness of the land of Egypt, so will I plead with you, saith YAHUAH ELOHIYM" (Ezekiel 20:35-36). The Gentiles, who may join Israel according to YAHUAH'S determination, will serve as handmaids and servants to Israel. Edom-Rome's religions of Judaism, Christianity, and Islam are not pathways to join Israel or become "spiritual" Israel because they are all pagan religions and have nothing to do with the Highest YAHUAH. Therefore, YAHUAH commands Israel to come out from among them and be separate so that they avoid partaking in the plagues that are about to come upon Edom-Rome and this Babylonian influenced world, "Wherefore come out from among them, and be ye separate, saith YAHUAH, and touch not the unclean thing; and I will receive you, and will be a Father unto you, and ye shall be my sons and daughters, saith YAHUAH Almighty" (2 Corinthians 6:17-18).

Choosing Israel meant that the Highest YAHUAH gave His Ruach (Spirit) to Israel and separated them as his righteous people. Israel is the only people to whom he gave his Spirit. The Spirit is not a god but his being, which encompasses his temperament as we understand the meaning of the word. He chose this seed of all he created to operate in righteousness. Therefore, he has declared in his word, "But over Yasharel he did not appoint any angel or ruach, for he alone is their ruler, and he will guard them and require them at the hand of his angels and his ruachoth, and at the hand of all his powers so that he may guard them and bless them, and that they may be his and he might be theirs from henceforth forever" (Jubilees 15:32). Being chosen, however, did not exempt Israel from the punishment that came as a result of disobedience. This punishment was the provision made by YAHUAH to redeem Israel back to himself through YAHUSHA, his anointed Son, whom he prepared to become the perfect lamb slain from the foundation of the earth, "Blessed be YAHUAH of Israel: for he hath visited and redeemed his people" (Luke 1:68). Yet, Edom-Rome took YAHUAH'S established word and changed its meaning and preached the message that redemption is a universal gift to all people on the condition of accepting YAHUSHA, whom they call Jesus.

YAHUAH only offered this gift of redemption to the chosen Israelites, the people of his covenant living among all nations since he had scattered them among the nations. This promise did not include the Gentiles who had held Israel captive. It is not even possible for it to include them since they have never covenanted with the Highest YAHUAH. So, it is problematic for redemption to come through a nonexistent covenant. Redemption means to buy back or to regain possession of something for payment. The Father sent YAHUSHA to prepare those whom he had first covenanted with, for the renewal of that covenant. He never called the Gentile nations his children because he had no relationship with them. Instead, he compares them to a drop of water from a bucket, "All nations before him are as nothing, and they are counted to him as less than nothing" (Isaiah 40:17).

The Covenant, the Highest YAHUAH, made, he made with Abraham, Isaac, and Jacob-Israel. He chose Israel to be his portion of the earth forever. To the other nations, he gave other spirits that would lead them astray from him. It was never YAHUAH'S intentions to take away the gods of the people that he gave to them. Therefore, in the kingdom of YAHUAH that is to come, people will continue to worship their gods, 'For all people will walk every one in the name of his god, and we will walk in the name of YAHUAH our ELOHIYM forever and ever," (Micah 4:5). However, all nations will worship the Highest YAHUAH as the ELOHIYM above all Elohiym.

Our Father, YAHUAH, always required the people of the other nations to give honor and respect to both him and Israel as they are his firstborn. He tells them to worship Him as the Highest ELOHIYM over all Elohiym. However, Edom-Rome has disrespected YAHUAH by replacing him and declaring their religious leaders, such as the popes of Rome, to be equal to YAHUAH. As Pope Pius V said, "The Pope and God are the same." And Pope Leo 13th agreed and stated, "We hold upon this earth the place of God Almighty." These popes do not understand how abominable these actions are in the sight of the Highest and the reason His wrath will come upon them. In Hebrew culture, one is required to respect one's elders as they still practice these traditions in Africa, today where the Hebrews have not been so influenced by the wicked Babylonian system of Edom-Rome. It requires giving the highest respect to the elder and the Highest. Edom-Rome replaced the teachings of YAHUSHA with a false Universalist doctrine called Catholicism. They determined that this should include everyone on the earth once they converted to the religion, accepted the crucifixion of Jesus' blood then the Holy 'spirit' would make them "spiritual" Israel.

In effect, Edom-Rome made YAHUSHA, or Jesus, the ELOHIYM of the Universe, and urged that he, Jesus wanted everyone to become his children, and promised that if they received Jesus as savior, they would become his son or daughter. Jesus, the Christ, became the God of New Testament believers, including Edomites, and they insisted that Jesus was not as harsh as YAHUAH, the ELOHIYM of Israel. Edom-Rome changed the Israelite laws and, instead, told believers in Jesus that because they were Gentiles, they did not have to obey YAHUAH's commandments since he had only given his Laws to the Israelites. But it was not just the keeping of the Law that could save anyone because salvation came from YAHUAH, and he had already chosen these people that would be saved. Therefore, Paul explained in his letter that obedience to the laws does not make one righteous; however, if we are righteous, we desire to obey the laws of the Highest YAHUAH. And, Israel can only be righteous because they are the chosen people of YAHUAH. But, Edom-Rome persecuted and killed the Hebrews for desiring to obey the laws of YAHUAH and labeled them heretics when they did so.

Therefore, YAHUAH has promised no mercy for Edom-Rome and any of their co-conspirators. The evil acts they perpetrated against YAHUAH'S chosen will return to them as they will reap what they have sown. Thus, YAHUAH will take revenge on them when he returns at the end of their reign of terror on the earth, 'For the day of vengeance is in mine heart, and the year of my redeemed comes," (Isaiah 63:4).

CHANGING THE IDENTITY OF YAHUSHA TO JESUS CHRIST

Through the introduction of Christianity, Edom-Rome transformed the HAMASHIACH of Israel into Jesus Christ, the God of Christianity. They did this by adding Greco-Roman ideologies and pagan philosophies to the Israelite teachings. One such creed was that the Messiah, who came in the flesh, was the God of the Gentiles and a divine messenger. The Church stated that if an individual accepted the call of Christ, he could become enlightened and emancipated, and would return to his true heavenly home at the end of time (Frend, 1984). They molded these ideas into their systems and associated them with the MASHIACH. They also believed that YAHUAH ceased just to be the ELOHIYM of Israel. Instead, they claim he became the ELOHIYM of the universe who was now far removed from the guiding and erratic being that controlled the affairs of Israel as portrayed in the Old Testament (Frend, 1984).

The Edomite Christians rejected the ELOHIYM of Israel and created another Elohiym, who is Christ. So, they do not find the path that leads to eternal life in this Edomite Christ. The truth, however, is that YAHUAH did not offer salvation to the Edomites because he will root them from off the earth. As Esdras explains what will take place when YAHUAH destroys humanity upon HAMASHIACH'S return, "For out of her (the earth) came all at first, and out of her shall all others come, and behold, they walk almost all into destruction, and a multitude of them is utterly rooted out," (2 Esdras 10: 10). YAHUAH did not send the HAMASHIACH to redeem all of humanity despite what the doctrine of Christianity says. YAHUSHA'S response to the Canaanite woman who wanted him to heal her child says it all, "But he answered her not a word. And his disciples came and besought him, saying; Send her away; for she crieth after us. But he answered and said, I am not sent but unto the lost sheep of the house of Israel" (Matthew 15:23-24). Biblical history proves that Israel's God, YAHUAH, is not the same as the god of the Christians, and although Edom-Rome has used Hebrew texts to expand the religion of Christianity, by adding and taking away many teachings to support their narrative. The covenant that YAHUAH will make with Israel will be the laws they could not keep on their own he will write in their heart and mind.

It was the early Christian church leader, Marcion (85-160 AD), who proposed the release of Christianity's shackles to the Law. He encouraged breaking the knot of keeping the law among

Christians. Marcion was a wealthy ship-owner and merchant who Polycarp labeled, "the firstborn of Satan" (Frend, 1984). The position he espoused was that Christ, was revealed by an unknown God for the salvation of all nations and was a different being from him who was ordained by God, the Creator for the restoration of the Jewish (Israel) state, and is yet to come (Frend 1984). He believed Jesus' "special and chief work was the separation of the law from the Gospel" (Marcion I.19). This Christ they supposed was another god for the Gentiles. Like the Chaldean god, who is upheld as a great object of love and adoration, a god through whom goodness and truth were revealed to humanity, so are the same characteristics found in Jesus, the God of Christianity (Hislop, 2012). The Chaldean god was a god they regarded as the predestined heir of all things, and on the day of his birth, they believed they heard a voice to proclaim, "The Lord of all the earth is born." In this Chaldean god, they styled the character of him as King of kings and Lord of lords. They also use the same characteristics to describe Jesus, the Christ, the god of Edom-Rome, and the god that the world follows.

Edom-Rome also removed and replaced the name of YAHUAH and YAHUSHA within the Hebrew scripts. They did this to eliminate the knowledge of the Highest YAHUAH as the Creator of the Universe and ELOHIYM of Israel. Edom-Rome presented a transliterated version of the name YAHUSHA which became Jesus or Iesus as it was first written. They wrote YAHUAH'S name as God or Lord. However, these words are titles and not names. Edom-Rome changed many of the Israelite's doctrines as Jesus became the god of the New Testament, while YAHUAH remained only the god of the Old Testament. The teachings offered by Edom-Rome stressed the importance of Jesus and the power of his name, which became more powerful than the Highest, YAHUAH. Therefore, they believed when they use the name of Jesus, and it is possible to get anything in his (Jesus') name. However, history shows the translators of the texts did not always spell the name Jesus with the letter 'J' since this letter did not exist in the English, Hebrew, Greek, or Aramaic alphabets. They only added it to the English alphabet in the seventeenth century, and the first spelling of Jesus

Black Icons of the Christian Church

with the letter 'J' they wrote in a secular way when they used it in June 1632 in an English brief prepared from the Court of the High Commission in London, England. It described the psalter as Jesus psalter (Matthew Phillips, 2013). Before this, the Edomites wrote the name of Jesus using the letter 'I' as seen in the 1611 version of the King James Bible "Now when Iesus was borne in Bethlehem of Iudea, in the days of Herod, the king, behold, there came Wise men from the East to Hierusalem," (Matthew 2:1). These changes in the names of YAHUAH and YAHUSHA has resulted in the descendants of Israel being deceived because they have believed in someone different from what YAHUSHA taught. Why he told the Pharisees in his day, "I have come in my Father's name, and ye receive me not: if another shall come in his own name, him ye will receive, (John 5:43). The Hebrew Israelites have lost the true teachings of YAHUSHA and why Israel, as the wife of YAHUAH, is still in the wilderness where the 'beast" has driven her where there is no truth.

The belief in a universal or catholic doctrine they thought made it possible for Edom-Rome to become one with Israel. They used Paul's writings to teach that because of Jesus, and he can adopt them into the family of Israel by being grafted into the good olive tree. Because of this possibility, Edom-Rome believed and taught that those who were not Israelites could now share in the Salvation that YAHUSHA brought to Israel. However, Edom-Rome knew this was false teaching, and they could not be grafted into Israel, but they changed the teachings to lead Israel away from the Highest to destroy them in this life as they knew their future for Israel in the kingdom to come was guaranteed. What Edom-Rome did cause Israel to act corruptly, and they replaced YAHUAH with graven images - a practice that the early ancestors of Israel knew brought death.

Rabbinic writings show that the Hebrew sages were against Edom-Rome. Still, once they instituted changing and dividing the divinity of YAHUAH into the form of a man, they called Jesus, the Christ, many of them became angry and surrendered to martyrdom rather than accept this teaching. History notes, how Edom-Rome changed the teachings of the only true church of

YAHUAH by replacing the divine attributes and personalizing them. They changed the name YAHUSHA to Jesus, the Christ, who they believed was one with the Father.

Edom-Rome, with its pagan ideas, had gods for every imaginary thing or virtue, and they also canonized saints. They believed that the Virgin Mary was the first of the vestal virgins and that she was the Divine purity personified, or made personal; Jesus, her son, was the Divine light personified or made personal; and Sophia, the Divine wisdom, made personal. They even made a god of the Spirit of God and called it God the Holy Ghost. They made this substantive in the likeness and body shape of a dove and is recorded in the New Testament. "The Holy Ghost descended in a bodily shape like a dove upon him, and a voice came from heaven, which said, Thou art my beloved Son; in thee, I am well pleased" (Luke 3:22). However, YAHUAH had spoken to Moses about these things, 'And YAHUAH commanded me to teach you statutes and judgments, that you might perform them in the land where you are going over to possess it. So watch yourselves carefully, since you saw none form on the day YAHUAH spoke to you at Horeb from the midst of the fire, lest you act corruptly and make a graven image for yourselves in the form of any figure, the likeness of male and female, the likeness of any animal on the earth, the likeness of any winged bird that flies in the sky, the likeness of anything that creeps on the ground, the likeness of any fish in the water below the earth," (Deuteronomy 4:14-18). The Ruach HaKodesh being formed in the shape of a dove and coming down on YAHUSHA is another false doctrine of the Edomite Romans.

ALTERING CEREMONIES AND RITES OF CHRISTIANITY

According to J.I. Mosheim, when Edom-Rome entered other nations with the gospel of Christianity, they believed, that it would be easier to introduce the forms or rites and ceremonies to those who were familiar with worshiping idols if Christianity also had idols. 'The leaders imagined that the nations would more readily receive Christianity when they saw the rites and ceremonies to which they (the heathens) had been accustomed established in the churches, (i.e., Christian churches,) and the same worship paid to Jesus and his martyrs (saints) which they had offered to their idol deities; hence in those times the religion of the Greeks and Romans differed little in its external appearance from that of Christians." (Vol. i. B, I, p.2, chap.4.). The Greeks and Roman always worshiped the pantheon gods. They also worshiped their ancestors and believed that they became gods.

Therefore, Jesus becoming god was not an event that happened to Jesus but a developing change in the thinking of those responsible for the change (Lloyd Geering, 1998). Geering (1998) furthers that the process continued to evolve, and even by the first century, Christians thought on this subject was still a long way away from the teachings proclaimed by the council of Chalcedon in 451AD. At this council, they proposed and ratified the doctrine of the divinity of Christ and the Trinity. These were doctrines that the early followers of YAHUSHA, led by Peter and James, still did not accept because they saw YAHUSHA from a Hebrew mindset, and in their view, YAHUSHA remained human like themselves; However, they believed he fulfilled the role of the HAMASHIACH but was not divine. This same schism was brewing from the First Council of Nice in 325AD when Emperor Constantine introduced these doctrines and added them to the Roman Christian church. However, after the fifth century, no one heard the Hebrew point of view anymore because Edom-Rome had full control of what Christians taught in the church; and the church became another pagan entity and not the bride of YAHUAH (Geering, 1998).

As a result of the changes made to the Christian Church, Jesus Christ, their savior god, was used to deceive Israel with a replacement faith and MASHIACH. And so, Hebrew Israelites must come into the knowledge of the truth about Jesus, the god of the Edomites, and understand the difference between him and YAHUSHA, the HAMASHIACH of Israel. According to Matthew Phillips (2013), Edom-Rome used revisionism to adopt the Gentile identity and codify it as a reform. They used Anti-Israelism, which they call anti-Semitism and, syncretism, the teaching that the adoption and grafting in of Gentiles are possible, to overtake the original intention of Hebrew Scriptures. He continues that this has been an outright exercise in reversed leveraged assimilation. Edom-Rome has reformed traditional practices of Israel into Christian practices and labeled them Judeo-Christian. They had substituted Jesus for YAHUAH and YAHUSHA, and have given Jesus the divine attributes of YAHUAH which goes against what YAHUSHA expressed when he was in Jerusalem, "I can of mine own self do nothing: as I hear, I judge: and my judgment is just; because I seek not mine own will, but the will of the Father which hath sent me' (John 5:30).

CHANGING TIMES AND LAWS

In revising the history of the earth, Rome, with its power, has sought to change the natural laws of how time is measured as well as the Moral Laws of YAHUAH. In the prophecies, they predicted that the fourth beast power would change times and laws. Edom-Rome, this beast power, has fulfilled this prophecy in these last days by doing just that, "And he shall speak great words against the Highest, and shall wear out the saints of the Highest, and think to change times and laws: and they shall be given into his hand until a time and times and the dividing of time," (Daniel 7: 25). Hence, it was Emperor Constantine who enforced the Roman-Babylonian change of the Sabbath day and other Hebrew Feast Days in 325AD. But, before Constantine, Rome had changed times and laws for centuries.

The New Encyclopedia Britannica explains that the origin of the calendric system used today is the Gregorian calendar. They trace it back to the Roman republican calendar, introduced by the fifth king in Rome, Tarquinius Priscus, who reigned from (616–

576BC). However, Constantine grafted the astrological planetary week system onto the Roman calendar by proclamation, making the first day of the week to align with the day of the sun, which would also be a day of rest and worship for all. He also imposed the sequence and names of the days of the week to the planetary week, so they became what we know them as today. With this official edict, they fused the market week and the planetary week into one continuous seven-day cycle named after the pagan gods of Rome. Therefore, the days of the week correspond to the planets: Apollo, the Sun god for Sunday, Diana, the Moon-god for Monday, Mars, the god of war for Tuesday, Mercury, the god of Woden, for Wednesday, Jupiter, the god of the sky and thunder for Thursday, Venus, the Roman goddess of love for Friday, and Saturn, the god of time for Saturday. This fact of Rome being the changer of times was confirmed in a letter by the Chancellor of Rome who boasted that indeed it was Rome who made these changes, "The Catholic Church claims the change was her act. And the act is a MARK of her ecclesiastical power and authority in religious matters." (C.F. Thomas).

Besides, the changes made to the Sabbath day Edom-Rome also divided the times into Before the Common Era (BCE) and (AD), which means the year of our Lord. This system of time change was devised during the middle ages in Europe. It was said to be a marker for the Christian Church to honor the year Jesus was born. They determined his birth to be in the year one and described the Latin word, Anno Domini, which means the year of our lord. They wanted Jesus to be born in the first year. However, scholars had found that this date does not correspond with the date found in New Testament history, which shows YAHUSHA'S birth to be before the death of Herod the Great, who died in the year 4BC. They wanted Jesus to be born at a certain time because Edom-Rome worshiped the stars, and they needed the time to coincide with the movements of the wandering stars they call planets. Thousands of years before they completed this act, Enoch declared that these wandering stars would move out of their courses, and those using them to tell the times and seasons would be wrong, "And many chiefs of the stars shall transgress the order prescribed. And these shall alter their orbits and tasks and not appear at the seasons prescribed to them. And it shall conceal the whole order of the stars from the sinners" (Enoch 80:10-12). The sinners are those of Edom-Rome using these stars to determine what the future would bring. And, because the stars do not move in their correct order, the times used by Edom-Rome are in error, and the times and seasons of the year are out of order. They have taken these observations of the stars and added them to the Christian festivals of Easter, which celebrates the goddess Ishtar and Saturnalia, which is a reference to the god of Saturn, the god of time that they celebrate the birthday of Jesus the Christ.

The Gregorian calendar in use today based on Scripture is also wrong about what the exact year is at present. Based on the Hebrew calendar which follows the lunar year dating back to

Adam, it shows we should be in about the year 5,780. However, this may also be inaccurate because of Israel's disobedience YAHUAH said that they, too, will lose track of the true time while in the diaspora. YAHUAH told Israel that he would not honor their feast days to him, because of their disobedience, and they would not know the correct times for these celebrations, "I hate, I despise your feast days, and I will not smell in your solemn assemblies' (Amos 5:21). Therefore, because YAHUAH has dispersed Israel and because all truth comes by and through them, thus, the world does not know what time it is. And, those who say they know are liars.

Despite Edom-Rome having ruled for over two thousand years, there are still different systems used to determine the year that we are in as there was never a consensus on which to use. Some nations use both the Gregorian calendar and their timetable. The calendar systems of Japan and North Korea base their calendars on the birth of their leaders and the Luna calendar. In the kingdom of Thailand, the calendar they use shows they are 543 years ahead of the Gregorian calendar, therefore, presenting the year 2019 as 2562BE, which they count since the era of the Buddha's birth. The people of Thailand place the Buddha's birth in the 11th century BC; however, scholars of Edom-Rome determined that he was more likely to be born in the 6th century BC. Although this change in his birth may just mean that Edom-Rome is trying to correct their timeline of historical facts, so they are distinct in claiming the oldest nation and Empire status next to Egypt.

USING ARAB ISLAMIC CO-CONSPIRATORS AGAINST ISRAEL

The true history of the earth shows that the religion of Islam was established around 1081 to 1097AD in sub-Saharan West Africa. However, my research shows that the followers of the Muslim faith were enlisted by Edom-Rome to destroy further the Hebrew Israelites living in West Africa. Since the Arabs were pagan worshipers who refused to join Edom-Rome's Christian religion, and the truth is that many of the Arab tribes were the brothers of Edom-Rome and had joined the conspiracy against the Israelites. The narrative presented as historical fact is that the Arabs rose in the 7th to 9th centuries and overcame the great Roman Empire, later ruling for hundreds of years. This conquering of Rome by the Arabs served several purposes - the Arabs could claim to have a prophet sent from their god Allah like Jesus, and Edom-Rome could use them as the scapegoat to destroy Israel while disguised as the Arabs.

Edom-Rome wrapped the religion of Islam into the practices of the Roman Christian Church. They also filled the Islamic holy book with passages taken from the New Testament about Mary, the mother of Jesus. In the Quran, they mention Maryam thirty-four times, and nineteen times in the Sura. Yet, they are a different religion from Catholicism. But the facts show that Islam

432

is one of the Mystery religions of Edom-Rome in which the female goddess, Allat, associated with fertility and war, is equal to Maryam. The rosary beads used by Catholics are also used by the followers of Islam and used while they pray the same purpose as the Edomite Catholic Christians. The Arabs employed the same tactics Edom-Rome used to convert the Israelites by the edge of the sword. They slaughtered hundreds of thousands of Hebrew Israelites who refused to convert or enslaved them. As a result, many Hebrews joined the Muslim religion, as evidenced by the Muslim populations throughout sub-Saharan Africa and the Middle East today. Islam eradicated the religion of Israel among the people of Hebrew descent in the area of Subsarahan Africa. And, there is no evidence that they ever lived in this area. In certain countries of Africa, it is not unusual for the population to consist of being almost 100% Islamic with no trace that the people of these regions were the Israelite Jews.

It took the powers of Edom-Rome to steal the land of Palestine for their Khazarian brothers. And it was the Muslim Arabs used by Edom-Rome to destroy the Israelites in Africa that they expelled from Judaea hundreds of years before. The Khazarian Jewish people claimed they were returning to their homeland, but they fail to reveal how and why they were removed from the land in the first place. However, there was one brave leader who questioned the validity of the Khazar Jews returning to the land of Palestine. And, it is alleged, for this reason, the President of Egypt lost his life. Edom-Rome used the Arab nations with the religion of Islam to wreak havoc wherever Hebrew Israelites settled throughout the Middle East and Africa. The truth of history, however, proves that this religion, too, has its foundation in Edom-Rome and for centuries used against the Israelites who had settled in Sub-Saharan Africa. In an excerpt from a book about Africa, the author makes these observations and recalled how the Ottoman Turks comport themselves toward the Hebrew Israelites who had settled in the lands they ruled during the time Israel was being expelled out of Europe. He writes;

> Many Jews also are scattered over the Region, some Natives boasting themselves of Abraham seed, inhabiting both sides of the River Niger: Others are Asian strangers, who fled thither either from the desolation of Jerusalem by Vespasian or from Judaea wasted and depopulated by the Romans, Persians, Saracens, and Christians: Or else such as came out of Europe, whence they were banished viz. Out of some parts of Italy in the year 1342, Out of Spain, in the year 1462. Out of the Low country in 1350, Out of France, in 1493, and Out of England, in 1422. These all different in Habit, and divided into several tribes, having no Dominion, though both wealthy and many, but despised of all Nations and so hated by the Turks, that they are not admitted to be Mahometans unless first Baptized: And then no otherwise used, than to receive their customs, and gather their Taxes.

The Ottoman Turks were nothing but the tool of Edom-

Rome chosen by them to implement their false religion into the communities of the Hebrew Israelites living in Africa. These Turks are the descendants of Alexander the Great and, therefore, are the seed of Esau-Edom, the Edomites. If they were serious about converting people to the Muslim religion, why would they force Israelites first to baptize as Christians before joining the Muslim faith? Why were Edomite Christians not forced to convert to Islam? So, if there was a war against Christians, why were there not more white European countries forced to convert to the Muslim faith? Europe should be abounding with white European Muslims. But, Edom-Rome tries to make the world believe that Turkey, a small Muslim country is the fourth beast destined to rise with a leader they call the Mardi who will force the religion of Islam by the sword throughout the earth. However, the prophecies tell us that Christianity and all those associated with it are the fourth beast power on the earth. Islam is another arm of Christianity used by Edom-Rome, the wicked people of the earth. And, are all part of the conspiracy against the Hebrew Israelites, the most hated of all people as Scripture says they would be.

---

[1] Pirke Elizer 24 is an aggadah-midrashic work on the Torah containing exegesis and retellings of Biblical stories. Traditionally, it has been understood to be a tannaitic composition which originated with the tanna Rabbi Eliezer ben Hyrcanus, a disciple of Rabbi Yohanan ben Zakai and teacher of rabbi Akiva and his disciples.

[2] Yalkut Shimoni or simply Yalkut is an aggadah compilation on the books of the Hebrew Bible.

CHAPTER
11

True Description of Israel

THE EDOMITES HAVE HIDDEN THEIR IDENTITY among the other nations of the earth, but more than that, they have gone to extreme lengths to obscure the identity of the Hebrew Israelites. And, although they describe the Israelites as the Negro, which means black, they differentiate between the black people who are descendants of Ham. They are not Negroes but are described as Arabs. These include the Egyptians, the Ethiopians, the Canaanites, and the Phonecians or Lybians as they are known today. They were able to tell the difference between these black people and the Negroes because of their cultural practices. And so during the time of the Transatlantic and Arab slave trades they only captured the Hebrew Israelites, the Negroes who they enslaved in the Americas and the Arab countries just as the

prophecy foretold, "And YAHUAH shall bring thee into Egypt again with ships, by way of which I spake unto thee, Thou shalt see it no more again: and there ye shall be sold unto your enemies for bondmen and bondwomen, and no man shall buy you' (Deuteronomy 28:68). Scripture also confirms the skin color of the Israelites when

Alessandro Longhi Portrait of a Young Black Man Italy (c. 1760s)

Solomon described himself, "I am black but comely." And Abraham Melamed shows further proof as it relates to the black skin color of the Israelites in a discourse found in the anti-Christian polemics in the Hebrew literature, which he concludes leaves no doubt that the Israelites were black or dark-skinned. Still, the Edomites had red or white skin. He noted. However, there appeared to be confused by the authors of these writings, as the Jews were deemed to be black and, therefore, ugly in comparison with the Christian, who was fairer and so more beautiful. He asserted that the empirical fact that the Jews had black skin worried the Edomites because they lived in a cultural mentality that they appeared to have internalized that black and ugly was a sign of degeneration and evil while beautiful and fair represented good and purity.

Other commentaries authored by sages such as Rashi and Abraham ibn Ezra on Isaiah 52:14 describe the black skin color of the Jews, "As many were astonished at thee, his visage was so marred more than any man and his form more than the sons of men." Rashi adds, "When many nations looked upon them in their abasement they said, why Israel

Icon of the Black Messiah

looked so marred, they saw how much blacker they were than other people, whom our own eyes behold." This description references two accounts in Scripture, one that shows how YAHUSHA looked in his physical, visible form during his crucifixion by the Romans. And, the other shows how the Israelites looked while they were in the siege; they lamented their condition why Edom rejoiced. They were dying of hunger while they watched from afar, as the enemy ravaged their crops. The account further describes their physical features at this time, "Their visage is blacker than a coal; we do not know them in the streets: their skin cleaves to their bones; it is withered, they become like a stick" (Lamentations 5:8). In an attempt to dismiss this fact about the black skin of the Jews, Rashi attempts to make this blackness as representative of the Israelites black heart; however, these verses of prophecy pronounce the skin color and condition of YAHUSHA and the Israelites at the time they were being devastated by Edom-Rome.

Jacob-Israel was and is a people of color or, as some may describe them as the Negroes. The Zondervan Bible Dictionary concurs and defines Israel's color when they described Ham, the youngest son of Noah, in comparing Shem, the eldest son of Noah. It states, "Ham the youngest son of Noah, born about 96 years before the Flood; and one of eight persons to live through the flood. He became the progenitor of the dark races, not the Negroes, but the Egyptians, Ethiopians, Libyans and Canaanites" (Gen 10:6-20). So, based on this definition, the white Jewish people claiming to be the descendants of Jacob cannot be because they are not Negroes, and therefore, cannot be descended from the tribe of Judah or any of the tribes of Israel. They claim to be Semitic, and they are the descendants of Esau, who are Edomites. Therefore, their Semitic roots came

Black Moses on Stained Glass, Augsburg, Germany, 12th Century

through him and not Jacob. Esau was the red son of Isaac, who mixed his seed with the nations; therefore, we see his skin color reproduced in the people of other Gentile nations.

The facts reveal that the true Israelites were black-skinned people then and now. Edom-Rome's revisionist history did not consider that these Negroes would one day awaken to the truth about their identity. The Highest YAHUAH made the skin color of Jacob and Esau different and an important factor in determining the dissimilarity between the two nations. Their names described who they would become from their birth. The main physical disparity between the Edomite Jewish convert and the Hebrew Israelite was the skin color. Therefore, Gamal Abdel

The Changer - Rudolph Ernst
(1854-1932)
A Moor and Edomite of Spain

Nasser, the first President of Egypt, described it best in a 1952 television interview when he said regarding the Israeli Jews returning to the land of Palestine, "The Europeans claiming to be the Jews are nothing more than Hebrew speaking Gentiles. You (the Jews) can never live here in peace because you left here black but came back white. We cannot accept you."

There is still other evidence that proves that the true Sephardic Jews of Spain were also black people. However, the white Edomite Jews have also attempted to replace them by appropriating their name and moving into the land of Palestine as Jews. Although, according to Rabbi Abraham Ben David, in describing the Negro Israelites, "A tradition exists with the (Jewish) community of Granada that they are from the inhabitants of Jerusalem, of the descendants of Judah and Benjamin."[1] And, Samuel S. Smith confirms the description of the Jews in Portugal and Spain as swarthy a word meaning black, as in the name Stuart, and implies the House of Stuart is where the Black kings that ruled the British Isles originated.[2] Therefore, the Sephardic Jewish people living in Palestine today have only appropriated the name Jews, but they cannot replace the Black Israelite descendants of Spain or Portugal. They are imposters and the Semitic descendants of Esau, the only red son of Isaac.

When Esau was born, Scripture described him as red and hairy all over. There is another word and definition in the same Zondervan dictionary that compares and contrasts the color of the Hebrew Israelites with the word "ruddy" a word used to refer to a red or fair complexion, in contrast to the dark skin of the Hebrew (1 Samuel 16:12, 17:42; Song of Solomon 5:10). Furthermore, Scripture confirms the color of the Judeans as it describes the color of YAHUSHA in the vision that John saw while on the Isle of Patmos, "And amid seven candlesticks one like unto the Son of man, clothed with a garment down to the foot, and girt about the paps with a golden girdle. His head and his hairs were white like wool, as white as snow; and his eyes were as a flame of fire, and his feet like unto fine brass, as if they burned in a furnace, and his voice as the sound of many waters" (Revelation 1:14-15). The skin of YAHUSHA'S feet was dark because they looked like they had been burned. The Hebrew Israelites fled from Jerusalem into the African Continent after the war of 70AD. However, some historians claim the Negro Hebrew Israelite also fled into the lands governed by the Roman Empire known as Europe. Indeed, this is true as evidence also shows that they lived as dispersed people throughout Europe even before the rise of the Greek and Roman Empires. The Hebrew Israelites had formed communities and claimed the thrones of England, Scotland, Ireland, and France. They were known as Jacobites, in Britain and ruled as the house of the Stuarts and Savoy. According to Mac Ritchie (1996), the Israelites, the Phoenicians, and the Chaldeans are said to have visited the British Isles at various periods and may have colonized them. The Hebrew Israelites ruled these lands, and the white Edomites were their subjects before Edom-Rome rose to power. He continues that the Gaelic writers discovered many affinities between the Hebrew and Gaelic tongues. The evidence he cites, however, is a mixture of truth with mythology based on Edom-Rome's false narrative created to support their deception. The photographs of paintings of Negro nobility who lived in the British Isles and throughout Europe are evidence that the Israelites had established a homeland in the British Isles even before the birth of YAHUSHA and remained a nation ruled by them until the 17th and 18th centuries. Edom-Rome, through deception and war, conquered the lands and replaced the Negro British monarchies with the Germanic white Edomites. Edom-Rome has concealed the history of the Jacobites' rule under the guise of the "Dark Ages." Howbeit, in Acts of the Apostle, the 29th chapter, Edom-Rome left this chapter out of the Canonized text, which confirms the truth about the Nobility of Britain. "And Sha'ul, (Paul) full of the blessing of HaMashiach, and abounding in the Ruach HaKodesh, departed out of Rome, determining to go into Spain, for he had a long-time purpose to journey thitherward, and was also minded to go from thence into Britain. For he had heard in Phoenicia that certain of the children of Yisra'el, about the time of the Assyrian captivity, had escaped by sea to the isles afar off, as spoken by the prophet, and called by the Romans Britain" (Acts 29:1-3). Historical evidence shows the dispersed Israelites of the Northern Ten Tribes ruled in Europe, which would have come under the Roman Empire at the start of the reign of Edom-Rome in 168BC.

Family Crest of Christie, Faineham, Faringham, Gorton, Gouton, Hardie Mordant, Mordaunt, Pannell, Pert, Shipley (Fairbairn Book of Crests - plate 129)

The dispersed of Israel lived throughout the known world, and although they were in the diaspora, YAHUAH said that the Israelites would still be kings, but if they acted wickedly, they and their kings would be consumed. Many of them fled into the African Continent, Phoenicia, Portugal, and Spain between 70 and 135AD, where large communities of black Hebrew Israelites were living. However, some of the Judeans migrated into the deserts of Africa. They became the people of the Songhai dynasty. These are some of those that were hunted by Edom-Rome throughout this region in Africa in the late 16th and 17th centuries characterizing the Israelites as heretics because they refused to obey Rome, "The idolaters are many in negro-land, upper, and lower Ethiopia and toward the great ocean except as we hunted before, some few by industry of the Portuguese and Spaniards have converted and baptized in several places."

After the rise of papal Edom-Rome, the Israelites who lived in Europe were forced into exile to the African continent. By the seventeenth century, papal Rome had conquered and slaughtered or expelled most of the Negro inhabitants of Britain, France, Denmark, Scotland and Ireland, and destroyed many of the artifacts that could prove that black Hebrew Israelites once ruled in Europe. What they did not destroy, they tried to white-out during the Renaissance. According to papal Edom-Rome, they used this time as a cultural movement that brought about the scientific revolution and artistic transformation of modern history in Europe. It marked the transitional period between the end of the Middle Ages and the start of the Modern Age, which arose in the fourteenth century in Italy and the sixteenth century in northern Europe (Wikipedia). Edom-Rome changed the complete history of the world using their so-called scientific

Family Crest of Buller, Gleame, Maniot, Mauley, Moore, Mordant, Morgan, Mure, Quadring (Fairbairn Book of Crests - plate 134)

evidence to support the great deception that has deceived the entire world.

CHANGING THE COLOR OF PEOPLE IN HISTORY

Another method used by Edom-Rome to deceive the world was changing the color of the original people on the earth. They changed the color of the Hebrew Israelites, YAHUAH'S chosen people. Historical evidence shows that the skin color of all people were different shades of brown and black. However, when Esau was born, he came out red and had hair all over his body. YAHUAH used this difference in Esau's color to distinguish the people who would rule the earth in the final days before His return. Blumenbach, an 18th-century scientist, developed theories in anthropology that showed empirical evidence to support racism as he compared the anatomy of the human skull and skin color and decided that white people were of a superior race. He then applied his classification to human beings and claimed that there were four races - the Caucasian or white race, the Mongolian or yellow race, the Malayan or brown race, and the Ethiopian or black race. Later, they added a red race of American Indians. Based on this data, Edom-Rome classified white people as the superior race and classified the black race as inferior. There are accounts in Rabbinical literature that prove that Edom-Rome always believed their color made them superior and is one reason they had such a perpetual hatred for the descendants of Jacob. However, these beliefs only became evident when the revised papal Roman Empire took full dominion over the earth with a created scientific hypothesis to support their beliefs.

A person's skin color was not always used to identify people in earlier times since all people were black with melanin that protected them from the sun. Instead, people identified with their tribe or family lineage. However, on occasion, they did identify people by the color of their skin, such as the Moors of Spain and Portugal, noted in Scripture as the descendants of Ham. These people were the original Phoenicians known as the purple people because their skin was so black. From this, they derive the word Moor from the Greek word mauros, which means black or dark. The Israelites were another group of people sometimes described by their color, "Now there were in the assembly was at Antioch certain prophets and teachers; as Barnabas, Simeon that was called Niger, and Lucius of Cyrene, and Manaen, which had been brought up with Herod, the tetrarch, and Saul" (Acts 13:1). The word for Niger is Latin for black. However, in Moorish Spain and Portugal, many of the Israelites of the northern tribes had settled in these lands hundreds of years before the rise of the Greek and Roman Empires. And, despite the late history of Edom-Rome, the original people who ruled in these lands were the descendants of Phut. People of color dominated and ruled throughout Europe until Esau and his descendants whited many of them out, killed them, or they were exiled into Africa.

Evidence fills the annals of history, which confirms the color of the Israelites and those called Jews. Rev. Samuel Stanhope Smith describes the color of the Jews in a geographical context, at the latter end of the eighteenth century. He poses that Jews were fair in Britain and Germany, brown in France and Turkey, Swarthy (black) in Portugal and Spain, olive in Syria and Chaldea, and tawny or copper-colored in Arabia and Egypt.

His Majesty George II - King of Britain

While these descriptions may have described the color of the Jews during that time in history, the descriptions may not tell the entire story since other people would have converted to the Jewish religion. Edom-Rome had banned the actual Israelites from following the tenets of their faith and had forced most of them to convert to Christianity and Islam over the centuries. The true descendants of Israel went into the diaspora and later captured and carried into various slaveries world-wide. And because they lost their identity and heritage, they no longer recognized they were Israelites. However, we can still identify the true bloodline Israelites as Negro, because of the signs of the curses written in Deteronnnomy chapter 28 that identifies them as the people. The writer, Paul Isaiah, writes about the Jews from

Niger, "I knew you to be a Jew, because you JEWS have a particular color of face different from the form of other men. Which thing hath often filled me with admiration, for you are black and uncomely, and not white like the Edomites?" The skin color of Jacob-Israel was always the opposite of Esau, who is Edom, the white people as they describe themselves.

After Edom-Rome conquered the lands, the Israelites had inhabited, they replaced the people of color with people that looked like them. Even the indigenous people and black Israelite slaves who they carried captive into other lands were whited out. In the 19th and 20th centuries, there were five nations that Edom-Rome colonized and imported Europeans to whiten the population. These nations included Brazil, Cuba, Jamaica, South Africa, and Australia. In Brazil, scientific racism supported whitening ideology. Edom-Rome used Darwin's theory of natural selection, which claimed the superiority of the white race to all others. Therefore, in 1880, white Brazilians sought to improve their society by lightening the population. Later, in the 1920s, they paid white Europeans to immigrate to Brazil to prevent Brazil from becoming a complete black nation. They called this process branqueomento. In Cuba, Edom-Rome encouraged interracial marriage and invested over one million dollars into recruiting European immigrants. In Jamaica, they imported over one thousand Germans to work in the government as they refused to hire experienced black workers and tried to white-out the Israelites living there with these Germans. However, these attempts to whiten Cuba and Jamaica failed as the societies remained with most people of color.

In 1820, in South Africa, 5,000 middle-class British immigrants flooded the country. They intended to replace the black South African with white immigrants. The white South African government made rules that kept the black South African out of certain areas, and the blacks became third-class citizens in their own country. If a white South African found a black South African in a white-only area, they were allowed to kill the black person. Later, the white South African invited more immigrants from Taiwan, South Korea, and Japan and identified them as honorary whites. In Australia, Edomite authorities had children with aboriginal women for two hundred years, and by the third generation, had bred out the blackness of the Aboriginals through biological assimilation. Then, for over one hundred years, they enforced a policy of cultural assimilation in which they removed the indigenous children under age 12 from their families and brainwashed them with the Edomite-European culture. These whitening processes of the Hebrew Israelites and other indigenous people were Edom-Rome's method to become the dominant race of people on the earth. However, Edom-Rome did not understand that the same process they used to whiten people of color also worked in reverse. YAHUAH subscribed that if Israel were to mix once with Edom-Rome or any other Gentile nation and did not continue to carry on the legacy, by the third generation, YAHUAH would accept the children back into Israel.

He told this to Israel as he said we should not abhor the Edomite or the Egyptian, "The children that are begotten of them shall enter the congregation of YAHUAH in their third generation" (Deuteronomy 23:8). However, this has no bearing on the truth of Scripture that also states; there is a time for every purpose under heaven even a time to hate those of our enemies who have tried to destroy Israel. "A time to love, and a time to hate, a time of war, and a time of peace" (Ecclesiastes 3:8). Therefore, this was not a call to love our enemies who wished to destroy Israel and root them from off the face of the earth.

TRUE HISTORY PROVES YAHUAH EXISTS

The accounts of Esau-Edom's interaction with Jacob-Israel verify that YAHUAH, the ELOHIYM of Abraham, Isaac, and Jacob, does indeed exist. And, there is still a remnant of his chosen people on the earth, despite the efforts of Edom-Rome to eradicate them. YAHUAH has protected this remnant for such a time as this as he continues to fulfill his purpose for Esau, who is Edom. The Edomites' claim that the accounts of Israel's history recorded in Hebrew Scriptures are myths or oral traditions passed down and written by unsophisticated shepherds living in the land of Palestine will not change the truth. The Jewish Edomites living in Palestine today claim that the ancient people of Israel only had an oral tradition and wrote nothing until the 10th century BCE is false. Because, Scripture shows that Noah wrote in a cepher, "And Noach wrote all things in a cepher as we instructed him concerning every kind of medicine. Thus, the evil ruachoth was prevented from hurting the sons of Noach. And he gave all he had written to Shem, his eldest son, for he loved him above all his sons' (Jubilees 10:13-14). There is evidence in Scripture that shows that it was the servants of YAHUAH who told Enoch to read and write in a book, "And the angel Uriel said unto me 'Observe, Enoch, these heavenly tablets and read what is written thereon, And mark every individual fact.'... And now, my son Methuselah, all these things I am recounting to thee and writing for thee, and I have revealed to thee everything, and given thee books concerning all these: So preserve, my son Methuselah, the books from my father's hand, and see thou deliver them to the generations of the world' (Enoch 81: 1; 82:1-2). Edom-Rome has stolen these books of Israel and hidden them within the Vatican walls. They pretend to be the people with a predisposition for books, but Scripture says it is Jacob who stayed near the house reading books to learn the ways of YAHUAH.

Recording information in a book happened long before Israel was ever a nation, as evidence shows many accounts of YAHUAH telling his servants to write what he had said in a book which, in Hebrew, is a sé-fer or scroll, "And YAHUAH said unto Moses, Write this for a memorial in a book, and rehearse it in the ears of Joshua: for I will put out the memory of Amalek from under heaven' (Exodus 17:14). In the book of Isaiah, when Israel had taken the counsel of others against YAHUAH'S instructions, YAHUAH told the prophet to write what would happen because of what they did in a book, "Now go, write it before them in a table, and note it in a book, that it may be for the time to come forever and ever' (Isaiah 30:8). YAHUAH always had his servants write in a book as he created them in his image with the ability to think and learn and then write what they had learned. Why would they not write? The servants and Prophets always wrote Israel's history, which is why Israel has the oldest written history, known as the Hebrew Scriptures. Edom-Rome as they arose as the fourth beast power took authority over these writings and added to them and took away portions that did not agree with their narrative. Israel is a nation that has no monuments standing today, which show where they once lived; however, they have the Hebrew Scriptures that record their history. And, although Edom-Rome has tried to eliminate the Hebrews of Scripture and replace them with their whited-out version, it is still the Negro Hebrew Israelites who the world will soon identify as the people of the book.

Besides, the truth written in Hebrew Scripture, researchers have found evidence that confirms and attest to the events recorded in them. For example, the real natural disasters that resulted from the ten plagues of Egypt. However, in trying to explain away the parallels recorded in Scripture, the author claims that the plagues only occurred because of a chain of natural phenomena triggered by changes in the climate and the environment. They want to attach the plagues that YAHUAH will bring upon them to what they call climate change. According to this theory, what happened was not the result of an angry, wrathful God. But from a Hebrew perspective, YAHUAH would not just be angry or wrathful but the avenger of his children whom the Egyptians had enslaved for over a hundred years. And when he brings down his wrath again, it would take vengeance on the people who tried to destroy his children and his earth. And, perhaps their theory is correct, that the plagues resulted from climate change, but Hebrew Scriptures record the full account of these plagues which supports the evidence of the scientists. It is important to note that archeologists now believe that the plagues occurred at the ancient city of Pi-Rameses on the Nile Delta, the capital of Egypt (Gray, 2010).

The researcher, John D. Morris (2001), has also confirmed the stories about the Flood and collected over 200 flood stories from around the world as reported by missionaries, anthropologists, and ethnologists. He surveyed the stories told and concluded that based on this evidence, the common story among all those reported was the story outlined below:

> Once there was a worldwide flood, sent by God to judge the wickedness of man. But there was one righteous family which he forewarned of the coming flood. They built a boat on which they survived the flood along with the animals. As the flood ended, their boat landed on a high mountain from which they descended and repopulated the whole earth.

Scriptures record YAHUAH would interact with the people of Israel, the descendants of Abraham, Isaac, and Jacob. And, he also created the other nations who would be Gentiles even those who would be Abraham's sons of which the servants of the Highest told Abraham would happen as YAHUAH only chose one of Abraham's seed, "And we returned in the seventh month and found Sarah with a child before us and we blessed him, and we announced to him all the things which had been decreed concerning him, that he should not die till he should beget six sons more, and should see them before he died; but that in Yitschaq should his name and seed be called: And that all the seed of his sons should be the other nations and be reckoned with the other nations; but from the sons of Yitschaq one should become a holy seed, and should not be reckoned among the other nations. For he should become the portion of EL ELYON, and all his seed had fallen into the possession of ELOHIYM, that it should be unto YAHUAH a people for his possession above all nations and that it should become a kingdom and priests and a holy nation," (Jubilees 16:16-18). Historical evidence confirmed by the other nations surrounding Israel when they lived in the Promised Land shows that the Israelites were a unique people, a nation whose ELOHIYM was the Highest YAHUAH. These nations respected the Israelites, feared them, and yet they hated them. These accounts of history help to settle the truth that the Highest YAHUAH, the ELOHIYM of Jacob-Israel, whose adversary,

Esau-Edom, are the main characters carrying out their roles today in the predetermined plan of the Highest YAHUAH.

---

[1] Rabbi Abraham Ben David (c. 1125-27 November 1198), also known by the abbreviation RABaD, Ravad or RABaD III, was a Provencal rabbi, a great commentator on the Talmud, Sefer Halachot of Rabbi Yitzhak Alfasi and Mishne Torah of Maimonides, and is regarded as a father of Kabbalah and one of the key and important links in the chain of Jewish mystics. He was born in the Provence, France, and died at Posquieres.

[2] Samuel S. Smith was a Presbyterian minister, founding president of Hampden-Sydney College and the seventh president of the college of New Jersey from 1795 to 1812.

CHAPTER
12

Israel's Blessed Hope

YAHUAH DELIVERED THE CHILDREN of Israel into the hand of Esau, who is Edom, to produce in them the righteousness that comes through adversity. The Highest YAHUAH chose only one Nation of people on earth as his portion and desired to refine them the same way gold and silver are purified by fire, which removes the dross caused by disobedience. The Prophet Zechariah forecasted how this the Most High's will would be fulfilled in the children of Israel, "And it shall happen, that in all the land, saith YAHUAH, two parts shall be cut off and die; but I shall leave the third. And I will bring the third part through the fire and will refine them as silver is refined, and will try them as gold is tried: they shall call on my name, and I will hear them: I will say, it is my people: and they shall say, YAHUAH is my ELOHIYM," (Zechariah 13:8-9). Most High needs his chosen people to be pure of any contamination. Therefore, he allowed Edom-Rome to administer the punishment to the children of Jacob-Israel for their fore-parents' disobedience to his laws, statutes, and commandments. Edom-Rome's deep-seated hatred and jealousy of Israel led them to increase the punishment and do far more to Israel than was necessary. As a result, the wrath of the Most High will come upon their children. "Because thou hast had a perpetual hatred, and hast shed the blood of the children of Israel by the force of the sword in the time of their calamity, in the time that their iniquity had an end: therefore as I live, saith YAHUAH ELOHIYM, I will prepare thee unto blood, and blood, even blood shall pursue thee' (Ezekiel 35:5-6). YAHUAH'S intentions were to have the children of Israel disciplined not destroyed, "Ye were sold to the nations, not for your destruction: but because ye moved YAHUAH to wrath, ye were delivered unto the enemies," (Baruch 4:6).

Not only did Edom-Rome go beyond what YAHUAH allowed in meting out punishments on Israel, but they were also hypocrites. While carrying out evil acts, they pretended they were also the holy people of YAHUAH and deceived Israel into joining with them. They replaced the Israelites with the likeness of themselves. Edom-Rome spread this deception to the rest of the world, who accepted the lie that YAHUAH had cast the nation of Israel away and replaced them with Edom. Edom taught that they were now the chosen ones and called the oracles of YAHUAH. Such false religious teachings continued the traditions of the mystery cults of Nimrod, who sought to reach heaven by building the Tower of Babel. This research was done to reveal to the children of Israel and all those who are interested in the fraud that Edom-Rome perpetrated against the entire world. They aimed to destroy Jacob-Israel and become the elected people of YAHUAH to whom the adoption pertained, "Who are Israelites; to whom pertaineth the adoption, and the glory, and the covenants, and the giving of the law, and the service of YAHUAH, and the promises' (Romans 9:4).

Howbeit, because Israel is the chosen people of YAHUAH, Edom-Rome could only execute punishments the Highest allowed. He permitted Edom to interpret the Hebrew TORAH falsely to suit their selfish purposes. They have been able to rule the earth for centuries as they hold authority over what is told about historical events, which has resulted in this great deceit. Many are now shedding light on the truth about Edom-Rome and the people of Israel. In an article about Jewish American History, the Documentation Foundation notes that the scheme that has been perpetuated by Edom-Rome is corruption at its core, hypocrisy at its most lethal, and is a good reason for YAHUAH to hate Esau, who is Edom. However, despite all that Edom-Rome has done to destroy and replace Israel, it is still YAHUAH'S choice and purpose to give Israel a good future, "For I know the thoughts I think toward you, saith YAHUAH, thoughts of peace, and not of evil, to give you an expected end. Then shall ye call upon me, and ye shall pray unto me, and I will hearken unto you' (Jeremiah 29:11-12).

THE COVENANT WITH ISRAEL

While the Hebrew Israelites lived in the Promised Land, everyone knew that they were the people who had covenanted with the Highest YAHUAH. It was also widely known they were awaiting the HAMASHIACH'S return to set up the kingdom that would deliver them from the bonds of sin and Roman oppression. Hence, the Judeans remained strong and returned yearly to their land for special feast days regardless of where they lived throughout the Roman Empire. It did not matter if they spoke Aramaic or Greek, or whether their life centered on the Temple at Jerusalem or on a synagogue in a town in Asia Minor, or whether they were Palestinian peasants or Alexandrian philosophers, the Judeans all formed part of the religious and cultural confederation that extended throughout the Greco-Roman world. They were nationalists and were dangerous when provoked (Frend 1985). Gunther Bornkamm agrees with and states, "The Jewish (Israelite) religion (is) unique among the religions of the world. In contrast with the Greeks and Orientals and other peoples of the time, the Judeans worshiped a God that 'had no image, no myth, and no cult practices whereby men might share in the natural-supernatural powers of the deity." He furthered that the animal sacrifices they made might turn away his wrath, but it could not identify the worshiper with him. So, while the Israelites were YAHUAH'S people, it did not confine them to their designated territory. The covenant that YAHUAH made with Israel bound them to Him and His will, and, amid every form of unrighteousness and wickedness, there was always a faithful remnant that would uphold the law and comfort themselves with conviction even when they were in captivity. They believed that YAHUAH would send his representative who, with supernatural power, would come and overthrow the heathen oppressor and restore Israel to its former glory. They knew that HAMASHIACH, the anointed One, would redeem and save Israel when he came (Frend, 1984).

Therefore, the covenant remained with Israel even though Jacob-Israel is in the wilderness of the people at this time. As Scriptures says, there is a remnant that remains faithful. Like the time in about 600BC, when the Northern Ten Tribes dispersed into the other nations, the Hebrew Israelites spoke the languages of the nations where they lived, but they did not forget who they were. However, the Judeans, who remained in Judaea, regarded these tribes as Greeks or Gentiles because they spoke the language of the Gentiles. It was this reason the inscription Pilate placed on the Roman cross of YAHUSHA showed three different languages spoken by the Hebrews. When Paul stated that he was an apostle to the Gentiles and wrote his letters to the Gentiles living in these areas, he was referring to the Hellenized Israelites living as Gentiles throughout the empire. Whenever he wrote about the Jews, he referred to the tribes of Judah and Benjamin still living in the land of Judaea known as Judeans, "And a superscription also was written over him in letters of Greek, and Latin, and Hebrew, THIS IS THE KING OF THE JEWS' (Luke 23:38). Pilate knew that it was necessary to have the inscription written in these languages because the dispersed Israelites throughout the empire were all considered Hebrew Israelites. However, they spoke the languages of the country where they lived and, the inscription addressed all Hebrews regardless of their location.

THE REDEMPTION OF ISRAEL

Edom-Rome knew that YAHUSHA HAMASHIACH came to redeem the dispersed tribes of Israel back to the Father YAHUAH. For this reason, they desperately anticipated hiding their involvement in the destruction of Israel throughout history. History shows Edom-Rome could always identify Israel because they were distinctive people with a unique culture. However, because for nearly three hundred and fifty years, the Israelites did not know their own identity, they could not defend who they were. The Israelites did not know their true heritage and, as Marcus Garvey stated, "People without the knowledge of their history and culture is like a tree without roots." As a result, Israel could not grow as people because they could not be nourished. However, Edom-Rome also had distinct characteristics that identified them as Edomites, Idumeans, Greeks, and Romans. These descendants of Esau, who is Edom, knew that YAHUAH favored Israel his chosen people; in fact, people all over the earth knew this to be true. Therefore, when HAMASHIACH came, he did not come to change or add anything to what YAHUAH had already established, "For the mountains shall leave, and the hills are removed; but My kindness shall not leave from thee, neither shall I remove the covenant of my peace, saith YAHUAH that hath mercy on thee' (Isaiah 54:10).

YAHUAH chose a people, he called Israel as his portion on the earth, and he gave the other people he created other gods for them to worship. Because he had chosen a people, there was no need to redeem the other nations as he had no covenant with them. This knowledge, however, did not prevent Edom-Rome from creating a grand scheme that substituted their god as the ELOHIYM of Abraham, Isaac, and Jacob to be the ELOHIYM of all nations. In their version, YAHUAH would adopt Edom-Rome into his family and become the Father ELOHIYM of Edom-Rome and the entire earth.

While YAHUAH is the Creator of everything in heaven and on earth, he is only the ELOHIYM of the righteous seed of Abraham, Isaac, and Jacob-Israel. He regards none other nation as his own, including Edom-Rome, and there was never a plan set in place to adopt them into his family. And, the idea that

YAHUAH is the ELOHIYM of all people is not scriptural. Edom-Rome has created this confusion by force conversions to their pagan religions that made people believe the God they served was the Creator ELOHIYM of the Universe and the Father ELOHIYM of all people. Howbeit, Scripture states that YAHUAH is the Father of the children of Jacob-Israel and this is why he punished them for breaking his covenant, "You only have I known of all the families of the earth: therefore I will punish you for all your iniquities," (Amos 3:2).

Thus, when the Kingdom comes, the Highest YAHUAH promises to redeem Israel and restore them and place them above all nations, "Oh, that the salvation of Israel was come out of Zion! When YAHUAH bringeth back the captivity of his people, Jacob shall rejoice, and Israel shall be glad' (Psalm 53:6). YAHUSHA came to earth for this expressed purpose, to become the perfect sacrifice that would pay the price for Israel's redemption back to the Father. Also, his coming and being born into the earth was supposed to be a sign to Israel as the Prophet Isaiah stated; 'Therefore YAHUAH himself shall give you a sign; Behold, a virgin shall conceive, and bear a son, and shall call his name Immanuel' (Isaiah 7:14). The name Immanuel means ELOHIYM with us, and YAHUSHA would be the promised Mashiach. He would receive power to rule in righteousness and to judge and make war with the enemy. When John saw him in the vision he had on the Isle of Patmos, he described him, "And I saw heaven opened, and behold a white horse, and he that sat upon him was called faithful and true, and in righteousness, he does judge and makes war. His eyes were as a flame of fire, and on his head were many crowns; and he had a name written, that no man knew, but he himself. And he was clothed with a vesture dipped in blood: and his name is called The Word of ELOHIYM" (Revelation 19: 11-13). When the KING OF KINGS and ADONAI OF LORDS returns to the earth, he is coming to make war with those who tried to destroy his seed, and he is not coming to redeem the wicked people of this earth. The Most High's redemption plan does not include all people, such as the Edomites, because they did not break YAHUAH'S laws as he had never given them the laws. Instead, it was only Israel who had been in covenant and had broken the laws, and he had to divorce his wife and cut them off. Therefore, only Israel needed cleansing with the blood of YAHUSHA. He died and was raised to new life so that he could be a new man and marry a new, born-again wife in a New Covenant. Thus, He paid the price with His life for Israel's return to the Father. Therefore, no other man could buy Israel out of captivity. It would take the blood of YAHUAH'S first begotten son to redeem them back to the Father ELOHIYM, "Kiss the Son, lest he is angry, and ye perish from the way, when his wrath is kindled but a little. Blessed are all they that put their trust in him' (Psalms 2:12).

YAHUAH turned his face away from Israel for a little while because of disobedience, and the only way they could return to Him is through this exchange, "For a small moment have I forsaken thee; but with great mercies will I gather thee. In a little wrath, I hid my face from thee for a moment; but with everlasting kindness will I have mercy on thee, saith YAHUAH thy Redeemer' (Isaiah 54: 7-8). As promised, the false teachings of Edom-Rome will soon cease and the wicked system they have created to destroy Israel will end, "Therefore the redeemed of YAHUAH shall return, and come with singing unto Zion; and everlasting joy shall be upon their head: they shall obtain gladness and joy, and sorrow and mourning shall flee away' (Isaiah 51:11).

ISRAEL GRAFTED BACK INTO THE OLIVE TREE

When the HAMASHIACH brings the kingdom of YAHUAH to the earth, he will graft them into their olive tree. Both the descendants of Jacob-Israel from the northern ten tribes they refer to as Israel or Ephraim and the Judeans, the southern tribes. In Paul's Epistle to the Hellenized Israelites living in Rome in the diaspora, he explained to them this grafting in process. He also clarified why YAHUAH had cut off some Judeans because of their unbelief in HAMASHIACH. However, Paul noted that YAHUAH would graft them in again if they believed in the HAMASHIACH. Yet, Edom-Rome took Paul's letter and used it to mislead and deceive those of the pagan religions that, somehow, Paul addressed these letters to all people, from all nations referred to as Gentiles. At the time, these people still knew they were Israelites but had adopted the ways of the Gentiles. History shows they lived in large Israelite communities in Rome and throughout Europe and Africa, where many of them rose to rulership and prominence in the established nations. Up to this time, the chosen people of YAHUAH had never lost their Israelite identity. Most of them still kept the Sabbath, met in synagogues, obeyed YAHUAH's laws, and observed and celebrated the feast days by returning to Jerusalem from all over the earth three times a year. These Israelites from the northern ten tribes whom Paul addressed were not Roman pagans, yet the Greek and Roman

pagan ideas and philosophies had influenced some of them. Paul reminded these dispersed Israelites who were returning to the House of Israel that they should not boast against the Judeans, who, because they did not accept the HAMASHIACH,

An Olive Tree with One Branch Cut Off

had also been cut off for unbelief. And because the Judeans were the actual good tree that remained, therefore, it would be easy to graft them back into their tree. He told them that the Judean root of the tree held them, which made it possible for YAHUAH to graft Israel back into the congregation of the righteous. Paul referred to those of the northern ten tribes as the wild olive tree, which the Judeans no longer considered being part of the house of Israel.

Paul then illustrated how the olive tree represented both branches of Israel. From this tree, YAHUAH cut one branch off while the other branch remained intact. However, YAHUAH also removed some branches from the good tree because of their unbelief. So, according to Paul, they too would have to rejoin the good branch of the olive tree again, 'And they also, if they abide not still in unbelief, shall be grafted in; for YAHUAH can graft them in again. For if thou were cut out of the olive tree wild by nature, and were grafted contrary to nature into a good olive tree: how much more shall these, which be the natural branches, be grafted into their own olive tree' (Romans 11:23-24)? Instead, Edom-Rome has attempted to use Paul's teachings to support their claim that Paul wrote to people outside of the Israelites known as Gentiles, which meant Edom-Rome. However, the Epistles prove that the audience Paul addressed specifically referred to the olive branch of the northern ten tribes living in the diaspora.

Edom-Rome took the events of YAHUSHA'S death, burial, and resurrection to misrepresent what the Highest YAHUAH only planned for his chosen people Israel. They then added the pagan beliefs and ideas of the Edomite Christians, which resulted in creating another religion - Christianity. Once Edom-Rome took control of the Israelites, they insisted that YAHUAH had now chosen them, and it was they who would rule in the kingdom of heaven, and therefore, Israel needed to obey them. Yet many Israelites still obeyed YAHUAH and refused to obey Edom-Rome, and therefore, became martyrs. In, several instances the Apostles entered Roman territories to preach and teach about the

HAMASHIACH to the lost sheep of the house of Israel. At these times, the Edomites and other Roman citizens became furious. They would sometimes arrest them for teaching "And brought them to the magistrates, saying, These men, being Jews, trouble our city, and teach customs, which are not lawful for us to receive, neither to observe, being Romans' (Acts 16:20-21). The Edomite-Romans at the time did not want the teachings of the Apostles because they did not believe in the MASHIACH or worshiped the Highest YAHUAH. However, the Apostles' message was for those Israelites who were Roman or Greek citizens and whose heritage lies in the bloodline of Israel. Paul knew that, like all Judeans, the Israelites were the chosen people of YAHUAH and that HAMASHIACH'S coming did not change the truth about being obedient to YAHUAH's laws.

YAHUAH sent Paul to the Israelites living in different territories of the Roman Empire. His letters and ministry addressed those who belonged to the wild branch of the olive tree. Paul knew these brethren as Hellenized Israelites who lived among the Greeks and Romans. Because they lived among these people, he also labeled them Gentiles. Whereas, those who identified as Judean Israelites, he addressed them as Jews. The Israelites in Paul's day were nationalistic and carried their culture wherever they settled. There were huge communities of Israelites throughout the Roman Empire, and no matter which country they lived in, Paul could always identify them. Today's imposter Jewish people have stolen the identity of the true Israelites and have copied their way of life by living in similar communities throughout the earth.

THE HEBREW ISRAELITES' RESPONSE

The evidence presented proves that YAHUAH's chosen people are the black descendants of Jacob-Israel, who now live among the other pagan nations in the diaspora, believing they are Gentiles. Many of them claiming they have Hamitic roots. But this research refutes that claim. While many are now being awakened to the truth, some still find it difficult to release the indoctrination instilled by their slave masters, or, in other words, Esau, who is Edom- the man of sin. Many awakened Hebrew Israelites still believe that YAHUSHA came to redeem the entire world so that he could save all people. But Scripture is consistent in its delivery, which refers to only one nation, Israel and one people, the Hebrew Israelites who are chosen by YAHUAH.

According to Van den Bissen, "The Hellenistic Judaism religion became the soil in which Christianity took root and gained strength. When they formed the early Christian church, Greco-Roman pagans included ideas that altered their doctrines, but they did not align with Hebrew Scriptures. Hence, our fore-parents adopted and received false religious teaching while their Edomite-Roman masters enslaved them. It is imperative, therefore, that Israel discerns the truth and identify the lies fed to them and the rest of the world by those who have held power over the scripts and scrolls of Israel for the past five hundred years. To come to this realization, the children of Israel also must put their trust in the power of the Highest and believe his unaltered words above anyone or anything else. The Highest YAHUAH has promised to reveal all things through his servants, the Prophets. He also guarantees that there are no mysteries, unlike those found in Babylonian mystery religious cults such as Christianity, Judaism, and Islam. Therefore, when understanding is unclear, Israelites must use discernment and trust that all scripture is given by inspiration of the Highest YAHUAH. Although Edom-Rome contaminated the Hebrew Scriptures, Israel must not fear that the Highest's words have become unusable. Edom-Rome only holds the power that YAHUAH has given them. Since the Most High's power is the ultimate authority, there is nothing that Edom-Rome can do without His permission.

As the Hebrew Israelites awaken at this point and time in history, they need to reclaim their stolen heritage by researching the truth for themselves. This truth must compel Hebrew Israelites to write their histories and support their statements with the proof found in Scripture. Edom-Rome has tried to discredit Hebrew Scripture, but they have given very little sourcing for the lies they have spread throughout history. Israel must use the words that our Prophets and foreparents taught against Edom-Rome to slay them with the pen. As the old English adage, I used as a mantra for my writing, states, "The pen is mightier than the sword." Today, Jacob's descendants must think and act like the Bereans, living in the diaspora. During that time, the apostles were teaching the Hellenized Jews scattered throughout the Roman Empire, the Israelites not only believed what the apostles taught them, but they also searched Scriptures to prove what was true. "These were nobler than those in Thessalonica, in they received the word with all readiness of mind, and searched the scriptures daily, whether those things were so" (Acts 17:11).

Also, since we do not wrestle against flesh and blood, but with the powers of darkness in high places, Israel must also pray to be led by YAHUAH and show a serious scholarship Edom-Rome cannot deny or contradict. The foundation of the research process must be the Hebrew Scriptures because it is the original truth of history. Even though Edom-Rome has influenced certain segments of Scripture, this would not be the only time that they did. For example, during the time of the Maccabees, the Greeks sought to alter the Torah, "And laid open the Cepher of the Torah, wherein the heathen had sought to paint the likeness of their images' (Maccabees 3:48). Still, the Hebrew Israelites of those times kept their faith and believed the Word of YAHUAH over anything Edom-Rome attempted to change.

Likewise, Hebrew Israelites must consult all history, and particularly, all the Hebrew literature, even those the Edomite Jewish people claimed to have authored. I found that many of these writings were produced by the descendants of Israel, and we must be willing to cross-reference to check for accuracy and truthfulness when used for reporting. We must realize who the descendants of Edom-Rome are and let the Scriptures confirm their character traits, which reveals the true identity of them. YAHUAH answered Habakkuk and told him to write the vision, which describes Esau-Edom. "For the vision is yet for an appointed time, but at the end, it shall speak, and not lie: though it tarry, wait, for it; because it will surely come, it will not tarry. Behold, his soul which is lifted, is not upright in him: but the just shall live by his faith. Yea also, because he is a proud man, neither keepeth at home, who enlargeth his desire as hell, and is as death, and cannot be satisfied, but gathereth unto him all nations, and heapeth unto him all people," (Habakkuk 2:3-5).

And above all, Israel must seek the Father YAHUAH and His will. And, let his Ruach lead, guide, direct, and give discernment of all written accounts. It is known that Esau, who is Edom, has revised both theirs and Israel's history and has deceived the world. And, what we know is based mainly on what Edom has written and provided. Therefore, to combat the influence of Edom-Rome, Israelites must remove themselves from among the Babylonian mystery religions, which have been used by Edom-Rome to keep them blinded and oppressed. I concur with the sociological theory of Karl Marx which states that religion is "the sign of the oppressed creature . . . the opiate of the people." As the lyrics of a Rap song performed by one of my Hebrew brothers declare and say it another way, "If religion weren't wack, they would take it from the Blacks."

EDOM-ROME'S PUNISHMENT AND FALL

The present age we live in Esau-Edom has dominion overall as the Roman Empire. However, it will end and, according to their timeline, they have ruled for over two thousand years. During their rulership, they have carried out untold devastation on the descendants of Jacob-Israel as well as YAHUAH'S earth. YAHUAH'S blessing upon Esau was that he would live in the earth's fatness, and indeed he did live by the edge of the sword. However, YAHUAH will deliver Jacob-Israel from the hand of Edom-Rome, and they will inherit the earth for an everlasting possession as prophecy forecasts, "And I will feed them that oppress thee with their own flesh; and they shall be drunken with their own blood, as with sweet wine: and all flesh shall know I YAHUAH am thy Savior and thy Redeemer, the Mighty One of Jacob," (Isaiah 49: 26). Jacob-Israel will receive the blessings of the Kingdom to come, in righteousness, as YAHUAH will write the laws on their heart and in their mind, and they will obey, and no one will have to tell them right from wrong. "For this is the covenant I will cut with the house of Yashar'el after those days, saith YAHUAH; I will put my Torah into their mind, and write them in their hearts: and I will be their ELOHIYM, and they shall be to me a people," (Hebrews 8:10). Esau and his descendants have received their portion in this age. And, soon, Jacob and his descendants will have the part YAHUAH has promised them in the kingdom to come.

The Highest YAHUAH created Esau for sin. He was the vessel, described by Paul, made for dishonor. From the same lump of clay came Esau, a tool for evil, while Jacob, created by YAHUAH for honor, "YAHUAH hath made all things for himself: yea, even the wicked for the day of evil," (Proverbs 16:4). YAHUAH turned the children of Jacob-Israel over to Edom for chastisement for their sins against him. They kindled the Highest's anger, "For he hath brought a nation upon them from far, a shameless nation, and of strange language, who neither reverenced old man nor pitied child' (Baruch 4:15). The prophecies that pertain to Esau, who is Edom, are definite, and Rome will fall just as the Targums of Genesis 15:12 reveals. "Terror that is Bavel (Babylon), the darkness that is Media (Medes and Persians), Greatness that is Greece and Fell that is Edom (Rome), that fourth kingdom is to fall and never to rise again forever and ever." The Targums show four kingdoms that would rule the earth and would enslave and hurt the descendants of Jacob-Israel, YAHUAH'S chosen people. And, Edom-Rome is the fourth and final empire of this Babylonian system destined to fall.

According to several modern Rabbinic writings, Edom-Rome has tried to hide the identities of themselves and the Greeks to minimize the punishments they will receive or to hide their evil actions against Israel because they are, in fact, hypocrites. They say that Edom-Rome was unlike the Greeks, whereas the Greeks threatened the physical existence of Israel; they had also enriched their Rabbinic culture. However, when Rome began its rule over Israel, the Roman Empire single-mindedly determined to destroy the Hebrew Israelite civilization. And, once Edom-Rome sent the Hebrews into exile, the damage was irreversible. Therefore, Edom-Rome as the ruling power that destroyed the people and the homeland of YAHUAH.

They say the atrocities committed against the Hebrew Israelites by both the Greeks and Edom-Rome is symbolic of Israel's ruthless enemy. Though the records of the Greeks depict that the acts they committed against the Hebrew Israelites were less violent, the Biblical history proves that both the Greeks and Edom-Rome were equal in their violence against the Israelites in the attempt to wipe them out. The commentary on the writings of the Hebrew sages claims the names of Esau and Amalek were used in the writings of the Rabbis to escape censorship and arrest by Edom-Rome. However, this does not square, knowing that Esau-Edom and Amalek are all Edomites as they are the progenies of Esau and the enemy of Jacob-Israel. The identities of Edom and Amalek the sages wrote before Edom-Rome was an empire because everyone knew the descendants of Esau was Israel's enemy. This white man claims to be of European descent ruling on the earth today. They are the true names of the enemy and are not symbols of any other people. The sages used the names of the actual people as they were not in fear of Rome because Edom-Rome had no power over them.

The nation of Edom-Rome has attempted to commit a complete genocide of the descendants of Jacob. In fact, for this reason, several prophecies foretell that YAHUAH will destroy them forever for this violence against Israel. Prophecy also predicts a sobering end-time event to transpire involving the descendants of Esau, who is Edom-Rome, which will, or should cause them to reflect and give pause, "Thus I will make mount Seir most desolate, and cut off from it him that passeth out and him that returneth. And I will fill his mountains with his slain men: in thy hills and thy valleys, and all thy rivers, shall they fall that are slain with the sword. I will make thee a perpetual desolation, and thy cities shall not return: and ye shall know that I am YAHUAH' (Ezekiel 35:7-9). Despite this warning and impending punishment, Edom-Rome shows little regard for what they know is coming. They continue to boast about their power because they have built vast armies and developed weaponry they say can destroy the entire earth. They somehow believe the weapons they have designed and built will prevent their destruction or make it possible for them to escape. But YAHUAH will not be mocked as Paul wrote in his letter to the Hellenized Israelites in Galatia, "Be not deceived, YAHUAH is not mocked for whatsoever a man soweth, that shall he also reap' (Galatians 6:7).

CONCLUSION

I wrote this book based on the information I uncovered to support my belief regarding the identity of Esau, who is Edom. The evidence has led me to believe that Esau, the elder brother of Jacob, is the white people of European descent who rule the earth today. However, I realized that I had no preponderance of evidence to support what I thought to be true. Therefore, I spent countless hours gathering proof from Scripture and corroboration I found in the secular historical records. These findings are what I used to substantiate my theories. The Highest gave Edom-Rome dominion to rule over the earth for the present dispensation. He also placed his chosen people, Jacob-Israel, into their hands. For centuries, the descendants of Esau-Edom have hidden their identity through a revised history of the earth. They have also mixed with the nations and taken the identity of the peoples they have mixed with, yet they still claim to be of European descent because they are white. To them, their whiteness makes them superior to all other people.

Throughout this research process, I have uncovered many lies mixed in with the truth. As a result, it was important for me to discern what truth was and then validate and compare information to substantiate my findings. One critical element of determining truth was my reliance on Hebrew Scriptures since these writings give the real story about the past, the present, and the future. Whenever I found truth in Scripture, I sought to establish it by locating two or three more witnesses as I believe that if something is true, then it is possible to verify and find evidence that supports this truth.

I hope that every Hebrew Israelite will pay attention to scripture, and the history the Highest speaks through his prophets and in the evidence I wrote in this book. For me, seeking the truth is not important just for the sake of having more knowledge. Still, it is important so that Israel may know the identity of Esau, but also that the Israelites may confirm who they are as we prepare for the coming kingdom of the Highest YAHUAH.

It is essential we, as Israelites, identify our enemy without a doubt so we may navigate their system with knowledge. After all, without knowledge, the people perish. And, it has been for our lack of knowledge about our identity and the identity of Esau-Edom that they have been able to destroy us for hundreds of years.

For centuries Edom-Rome convinced the children of Israel that if something were in a book, they would never find it. In this statement, there is a great irony because Israelites are the people of the book. The evidence of Scripture and history shows the Negro Hebrew Israelites are, indeed, the children of the Highest. This fact is confirmed in the TORAH and the Prophets. It is the reason that Edom-Rome burned so many of the books and scripts of Israel and prevented them from learning to read the English language during slavery. Edom-Rome created a book called the New Testament and added it to the Torah, and claimed the entire Hebrew scriptures as the Christian Holy Bible. However, this book is the actual history of the Israelites, the chosen people of YAHUAH. Therefore, we must return to it to find out about our truth. We must form our conclusions based on facts we can prove in other sources. For example, many doctrines imply different teachings that Edom-Rome has inserted in the Hebrew Scriptures, which are not original to the Hebrew Israelites' understanding. These human-made ideas and philosophies Edom-Rome twisted to deceive further the children of the Highest YAHUAH and the other nations on the earth. Therefore, we don't need to accept these false doctrines to believe that the scripts and history belong to the Hebrew Israelites. Though, we must still be cautious when judging the motives of some historians. The Scriptures admonish us to fear the Highest and seek the truth and serve him in spirit and truth, "Only fear YAHUAH, and serve him with all your heart: for considering how great things he hath done for you," (1 Samuel 12:24).

I realize that Israel is not just a religious organization. Instead, it was an established nation that Edom-Rome scattered throughout the earth by warfare and economic hardship. Edom-Rome has either destroyed most of Israel's records, stolen many of its scripts, or has hidden them away in the vaults of the Vatican. However, we must reclaim our heritage, and the only way to achieve this is to seek the truth and write about it using the same evidence that Esau understands. If we just speak and preach the truth, they will continue to ignore the facts and refuse to listen. But they cannot ignore written truth with references. I believe that history would be bare if those in power did not have access to our Hebrew writings and knowledge of the Hebrew Israelites' history despite what they have said about how the Greeks influence the world's history.

Enoch prophesied that Edom-Rome would alter and pervert the words of the Highest. He said that Esau would tell lies about himself and his people and that the wicked would write their books concerning their words. The words written by Enoch have come to life as the Israelites awaken to the truth and are writing their history in books with evidence. Enoch said that we would write the truth according to the words of the Holy Great One "But when they write all my words in their languages truthfully, and do not change or minish ought from my words but write them all down truthfully all I first testified concerning them. Then, I know another mystery, that books will be given to the righteous and the wise to become a cause of joy and uprightness and much wisdom. And to them shall the books be given, and they shall believe in them and rejoice over them, and then shall all the righteous who have learned from there all the paths of uprightness be recompensed" (Enoch 104:11-13).

I have attempted to retrace the history of Esau, who is Edom, from his birth, and in doing so, I also retraced Jacob's sojourn. I discovered that the connection between Esau and Jacob is relevant and that it is difficult to separate the two and write about one without including the other. Edom-Rome has limited the Canonized scriptures in its scope as it concerns Esau. Because they are Edom-Rome, they have only chosen to publish scriptures in the Canonized text that supported their narrative. However, it is possible to find relevant information in other Biblical texts, including the Talmud and the Rabbinic writings since these writings, too, do not belong to the imposter Jewish people but to our forefathers, whom YAHUAH gave the understanding, the laws, the glory, the covenant, and the promises.

We must understand what has happened to Israel and then seek the truth through YAHUSHA how to return to the Father. Esau, who is Edom, has used various schemes and plans to keep Israel in a state of confusion as they awaken out of this Greek-influenced Babylonian system, which has resulted in more confusion. Edom-Rome caused the nation of Jacob-Israel to scatter to the four corners of the earth. Today, we identify them as the revived papal Roman Empire. The identities of these two people, Esau and Jacob, are intimate and linked to prophecies of the "end" times. If there is no Esau, then there is no Jacob. Therefore, we must identify Esau, who is Edom.

We must return to our Hebrew roots and strive to obey the Laws of the Highest not just in the law's letter but in the spirit as YAHUSHA admonished us, "Ye have heard it was said by them of old time, Thou shalt not kill, and whosoever shall kill shall be in danger of the judgment: but I say unto you, that whosoever is angry with his brother without a cause shall be in danger of the judgment: and whosoever shall say to his brother, Raca, shall be in danger of the council: but whosoever shall say, thou fool shall be in danger of hellfire," (Matthew 5:21-22). I understand and believe that because we were a Nation and not just a religion, it is unnecessary to start a church or an assembly or even to join an assembly because Israel, the Nation, and its people are the church. Therefore, it is not a place where we can go to or assemble at this time. We do not have to use the model of Christianity because its foundation is found in pagan Rome and will lead to false religion,

481

"For we are the circumcision, which worships YAHUAH in the spirit, and rejoice in YAHUSHA, and have no confidence in the flesh' (Philippians 3:3). Therefore, we must return to the principles that made the world envy us as a great Nation. Our Father chose a people to be his own, physical people led by his Spirit and given laws that governed their behavior in every aspect of their life. We lived in the Land of Promise, and we will again, the Most High willing. And, it is his will to return the Israelites to the Land which is our true homeland, "For YAHUAH will have mercy on Jacob, and will yet choose Israel, and set them in their own land: and the strangers shall be joined with them, and they shall cleave to the house of Jacob. And the people shall take them, and bring them to their place: and the house of Israel shall own them in the land of YAHUAH for servants and handmaids: and they shall take them captives, whose captives they were; and they shall rule over their oppressors' (Isaiah 14:1).

At this time YAHUAH will administer healing to all of Israel, "Behold, at that time I will undo all that afflict thee: and I will save her that halteth, and gather her that was driven out, and I will get them praise and fame in every land where they have been put to shame. At that time will I bring you again, even in the time that I gather you: for I will make you a name and a praise among all people of the earth, when I turn back your captivity before your eyes, saith YAHUAH," (Zephaniah 3:19-20). Thus, the children of Israel must come out from among the confusion of this Babylonian influenced system and return to the Father, "Flee out of the midst of Babylon, and deliver every man his soul: be not cut off in her iniquity; for this is the time of YAHUAH'S vengeance; he will render unto her a recompense," (Jeremiah 51:6). We must seek the Most High with all our hearts and pray like Manasseh did when he repented of his sins;

MANASSEH'S PRAYER OF REPENTANCE

O YAHUAH, EL SHADDAI, of our fathers, Abraham, Isaac, and Jacob, and of their righteous seed; who have made heaven and earth, with all the ornament thereof; who have bound the sea by the word of your commandment; who have shut up the deep and sealed it by your terrible and glorious name; whom all men fear and tremble before your power; for the majesty of your glory cannot be borne, and your angry threatening toward sinners is importable: But thy merciful promise is immeasurable and unsearchable; for you are EL ELYON, of great compassion, long-suffering, very merciful, and repent of the evils of men. You, O YAHUAH, according to your great goodness, have promised repentance and forgiveness to them that have sinned against you: And of your infinite mercies have appointed repentance unto sinners, that they might be saved. You, therefore, O YAHUAH, that art the ELOHIYM of the just, as to Abraham, and Isaac, and Jacob, which have not sinned against you; but you have appointed repentance unto me that am a sinner: For I have sinned above the number of the sands of the sea. My transgressions, O YAHUAH, are multiplied: My transgressions are multiplied, and I am not worthy to behold to see the height of heaven for the multitude of my Torahless deeds. I am bowed down with many iron bands that I cannot lift up my head, neither have any release: For I have provoked your wrath, and done evil before you: I did not do your will, neither kept I your commandments: I have set up abominations, and multiplied offenses. Now, therefore, I bow the knee of mine heart, beseeching you of grace. I have sinned, O YAHUAH, I have sinned, and I acknowledge my Torahless ways: Wherefore, I humbly beseech, forgive me, O YAHUAH, forgive me; and destroy me not with my iniquities. Be not angry with me forever by reserving evil for me; neither condemn me to the lower parts of the earth. For you are ELOHIYM, even the ELOHIYM of them that repent; and in me, thou wilt shew all your goodness: for you will save me that am unworthy according to your great mercy. Therefore, I will praise you forever all the days of my life: for all the powers of the heavens do praise you, and yours is the glory forever and ever. Amen.

SCRIPTURE REFERENCES

CHAPTER 1

Genesis 17:1	Malachi 2:9	Jeremiah 49:10
Genesis 17:4-5	Jasher 47:6	Job 9:24
Genesis 17:19	Amos 9:7, 9	Jubilees 20:12-13
Genesis 25:23	Jasher 26:17	4 Ezra 12:22-25
Genesis 25: 25	Jubilees 19:16-18	2 Esdras 11: 1-2
Genesis 25:34	Jubilees 19:21	Daniel 7:20-23
Genesis 25:30	Deuteronomy 7:6	2 Esdras 6:9
Genesis 36:1	Genesis 10:9	Psalms 83:5-8
Genesis 36:43	Jasher 27:1-12	Daniel 2:31-34
Genesis 3:15	Jasher 7:30	Daniel 2:28
2 Samuel 22:27	Jasher 8:4	Daniel 2:44
2 Esdras 8:1	Jasher 27:12	Daniel 2:43
Malachi 1:2-3	Genesis 27:9-10	Revelation 6:7-8
Jubilees 15:30-31	Jubilees 26:21-24	2 Esdras 11:40
Numbers 12:10	Genesis 27:38	Revelation 6:9-10
Genesis 25:26	Jubilees 26:33	Daniel 7:17-18
Song of Solomon 1:5	2 Esdras 10:10	
	Ezekiel 35: 5-6	

CHAPTER 2

Jasher 29:36	Jasher 31:63	Jasher 47:6
Jasher 31:37	Jubilees 35: 9-12	Jasher 47:7
Jasher 31:48	Jubilees 35:18-27	Jasher 47:22-23
Jasher 31:51	Jasher 47:5	Jasher 47:1-33

CHAPTER 3

Jasher 29:14	Jasher 30:25	Jubilees 29:18

Jasher 30:27	32: 27	Jubilees 8: 25-30
Jasher 30:29	Jeremiah 23:19-21	Jasher 90:10-11
Genesis 10: 6	Ezekiel 37:21-22	Jasher 60: 1
Jasher 57:18	Ezekiel 7:22	Jasher 60
Jubilees 8:12-13	Isaiah 66:1-2	1 Maccabees 1:1-3
Jasher 57	Jubilees 37:23	Genesis 10:4-5
Jasher 57:41-42	Ezekiel 35:2-6	Jubilees 16:26
Genesis 36	Obadiah 1:3	Deuteronomy 4:19-20
Matthew 13:3-8	Genesis 36:8	
Jasher 30:21-22	Psalm 2:7-8	Jasher 60:7-9
Genesis 36:40-43	Jubilees 38:1-2	Revelation 2:12-13
Genesis 36:20-21	Joshua 10: 13	Jeremiah 29:14
Jubilees 38:15-25	2 Samuel 1:18	Ezekiel 36:4-5
Romans 9:10-13	Jasher 62:27	Proverbs 16:4
Romans 9:14-20	Jasher 64:14-18	Psalm 2:1
Deuteronomy 28:64	Jasher 64:19-24	Isaiah 14:1
Isaiah 40:17	Jasher 64:29	Matthew 24:31
Isaiah 54:17	Jasher 64:50	Genesis 36:1
Deuteronomy 32: 21-24	Jasher 64:46	Genesis 36:8
Deuteronomy 32:26	Jasher 58:28	Genesis 27:22
Deuteronomy	Jasher 67:5-7	Romans 9:11-13
	Jasher 67: 8-10	Daniel 7:23
	Genesis 9:27	Malachi 1:4
	Genesis 10:2-5	

CHAPTER 4

Jasher 74: 5-6	Exodus 17:15-16	2 Samuel 8:14
Jasher: 74	1 Samuel 15:2-3	1 Kings 9: 26
Jasher 74:18	Additions to Esther 8:9	1 Kings 11:14
Jasher 74: 21-23		2 Kings 3:14
Jasher 84:25-2	1 Samuel 14:47	2 Kings 14:7
Genesis 36:16	Jubilees 26:34	2 Chronicles 25:11-12
Exodus 17:11	1 Chronicles 18:12	

| 2 Kings 14:21 | 2 Chronicles 28:16- | 2 Chron. 28: 19-22 |
| Amos 1: 11-12 | 18 | Isaiah 14:24-25 |

CHAPTER 5

Obadiah	Ezekiel 35:10	1 Maccabees
1:9-10,13-14	1 Esdras	5:24-26
Lamentations 4:18-	4:47; 50-53	2 Maccabees
21	2 Maccabees	10:14-15
Jeremiah 52:12-13	10:14-15	Baruch 4:3
Psalm 137:7-9	1 Maccabees 3:48	Revelation 2:9
Obadiah 1:18	1 Maccabees 5:2	John 8:44
1 Esdras 4: 45	1 Maccabees 5:3	Revelation 3:9

CHAPTER 6

Matthew 2:3-6	Jeremiah 30:7	2 Kings 17:18
Matthew 2:18	Roman 9:4	Romans 11: 32
John 8:49	2 Peter 3:8	Romans 11:12
Acts 25:13-14	2 Thessalonians	Jeremiah 30:16
Matthew 24:4-5	2:8-9	Daniel 7:25-27
Matthew	Ezekiel 5:12	Daniel 7:7
24:15-17, 21	Jeremiah 30:7	Acts 22:25
Matthew 24:15	Deuteronomy	
Matthew 24:34	28:64	
Matthew 24:21-22	Jeremiah 30:8-10	

CHAPTER 7

Act 1:6-8	1Timothy 4:1	2 Thessalonians 2:3
Matthew 2:23	Matthew 24:24	Revelation 17:3-5
Matthew 13: 24-28	Romans 11:26-27	Jubilees 15:32
Matthew 13:37-42	Isaiah 45:7	John 10:1
1 Samuel 16:7	Ezekiel 20:34	Revelation 13:4
Romans 1:16-17	Matthew 23:28	Wisdom of
2 Timothy 3:16-17	Ecclesiasticus 24:23	Solomon 5:1-2

Baruch 6:39

Matthew 5:17-18

Revelation 12:16-
17

Revelation 17:3-5

Romans 9:29

Revelation 11:8,
11-12

Acts 15:7

Isaiah 60:14

Zechariah 11:4-5

CHAPTER 8

Enoch 89:12

Leviticus 11:7

Genesis 25:25

Genesis 25:34

Jeremiah 24:9-10

Psalms 2:1-3

Ezekiel 36: 5

Ezekiel 11:17

Acts 15:5

Mark 7:7

Hosea 13:14

Genesis 33:12

1 Peter 2:9

Genesis 9:11-13

Zephaniah 3:8

Revelation
13:16-18

Ezekiel
39:25, 27-28

Revelation 14:8

Joel 3:3

Deuteronomy
28:41

Job 9:24

Psalm 58:3

Deuteronomy
28:68

Acts 29:1-3

CHAPTER 9

Genesis 1:1-5

Isaiah 45:7

John 11:9

Revelation 21:25

Romans 9:11-13

Hebrews 12:11

2 Maccabees 6:12

Revelation 15:1

James 1:13-15

1 John: 2:16

Ecclesiastes 3:1-3

Genesis 3:22-23

Jeremiah 10:16

Revelation 4:11

Proverbs 3:11

2 Esdras 6:6

2 Esdras 6:8-9

Ecclesiasticus 2:5

2 Esdras 15:5

Malachi 3: 2-3

Esdras 8:2-3

2 Esdras 9:13

Psalm 24:1

Wisdom of
Solomon 15:7

Deuteronomy 14:2

Psalm 78:5-7

Jeremiah 3:8

Psalm 110:4

John 3:3

Jeremiah 31:33

Hebrews 8:8-11

Malachi 4:6

Isaiah 45:17

2 Esdras 6:55-56

Romans 9:20-21

2 Esdras 8: 41

John 15:16

Ecclesiastes
12:13-14

Daniel 7:27

Joshua 24:31

Deuteronomy
28:64

Deuteronomy
28:25

Deuteronomy
28:32

Deuteronomy 28:36	Obadiah 1:8-10	Obadiah 1:8
Deuteronomy 28:48	Revelation 21:12	Hebrews 12:7-8
2 Esdras 8: 50	Jubilees 15: 31	Ecclesiasticus 35:18
John 19:11	Psalm 83:3-4	Baruch 2: 30-33
Acts 29: 20	Hosea 4:6	Revelation 12:14
Zechariah 13:8-9	Jeremiah 13:23	Revelation 12:17
	Ezekiel 35:5-6	
	Isaiah 46:9-10	

CHAPTER 10

1 Timothy 6:20-21	Ecclesiastes 3:8	Deuteronomy 4: 19-20
Jubilees 12: 16-17	Jeremiah 49:10	Obadiah 1:8-10
Isaiah 66:1	Jubilees 23:23	Isaiah 63:4
1 Thessalonians 5:21	Joel 3:20-21	2 Esdras 10: 10
Jeremiah 31:37	Deuteronomy 28:45-46	Matthew 15:23-24
Genesis 1:14	Jubilees 8:22-24	Hebrews 10:16
Deuteronomy 4:19-20	Amos 9: 9	Matthew 2:1
Jubilees 2:9	Jeremiah 46:27	John 5:43
Enoch 80:11-17	Ezekiel 36:24	Luke 3:22
Joshua 10:11-13	Matthew 23:28	Deuteronomy 4:14-18
Additions to Esther 13: 9-11	Ezekiel 20:35-36	John 5:30
2 Esdras 6:8-10	2 Corinthians 6:17-18	Daniel 7: 25
Daniel 2:43	Jubilees 15:32	Enoch 80:10-12
Luke 6:44	Luke 1:68	Amos 5:21
Matthew 7:26-27	Isaiah 40:17	Jubilees 16:16-18
	Micah 4:5	

CHAPTER 11

Deuteronomy 28:68	Lamentation 5:8	Acts 29:1-3
Isaiah 52:14	Genesis 10:6-20	Acts 13:1
	Revelation 1:14-15	Deuteronomy 23:8

Ecclesiastes 3:8   Enoch 81:1; 82:1-2   Isaiah 30:8

Jubilees 10:13-14   Exodus 17:14

CHAPTER 12

Zechariah 13:8-9   Psalm 53:6   2 Timothy 3:16

Ezekiel 35:5-6   Isaiah 7:14   Acts 17:11

Baruch 4:6   Revelation   Maccabees 3:48

Romans 9:4   19: 11-13   Habakkuk 2:4-5

Jeremiah 29:11-12   Psalms 2:12   Isaiah 49: 26

Luke 23:38   Isaiah 54: 7-8   Hebrews 8:10

Isaiah 54:10   Isaiah 51:11   Proverbs 16:4

2 Esdras 6:56   Romans 11:23-24   Baruch 4:15

Amos 3:2   Acts 16:20-21   Obadiah 1:10

CONCLUSION

1 Samuel 12:24

Enoch 104:11-13

Matthew 5:21-22

Philippians 3:3

Isaiah 14:1

Zephaniah 3:19-20

Jeremiah 51:6

REFERENCES

ABARIM Publications, (2014, 2017). Zepho meaning Zepho in Biblical Hebrew.

ABS Contributor, (2013). When Black Men Ruled the World: 8 Things the Moors Brought to Europe. Atlanta Black Star.

Alfred, H. A History of Arabs in the Sudan. P. 199.

ANONYMOUS (1920). The International Jew: the World's Foremost Problem. A Reprint of a Series of Articles Appearing in The Dearborn Independent from May 22 to October 2, 1920.

Baring-Gould, S. (1881) and Ginzberg (1909). The Secret of Shem Second Part. The Older of the two will Serve p. 217 (9), pp.314 (10).

Beaty, J. (1954). The Iron Curtain Over America. Author.

Bell, J. (1790). Bells New Pantheon or Historical Dictionary of the Gods, Demi-Gods, Heroes, and Fabulous Personages of Antiquity Vol. 2. (p.5). London: British Library.

Ben-David, A. History of Sephardic Jews C-11th-12th.

Ben Israel, M. Edom the Red People of Antiquity, the Prophets, and Hagiography. The Translator, 4 Castle-Street, Hounds ditch p. 218.

Berlin, N.Z.Y. Commentary Haamek Davar on Genesis https://www.sefaria.org/Haamek_Davar_on_Genesis?lang=bi

Bible Hub (2017, May 8). Topical Idumea ATS Bible Dictionary. Retrieved from http://biblehub.com/topical/i/idumea.htm

Biblical Facts: Edomites (2017, May 8). Retrieved from http://www.davidandsindy.com/HTMLKJV/torrey/torr0175.htm

Biblical Facts EDOMITES (Idumea), http://www.ordination.org/edomites.htm

Blank, W. (2017, May 9). Javan. Retrieved from http://www.keyway.ca/htm2003/200330706.htm

Brett, T. The Esau-Rome Connection.

Browne, T. Ionian- Yawan: The Works of Sir Thomas Browne. P 177.

Bruder, E. The Black Jews of Africa. P. 116.

BURCKHARDT. Idumea, Catholic Encyclopedia,
   http://www.newadvent.org/cathen/07638a.htm

Bryant, T. A. (1994). Zondervan Compact Bible Dictionary: Harper
   Collins Christian Publishers.

Cambridge University Press. (2008). Cambridge Dictionary online.
   Retrieved on April 23, 2008, from the website temoa: Open
   Educational Resources (OER) Portal at
   http://temoa.tec.mx/node/324

Carpenter, W. (1885).One Hundred Proofs That the Earth Is Not a
   Globe.

Carr, F. W. (2003). Germany's Black Holocaust: 1890-1945. Firpo
   Wycoff Carr, Author.

CEPHER Bible (2017).Library of Congress-in-Publication Data,
   Cepher Publishing Group, LLC Everett Washington: Cepher
   Publishing Group, LLC.

Chambers Biographical Dictionary, ISBN 0-550-18022-2, page 1,
   (Abarbanel) Esau known as Edom.

Chronological Life Application Bible KJV. Tyndale House Publishers

Classical Baby Names: Biblical Timeless Names for Modern Parents.

Cohen, G.D. Esau as Symbol in Early Medieval Renaissance: Edom,
   Israel's Brother, and Antagonist. pp. 93119-20

Corbet, G. J. (2016). Solving the Enigma of Petra and Nabateans,
   Who were the Nabateans? Originally published in 2012. Retrieved
   from http://www.bblicalarchaeology.org/daily/ancient-near-
   eastern-world/solving-the -enigma-of-petra-and-the-Nabataeans/

Crane, O. T. (1890). The Samaritan Chronicle or the Book of Joshua,
   Part 1 The Son of Nun. New York: John B. Alden Publisher.

Cresson, W. (Michael Boaz). Origin of Edom, Babylon, and Rome, or
   Christianity.

Daly, K. N. Greek, and Roman Mythology. P. 89.

Davidy, Y. Germany and Edom 2nd Edition.

De Benoist, A. (2011-12). Rome-Edom: The Image of Rome in Judaism. Noahide-The Ancient Path A Resource of Jewish Noahide and Other Information.

Dicon Dicou, S. Edom, Israel's Brother, and Antagonist: The Role of Edom in Biblical Prophecy and Story.

Dictionary of Greek and Roman Biography and Mythology by Smith 1800s.

Dubay, E. (2000). Flat Earth Conspiracy. Astronomer, Fred Hoyle

Dubay, E. (2014). The Flat Earth Conspiracy. Author.

Dudley, Dean (1880). History of the First Council of Nice: A World's Christian Convention AD 325; With A Life of Constantine. C.W. Calkins & Company Publishing.

Editors of Time-Life Books. Feats and Wisdom of the Ancients. Bloomsbury Street, London: Caxton Publishing Group.

Eliezer, P. Chapters of Rabbi Eliezer https://www.sefaria.org/Pirkei_DeRabbi_Eliezer.24?lang=bi

Encyclopedia of The Bible. (2017, May 9) Javan. https://www.biblegateway.com/resourcess/encyclopedia-of-the-bible/Javan

Fishberg, M. The Jews of Jamaica. P. 149.

Frend, W. H. C. (1984). The Rise of Christianity. Philadelphia: Fortress Press.

Gaster, M. (1899). The CHRONICLES OF JERAHMEEL or the Hebrew Bible Historiale. Royal Asiatic Society, London.

Gerring, Lloyd (1998). Volume 11-5, How Did Jesus Become God and Why? West Star Institute.

Glueck, Nelson (1947). The Civilization of the Edomites.

Gonzalez, J. L. (1984). The Story of Christianity. San Francisco: HarperSanFrancisco. A division of Harper Collins Publishers.

Hanko, R. (2007). The Arian Controversy. Reformed Perspectives Magazine, 9(10), March 4th -10th.

Hardins, A. (1901). What is Christianity? Second Edition. New York: Putnam Press.

Harper's Bible Dictionary (1817). San Francisco: Harper & Row, Publishers.

Hebrew Roots Bible (2012). DitoPlex, LLC Everett, Washington www.bibleplex.com

Hislop, A. (2012). The Two Babylons: Or, The Papal Worship Proved to be the Worship of Nimrod. United States of America: Renaissance Classics.

History of Macedonia. ORG.

Horn, Ame. Eusebius of Caesarea p. 107.

Howell, Elizabeth (2015). Guide to Space How Long Have Humans Been On Earth?

Humans Are Free.com; Humans are Free. The Unholy Trinity of Globalist Control: The Vatican, the city of London, and Washington D.C. Online Article.

James Francis Edward Stuart. Retrieved from realhistoryww.com

Jewish-American History Documentation Foundation, (2018). Lathrup Village, MI, 48076.

Jewish Encyclopedia: Archelaus: Banishment and Death. Retrieved from (http://jewishencycyclopedia.com/view.jsp?artid=1729&letter=A& Search=Herod%20Archelaus #20Archelaus#5201)

Jewish Encyclopedia: Edom, Idumea. 1906.

Josephus, F. (1998). Josephus: The Complete Works. Nashville, Tennessee: Thomas Nelson Publishers, Inc.

Justasheep. (2012, June 7). UNSEALED PROPHECY: Speculation about Kittim. Retrieved from http://unsealedprophecy.wordpress.com/2012/06/07/speculation-about-kittim/

Kahn, Z. (1880). Mi-Mizrah u-mi-Ma'arav, (1899), ;idem, in: Festschrift. . Berliner (1903), Heb. Pt., 80-90; E.E. Urbach, in REJ, 100 (1935), 49-77; Joseph Official, Yosef ha-Me-Kanne, ed. By J. Rosenthal (1970) intro.

Koestler, A. (1976). The Thirteenth Tribe: The Khazar Empire and Its Heritage. New York: Random House, Inc.

Kohen, E. Isaurian Kings: History of the Byzantine Jews. P. 25.

Lendering, J. (1995-2017). Edomites- Edom: Iron Age kingdom. Retrieved from http://www.livius.org/articles/people/edomites/

Levin, M. (2016). Do West and Christianity Represent Esau and Edom? Daily Minyan Online Article.

Map of Ancient Israel – Idumea – Bible History Online Israel in the First Century: More about Ancient Idumea. Retrieved from http://www.bible-history.com/geography/ancient-Israel/idumea.html

Martin, W.C. (1964). The Layman's Bible Encyclopedia: Nashville, Tennessee. The Southwestern Company,

McGonigle, T. D. & Quigley J. F. Thomas D. (1988). History of the Christian tradition (Vol. 1 p 39), Paulist Press.

Melamed, A. (2003). The Image of the Black in Jewish Culture: A History of the Other. London and New York: Routledge Curzon.

Merriam-Webster's School Thesaurus (1989). Merriam-Webster Incorporated: United States of America.

Michelet, J. History of the Roman Republic p. 294.

Miller, T. CONSTANTINE CHANGED CALENDAR. Light Bearer Ministries International. Retrieved from www.lightbearerminiatries.org/files/9413/8038.../Constantine_Changed_Calendar.pdf

Missler, C. (2017, April 24). Who Are the Edomites? Retrieved from http://khouse.org/articles/2010/920/

New Unger's Bible Dictionary (1957). Chicago: The Moody Bible Institute.

Nigosian, S.A. (2000). World Religions. Hampshire and London: PALGRAVE.

NJOP/Jewish Treats (2014). Ishmaelites and Edomites. Jewish Treats Juicy Bits of Judaism Daily.

On Philo, see H.A. Wolfson's magisterial Philo: Foundations of Religious Philosophy in Judaism, Christianity, and Islam, two vols. (Cambridge, Mass. Harvard University Press; London: Oxford University Press, 1947), and Henry Chadwick's chapter "Philo," in The Cambridge History of Later Greek and Early Medieval Philosophy, ed. A. H. Armstrong (New York and Cambridge: Cambridge University Press, 1967), pp. 137-157.

Orr, J. M.A., General Editor. Bible Study Tools Jewish-Encyclopedia International Standard Bible Encyclopedia, "Entry for 'JEUSH' International Standard Bible Encyclopedia." 1915.

Realhistoryww.com

Roberts, A. & Coxe, J. D. (1895). St. Ignatius of Antioch: The Epistles. New York: Christian Literature Publishing Co.

Roberts, A., Donaldson, J. & Coxe, A. C. (2012). St. Ignatius of Antioch: The Epistles. (New York: Christian Literature Publishing Co., 1885). Veritatis Splendor Publications.

Rocca, S. (2015, March 30). Herod's Judaea: A Mediterranean State in the classic World. Retrieved from (https://book s. google.com/books.

Rogers, J.A. (1952). Nature Knows No Color-Line: Research Into the Negro Ancestry in the White Race. Renewed, 1980.

Rudd, S. (2017, April 21). The Edomites, 'The Historical Transjordan territory of the Edomites in the Bible, Historical Survey 1950-500 BCE.' Retrieved from http://www.bible.ca/archeology/bible-archeology-edomite-territory-mt-seir.htm

Sanders, R. (1977). Lost Tribes and Promised Lands. New York and Putney Vermont. Author.

Sands, S. (2009). The Invention of the Jewish People. London and Brooklyn, New York: Verso.

Scheifler, M. (2018). Vicarius Fili Dei 666, the Number of the Beast. Retrieved from Michael Scheifler's Bible Light Homepage.

Seekins, F.T. (2009). Hebrew Word Pictures, How Does The Hebrew Alphabet Reveal Prophetic Truths? Frank T. Seekins.

Selwood, D. (2015). It was Thomas Cromwell who destroyed all evidence of Black Rule in Britain. Article Daily Telegraph Media Group Limited January 2015.

Sermon of 1 Corinthians 10:19-24, Calvin Opera Selecta, Corpus Reformation Vol. 49, 677 (Philip Stallings). The Biblical Flat Earth Society, Founder.

Shaver, D.A. (2012). The Books of Enoch, Jubilees, and Jasher. Derek A. Shaver, Author.

SlaveVoyages.org, Emory University-Voyages database

Smith, W. Dr. (1901). Edom, Idumaea, or Idumea, Smith's Bible Dictionary. "Entry for 'Edom, Idumaea or Idumea.'"

Sophie's Blog. (2017). Why is Christianity Associated with Edom (Esau) and Rome? Jesus is Not for Jews.

Stangroom, J. & Garvey, J. (2006). The Great Philosophers from Socrates to Foucault. New York: Barnes & Noble, Inc.

Stem, S. (2000). Jewish Identity in Early Rabbinic Writing, pg. 19.

Strong, J. (1890, 1980). Abingdon's Strong's Exhaustive Concordance of the Bible: Madison, N. J. Library of Congress Cataloging in Publication Data.

The Arian Controversy (2007). Reformed Perspectives Magazine. Volume 9 (10).

The Columbia Electronic Encyclopedia. (2013). Idumea. Retrieved from www.cc.columbia.edu/cu/cup/

The Editors of Encyclopedia Britannica. Nabatean People

The Epistles of Ignatius to the Smyrnaeans. Translated by Alexander Roberts and James Donaldson. From Ante-Nicene Fathers Vol. 1. Edited by Alexander Roberts, James Donaldson, and A. Cleveland Coxe. Buffalo, NY: Christian Literature Publishing Co. 1885.

Revised and edited for New Advent by Keven Knight. http://www.newadvent.org/fathers/0109.htm.

The First Book of Dionysius of Halicarnassus About the History of the Romans. Chapter 28:1-19.

The Great Soviet Encyclopedia, 3rd Edition. (1970-1979). Edom. © 2010 the Gale Group, Inc.

The Habakkuk Scroll Part 1, The Kittim. Retrieved from http://www.world-destiny.org/habtheme.htm

'The Historical Transjordan territory of the Edomites in the Bible, Historical Survey 1950-500 BCE.'

The Holy Bible 1611 Edition, King James Version (2010). Peabody, Massachusetts. Hendrickson Publishers Marketing, LLC.

The International Standard Bible Encyclopedia. Idumea. IDUMAEA; IDUMAEANS Bible answers for almost all your Questions by Elmer Towns.

The New Oxford Annotated Bible with the Apocrypha and Editions to Esther (2007). Oxford New York. Oxford University Press, Inc.

The Septuagint with Apocrypha (1986, 2017). The United States of America. Hendrickson Publishers Marketing, LLC.

The Works of Sir Walter Raleigh. Mecca. P. 83

Thompson, W.T. The Battle Flag of North Virginia: A symbol of white supremacy?

https://civilwardocs.weebly.com/the-battle-flag.html

Weisman, C. (1996). Who is Esau-Edom? Fifth Edition. Apple Valley MN: Weisman Publications.

Weitzmann, K. (1978). The Icon: Holy Images--- Sixth to Fourteenth Century. New York, New York: George Braziller, Inc.

Weisman, C. (1996). Who is Esau-Edom? Fifth Edition. Apple Valley MN: Weisman Publications.

Where is Edom Today? And what is Edom's name today? Retrieved from http://www.lavistachurchchrist.org/LVanswers/2005/09-24.htm

Who were the Nabataeans? Nabataean History. Retrieved from http://nabataea.net/who.html

Wikipedia, the free encyclopedia. (2017, June 13). Ancient Jewish History (c. 1500 BCE-63 BCE). Retrieved from https://en.wikipedia.org/wiki/Jewish-history

Wikipedia, the free encyclopedia. (2017, May 8). Antipater the Idumean. Retrieved from https://en.wikipedia.org/wiki/Antipater_the_Idumaean

Wikipedia, the free encyclopedia. (2017, June 13). Biblical Archaeology. Retrieved from https://en.wikipedia.org/wiki/Biblical_archaeology

Wikipedia, the free encyclopedia. (2017, June 13). Canaan. Retrieved from https://en.wikipedia.org/wiki/Canaan#History

Wikipedia, the free encyclopedia. (2017, April 6). Edom, Retrieved from https://en.wikipedia.org/wiki/Edom

Wikipedia, the free encyclopedia. (2017, June 13). Elephantine Papyri. Retrieved from https://en.wikipedia.org/wiki/Elephantine_papyri

Wikipedia, the free encyclopedia. (2017). Eusebius of Nicomedia. Retrieved from https://en.wikipedia.org/wiki/Eusebius_of_Nicomedia

Wikipedia, the free encyclopedia. (2016). Do west And Christianity Represent Esau and Edom?

Wikipedia, the free encyclopedia. (2016). First Jewish-Roman Wars. Retrieved from

Wikipedia, the free encyclopedia. (2017). The Herodian Kingdom, Retrieved from https://en.wikipedia.org/wiki/Herodian_kingdom

Wikipedia, the free encyclopedia. (2017, June 13). Herodian Dynasty. Retrieved from https://en.wikipedia.org/wiki/Herodian_dynasty

Wikipedia, the free encyclopedia. (2017, June 13). History of Ancient Israel and Judah. Retrieved from https://en.wikipedia.org/wiki/History_of_ancient_Israel_and_Judah#Roman_occupation

Wikipedia, the free encyclopedia. (2017, June 13). History of the Jews in the Roman Empire. Retrieved from https://en.wikipedia.org/wiki/History_of_the_Jews_in_the_Roman_Empire

Wikipedia, the free encyclopedia. (2017, June 13). History of the papacy. Retrieved from https://en.wikipedia.org/wiki/History_of_the_papacy

Wikipedia, the free Encyclopedia. (). Judaic Views of the Amalekites.

Wikipedia, the free encyclopedia. Gleason's New Standard Map of the World. Retrieved May 28, 2019, from https://www.google.com/url?sa=i&source=images&cd=&cad=rja& uact=8&ved=0ahUKEwixxsuKir_iAhWUqp4KHY4gC04QMwhQ KAAwAA&url=https%3A%2F%2Fcommons.wikimedia.org%2F wiki%2FFile%3AGleason%2527s_new_standard_map_of_the_wo rld_-_on_the_projection_of_J._S._Christopher%2C_Modern_College %2C_Blackheath%2C_England%3B_scientifically_and_practically _correct

Wikipedia, the free encyclopedia. (2017, June 13). Jewish History. Retrieved from https://en.wikipedia.org/wiki/Jewish_history

Wikipedia, the free Encyclopedia. (2017, May 19). Kittim. Retrieved from, https://en.wikipedia.org/wiki/Kittim

Wikipedia, the free encyclopedia. (2017, June 13). Israelites. Retrieved from https://en.wikipedia.org/wiki/Israelites

Wikipedia, the free encyclopedia. (2017, June 13). List of Hasmonean and Herodian Rulers. Retrieved from https://en.wikipedia.org/wiki/List_of_Hasmonean_and_Herodian _rulers

Wikipedia, the free encyclopedia. Map of Palestine under the Herods. Retrieved May 28, ,2019 from https://www.google.com/url?sa=i&source=images&cd=&cad=rja& uact=8&ved=0ahUKEwjM4Oe7lr_iAhVJqZ4KHfkWBt8QMwhG KAAwAA&url=https%3A%2F%2Fwww.biblestudy.org%2Fmaps %2Fpalestine-under-the-herods.html

Wikipedia, the free encyclopedia. Map of Negroland. Retrieved May 28, 2019 from https://www.google.com/url?sa=i&source=images&cd=&cad=rja&

uact=8&ved=0ahUKEwjXj-
24iL_iAhUH7J4KHe1ABykQMwhsKAAwAA&url=https%3A%2
F%2Fen.wikipedia.org%2Fwiki%2FNegroland

Wikipedia, the free encyclopedia. United Nations Logo. Retrieved
May ,28, 2019 from
https://www.google.com/url?sa=i&source=images&cd=&cad=rja&
uact=8&ved=0ahUKEwjh-f_sjb_iAhXNl54KHY28BG0QMwi-
AShdMF0&url=https%3A%2F%2Fwww.mayimachronim.com%
2Ftag%2Fnoah

Wikipedia, the free encyclopedia. Phoenicia the Land of Phut or
Carthage. Retrieved May 28, 2019 from
https://www.google.com/url?sa=i&source=images&cd=&cad=rja&
uact=8&ved=2ahUKEwj8wr_3j7_iAhWEqp4KHWz-
Bd84ZBAzKAMwA3oECAEQBA&url=https%3A%2F%2Fipfs.io
%2Fipfs%2FQmXoypizjW3WknFiJnKLwHCnL72vedxjQkDDP1
mXWo6uco%2Fwiki%2FPhoenicia.html

Wikimedia, the free encyclopedia. United Nations Logo. Retrieved
May 28, 2019 from
https://www.google.com/url?sa=i&source=images&cd=&cad=rja&
uact=8&ved=0ahUKEwjWpoKLi7_iAhWNoJ4KHeE9B6cQMwh3
KAAwAA&url=https%3A%2F%2Fcommons.wikimedia.org%2F
wiki%2FFile%3ALogo_of_the_United_Nations

Wikipedia, the free encyclopedia. Map of Edom in Mount Seir.
Retrieved May 28, 2019 from
https://www.google.com/url?sa=i&source=images&cd=&cad=rja&
uact=8&ved=0ahUKEwiv5ciOkb_iAhVPtZ4KHQXoA1IQMwiBA
SgjMCM&url=https%3A%2F%2Fwww.youtube.com%2Fwatch
%3Fv%3DlApGTESzK9s&psig=AOvVaw3sJPNR7PQlonDEOLh
5d0-p&ust=1559164122769164&ictx=3&uact=3

Wikipedia, the free encyclopedia. The Hasmonean Dynasty Chart.
Retrieved May 28, 2019 from
https://www.google.com/url?sa=i&source=images&cd=&cad=rja&
uact=8&ved=2ahUKEwjy-
Z6Blr_iAhVXoZ4KHUXwCLU4ZBAzKBwwHHoECAEQHQ&u
rl=https%3A%2F%2Fadammaarschalk.com%2Ftag%2Fantiochus
-

epiphanes%2F&psig=AOvVaw1FY0WrMezIy59H1d1JNXI4&ust=
1559165415508527&ictx=3&uact=3

Williams, J. J., Hebrewisms of West Africa: From Nile to Niger with the Jews. United States of America: African Tree Press.

Williams, J. J. (1921). Hebrewisms of West Africa. African Tree Press Manufactured in the USA January 2016.

Williams, S.J. (1932). WHENCE THE "BLACK IRISH" OF JAMAICA? New York: Dial Press Inc.

Windsor, R. R. (1988). From Babylon to Timbuktu: A History of the Ancient Black Races Including the Black Hebrews. Atlanta, Georgia: Windsor Golden Series.

Zacuto, A https://en.wikipedia.org/wiki/Abraham_Zacuto

Zampano, G. (2019, April 12). Pope Kisses Feet of South Sudan's Leaders to Encourage Peace. Associated Press. In World News, Nassau Guardian.

ABOUT THE AUTHOR

Dr. Bonnie V. Franks has returned to her Hebrew roots and is now known by those who have read her book Dr. Beneyah Yashar' el the name she chose from the Slave Manifest of a slave ship. Upon further research, she found that the Hebrew meaning is "Construction." This meaning got her attention as she realized the Highest YAHUAH named her for the purpose, for which he called her to construct the real history of the Hebrew Israelites. Born in the Bahamas, she received her early education. She then furthered her studies at Prairie View A&M University, Prairie View, Texas, where she completed her Bachelor's and Master's degree in Education. She later finished her doctoral studies in Educational Leadership at the Nova Southeastern University of Florida.

Dr. Franks has experienced teaching at every level, from Kindergarten to University. Her last teaching position was five years in Shanghai, China, as Academic Manager of the International Department of Shanghai World Foreign Language Primary School, where she taught and supervised foreign teachers of English.

Harboring a deep, long-standing interest in her past, future, and purpose, her China experience led to the discovery of the identity of her ancestors. She learned that the Black Slaves brought to the Western world aboard slave ships during the Transatlantic Slave Trade were, in fact, descendants of the Tribes of Israel known as the Hebrew Israelites.

The knowledge prompted asking some fundamental questions and looking further for the answers to; why the Europeans chose the people from the African Continent to enslave? Who were the people responsible for the enslavement of these "African" people? And also important was why there was a distinction made between the Black people of Egypt, Ethiopia, Libya, Algeria, and Morocco, people known to be the true descendants of Ham the progenitor of the dark races.

As, the Black Hebrew Israelites of this tragedy awaken to the truth about their identity, they must come to know, with documented certainty, the significance of the people who perpetrated such heinous acts against their ancestors as well as on the Israelites still living in the diaspora, today. This book will confirm the truth about Esau, who is Edom and Rome, Jacob's twin brother ruling as the Edomite Romans today.

And so, it is imperative, that as they come to the close of this age, that the descendants of slaves in the diaspora scattered to the four corners of the earth develop and embrace an awareness of whom and whose they are and also identify the true enemy of the actual Israelites.

Made in the USA
Monee, IL
03 June 2020